Christ
Our
Passover

Christ
Our
Passover

By

Stephen Charnock

Sovereign Grace Publishers, Inc.
P.O. Box 4998
Lafayette, IN 47903

ISBN 1-58960-016-9

Printed In the United States of America
By Lightning Source, Inc.

CONTENTS

6

PREFACE

Since everyone instructed unto the kingdom of Heaven is to bring forth out of his treasure things both new and old (Matthew 13:52), we are bringing out something old for your delight.

STEPHEN CHARNOCK needs little introduction to many of you who have had the soul-lifting pleasure of reading his unmatch-able work, The Existence and Attributes of God (one of our 1958 productions). Who knows God like Charnock knew God? At the very least, everyone can learn of God from him.

Now you are about to find that he that knows God must also know the Christ, who is called the Son of God, the express image of His person, etc. In the aforementioned book, Stephen Charnock showed many times his grasp of the work of Christ. You are now to get up closer, to see more clearly through the dark mystery which natural eyes will not penetrate. Even spiritual eyes sometimes need an experienced guide to realize fully what is the meaning and purport of the death and communion of Christ.

Here you will first read the tender, spiritually passionate story of Christ, sacrificed as our Passover - - the why of it, the acceptable-ness of it, the voluntariness of it, the necessity of it. Then you will be exalted as you read of the exaltation of Christ, and find out the necessity of it.

From this point you will find yourself communing with the Lord as you read of His communion. How powerfully does Char-nock set forth the meaning and end of the Lord's Supper. Here is meat that altogether too many Christians know little of. Here is drink that will fill you full of spiritual glow. Once you begin to know Him like this, you will be crying out with far more fervor, O that I might know Him, and the power of His resurrection, and the fellowship of His sufferings, being made conformable unto His death; if by any means I might attain unto the resurrection of the dead.

Come, let us reason together! Do you not need to walk this path to the knowledge of Christ in His death and resurrection? Do you not want to be brought into such sweet communion with Him? Yea! and more so, for my poor words will not express your longing to know of such things. Yet the words of Stephen Charnock will go a long way to lead you into His presence, where words are no longer necessary. May God bless these pages to your edification.

THE LIFE OF THE AUTHOR

Stephen Charnock was born in the parish of St. Catherine Cree, London, in the year 1628. He was the son of Richard Charnock, a solicitor. He entered the famous Emmanuel College, known for its independent, puritan spirit, at Cambridge in the year 1642. There he obtained the degrees of B.A. and M.A. by 1649. His B.D. he obtained later.

He entered Cambridge without spiritual life, but it was not long after that he came to know God as the True God, and Christ as his Lord and Savior, for we read in his funeral sermon (preached by Mr. Johnson), "The deed or gift, or rather copy of it, which showed his title to heaven, I believe perished with his books in London's flames, and I have forgotten the particular places of Scripture which he was wrought upon, and which were there inserted.' It seems Charnock had written an account of his conversion, but it had been burned along with a number of his books in London. Now when he is only 18 years old, Mr. Johnson meets him and describes him "as venerable and grave, like an aged person from his youth."

Mr. Johnson continued in this vein, "He would deeply search into and prove all things, and allow only what he found pure and excellent. In this I had him in my heart at my first acquaintanceship with him in Cambridge thirty-six years since. I found him one that, Jonah-like, had turned to the Lord with all his heart, all his soul, and all his might, and none like him; which did more endear him to me. How had he hid the word of God in a fertile soil, in a good and honest heart, which made him flee youthful lusts, and antidoted him against the infection of youthful vanities. His study was his recreation; the law of God was his delight. Had he it not . . . engraven in his heart? He was as choice, circumspect, and prudent in his election of society, as of books, to converse with; all his delight being in such an excelled in the divine art of directing, furthering, and quickening him in the way to heaven, the love of Christ and souls. Most choice he was of the ministers that he would hear; what he learned from books, conversation, or sermons, that which affected and worked most upon him he prayed over till he was delivered into the form of it, and had Christ, grace, and the Spirit formed in him. True, he had been in darkness, and then he said full of doubtings, fears, and grievously pestered with temptations. How often have we found him (as if he had lately been with Paul caught up into the third heavens, and heard unspeakable words) magnifying and adoring the mercy, love, and goodness of God."

8

Charnock was a deep and laborious student all his life. His works show this. Not only was he a wide reader of all that was counted worthy in his day, but he spent long hours of meditation upon the things that he read. Such prolonged, deep contemplation sets his writing upon a higher plane than the writings of others, either in his own age, or in subsequent years. Neither did he neglect the Scriptures, but rather hour upon hour searched and compared, and attempted to interpret Scripture by Scripture. What a commentary this is upon those who test Scripture by their own standards, tastes, and predilections!

Charnock acquired the knowledge of many languages, and a very intimate knowledge of medicine as practised in his day. The only thing which kept him from being a physician of bodies was the impelling force he felt leading him to be a physician of souls. Even before he left college he was God's instrument in converting seven or eight persons who heard him saying, "Come and see Jesus," etc. following the example of the women of Samaria. Upon leaving college he tutored in a private family a while, but returned to his preaching point in Southwark to minister to those before converted under his preaching. However, he set his sights upon a fellowship at Oxford, and in 1650 he obtained a fellowship in New College. There at Oxford he was awarded other honors, being made joint-proctor in 1654. He was of course associated with Thomas Goodwin, then president of Magdalene College at Oxford, and John Owen, the vice-chancellor at the time.

Oliver Cromwell, however, appointed Charnock to be one of the chaplains to his son in Dublin, and while there he also ministered to the church of St. Werburgh, and lectured to Christ Church as well. This Sunday afternoon lecture was attended by virtually every well-known saint, as well as by huge, overflowing crowds of the Irish churches, both near and afar. This ministry continued, apparently, until 1660, at which time he was forced to return to England, and from this time he never had a settled church to which he might minister the riches of the grace of Jesus Christ, his Beloved Lord. Like John Owen, he was thrown upon study, and probably it was during these 12 to 15 years of public obscurity that his memorable, yea, unforgettable, work on the Attributes of God was formed and completed. He in the meanwhile belonged to the famous church in London over which Thomas Goodwin so sweetly ruled, a church so full of famous names, authors, preachers, etc. as to be considered almost a scholars church.

About 1675, Charnock was called to minister jointly with equally judicious Thomas Watson in Crosby Hall. Here he remained until his death in 1680. He died July 27, 1680 at a comparatively early age, 52.

A DISCOURSE OF CHRIST OUR PASSOVER.

For Christ our passover is sacrificed for us.—1 Cor. V. 7.

THE words are a reason of the apostle's exhortation to the Corinthians to cast out the incestuous person, in regard of the contagion which might be by so ill an example dispersed to others, as a leaven spreads its vapours through the whole lump: ver. 6, 'Know you not, that a little leaven leaveneth the whole lump?' And having used this similitude of leaven, he pursues it in allusion to the custom of the Jews before the celebration of the passover, according to the command to have no leaven found in their houses at that time, upon the penalty of being cut off from the congregation of Israel; and with respect to the true design of that ceremonial injunction, exhorts the Corinthians to 'purge out the old leaven,' viz., that person from their society, lust from their hearts, every member of the old Adam, that they might be a new lump, answering their holy and heavenly calling. The reason of this exhortation is in the words: 'For Christ our passover is sacrificed for us,' and by his death hath taken away the sin of the world.'*
As the sacrifice of the paschal lamb represented the sacrifice of Christ, so the manner wherein the Israelites celebrated that solemnity with unleavened bread represents the manner wherewith we ought to celebrate the death of the Redeemer of the world. As therefore our true passover, which is the Lord Jesus, hath been sacrificed for us, let us daily celebrate the memory of it in a manner worthy of so great a grace. As, therefore, the Jews abstained from all leaven in the time of the figure, let us not only abstain from, but purge out, all things contrary to God, because for this end Christ was sacrificed for us. As the passover was a type of Christ, so the unleavened bread was a type of Christians, and of their innocence and purity of life.† And that 'because you are unleavened,' *i. e. de jure*, you ought to be so; for that is said in Scripture sometimes to be *de facto* which ought to be, as 'the priest's lips preserve knowledge,' *i. e.* ought to preserve knowledge.‡ 'Εκκαθάρατε, purge out, is more emphatical and pressing than a simple purging: purge it out wholly, that nothing may be left in you, that you may be such as a new lump did figuratively signify.
Christ our passover. The institution of this solemn figure is particularly set down Exod. xii. 3–5, &c. It was appointed by God as a memorial,§

---

* Amyraut in loc; Estius in loc. ‡ Pareus in loc.
† Menoch. § Daillé, Serm. sur 1 Cor. v. 7.

both of the Israelites' slavery in Egypt and their deliverance from it. After they had been about two hundred years in that country, God, mindful of his promise, sets upon their delivery ; and since all the former miracles had proved unsuccessful for the bending Pharaoh's heart to give the captives liberty to depart, God designs the slaying of the first-born of every Egyptian family, and thereby sending the greatest strength of the nation to another world. Upon this occasion he orders the Israelites, by Moses, to slay the lamb the fourteenth day of the first month (which answers to our March), and sprinkle the posts of their doors with the blood, and feast upon the flesh of it in their several families ; and that night the angel comes and mortally strikes every first-born, none escaping but those who observed this command of God, and had sprinkled their door-posts with the blood of the slain lamb ; every house besides being made that night a house of mourning. It was an earnest of the Israelites' deliverance, and the Egyptians' calamity.

Obs. 1. God's greatest mercies to his church are attended with the greatest plagues upon their enemies. The salvation of man is the destruction of sin and the devil ; the passover was the salvation of Israel and ruin of Egypt.

2. God provides for the security of his people before he lays his wrathful hand upon their adversaries. He provided a Moses to conduct them, an ordinance to comfort and refresh them, before he shoots his arrows into the Egyptians' hearts. God settles this passover as a standing ordinance in the church, a feast throughout their generations, to be kept by an ordinance for ever, Exod. xii. 14 ; so that it was not only a memorial of a past and temporal deliverance, but the type of a future and spiritual one. As all the sacrifices were types of what was to be performed in the fulness of time in the person of the Messiah, so this was a great and signal type, and had its truth, reality, and efficacy in the death of the Redeemer.

Christ the passover, i. e. the paschal lamb. The lamb was called the passover ; the sign for the thing signified by it : 2 Chron. xxxv. 11, ' And they killed the passover,' *i. e.* the lamb : for the passover was properly the angel's passing over Israel, when he was sent as an executioner of God's wrath upon the Egyptians. So Mat. xxvi. 17, ' Where shall we prepare for thee to eat the passover ?' *i. e.* the paschal lamb.

Our passover : our paschal lamb. He is called ' God's Lamb,' John i. 29. God's in regard of the author, ours in regard of the end ; God's Lamb in regard of designation, ours in regard of acceptance.

Our passover. Not only of the Jews, but of the Gentiles. That was restrained to the Israelitish nation, this extends in the offers of it to all, and belongs to all that are under the new administration of the covenant of grace.

For us, ὑπὲρ ἡμῶν. Not only for our good, but in our stead, to free us from eternal death, to purchase for us eternal life ; sacrifices were substituted in the place of the transgressor, and received the stroke of death which his sin had merited. The title of the paschal lamb is given here to Christ, not only in regard of his meekness and innocence, but in regard of his being a sacrifice, whence he is called ' the Lamb slain,' Rev. v. 12 ; the Lamb that ' redeems us by his blood,' 1 Pet. i. 18. Here we have,

1. A description of Christ in the type, *passover.*
2. The end of his death.
(1.) *Finis cujus,* a sacrifice.
(2.) *Finis cui,* our, for us.
Three doctrines may be observed from the words,

1. Christ is our passover.
2. Christ is a sacrifice.
3. Christ is a sacrifice in our stead.

1. For the first, Christ is our passover. In allusion to this, he is so often called a Lamb, as also in allusion to the lambs offered in the daily sacrifice, but especially in relation to the paschal lamb, which did more fully express both the nature of his sufferings and the design of his office. You do not therefore find him expressed in the New Testament by the name of any of those other animals which were figures of him in the Jewish sacrifices, but only by this of a lamb, as being more significant of the in- nocence of his person, the meekness of his nature, his sufficiency for his people, than any other.

(1.) The design of the passover was to set forth Christ. All the sacri- fices, which were appointed by God as parts of worship, were designed to keep up the acknowledgment of the fall of man, his demerit by sin, and to support his faith in the promised Redeemer; for they being instituted, not before the fall, but probably immediately after the first promise of the seed of the woman, did all refer to that seed promised, whose heel was to be bruised, as to the foundation of their institution; and being unable of them- selves to purge the sin of a rational creature, and the spiritual substance of the soul, they must refer to that which was only able to do it: Heb. x. 8, 'Sacrifice and offering, and burnt-offerings, and offering for sin, thou would- est not, neither hadst pleasure therein; then said I, Lo, I come to do thy will:' the will of God manifested in the first draught and agreement in heaven, and shadowed in all the sacrifices under the law. When sacrifices of themselves were not, nor could be, grateful to God, nor the blood of an animal give a due compensation to an offended God for the sin of man, then said Christ, 'Lo, I come,' as the person represented by those pictures, as the body signified by those shadows. All those institutions not being designed for any other virtue in themselves, but as notices of the intent of God, and the methods he designed for the taking away of sin by the promised seed; that it was to be by blood and death, that this was the agreement between God and the seed so promised; therefore they were in all those doleful spectacles of blood and slaughter to look through that veil to the calamities the promised seed should endure for the taking away of sin, and have a prospect of the heinousness of sin, and the sharpness of the suffer- ings of the Messiah, in the groans and strugglings of those dying creatures. So the design of this passover was ultimately to represent the Messiah to them, by whose blood they were to have a spiritual deliverance from sin and Satan, as by the blood of the lamb they had a deliverance from the sword of the destroying angel, and afterwards from Pharaoh and the Egyp- tian pressures. He is therefore called the Lamb of God, as being shadowed by the paschal lamb of the Old Testament. All things under the law were but shadows of things to come, Heb. x. 1. Christ is the real accomplish- ment of all; he is our mystical, spiritual, heavenly, perfect passover; therefore those words, which are immediately spoken of the paschal lamb, and did immediately respect the passover, Exod. xii. 46, 'Neither shall you break a bone thereof,' and Num. ix. 12, are said to be fulfilled in Christ the antitype, as if they had been immediately pronounced of him when they were spoken of the paschal lamb: John xix. 36, 'For those things were done that the scripture should be fulfilled, A bone of him shall not be broken.' And, indeed, if we consider all the circumstances in the institu- tion, they seem not worthy of the wisdom of God, nor are capable of having any reason rendered for them, if they be not referred to some other mystery;

and what can that be but the Redeemer of the world represented thereby? Why should so much care be in the choice and separation of a lamb?* What virtue had the blood of a poor animal to secure the house and the life of the first-born against the sword of a strong and invisible angel? Was the sprinkling of the blood upon the posts a necessary mark for the angel, as though he had not understanding enough to distinguish between the houses and children of the Israelites and Egyptians? Could not God have signified his pleasure to the angel without such a mark, and given him directions for the security of his people? How can we think God should appoint so many ceremonies in it, lay such a charge upon them for the strict observation of them, if he designed it not as a prop to their faith, a ground to expect a higher and spiritual deliverance by the blood of the Messiah, as well as a trial of their obedience, a memorial of their temporal deliverance, and a sign for the direction of the angel in the execution of his commission?

(2.) The believers in that time regarded it as a type of the Messiah: Heb. xi. 28, 'Through faith he,' *i. e.* Moses, 'kept the passover and the sprinkling of blood, lest he that destroyed the first-born should touch them.' It was an illustrious testimony of Moses his faith to rely upon the promise and good will of God, and keep the passover, when the blood of a lamb seemed so improbable a means of preserving the Israelites from the destroying angel's sword. Yet certainly Moses his faith pierced further, and looked through this shell to the kernel, through this sign to the thing signified by it. Moses could not have 'esteemed the reproach of Christ,' ver. 26, had he not known Christ; and we cannot suppose so illustrious a prophet, that had such an estimation of Christ as to value his reproaches, did terminate his faith upon the outward action and the bare type, but pierced further to the promised seed, as well as Abel in his sacrifice. It is not likely that his faith stuck only in the effusion of the blood of an animal, and did not see the effusion of the blood of the Messiah, whose reproach he had been so willing to bear. It had been too low a faith for so great a man, not to regard the spiritual deliverance promised to be wrought by the bruising the heel of the seed of the woman. Who can think Moses utterly ignorant of the design of that promise? And if not, who can think his faith should terminate in the outward sign, and that the apostle should give such encomiums to a faith of no higher an elevation than that which respected the command of God in that present affair? Moses his faith had been great in former commands; why should the apostle skip them, if he had not designed to shew his faith in the Messiah figured in the passover? The apostle doth not speak of faith in God simply considered in that chapter, but of faith in the mediator, or high priest, which he had discoursed of throughout that book. How could the ancient believers eat the same spiritual food, and drink of the same spiritual rock, which was Christ, without faith in him, and respecting him as the object of faith in that rock and manna, 1 Cor. x. 3, 4. Some of the Jews acknowledge that the Messiah is to come exactly on that day wherein the passover was offered when they fled out of Egypt;† and to redeem Israel the fifteenth day of the month Nisan, which was the day wherein Christ by his death redeemed the world. They came out of Egypt the first month, when the moon was at the full, and in the same month, and the same appearance of the moon, did Christ procure our spiritual liberty by his death.

(3.) The paschal lamb was the fittest to represent Christ. It was a sacri-

* Daillé, Serm. sur 1 Cor. v. 7.
† Eugubin. in Exod. xii., Masius in Josh. v. 10, tells us out of the Talmud that this was the opinion of the ancient Jews.

fice and a feast; a sacrifice in killing it and sprinkling the blood, a feast in their feeding upon it. It represents Christ as a victim satisfying God, as a feast refreshing us; he was offered to God for the expiation of our sins, he is offered to us for application to our souls. The apostle mentions one in the text, the other in the verse following, 'therefore let us keep the feast.' A lamb is both clothes and meat; Christ is clothing to us by his righteousness to cover our nakedness, and food to us by his body and blood to satisfy our appetite, a sacrifice and a feast for us.

The truth of this proposition will appear,

[1.] In the resemblance between the paschal lamb and the Redeemer.

[2.] In the effects or consequents of it.

[1.] In the resemblance between the paschal lamb and the Redeemer.

First, A lamb is a meek creature. It hurts none, is hurt by all; it hangs not back when it is led to the slaughter, it cries not when it is stuck; no greater emblem of patience to be found among irrational creatures. To this the prophet likens our Saviour, when he saith, Isa. liii. 7, 'He was brought as a lamb to the slaughter, and as a sheep before the shearers is dumb, so he opened not his mouth.' How strange was his humility in entering into such a life! How much more stupendous in submitting to such a death, as shameful as his life was miserable! For the Son of God to be counted the vilest of men, the sovereign of angels to be made lower than his creatures, the Lord of heaven to become a worm of the earth, for a creator to be spurned by his creatures, is an evidence of a meekness not to be paralleled. The soldiers that spat upon him and mocked him met not with a reproachful expression from him. He held his peace at their clamours, offered his back to their scourges, reviled them not when he lay under the greatest violence of their rage, was patient under his sufferings, while he was despised more than any man by the people. His calmness was more stupendous than their rage, and the angels could not but more unexpressibly wonder at the patience of the sufferer than the unmercifulness of the executioners. He was more willing to die than they were to put him to death; he suffered not by force; he courted the effusion of his blood when he knew that the hour which his Father had appointed, and man needed, was approaching. Neither the infamy of the cross, nor the sharpness of the punishment, nor the present and foreseen ingratitude of his enemies, could deter him from desiring and effecting man's salvation. He went to it not only as a duty, but an honour, and was content for a while to be the sport of devils, that he might be the spring of salvation to men. And when he was in the furnace of divine wrath, and deserted by his Father, he utters a sensible, but not a murmuring, expostulation; he received our sins upon his shoulders, to confer his divine benefits upon our hearts; he endured the contradiction of sinners against himself; he despised the shame, submitted to the cross; his own worldly reputation was of no value with him, so he might be a sacrifice for the redemption of forlorn man; and, in the whole scene, manifested a patience greater than their cruelty. From this paschal lamb typifying the Redeemer, the Jews might have learned not to expect a Messiah wading through the world in blood and slaughter, sheathing his sword in the bowels of his enemies, and flourishing with temporal victories and prosperity; but one meek, humble, and lowly, suiting the temper of the lamb which represented him in the passover.

Secondly, It was to be 'a lamb without blemish,' Exod. xii. 5. It was to be entire in all its parts, sound, without bruise, scab, or maim; and the reason why it was separated four days before the killing of it was, that they might have time to understand whether it had any spot or defect in it. So

is the Lamb of God ; he was holy in the production of his nature, as well as
in the actions of his life. Though he was of Adam's substance, he was not
contained in Adam's seminal virtue ; he was conceived by the Holy Ghost,
therefore unblemished in his conception, unspotted in his birth. From the
first moment of his conception, he was filled with all supernatural grace according to the capacity of his humanity ; his union with the divine nature
secured him against the sinful infirmities of our nature, and made all supernatural perfections due to him, whereby he might be fitted for all holy
operations. As he was that holy thing in his birth, Luke i. 85, so he was
righteous to the last moment of his life. The law of God was within his
heart, signified by the tables of the law laid up in the ark, a type of his
human nature, which possessed in a sovereign degree all the habits of the
most accomplished righteousness that ever was in the world ; to which
Peter alludes, 1 Peter i. 19, ' a lamb without blemish and spot,' a divine
idea of all virtue, who infinitely surpassed all the holiness of men or angels.
The apostle multiplies expressions to declare it, and all little enough to express it : Heb. vii. 26, ' Holy, harmless, undefiled, separate from sinners.'
He was like us in our nature, but not in our blemishes ; he had our flesh,
but without the least stain of imperfection ; he had the likeness of sinful
flesh, but there was not any inherency of sin in him, or adherency of it to
him in the assumption of our nature, Heb. iv. 15 ; as the serpent upon the
pole had the likeness, but not the venom of the serpent. He was not subjected to our sin, as he was to our natural infirmities ; he had the form of a
servant, without the impurities of our slavery, and in all the days of his
flesh was not found guilty of one inobservance to God or man. It was
necessary he should be so. Had he been obnoxious to sin, he had not been
able to take away the sins of the world. No impure person could have made
our peace with God, because he could not have made his own peace, nor
have procured quietness in his own conscience ; he could not have merited
for himself, much less have wrought any righteousness for others.

Thirdly, The lamb was to be chosen and set apart three days, and killed
the fourth in the evening, Exod. xii. 6, or ' between the two evenings,' as it
is in the Hebrew. Our Saviour was separate from men, manifested himself
in the work of his prophetical office three years and upwards, before he was
offered up as a sacrifice in the fourth year, after he had been solemnly
inaugurated in the exercise of his office. Their keeping the lamb in custody,
and tying it at the feet of their beds, that, being in view, it might mind them
of their servitude in Egypt, and deliverance from thence by the mighty hand
of God, noted the humiliation of Christ before his death, which is called his
prison, and therefore the beginning of his exaltation is called a ' taking him
from prison and from judgment,' Isa. liii. 8. As the lamb was set apart the
tenth day, so some observe* that, in answer to the type, Christ did on the
tenth day solemnly and in triumph enter into Jerusalem, and by the same
gate through which lambs were led to sacrifice ; and he was crucified that
very day and time wherein the paschal lamb was to be slain, between the
two evenings, *i. e.* the declining of the sun from noon, which was the first
evening, and the setting of it, which was the second ; for it was about the
ninth hour, or three in the afternoon, the usual time wherein they killed the
passover, that Christ was offered up as a complete sacrifice to God, Mat.
xxvii. 46–50. It was ordered by God to be killed in the evening, to signify
the sacrifice of the Messiah in the evening of the world. He was crucified
at the end of the second age of the world, the age of the law, and the beginning of the third age, that of the gospel, which is called in Scripture
* Gerhard. loc. commun.

' the last times,' Heb. i. 2 ; and ' the ends of the world,' 1 Cor. x. 11 ; which Peter alludes to when he resembles him to the paschal lamb without blemish, 1 Peter i. 19, 20, 'manifested in these last times for you.' The death of Christ was in the first evening of the world. The sun is turned ; the world shall not last so long after the coming of Christ as it did before ; the state of the world is far declined, and the consummation of all things is not far off, since more than sixteen hundred years are past since the first evening began.

Fourthly, The lamb was to be roasted with fire whole, Exod. xii. 4, 8, 9, not sodden ; to put them in mind of the hardship they endured in the brick kilns of Egypt, and as a type of the scorching sufferings of the Redeemer, whose 'strength was dried up like a potsherd,' and his ' tongue cleaved to his jaws,' Ps. xxii. 15, probably alluding to this roasting of the paschal lamb. He bore the wrath of that God who is a consuming fire, without any water, any mitigation or comfort in his torments. It may note also the gradual rising of the suffering of Christ. As his exaltation was not all at one time, but by degrees, so were his sufferings, by outward wounds, cutting reproaches, and inward agonies. The pains of the body are unexpressible in regard of the nervousness, and therefore sensibility of those parts, his hands and feet, which were pierced upon the cross. The consideration of those millions of sins laid upon him could not but be an unexpressible grief to the pure nature of Christ, had there been nothing of the wrath of God mixed with it. But his bodily death and grief was not all, the wrath of God dreadfully flamed out against his soul : there was the principal seat of the sufferings of Christ, because the soul is the principal seat of that sin for which he suffered. What should have been inflicted on us was inflicted on him ; but we had not only merited the death of the body, but a death joined with the curse of God tormenting the soul. He tasted death, that death which the devil had the power of, that death which men feared, Heb. ii. 9, 14, 15, which is the weight of that eternal death due to sin. How sharp must that be which had the bitterness of a thousand deaths, for those millions of sins which Christ bore in his body, every one of which had deserved an entire death from the hand of God ! How grievous was that death, since he that was more courageous than all the martyrs sweat drops of blood at the approach of the cross, and when he was upon it uttered that terrible complaint, ' My God, my God,' &c., words which never came out of the mouth of any of the martyrs in the strength of their torments ; so that the sufferings of Christ were of that weight that a mere creature would have sunk under them, not only the holiest man but the highest angel.*

Fifthly, Not a bone of the paschal lamb was to be broken, Exod. xii. 46, which, according to the opinion of some,† signified that kind of death to which the breaking of the bones belonged, and that was crucifixion, it being the custom to break the bones of malefactors, that their punishment might be shortened. This was fulfilled in our Saviour, John xix. 36. Death had not a full power over him, he was not broken to pieces by the greatness of his sufferings, but surmounted his enemies upon the cross, and was reserved entire for a resurrection.

There may be other resemblances noted. As the lamb was to be a male, which implies the perfection and strength of the sacrifice, not above a year old, the sufferings of Christ were in the prime of his age.

[2.] There is a resemblance in the effects or consequents of the passover. *First*, The diverting the destroying angel by the sprinkling of the blood

---

* Daillé, Sermons sur Jean iii. Serm sur Gal. iii. p. 613.
† Pearson on the Creed, p. 408.

upon the posts, to be a mark to the angel to spare the firstborn of such houses, was the main end expressed in the institution, Exod. xii. 12, 13. Their preservation could not be merited by the blood of an animal. It had a higher cause, the blood of Christ, which was represented by it; to which purpose the observation of Chrysostom is remarkable: As the statues of kings, though they are inanimate things, yet are sanctuaries to preserve those that fly to them, not because they are statues, but because they represent the prince, so the blood of the lamb preserved the families, not because it was blood, but because it represented the blood of the Messiah. This blood quenched that fire of wrath we had merited, turns away that vengeance which would else consume us. By virtue of this sacrifice we ' pass from death to life,' John v. 24. When God shall judge the world, he will pass over those whom he sees sprinkled with the blood of his well-beloved, and turn from them the edge of that consuming sword which shall strike through the hearts of those that are without this blood of sprinkling. It is only under the warrant of this blood that we can be safe. The Redeemer's blood shed for us and sprinkled on us preserves our souls to eternal life. As the destroying sword did not touch the Israelites, so condemning wrath shall not strike those that are under the protection of it; death shall have no power over them. The blood of the paschal lamb wrought a temporal deliverance, and this blood a spiritual and eternal one.

Secondly, Upon this succeeded that liberty God had designed for them, Exod. xii. 31. As it secured them from death, so it was the earnest of their deliverance, and broke the chains of their slavery. The death of Christ is the foundation of the full deliverance of his people, and the earnest of the fruition of the purchased and promised inheritance. This was the conquest of Pharaoh, upon which soon after followed his destruction. Pharaoh's heart was not bent till the celebration of this passover; that which succeeded upon it laid him more flat than all the former plagues whereby he had smarted. The promises concerning the Messiah, and the sacrifices which were types of him, terrified the devil, Pharaoh's antitype; but only the blood of Christ shed conquers him and pulls captives from his chains. The Israelites' slavery ended when their sacrifices were finished; the efficacy of this divine passover delivers men from a spiritual captivity, under the yoke of sin and the irons of Satan, instates them in the liberty of the children of God, whereby they become a holy nation, a royal priesthood, a free and peculiar people. This strikes off the shackles, works an escape from the pressures of spiritual enemies, changeth a deplorable captivity into a glorious liberty, and reduceth Satan to so impotent a condition, that all his strength and all his stratagems cannot render him master of that soul that is once freed from his chains; as after this passover the Egyptian strength was so scattered that they were as ready to force that people to their liberty as before they were desirous to detain them their slaves, and were never able to reduce them to their former chains.

Thirdly, After this passover they do not only enjoy their liberty, but begin their march to Canaan, the promised and delightful land. They then turn their backs upon Egypt and their faces towards Canaan, and after a pilgrimage in the desert they enter the land flowing with milk and honey. So by the merit of the sacrifice of Christ the true Israelite turns his face from earth to heaven, from a world that lies in wickedness to an inheritance of the saints in light, and travels towards Canaan, whither he shall be sure to enter after he hath finished his pilgrimage, to feed upon the milk and honey, the glory and happiness proper to that state. Then shall all the ends of this passover be fulfilled and completed in the kingdom of God, Luke xxii. 16, and the soul remain for ever in a glorious state beyond the reach of its former tyrants, free from all fear of slavery, for ever rejoicing in the happy accomplishment of the promises of God. In short, as after the celebration of this passover in Egypt, all the promises of God to them began to take place and pass into performance, so by the death of Christ, the true passover, all the promises were made *yea and amen* in him, and began to be made good to every believer.

The use.

1. Of information, Is Christ called our passover ? Then

(1.) The study of the Old Testament is advantageous. The apostle here writes to the Corinthians, among whom were not only Hellenists but Gentiles, who could not understand the nature and ends of the passover without the knowledge of the Old Testament. By this they are implicitly directed to the study of it. The Old Testament verifies the New, and the New illustrates the Old ; the Old shews the promises of God, and the New the performance ; what was predicted in the Old is fulfilled in the New. By comparing both together, the wisdom of God in his conduct is cleared, and the truth of God in his word confirmed. The Old Testament delivers the types, the New interprets them ; the Old presents them like money in a bag, the New spreads them, and discovers the value of the coin. The Israelites in the Old felt the weight of the ceremonies, believers in the New enjoy the riches of them.

(2.) Upon what a slender thread doth the doctrine of transubstantiation hang. Christ is here called the passover. Was the paschal lamb therefore substantially the body of Christ ? Were those lambs that were slain in Egypt, or at any other time, in the celebration of this ordinance, transubstantiated into Christ ? Yet Christ is absolutely here called the passover, and in other places the Lamb, as the bread in the sacrament is called his body, or the wine his blood. Christ is said to be the rock of which the Israelites drank, 1 Cor. x. 4 ; was the rock, or the water that flowed from it, transubstantiated into Christ ? But in Scripture the name proper to the thing represented is given to that which represents it. The lamb is called the passover, because it is a memorial of the angel's passing over the Israelites' families ; and not only called so at the first institution, but above fifteen hundred years after that miraculous mercy. So the bread and wine are called the body and blood of Christ, because they are memorials and signs of his body and blood. If the church of the Jews spake figuratively in the case of the passover, what difficulty is it that Christ should call the memorials of his body and blood by the name of the things they signified ?

(3.) It gives us a probable reason for the change of the Sabbath from the seventh day to the first. That it is changed is evident by apostolical example. It is probable that from the creation the year began in September, the autumnal equinox, the fruits being on the trees at the creation ;* but now God orders the beginning of the year from the time of this first passover, and the consequences following upon it, their deliverance from Egypt, which was in March, the vernal equinox : Exod. xii. 2, ' This month shall be unto you the beginning of months ; it shall be the first month of the year to you.' Had the year began from March at the beginning, it had not been so proper to command them to begin it from that month, which they had always observed before as the beginning of the year. The Israelites had been as it were buried in Egypt, and this being the month of their resurrection, should be the first month of the year. This change of the beginning of the year gives us a probable reason of the change of the Sabbath. If the beginning of the year were changed upon the account of the type, a day might well be changed upon the account of the antitype. If this in the figure were counted greater than creation, that the month of the world's

* Lightfoot's Gleanings on Exod. xii. 2.

creation must give place to it, the substance of this figure appearing might well be the cause of the change of a day, and the seventh day of the creation give place to the first day of the perfection of redemption.

(4.) The ancient Jews were under a covenant of grace. Christ was the end, the spirit, the life of their sacrifices. The passover, rock, sacrifices, manna, were the swaddling-bands wherein he was wrapped. They ' ate of the same spiritual meat, drank of the same spiritual drink;' the ' rock which followed them,' cherished them, and watered them, ' was Christ,' 1 Cor. x. 3, 4. Christ to come was set forth to them as an object of faith. Christ was the rock, the passover sacramentally. Their sacraments and ours were the same *in re,* though diverse in signs. Hence their sacraments are attributed to us, circumcision and the passover, spiritually; ours in the same manner to them, baptism and the Lord's Supper, 1 Cor. x. 2, 3. They indeed had Christ, as it were, in his infancy; we in his ripe and full age. They had him under the obscure veils of lambs, bullocks, goats; we have him in his person. They had the sun under a cloud; we the sun at noonday in his glory.

2. Comfort; in the security Christ procures. The destroying angel was not to enter into any sprinkled house, no passage was afforded to him. The wrath of God, or the malice of the devil, can have no power over them that are sprinkled with the blood of Christ. In the efficacy. The blood of the lamb was but a sign of that deliverance of the Israelites, but could not purge their defiled consciences; but the blood of our Lamb hath merited our salvation, can cleanse our consciences from dead and condemning works to serve the living God, and rejoice in him, who, without this sprinkling, will be to us a consuming fire. As the passover was killed, that he might be their food as well as their security, so was Christ crucified, that he might be our atonement and our nourishment, our shield and our food, to make us partakers of his benefits by a spiritual application, and a close incorporation of us with himself. This comfort is the greater, by how much the tyrant we are delivered from is more dreadful than Pharaoh; whose design is not only, like his, to afflict our bodies, but tumble our souls and bodies into the same hell with himself. It is from the wrath of God our passover hath delivered us; and what is the anger of Pharaoh to the fury of an offended Deity, kindled against us by our multiplied transgressions? It is true, deliverance is yet but begun; it is not yet perfect; miseries and spiritual contests are to be expected. Pharaoh will pursue, but shall not overtake; the sea shall ruin the Egyptians, but secure the Israelites; death shall not swallow up those who are sprinkled with this holy blood. Consider also, if God were so punctual to his word in so light an instance as the blood of the lamb, he will be as stedfast to it in so great an instance as the blood of his Son beheld cleaving to the soul.

3. Exhortation.

(1.) Thankfully remember this passover. A redemption from divine wrath, a spiritual life and liberty, the fruits and purchase of this lamb, are incomparably beyond the temporal deliverance conferred upon the Jews. The giving thanks was a duty annexed to the eating of the paschal lamb, wherein they blessed God for the mercy shewed to their fathers in bringing them out of Egypt.* How infinitely more precious is the blood of the Son of God than the blood of a silly animal! How highly doth the benefit of the one surmount the immediate fruit of the other! And is it not fit our praises should surpass those of the Jews for the old passover? Remember it with bitterness. The Israelites ate the passover with bitter. herbs; shall

* Buxtorff's Synag. Jud. cap. xiii.

we be without it when we consider the cause of our slavery, and the means of our deliverance ? A bitterness of soul will make the taste of the benefit of Christ more delicious.

(2.) Inquire whether he be our passover. He is our passover, but is he a lamb eaten by us, owned by us ? He is ours by the gift of God, but is he ours by the acceptation of our souls ? It is the most useful, most necessary inquiry we can make. All the comforts of possessions in the world consists in the word *mine, ours*, and the use as ours ; all the comfort of spiritual mercy consists in property, possession, and fruition. If he be our Lamb, we must be like him, we must learn of him. As he is the cause of our expiation, he must be the copy of our imitation : Mat. xi. 29, ' Learn of me, for I am meek and lowly, and you shall find rest unto your souls.' No rest without a sense of sin, and humiliation for it. This Lamb is ours in the liberty, life, glory, and rest he hath purchased, when we are like him, when we learn of him.

(3.) Have faith in the blood of Christ. The killing the lamb signified the death of Christ, the sprinkling the blood signified the application of it by faith. It was not the blood contained in the veins of the lamb, or shed upon the ground, that was the mark of deliverance, but sprinkled upon the posts ;* nor is it the blood of Christ circulating in his body, or shed upon the cross, which solely delivers us, but as applied by faith to the heart. That was sprinkled upon every house that desired safety, and this upon every soul that desires happiness. Satan will have an undoubted right over all that are without the token of this blood, as the destroying angel had over every house that was not sprinkled with the blood of the passover. This was the sanctuary of the Israelites, the want of it, the death of the Egyptian first-born, from the prince to the peasant, from him that sat upon the throne to him that was in the dungeon, Exod. xii. 29. Without this blood of sprinkling, neither prince nor beggar can possibly escape ; the one's grandeur cannot privilege, nor the other's misery procure a pity. The blood was to be taken and put upon the posts ; this condition was requisite. To have a part in the great passover of our Lord, the condition is to ' sprinkle our hearts' by faith with his blood, 1 Pet. i. 2. Had an Israelite's family neglected this, it had felt the edge of the angel's sword ; the lamb had not availed him, not by a defect of the sacrifice, but by their own negligence or contempt of the condition. Or had they used any other mark, they had not diverted the stroke ; no work, no blood, but the blood and sufferings of the Redeemer, can take away the sin of the world ; without it, every man in the world lies in the sin of his nature, under the wrath of God. If anything else in the world had a virtue for it, it could not prevail, unless God would accept it, because he did not appoint it. This only is designed to be our passover ; where else can we find any remedy against the stings of our consciences, any ease under the weight of our sins, any consolation against divine wrath ?

(4.) Let us leave the service of sin. The Israelites after this passover did no more work at the brick-kilns of Egypt ; they ceased to be Pharaoh's slaves, and began to be the Lord's freemen. God intended no more to turn them to their former labour ; he would have them eat their passover with their loins girt, in the habit of travellers. We must be in a readiness to leave the confines of Egypt, all commerce with, and service of sin and Satan, and have our faces set towards Canaan, our steps directed to observe his commands for our rule, to attain his promises for our comfort, and go

* Durant *Agneau Paschal.*

forward rejoicing in his goodness, celebrating his name, offering our souls and bodies to him, which is a reasonable service to Christ our passover.

Doct. 2. Christ is a sacrifice, ἐθύθη. The word θύειν properly signifies to kill as a sacrifice.* Some dispute whether the paschal lamb was a sacrifice, because in a sacrifice something was offered to God, either in whole or in part, but the paschal lamb was not offered to God, but eaten by the people; it was killed to the end that the blood should be sprinkled upon the posts of the doors, and therefore it is rather a sacrament than a sacrifice. Again, the Jews did not sacrifice out of the temple, and therefore in their captivities they did not sacrifice, but both then and now they celebrate the passover. Others again think it a sacrifice, because the sprinkling of the blood upon the posts was, in a manner, an offering it to God to turn away his wrath (Exod. xxxiv. 25, 'Thou shalt not offer the blood of my sacrifice with leaven, neither shall the sacrifice of the feast of the passover be left until the morning'), and a means of reconciliation to him: Deut. xvi. 2, 'Thou shalt therefore sacrifice the passover unto the Lord.' But whether properly a sacrifice or no, yet it was significative of the propitiating blood of Christ, the future grand sacrifice, by virtue of which we have our deliverance. The apostle might here allude to the passover and other sacrifices, all which did prefigure the spiritual redemption by the Messiah. A sacrifice is defined to be a religious oblation of something consecrated and dedicated to God, by the ministry of a priest, according to God's institution, to be destroyed, for a testimony of the worship of God and an external symbol.†

I shall lay down some propositions for the illustrating this doctrine.

1. Sacrifices were instituted as types of Christ.

(1.) They were instituted by God. No satisfactory reason can be rendered of the custom of sacrificing, derived from the first age of the world, practised by all nations, till the appearance of the gospel abolished it in those places where it shone. It could not be a dictate of the law of nature inscribed in all men's hearts, for then they would have been of force still. Christianity doth not extinguish any beam of natural light, but adds a clearness to it; it abolisheth only what was corrupt, or only ceremonial. Though natural light could not invent them, yet it made them entertainable by all, while they were stung with the conscience of sin and expectations of vengeance. Men might know that they were unlike to what they were in their creation; they found their light darkened, their beauty defaced, and might suppose that a God of infinite goodness did not send them forth in such a shape out of his mint; this deformity must come upon them for some provocation, and by the means of their own sin. They also found the marks of God's anger upon them, saw and felt his thundering judgments in the world; they had a notion of the vindictive justice of God; they had frequent manifestations of it upon themselves and others. This the apostle affirms generally of the heathens: Rom. i. 32, 'They knew the judgment of God, that they which commit such things are worthy of death;' they had a sentiment of God and revenging justice in their consciences, that it did not become the holiness and righteousness of the divine nature to let their rebellions remain unpunished. The apostle speaks not there of any supernatural revelation, but the natural manifestation by the creatures, whereby his justice was discovered, as well as his eternal power and Godhead. Upon this account sacrifices were practised among them, as seeming to them congruous means

* Θύειν ἱερεῖα. Θύειν θυσίας. Stephan.
† Cloppenburg. de Sacrificiis, p. 4. Owen against Biddle, p. 479.

for the expiation of sin, and to put a stop tó the wrath of God, either feared by them or already kindled among them. For by this action they confessed their desert of death for their crimes, acknowledged God's sovereignty and right over all they had, and owned his mercy in accepting in their stead the life of an irrational animal. For when men are sensible of the anger of God, the next thought in order is how to escape it. When men see a magistrate suffer murders and violences in a nation to go unpunished, they generally have an horror of it, and expect some judgment of God, till an expiation be made by the death of the offender. And could they reasonably think God to be void of that virtue of justice, which is commendable over all the world by the light of nature, when those perfections of human nature, left in the midst of corruption, are but as little sparks to those which are infinite in God? They were at first instituted by God; though we have not the institution of them in express words, yet we have the practice in Abel, Gen. iv. 4; afterwards in Noah, Gen. viii. 20, Noah offered burnt offerings on the altar. And since the apostle, Heb. xi. 4, speaks of Abel's offering a sacrifice in faith, it must be God's command; for no act of worship of a human invention can please God. The demand might be made, Who hath required those things at your hands? It had not been formally good unless offered in faith; nor had it been a fit ground or medium of faith without a divine stamp upon it. If the foundation were not divine, the act could not be acceptable.

(2.) No other reason can be rendered of the institution of them, but as typical of the great sacrifice of the Redeemer. The Scripture gives us the only account of this; all nations in the world without the Scripture are in the dark as to the design of those sacrifices, though they practised them conformably to the sentiments of their consciences. The institution of them from the beginning of the world cannot reasonably be concluded to be for any other end than to prefigure some sufficient sacrifice, able to appease the wrath of God, and pacify the consciences of men, and to instruct men in what was to be brought upon the stage in time, in the exhibition of the person of the Redeemer. In the state of innocence we find no mention of them, nor could they have had any place had man continued in his created rectitude and integrity. The covenant of works, which then was the rule and ground of man's standing, required not faith in a Redeemer, and therefore implied no such act as sacrificing. Man then had no relation to God but as a creature, and persisting in obedience could not by the righteous law of God be subject to death, and therefore no other subjected to death for him; for to have any one to die for us implies that we had merited death ourselves. It cannot enter into the reason of man to imagine what use they could be for in that state. Death was not due to the righteousness of man's nature, but to his corruption. Adam stood upon his own bottom, and was the foundation of all his posterity, and no person was substituted in his room. What could sacrifices then represent? Whereof could they be typical? Could they be for the confession of sin? There was none to confess. Could they be to represent a death deserved? There was no crime committed whereby to merit it. Could it be to typify Christ to come? There was no revelation of him till after the fall, Gen. iii. 15. And supposing (as some do) that Christ should have been incarnate had man persisted in his first integrity, yet none suppose that Christ should have been crucified in that nature without the entrance of sin. What end could be supposed of shedding his blood? For satisfaction of justice? Justice was not provoked. For example? Man, perfect in all virtue, needed none; besides, he was not capable of the exercise of suffering virtues, who was not capable of suffering in that state. They were appointed therefore after the fall, as the representations of this sacrifice, so necessary for the expiation of sin. And some conclude with probability that they were put in practice immediately after the making the promise of the seed of the woman (though there be no express scripture for it), from Gen. iii. 21, ' God made them coats of skins,' which probably were the skins of slain beasts, very likely consumed by fire from heaven, as the Jews say Abel's sacrifice was, which was a token of God's acceptation of it. This was probably done for the confirmation of the truth of the promise, the clearer representing the design of it to them, by substituting another in the room of the offender, and comforting them thereby, since ' without shedding of blood is no remission,' Heb. ix. 22. And of those sacrifices the skins were appointed to be the garments of the first man and woman, to put them in mind of their apostasy, and the way of their recovery, and the righteousness of another, wherein they were to stand before God. But howsoever it be, we cannot suppose Abel to be the first that offered sacrifice, and that 129 years should run without the offering of any.* It is likely Abel was slain in that year, because Seth was born in the 130th year of Adam's age, Gen. v. 3. Indeed sacrifices, as they looked backward, could be no other than a transcript of the agreement between the Father and the Son, of the one's paying, and the other's accepting the price of blood for the redemption of man ;† and as they looked forward, a type of the real performance of the sufferings on the one part, and the acceptance of them on the other part, when the fulness of time should come wherein they were actually to be undergone. This tradition of sacrifices was handed down to all nations of the world, but the knowledge of the end of them was lost. Yet in an exercise of reason they might rise to a consideration, that this low blood could not be a compensation for sin, as not being proportioned to the dignity of him with whom they had to do. But as to the true end of them, the representation of a higher sacrifice, they were not able to discern it by all the reason in the world, after they had lost the revelation of it. By the way, this adds a credit to the Scripture, since it gives us an account of the reason of that which was practised by all nations, which they could not without revelation render any tolerable reason for. The Scripture makes it plain. God would have a representation of that which the Redeemer was to offer in the fulness of time for the abolition of sin. As men always need a satisfaction of the justice of God, so God would have it that in all their worship there should be a mark of this necessity, and some presage that one day there should be a sacrifice eternally efficacious, the reality of which was represented by this figure.‡

(3.) Christ did really answer to these types. They were all Christ in a cloud ; the substance did answer to the shadows, and he was used in such a manner as the figures of him were. Christ was a victim put in the place of the sinner to appease the anger of God ; and as sins were laid upon the head of the sacrifice, so God ' put upon him the iniquities of us all,' Isa. liii. 6. In regard of this typicalness of the legal administration, Christ is often called a lamb, and ' the Lamb of God,' John i. 29, and ' a Lamb slain from the foundation of the world,' not only in the decree, but in the type of him, the first sacrifice mentioned in Scripture, which was a firstling of the flock, Gen. iv. 2, 4, Abel being a keeper of sheep. To those figures of him he seems to refer in his last speech upon the cross, John xix. 30, ' It is finished.' The whole design of the daily and extraordinary sacrifices was

---

* Cloppenburg. de Saçrific. pp. 12, 13.
† Owen on Hebrews, vol. ii. Exercit., p. 61, much changed.
‡ Amyraut sur Hebr. vii. p. 50.

completed, the demerit of sin and severity of divine justice were manifested, and the truth of God, as well as his love, made glorious therein; upon which followed the rending of the veil, and the setting heaven open for the entrance of all that believed in him, to approach to God upon the account of this sacrifice.

2. The sacrifices thus instituted were of themselves insufficient, and could not expiate sin, they must therefore receive their accomplishment in some other. Being but shadows by their institution, they could make nothing perfect, Heb. x. 1, 11, where, and in the following verses, the apostle lays the glory of the legal sacrifices in the dust; nor really atone, though they typically did, they did but evidence the guilt of sin and misery of men, whence the law is called a minister of death.

(1.) It was not consistent with the honour of God to be contented with the blood of a beast for an expiation of sin. How could there be in it a discovery of the severity of his justice, the purity of his holiness, or the grandeurs of his grace? How would he have been known in his infinite hatred of sin, if he had accepted the blood of an abject animal as an atonement for the sin of a spiritual soul? Was it becoming the majesty of God, who had denounced a curse in the law upon the transgressors of it, and published it with so terrible a solemnity, as thunders, lightnings, earthquakes, which made it pass under the title of a fiery law, Deut. xxxiii. 2, in regard of the severe menaces against the transgressor, to make so light of it, to accept the mangling a few beasts in the place of the offender against it?* Should he appear on mount Sinai with ten thousand of his angels in the giving of it, to let all the threatenings of it vanish into smoke? Was it likely all those curses should be poured out upon a few irrational and innocent creatures, who had never broken that law? Can it be imagined, that after so terrible a proclamation, he should acquiesce in so light a compensation as the death of a poor beast? No man can reasonably have such despicable thoughts of the majesty, justice, and holiness of God, or the vileness of sin and greatness of its provocation, as to imagine that the one could be contented, or the other expiated, by the blood of a lamb or bullock. Our own consciences will tell us that if God will have a sacrifice, it must be proportioned to the majesty of him whom we have offended, and the greatness of the crime we have committed.

(2.) They have no proportion to the sin of man. The sin of a rational creature is too foul to be expiated by the blood of an irrational creature; nor could the blood of a human body, though the first-born, the strength and delight of man, Micah vi. 7, much less of a beast, bear any proportion to the sin of the soul: Heb. x. 4, 'It is not possible that the blood of bulls and goats should take away sin.' The butchery of so poor a creature cannot be any compensation for that which is a disparagement of the Creator of the world. What alliance was there between the nature of a beast and that of a man? An inferior nature can never atone the sin of a nature superior to it. There is indeed in the groans of those dying creatures some demonstration of God's wrath, but no bringing in an everlasting righteousness, nor any vindication of the honour of the law.

(3.) The reiteration of them shews their insufficiency.† Had the wrath of God been appeased by them, why should the fire burn perpetually upon the altar? Why should it be perpetually with the carcases of beasts? As often as they were offered, a conscience of sin was excited in the presenter of them, iniquity was called to remembrance, Heb. x. 2, 3. The whole scene of that administration loudly published that the wrath against sin was

* Amyraut, des Religions, p 309, 310.   † Jackson, vol. ii. 292.

not appeased, the guilt of the soul not wiped off. If a man had presented a sacrifice for his sin one day, and fallen into the same, or another, before night, he must have repeated his sacrifice for a new expiation; had there been ability in them to perform so great a thing, there had not been a repetition. They were rather a commemoration of sin, and confessions of it, than expiations of any; rather accusers than atoners.

(4.) God had often spoken slightly of them. He resembles them to the 'cutting off a dog's neck,' when done with an unholy heart, Isa. lxvi. 3. While the temple stood, he struck their fingers off from hanging upon them, Isa. i. 11–13; indeed, he would 'not reprove them for their offering,' Ps. l. 8, but he would not have them place their justification in them. He professeth he had no delight in them, Ps. xl. 6. If all sacrifices of the law were not of such value as love to him and fear of him, they could not expiate; and if that which was more excellent than those were too weak to effect it, an utter inability must remain in the other. He doth frequently predict the abolition of them, and hath destroyed the temple to which he had affixed them, which remains in desolation without a sacrifice to this day. Besides, he never provided a typical remedy for all sins in them; some transgressors were to be cut off without a sacrifice for them, according to the judicial law, the rule of the government of that people; upon which account David argues that God did not delight in them: Ps. li. 16, 'Thou desirest not sacrifice, thou delightest not in burnt-offerings,' because he had provided no sacrifices for those sins David at that time was guilty of; whereupon he desires, ver. 18, that God would 'do good to Sion in his good pleasure;' bring forth that Redeemer out of Sion which he had promised, whose sacrifice, being a sacrifice of righteousness, should be infinitely delightful to him. Since, therefore, it is unbecoming the majesty of God to be satisfied with the blood of a calf or goat, since it bears no proportion to the sin of man; since he never intended those institutions to be perpetual; since the threatenings of the law must, if God be a God of truth, have their accomplishment either in the person offending, or in some undertaker for him, capable to bear them in his stead; there must be some other sacrifice suited to the majesty of God, able to make an expiation proportionable to the sin of man, a sacrifice able to remove the guilt and pacify the conscience, a rest for God and a security for the creature. The natural order of things requires, and the whole design of those legal institutions declares, that as he that keeps the law should have a reward from the goodness of God, so he that breaks it should endure a punishment from the justice of God; and every man being a breaker of the law, must either sink under the menaces of it, or present a sufficient sacrifice to God to avert his wrath, a precious blood that may quench the flames of his anger, that God may say to the sinner, 'I have found,' and accepted, 'a ransom' for thee. And what is said of this may be said of all our duties and performances, the staves upon which men naturally lean for acceptation of their persons. They can no more be acceptable in themselves to God, or remedies for man, than the legal sacrifices, which had no merit in themselves, but represented that which was grateful to God and meritorious for the creature; and whatsoever virtue and efficacy they had was not from themselves, but from that which they shadowed.

3. Proposition. Such a sacrifice, therefore, is necessary for a sinful creature. No creature can be such a sacrifice. As the apostle argues, 'If righteousness be by the law, then was Christ dead in vain,' Gal. ii. 21. Upon the same account it may be concluded, if expiation could be made by a creature for himself, in vain did God send his Son to be a propitiation for sin. Had

man himself been sufficient for it, God's sending his Son had rather appeared an act of cruelty to Christ than of mercy to us.   Who could think God should expose the delight of his soul to our infirmities and a shameful death, if a sufficient sacrifice could have been found elsewhere ?   Besides, the wrath of God being so terrible that the human nature of Christ trembled at it, how is any creature ever able to bear the horror of it, and stand as a sacrifice under the weighty strokes of that justice ?

(1.) What is a sacrifice for sin must be pure and sinless.   God will not accept a defiled offering.   He that provokes him by his own offence is not capable of appeasing him for his own or another's.   The least blemish in a typical lamb rendered it unfit for the altar.   God is infinitely pure who is offended ; the law is exactly holy which is contemned.   A compensation cannot be made to a holy God and a righteous law by the criminal without enduring an infinite penalty, which, because it cannot be *intensive* so, must be *extensive*, infinite in point of duration, *i. e.* since it cannot be infinite it must be perpetual.   As he would be always suffering, so he would be always sinning, and wrath can never be appeased by that which provokes it at the same time it endeavours to pacify it.   What is displeasing can never be capable of pleasing an infinite holiness.   If a man had but one sin, and thought to expiate that by anything he could do, he would still need another sacrifice to expiate the sin of the former, and so would be always satisfying and always sinning, since ' there is no man that doth good and sins not,' *i. e.* in the doing of it, Eccles. vii. 20 ; he could not possibly find anything in himself or in any corrupted creature, where he might rest his foot with any content and security.   Where any sin is, though but one, there can be no merit.   Whatsoever is done after all our strength is gone is done by the grace of God.   In that case God deserves service of us, but we deserve no acceptation from him.   Since, therefore, we are not able since our fall to do one good work, we are not able to offer one acceptable sacrifice, how can man then satisfy for himself, any more than a man that owes a shilling pays that by borrowing two, whereby he is so far from paying his debt that he increaseth it ?

(2.) An infinite sacrifice is necessary for a sin in some respects infinite ; for every sin entrencheth upon the honour of an infinite God.   An infinite sacrifice is due for an infinite offence.   God is infinite in his glory, which is impaired, infinite in his sovereignty, which is degraded ; the sacrifice must be of as great a dignity as the offence was of malignity.   It must be fully proportioned to the sin of man and the majesty of God.*   What man, nay, what creature is capable of such a proportion ?   The condition of his nature is too low, and the limits of his dignity too strait, to correspond with such an effect.   The drop of a bucket and the dust of the balance are of too vile a nature to be a satisfactory sacrifice to God.   All men are no more, Isa. xl. 15–17, nay, ' worse than nothing and vanity,' and therefore all men in the world put together would be so far from redeeming themselves by a sufficient sacrifice, that as themselves, so their sacrifice, would be worse than nothing and vanity, and would be overwhelmed under the punishment due to their offence.   Finite bears no proportion to infinite, therefore a finite sacrifice carries no equivalent compensation in it for an infinite wrong ; so that neither length of time nor strength of nature can ever make a recompence for that offence, which increaseth in proportion according to the dignity of the person against whom it is committed.   If every hair of our head were a soul, and every soul a sacrifice, all would be too poor an amends for that glorious God wronged by us, though it had been but by one act of rebellion ; for man cannot do any act of that value

* Amyraut, des Religions, p. 395.

in the nature of satisfaction, as one act of sin is injurious in the nature of
wrong. Upon the same account of finiteness no angel could be a proportionable sacrifice to the justice of God for the sin of man ; for, though the
excellency of the angelical far transcends the nature of man, yet it cannot
equal the dignity of God.* They are creatures, and an unconceivable distance is perpetually between creatures and the Creator ; therefore saith Job,
chap. iv. 18, 'He puts no trust in his servants, and his angels he chargeth
with folly.' All the excellency of the angelical nature is despicable compared with God, and if God did not secure them they would fall ; if God
did not preserve light in them, they would be darkness as well as we. If
they could not because they are creatures, man could not because he was a
sinful creature ; 'Thousands of rivers of oil, and thousands of rams,' would
have borne far less proportion to the Creator of them, or to sins against
him, Micah vi. 6, 7.

(3.) Necessary, in regard of the justice of God, which is an immutable
and infinite perfection of the divine essence. As God is so infinitely holy as
it is impossible he should not but hate the least sin, so he is infinite in his
justice, and cannot let any sin go unpunished, since he hath declared by his
law, that 'cursed is he that continueth not in all things of the law to do
them,' and that it was irrevocably passed, that 'in the day man ate of the forbidden fruit he should die the death,' Gen. ii. 17. As the perfection of his
nature requires that he should have for sin an implacable aversion, so the
same perfection requires that justice be not appeased without punishment.
Since God therefore would have a sacrifice for sin, to have one disproportioned to his infinite dignity and justice, had been the same as to have none
at all. An infinite sacrifice cannot be offered but by an infinite person ; it
is necessary therefore that one of the persons of the Trinity should be this
sacrifice, and it was most congruous to the wisdom of God, upon several
accounts, that it should be the second. This sacrifice is necessary at least
in point of becomingness. As God is the author of all things, and placed them
in a rectitude from which they departed by their own folly, and sullied that
glory they were created to manifest ; it became him to bring things into
order again by such a method as should manifest his hatred of that disorder
sin had introduced into the world, and how strict a guardian he would be of
the eternal order of things, and of those sacred laws whereby he governs the
world : Heb. ii. 10, 'It became him for whom are all things, and by whom
are all things, in bringing many sons to glory, to make the captain of their
salvation perfect through suffering.' As God had made all things for his
glory, so it was fit his Son, becoming the head of the world, should be put
in such a posture as to shew forth the glory of God in the most illustrious
manner. Now, in the sufferings of Christ, the justice of God flames more
bright than it could in any creature, and shews itself inflexible against sin ;
the treasures of his grace are wider opened than could be in any other act,
and his wisdom sparkles more gloriously in bringing men to glory by punishment ; and since he made all things, and that for himself, it became him
after the apostasy of man and the defacing the creation, to restore things in
such a way as might conduce most to his own glory and the happiness of
the creature.

4. Proposition. Christ only was fit to be this sacrifice. Whatsoever any
creature could have done had been a debt of duty, and that could not have
made a compensation for a debt of rebellion. Whatsoever a mere creature
could do was by the gift of God, and therefore could not merit anything at
the hand of God. Whatsoever is meritorious must be our own, as well as

* Amyraut, des Religions, p. 335.

that which is not due. Besides, from any other hand God would have received less than the offence merited; at the best, it would have been but a feigned and partial satisfaction, which had not been congruous to the wisdom and justice of God, since he determined it necessary to have a sacrifice. But Christ in his divine nature was 'equal with God,' Philip. ii. 6, and therefore in his person was answerable to the dignity of the person offended; and as he was in the form of a servant and innocent, he offered that which was not due from himself and upon his own account to God; for though as a creature he was bound to the obedience of the precepts of the law, yet as an innocent creature he was not obliged to the penalties of the law: suffering was in no wise due upon his own account. And he was without blemish. Had he been a criminal, he could not have been a remedy. He had also an alliance with both parties; he could treat with God as partaking of his glory, and be a sacrifice for man as partaking of the infirmities of his nature. He had a body to bear the stroke due to a victim, and a divine nature to sustain him under it. He had a human nature to offer as a sacrifice, and a divine nature to render it valuable and infinitely meritorious; being God and man, he wanted not a fitness to accomplish so great an undertaking. If he had not been man, he could not have been a sacrifice; and if he had not been God, he could not have been a remedy.

5. It was necessary, in regard of his office of priesthood, that he should be a sacrifice. He was constituted as 'a priest for ever,' by an oath, Ps. cx. 4. Now, he could not be a priest without a sacrifice; a priest and a sacrifice are relatives: Heb. v. 1, 'Every high priest taken from among men, is ordained for men in things pertaining to God, that he may offer both gifts and sacrifices for sins. It is therefore of necessity that this man have something to offer,' Heb. viii. 3. As he was a prophet, he was to have a doctrine to teach; as a king, he was to have subjects to govern; as a priest, he was to have a sacrifice to offer; as he was a prophet, he was to deliver something from God to men; as he was a priest, he was to present something for man to God; as a prophet, he was to teach men obedience to God; as a priest, he was to make God propitious to men; that which he was to offer must be expiatory, that is the proper notion of a sacrifice; the other offerings are termed gifts. If he had offered the blood of bulls and goats, we had been in the same case we were in before; the insufficiency of them had not been removed by the dignity of the offerer; they could never in their own nature be proportioned to the dignity of the wronged sovereign, or be adequate to the punishment the criminal had deserved. The impossibility of their taking away sin is positively asserted, Heb. x. 4. The transcendent excellency of the priest could never alter the disproportion between the justice of God provoked by sin, and the death of the miserable beast for it; though the person offering had been greater, the thing offered had been the same; besides, the offending nature had not suffered, but a nature inferior to it. They must have been always offered, the repetition of them must have been continued, and had that been a proper employment for the Son of God, to have been always imbruing his hands in the blood of animals? But a sacrifice must be offered by him (if he did not offer one, he was no priest), and none but himself was a sacrifice worthy to be offered by so great a priest. He offered but once, and it was himself he offered, Heb. vii. 27. And this was so spotless, Heb. ix. 14; and of so sweet smelling savour, Eph. v. 2, that it need not again be repeated, Heb. ix. 28. His unblemished 'soul was made an offering for sin,' Isa. liii. 10. For being a priest of another kind than the legal priests, he must have a sacrifice of another kind.

6. Proposition. Jesus Christ, then, was a sacrifice in his human nature. To this end a body was prepared for him, to be substituted in the place of those sacrifices wherein God had no pleasure: Heb. x. 5, ' Sacrifice and offering thou wouldst not, but a body hast thou prepared me.' Cited out of Ps. xl. 6, ' Mine ears hast thou opened' (as some* think figuratively, the ear being taken for the whole body, because obedience is learned by the ear, the instrument of hearing the will of another). The will of God was, that he should be an offering in this body: Heb. x. 10, ' By which will we are sanctified through the offering of the body of Christ once for all.' And his soul was an offering for sin, Isa. liii. 10. The first promise evidenced, that though the seed of the woman should tear up the empire of the devil, which by the law he had over sinners, yet it should be by the suffering something from him, by having his heel bruised. There was an obedience to the law to be performed, without which he had not been capable of being a sacrifice ; the penalty of the law to be endured, without which he could not be an actual sacrifice. Neither of those could be but in the human nature; obedience to the law is not consistent with the sovereignty of God ; according to his divine nature he was under no law. Suffering was impossible to the Deity ; it is the property of God to be immutable and impassible. His human nature therefore was the sacrifice ; for as he was made of a woman, whereby he took our nature, as he was made under the law, whereby he subjected himself to our obedience, he ' redeemed us from under the law,' from our condemnation, Gal. iv. 5. He that was to break the serpent's head, i. e. to dissolve the power which, as an executioner, he had from an offended God, was to be the seed of the woman. And this he effected by his death and bloody sacrifice, appeasing the wrath of God, and thereby destroying the power of the jailor, which he obtained by the entrance of sin and the curse of the law : Heb. ii. 14, ' Through death he destroyed him that had the power of death,' i. e. the devil. This sacrifice was both of soul and body, as the threatening was, ' In the day thou eatest thou shalt die the death,' i. e. be subject to the death and condemnation both of soul and body. As the reward of goodness respects the entire man, composed of soul and body, so doth the punishment of sin, which hath corrupted one as well as the other. The sacrifice therefore to be offered for the appeasing that wrath, and removing that curse, was to consist both of soul and body.

7. Proposition. That whereby this sacrifice was sanctified was the divine nature. Every sacrifice was sanctified by the altar, Mat. xxiii. 19. There must be something to add an infinite value to the sufferings of his humanity,† which could be nothing but the divine nature, and union with it. Nothing but that which is infinite can confer an infinite value on that which is finite. The infiniteness of dignity resides in the divine nature and essence, and the infiniteness of dignity is as incommunicable as the infiniteness of essence. For it hath its root and foundation in the infiniteness of being, and the one is but the reflection of the other. It is impossible to add a dignity without limits, but one must attribute an essence without bounds, as it is impossible that anything can possess the lustre and enlivening virtue of the sun but the sun itself. The human nature suffered, and the divine nature sanctified the humanity, and by reason of this admirable union, and the reflection of the divinity upon the humanity, what was done to the human nature upon the cross, is ascribed to the whole person. They ' crucified the Lord of glory,' 1 Cor. ii. 8. And God ' purchased the church with his own blood,' Acts xx. 28. It was this made his sufferings acceptable to God, whose justice was to be satisfied ; and efficacious for

---

* Owen against Biddle, p. 477.   † Amyraut, des Religions, p. 336.

man, whose happiness and commerce with God were to be restored, and his indigencies to be supplied. Thus some interpret Heb. ix. 14, 'Through the eternal Spirit he offered himself to God,' understanding by eternal Spirit his Deity ; not that he suffered in his divine nature, but by virtue of that presented himself to his Father a most acceptable sacrifice. So that he had a human nature to serve for a sacrifice, and an eternal spirit or divine nature, wherein he subsisted, from whence that sacrifice derived an infinite dignity, as gold, which hath a lustre of itself, hath a greater when the sun shines full upon it. We may see here how Christ was a priest, sacrifice, altar, in several respects : a priest in his person, a sacrifice in his humanity, the altar in his divinity. He was the offerer and the sacrifice, both are expressed : Eph. v. 2, 'He offered up himself.' Active as a priest, passive as a victim ; as one, offering ; as the other, offered. Upon this account of his blood being offered by his person, he is called God in the act of oblation of his blood for the redemption of the church, Acts xx. 28, 'which he,' referring to God, 'hath purchased with his own blood.' The Jews and soldiers were not the priests, as some affirm. They were the instruments of slaying him, but not with the intention of a sacrifice. They were instruments in it, but could not force him to it. His death was intended by them ; his death as a sacrifice intended by himself ; his laying down his life was of himself, John xx. 18, which is not meant barely of his death, but of his death as respecting his sheep, ver. 15, and indeed unless it had been voluntary, it had not been savoury.

8. Proposition. Upon the sacrifice of Christ all his other sacerdotal acts depend, and from thence they receive their validity for us. It is fit therefore we should well understand and often consider this sacrifice, which is the foundation of all our peace and comfort in reference to God. This was the chief thing God eyed in the first declaration of him, Gen. iii. 15, in the serpent's bruising his heel ; nothing but this spoken of. His resurrection was first represented in the safety of Isaac, after he was designed to death, and other things not till after that successively ; God making the light to dawn upon them by degrees.

(1.) This was the ground of his ascension and entrance into heaven as a priest. The high priest was not to enter within the veil without blood ; what was in the type, was to be answered in the antitype. An expiatory sacrifice was necessary to precede his ascension to heaven ; the sacrifice must be offered upon the earth, as the legal sacrifices were without,—heaven was no place for slaughter,—and with his blood he was to enter. Heaven's gates had been shut against him without it. Death was the penalty threatened, if the legal high priest ventured to step into the holy of holies without blood. The apostle argues from this, Heb. ix. 7, 'Into the second went the high priest alone once every year, not without blood, which he offered for himself, and for the errors of the people,' and ver. 25. According to this type, Christ by his own blood entered once into the holy place. How and in what order ? After he had obtained redemption for us, Heb. ix. 12, which is ascribed to his death, ver. 15. His entrance into heaven, and what he doth for us there, is laid upon the account of his death as a sacrifice upon the earth ; by virtue of which he went to heaven to present it to God, and apply it to us. And besides, all his royalty and power, whereby we have security and protection from him, depends upon this ; for it is because of that obedience to blood and death which he rendered to God, that he hath given him a name above every name, and advanced him to a sovereign power : Philip. ii. 8, 9, 'Wherefore God also hath highly exalted him ;' *wherefore*, referring to his death, ver. 8.

(2.) This is the foundation of his intercession. There are two functions of Christ's priesthood, oblation and intercession;* they are both joined together, but one as precedent to the other. The legal high priest, when he had first cut the throat of the sacrifice without (upon the day of the anniversary sacrifice), was not esteemed by that act to have completed his propitiation, till he had entered into the sanctuary, and sprinkled the blood of the sacrifice with his finger; so the propitiation made by our Redeemer was not fully complete till he entered into heaven to exercise his intercession. Yet the oblation precedes the intercession, and the intercession could not be without the oblation. It was with the blood of the victim, and no other blood, he was to enter. Without the oblation he would have had nothing to present in his intercession. They are placed in this order by the apostle, 1 John ii. 1, 2. He is first a sacrifice for propitiation, then an advocate for intercession. What he doth as an advocate, is grounded upon what he did as a sacrifice; and, were it not so, the apostle's arguing would not be valid, who placeth our salvation by the life of Christ upon our reconciliation by the death of Christ, Rom. v. 10. Indeed, he could not have been admitted, according to the type, as an advocate, but as being the high priest, and a high priest he could not have been without a sacrifice.

(3.) This is the foundation of all the grace any have. The conveyance of all the gracious love of Christ is through this channel. In redemption by his blood, the riches of the grace of God abounded, and that with the marks of the highest wisdom, Eph. i. 7, 8. All had laid buried from the view of man, and the fruition of men, without this sacrifice. This did commend his love, as well as satisfy his justice. His wrath had not been appeased, nor his grace drawn out to us without it; nor could the Redeemer lay any claim to any grace and mercy for those for whom he came, unless he had suffered for them as well as taken flesh for them. His offering himself, Isa. liii. 10–12, precedes his having a seed. The being and beauty of his seed depend upon the efficacy of his meritorious sacrifice. The offering his soul goes before the pardon of our sin; the payment of the ransom before the sprinkling it on us; the sealing of the covenant before the making good the covenant; his sufferings before his triumph, and the streams of his blood before the treasures of his grace. Upon the account of this sacrifice we enjoy the presence of God, protection against the enemies of our salvation, and receive the blessings necessary for our souls. By all this it appears that Christ is a sacrifice. This was his intent in coming. His death as a sacrifice was his intention in the assumption of our flesh; the prophecies predicted it, the types represented it; this he pursued, for this he thirsted. The accomplishment of this fiery baptism was the matter of his longing, his thoughts were never off from it, his will shrunk not from it; when his human will shewed some reluctance, it quickly returned to its fixedness: nothing could deter him, nothing could divert him. When he undertook to be mediator, he undertook to be a sacrifice, as a thing necessarily annexed to that office for the honour of God's justice, and the preservation of the rights of his sacred law. Upon which account, when the apostle speaks of this mediator, he adds with the same breath, 'who gave himself a ransom for all,' 1 Tim. ii. 5, 6. After the title of mediator follows 'the blood of sprinkling,' Heb. xii. 24. A mediator he was by means of his death, Heb. ix. 15. It is with good reason, therefore, that in our creed there is so quick a passage from the nativity of Christ to his passion, without any mention of the acts of his life, because he was incarnate, that he might be crucified.

The essence of a sacrifice consisted,

* Amyraut, Serm. sur Heb. ix. p. 187.

[1.] In the slaying or destroying it. [2.] In the offering it to God. Both were done in Christ.

[1.] In the slaying or destroying it. The shedding of the blood, the seat of the spirits, which are the instruments of action, was necessary to an ex-piatory sacrifice. The scape-goat, indeed, is called a sacrifice, Lev. xvi. 5, which was not slain in the temple, nor burned, but sent into the wilderness; and, as the Jews tell us, destroyed by being thrown down a rock, to which purpose men were appointed, who were to give notice of it by some signals from hill to hill, at a convenient distance, before which notice the congrega-tion at Jerusalem did not dissolve. But the other expiatory sacrifices were devoured by fire; fire being the highest representation in the world of the justice of God. The sufferings of Christ extended to soul and body. He was scorched by the wrath of God, Ps. xxii; 'His soul poured out to death,' Isa. liii. 12, alluding to the blood of the sacrifices poured out; and his human nature dissolved by the separation of the soul and body.

[2.] In the offering it to God. Oblation to God was a main part of the sacrifice; so 'Christ offered himself to God,' Eph. v. 2. To God, as es-sentially considered, whereby the whole right of rectorship and dominion was acknowledged belonging to God. Had the death of Christ been only for example, it had not been offered to God, who was not capable of any example to be set him. It being, therefore, offered to him, manifests it to be a sacrifice.

Doct. 3. Christ was sacrificed for us. ὑπὲρ, when joined with suffering for another, always signifies in another's stead and place. It is so used, Rom. v. 7, 'For a good man some would even dare to die;' *i. e.* instead of a good man, to free him from the death he was designed to, not only for his sake; so Gal. iii. 13, 'He was made a curse for us,' *i. e.* in our stead, suffering the curse due to us for our sins. He is called 'the Lamb of God,' in regard of God's designation of him; our lamb, our passover, in regard of his substi-tution in our place; as he died to appease the wrath of God, his death referred to the justice of God; as that justice flamed out against us, his death referred to us; he was a screen between the heat of wrath and the sufferings of the creature; a mediator, respecting God for his satisfaction and glory, respecting us for our reparation and grace.

This will be cleared, if we consider,

1. That Christ could not be a sacrifice for himself.* The Messiah was to be cut off, but not for himself,' Dan. ix. 36; he needed no sacrifice for him-self, as the other high priests did; they were sinners, he was harmless; they being encompassed with infirmities, needed, or ought to offer sacrifices for themselves, Heb. v. 2, 3; he was 'a lamb without blemish,' 1 Peter i. 19, who 'knew no sin, nor was guile found in his mouth,' nor did he ever do any thing displeasing to his Father, John viii. 29. He needed no glory to be purchased for him, for he was from eternity happy in the same essence with the Father, being 'God blessed for ever, over all,' Rom. ix. 5, having the command over all, and wanting nothing to a perfect blessedness. The sacrifices, which were types of him, could not be for themselves; they were not capable of sinning, as wanting a rational nature, and therefore a sinful nature. A beast was not capable of sin, because not capable of a law, and therefore its blood was not due for any sin of its own. Christ had no sin, none actual; 'no guile was found in his mouth,' 1 Peter ii. 22: nor original; that was stopped by his extraordinary conception by the Holy Ghost, which rendered him immaculate.

2. Sacrifices implied this. They had a relation to the offerer, and were substituted in his place. The substitution of the sacrifice in the place of the offenders, was always supposed by the heathen; hence did the offering of human victims arise, their opinion being that they could not present to God a nobler creature in their stead than one of their own nature. The notion of all sacrifices was, that they were in the place of a sinner to appease the offending* deity, and exempt the guilty person from punishment. And the actions about the Jewish sacrifices manifested this: the offerer laid his hand upon the head of the beast, signifying by that ceremony its consecration to God, and owning the translation of his guilt upon that creature, and putting it in his place to undergo the punishment deserved by his sin, Lev. iv. 24–29. And in this action of laying on hands, both hands, and with all their strength, as the Jews tell us, confession of sin was made by the presenter of the sacrifice, which signified also the disburdening of his guilt upon the head of the victim. By those actions was manifested a transferring of sin from the offender to the sacrifice, and of the death due to the criminal in like manner; besides, the pouring out of the blood, wherein the soul of the beast was supposed to be, was destined for the expiation of the sin of the soul of the offerer, Lev. xvii. 11–14; not that the blood is properly the soul, but because the vital spirits, which are the instruments of action, and conveying the virtue of the soul to particular members, are seated in the blood.

3. The whole economy of Christ is expressed in the whole Scripture to have a relation to us. All things preparatory to his sufferings were for us; some were first given to him, before he was given for them: John xvii. 9, he took flesh for us; Isa. ix. 6, ' Unto us a child is born;' for us he had a ' fulness of grace' in his human nature, John i. 16; for our sakes he did dedicate himself, that we might be sanctified, John xvii. 19; for us he gave himself, Gal. ii. 20; in the very moment of his sufferings, our iniquities were laid upon him, that health, by his stripes, might be derived to us. Christ was a common person for us, as the scape-goat was common to the whole congregation, Lev. xvi. 21, representing all of them; Christ was a common person for us, as Adam was, to whom, in this regard, he is compared: Rom. v. 14, ' Who is,' i.e. Adam, ' the figure of him that was to come.' The apostle compares one Adam and one Christ; he illustrates the condition and the actions of the one by the condition and actions of the other, what happened to us by Adam and what happened to us by Christ. This typicalness of Adam cannot be in any other regard than as he was a common person, representing all that were in his loins by natural generation. In this regard Christ is called ' the second man,' 1 Cor. xv. 47: ' The first man is of the earth earthly, the second man is the Lord from heaven.' Not that he was the second man born in the world (for many ages were run before his incarnation) but the second common root in the world. As when Adam, being the first root of mankind in a natural way, fell, the curse came upon him and all his posterity, and the standing punishments pronounced against him did reach, and were meant of all his posterity, Gen. iii. 19, not only of Adam personal, but of Adam as a representative, and so of all those who were not yet born into the world; as we sinned in Adam as a common root of natural generation, so we were all sacrificed in Christ as a common head of all that are in him by a spiritual union: the one merited death and damnation for all that descend from him; the other life and salvation for all that believe in him.

4. Our sins were imputed to him as to a sacrifice. Christ the just is put in the place of the unjust to suffer for them; 1 Pet. iii. 18. Christ is said to bear sin as a sacrifice bears sin, Isa. liii. 10–12. His soul was made an

* Qu. ' offended '?—ED.

offering for it; but sin was so laid upon the victims, as that it was imputed to them in a judicial account, according to the ceremonial law, and typically expiated by them. Christ had not taken away our sins as mediator, had he not borne the punishment of them; as a surety, 'He was made sin for us,' 2 Cor. v. 21, and he bare our sins, which is evident by the kind of death he suffered, not only sharp and shameful, but accursed, having a sense of God's wrath linked to it.

(1.) It cannot be understood of the infection of sin. The filth of our nature was not transmitted to him. Though he was made sin, yet he was not made a sinner by any infusion or transplantation of sin into his nature. It was impossible his holiness could be defiled with our filth.

(2.) But that our sin was the meritorious cause of his punishment. All those phrases, that Christ 'died for our sins,' 1 Cor. xv. 3, and was 'delivered to death for our offences,' Rom. iv. 23, clearly import sin to be the meritorious cause of the punishment Christ endured. Sin cannot be said to be the cause of punishment but by way of merit. If Christ had not been just, he had not been capable of suffering for us;* had we not been unjust, we had not merited any suffering for ourselves, much less for another. Our unrighteousness put us under a necessity of a sacrifice, and his righteousness made him fit to be one. What was the cause of the desert of suffering for ourselves was the meritorious cause of the sufferings of the Redeemer after he put himself in our place. The sin of the offerer merited the death of the sacrifice presented in his stead.

(3.) Our sins were charged upon him in regard of their guilt. Our sins are so imputed to him, as that they are not imputed to us, 2 Cor. v. 19, and not imputed to us, because he was made a curse for us, Gal. iii. 13. He bore our sins, as to the punishment, is granted. If he were an offering for them, they must in a judicial way be charged upon him. If by being made sin be understood a sacrifice for sin (which indeed is the true intent of the word sometimes in Scripture), sin was then legally transferred on the antitype, as it was on the types in the Jewish service by the ceremony of laying on of hands, and confessing of sin, after which the thing so dedicated became accursed, and though it was in itself innocent, yet it was juridically and *substitutive* nocent.† In the same manner was Christ accounted, as on the contrary believers are personally nocent, but by virtue of the satisfaction of this sacrifice imputed to them they are judicially counted innocent. Christ, who never sinned, is put in such a state as if he had; and we, who have always sinned, are put into such a state by him as if we never had. As we are made righteous in him, so he was made sin for us. Now, as justifying righteousness is not inherent in us, but imputed to us, so our condemning sin was not inherent in Christ, but imputed to him. There would else be no consistency in the antithesis: 2 Cor. v. 21, 'He hath made him to be sin for us, who knew no sin.' He knew no sin, yet he became sin. It seems to carry it further than only the bearing the punishment of sin. He was judicially charged in our stead with the guilt of sin. Our iniquities were laid upon him, Isa. liii. 6. He had spoken, ver. 5, of his bearing the chastisement of our peace, the punishment of our sin, and then seems to declare the ground of that, which consisted in God's imputation of sin to him in laying upon him the iniquities of us all. What iniquities? Our goings astray, our turnings every one to his own way. He made him to be that sin which he knew not; but he knew the punishment of sin; the knowledge of that was the end of his coming. He came to lay down his life a ransom for many. He knew not sin by an experimental inherency, but he knew it

* Ball on the Covenant, p. 278.   † Turretin.

by judicial imputation. He knew it not in regard of the spots, but he knew it in regard of the guilt following upon the judgment of God. He was righteous in his person, but not judicially or juridically pronounced righteous as our surety till after his sacrifice, when he was 'taken from prison and from judgment,' Isa. liii. 8. Till he had paid the debt, he was accounted as a debtor to God.

[1.] The apostle distinguisheth his second coming from his first by this : Heb. ix. 28, 'He shall appear the second time without sin unto salvation.' It is not meant of the filth of sin, for so he appeared at first without sin, but without the guilt of sin which he had at his first coming derived, or taken upon himself to satisfy for, and remove from the sinner. He shall appear without sin to be imputed, without punishment to be inflicted. At the time of his first coming, he appeared with sin, with sin charged upon him, as our surety arrested for our criminal debts. He pawned his life for the lives which we had forfeited, and suffered the penalty due by law, that we might have a deliverance free by grace. In his first coming, he represented our persons as an undertaker for us ; our sins were therefore laid upon him. In his second coming, he represents God as a vicegerent, and so no sin can be charged upon him.

[2.] He cannot well be supposed to suffer for our sins, if our sins in regard of their guilt be not supposed to be charged upon him. How could he die, if he were not a reputed sinner ? Had he not first had a relation to our sin, he could not in justice have undergone our punishment. He must in the order of justice be supposed a sinner really, or by imputation ; really he was not, by imputation then he was. How can we conceive he should be made a curse for us, if that which made us accursed had not been first charged upon him ? It is as much against divine justice to inflict punishment where there is no sin, as it is to spare an offender who hath committed a crime, or to clear the guilty, which by no means God will do, Exod. xxxiv. 7. The consideration of a crime precedes the sentence, either upon an offender or his surety. We cannot conceive how divine justice should inflict the punishment, had it not first considered him under guilt. Though the first designation of the Redeemer to a suretyship or sacrifice for us was an act of God's sovereignty, yet the inflicting punishment after that designation, and our Saviour's acceptation of it, was an act of God's justice, and so declared to be : Rom. iii. 26, 'to declare his righteousness, that he might be just,' that he might declare his justice in justification, his justice to his law. Can this highest declaration of justice be founded upon an unjust act ? Had that been justice or injustice to Christ, to lay his wrath upon the Son of his love, one whose person was always dear to him, always pleased him ; had he not stood as a sinner juridically in our stead, and suffered that sin, which was the ruin of mankind, to be cast with all the weight of it, upon his innocent shoulders ? After by his own act he had engaged for our debt, God in justice might demand of him every farthing, which, without that undertaking, and putting himself in our stead, could not be done ; which submission of his, and compliance with it, is expressed twice, Isa. liii. 7, by his not opening his mouth ; and no wrong is done to a voluntary undertaker. Add this too. It is from his standing in our stead as guilty that the benefit of his death doth redound to us. His death had had no relation to us, had not our sin been juridically adjudged to be his ; nor can we challenge an acquittance at the hands of God for our debts, if they were not our debts that he paid on the cross. 'He was wounded for our transgressions, he was bruised for our iniquities,' Isa. liii. 5. The laying hands upon the head of the sin-offering was necessary to make it a sacrifice for the offender, without which ceremony it might have been a slain but not a sacrificed beast.   The transferring our iniquities upon him must in some way precede his being bruised for them, which could not be any other way than by imputation, whereby he was constituted by God a debtor in our stead, to bear the punishment of our sin.   He being made sin for us, our sin was in a sort made his ; he was made sin without sin, he knew the guilt without knowing the filth, he felt the punishment without being touched with the pollution.   Since death was the wages of sin, and passed as a penalty for a violated law, Rom. vi. 23, it could not righteously be inflicted on him had not sin first been imputed to him.   In his own person, he was in the arms of his Father's love ; as he represented our sinful persons, he felt the strokes of his Father's wrath.

5. The sufferings of this sacrifice are imputed unto us.   He took our sins upon himself, as if he had sinned, and gave us the benefit of his sufferings, as if we had actually suffered and satisfied.*   He ' offered one sacrifice for sin for ever,' Heb. x. 12, *i. e.* ' to take away sin,' if you compare it with ver. 11 ; to remove the wrath due to us by reason of iniquity was the end he aimed at.   As our sins were imputed to him for punishment, so his sufferings are imputed to us for acceptation : Eph. i. 6, 7, ' Who hath made us accepted in the beloved, in whom we have redemption through his blood.' Christ had the relation of an undertaker for us, and we the relation of debtors to God.   Our debts then being charged upon him, his payment must be imputed to us ; the surety and the principal are legally regarded as one person, so are the representative and the persons represented by him. As Adam and all mankind were as one person, and as all Israel were called Jacob from the common root of them, so Christ and believers are as one person, and what he did, is as if a believer himself did it, as the suffering of the sacrifice was accepted in lieu of the life of the sinner.   By the stripes of our sacrifice we are healed, Isa. liii. 5, an exchange is made, stripes to him, health to us ; he was made a curse that we might be freed from the curse, Gal. iii. 13.   The first thing rising upon faith from the sufferings of Christ is a non-imputation of sin : 2 Cor. v. 21, ' Not imputing their trespasses unto them.'   They are not imputed to a believer, because borne by the undertaker for him.   The main end of his death as a sacrifice was to communicate a righteousness to us : Gal. ii. 21, ' If righteousness come by the law, then Christ is dead in vain.'   If this were the main or only thing that would make the death of Christ a mere vanity, then the great and main end of his death was to procure a complete righteousness for us, a righteousness whereby he was to be glorified, a righteousness whereby we might be justified ; his sufferings procured it, his resurrection endured it, Rom. iv. 25. All the world stands guilty before God, cannot present God with a righteousness of their own commensurate to the law ; not one act any man can do can bear proportion to it, all strength to do anything suitable to it was lost in Adam.   Since no righteousness of our own can justify, it must be the righteousness of the Son of God which must be imputed to us, in the same manner our sins were imputed to him.   As it is accepted by God for us, so it is accounted by God to us : 2 Cor. v. 21, ' He hath made him to be sin for us, who knew no sin, that we might be made the righteousness of God in him.'   Sin was in us, but charged upon Christ ; righteousness is in Christ and imputed to us ; therefore the apostle adds *him*, to signify that it is not our own righteousness, but another's, not inherent in us, but imputed to us.

The redounding of these sufferings to us ariseth,

1. From the dignity of the person undertaking to be a sacrifice for us,

* Turretin.

and the union of our nature with his. He assumed our nature that he might be a common person, and stand in our stead; he had not been a fit representative of us without it. But the main consideration is, ' the fulness of the Godhead dwelling in him bodily,' Col. ii. 9, and his being the man God's fellow, Zech. xiii. 7, whereby what he did and suffered in our stead became, according to the value of the person performing it, infinitely meritorious for those for whom he suffered, being infinitely more than all the obedience of men and angels, and more meritorious of happiness than sin could be of misery. As infinite sin deserves an infinite punishment, because it receives its aggravation from the dignity of the person against whom it is committed, so the sufferings of Christ, though finite in regard of his human nature, received an infinite value from the infiniteness of his person, equivalent to the debts of all that come to him. Sin is finite in regard of the subject, infinite in regard of the great God against whom it is. The sufferings of Christ are infinite in regard of the subject, and infinitely please the governor of the world, unto whom the offering is made, and therefore are of more force to convey a righteousness and beauty to the creature, than sin is to convey guilt and filth. Though sin abounded, grace did much more abound, Rom. 5.

2. From union with this infinite person by faith. All believers have a communion with him in his death: 2 Cor. v. 14, ' If one died for all, then were all dead.' All were accounted as dying, and bearing the wrath of God, by God's reckoning that death to them. As the sin of Adam is imputed to all his natural posterity, as being one with him in his loins, so are the sufferings of Christ imputed to all his spiritual seed, Rom. v. 18, as being one with him in a real union. Hence we are said to be ' crucified with Christ,' Rom. vi. 6, and ' risen with him,' Eph. ii. 6, as in the person representing us, as if the same wrath endured by Christ had been endured by us, and the same acquittance given to Christ had been given to us by God together with him; for all his meritorious passions were endured by him in the name of his elect, and for their use, and are fully belonging in the fruit and benefit of them to every believer. What Christ as a mediator did personally do, redounds in the benefit of it to Christ mystical, and is reckoned to every member of his body; we are made, we, and every one of us that believe, are made the righteousness of God in him. Well then, Christ bearing our iniquities is the cause of our justification: Isa. liii. 11, ' By his knowledge shall my righteous servant justify many, for he shall bear their iniquities.' If our sin had not been imputed to him, his righteousness could not be accounted to us; the commutation is clear, he first bears our iniquities that we might partake of his righteousness.

Use. If Christ be a sacrifice,

1. We may see the miserable blindness of the Jews in expecting the Messiah as a temporal conqueror. The Jews wait for such a one to this day. Though the promises represent spiritual deliverances under temporal grandeurs, not to raise carnal hopes but spiritual apprehensions, yet are there not multitudes of places which speak of sufferings, misery, death? Is not his heel to be bruised, his garments to be parted, a restoration to be made by him of what he took not away? Are not the sacrifices of the law to be perfected, his soul to be made an offering for sin, wounds made for transgression, his hands and his feet to be pierced? It was not by the slaying the bodies of men that he is to ' make reconciliation for the iniquities' of men, Dan. ix. 24. How can he be a conqueror of kingdoms who is to be cut off, and the city where he was to be destroyed as with a flood, and the desolations of it to be determined? ver. 25, כרת, penally cut off, as it signi-

fies, Lev. xvii. 4, as one was cut off that had no sacrifice allowed for him.*
The right apprehensions of the promises concerning the Messiah in the Old
Testament, what he was to be, what he was to do, cannot let you be ignorant
of him in the New. How do those poor people overturn at once the whole
design of that divine law they seem to reverence in the highest degree !
What blindness will seize upon the hearts of men, even under the oracles of
God, if the Spirit of God doth not vouchsafe to enlighten them !

2. If Christ be a sacrifice, it shews the necessity of a satisfaction to the
justice of God, and a higher satisfaction than men could perform. Blood
must satisfy justice, and no blood but that of the Son of God could be a
sufficient and valuable propitiation. If mere mercy could or would have
pardoned, it might have done it with or without the blood of the poor
creatures mangled under the law. But, alas ! neither the blood of those,
nor the blood of a rational creature, could take away sin. Less than death
justice could not demand ; death was settled by the immediate order of God
as the penalty of the law. The law, then, after transgression, could not be
vindicated in its honour without death. A God of infinite goodness delights
not in the shedding the blood of his creatures, nor can we suppose him to be
pleased with the effusion of the blood of animals. The institution of the
legal sacrifices could not be exemplary to man. What virtue could the
pangs of a dying beast represent to him ? No other ends can be imagined
but an acknowledgment of guilt, the desert of sin, the debt of death, the
necessity of a higher satisfaction, and the raising them up to a faith in the
promise of God, that another valuable sacrifice should be put in the room
of the sinner, to take away that sin, which the blood of beasts and the eternal
groans of men were not able to remove.

3. Christ, as sacrificed, is the true and immediate object of faith. We
are revolted from God, and are made uncapable of performing the terms of
the first covenant. The precepts of the law are too holy for our corrupt
nature, the penalties of the law too grievous to be borne by our feeble nature ;
a remedy must be looked after. When the venom of sin begins to work in
the conscience, and the thunder of the law alarms it to judgment, and the
punishment due to sin is presented in the horrors of it, the question immediately is, Whether there be any remedy, and where ? How forgiveness of
sin is to be attained ? The only remedy is proposed in Christ, and Christ
as a sacrifice. It is not Christ risen, or ascended, or exalted ; not Christ
only as the Son of God, or the head of angels ; not Christ as the creator of
the world, or by whom all things consist ; but Christ as answering the terms
of the first covenant, as disarming justice : and this he did as a sacrifice.
By this he bore the curse, by this he broke down the partition wall, by this
he joined apostate man and an offended God. This is that true faith pitcheth
on, daily revolves, and daily applies to. This is the first object of the soul,
Christ made sin, Christ bearing the punishment, Christ substituted in the
room of the offender. His resurrection and ascension come in afterward to
ascertain the comfort. But as his being a sacrifice is the foundation of his
being an advocate, a prince, a Saviour, to give repentance and remission of
sins, so it is the foundation of peace in ourselves. This is that which pacifies
God, and only what pacifies God can pacify conscience. This death as a
sacrifice purchased our comfort, because it purchased the comforter. Christ
begged not the Spirit before he died, John xvi. 7 ; he assures them he could
not come, unless himself went ; and he could not have gone with any success to heaven, if he had not shed his blood ; justice would have stopped
his entrance : Luke xxiv. 26, ' Ought not Christ to have suffered those

* Owen.

things, and to enter into his glory ?' Suffering was to precede his glory. Besides, our comfort lies in his being an advocate. But how is he an advocate ? With his blood in his hands. It is by his blood he speaks in heaven, and by his blood faith speaks to God. He paid the debt in his suffering, and pleads the payment in his glory. The payment went before the plea in order of nature, and our eyeing the payment precedes our eyeing the plea in order of faith. Both respect God as the rector. Christ, without his garments rolled in blood, could not be answerable to God, nor acceptable to a sinner. Faith is therefore called ' faith in his blood,' Rom. iii. 25. As faith is the instrument of justification, so it must eye the cause of our justification, and under that notion wherein it is the cause ; and that is Christ as groaning and offering up himself to God a ransom, a righteousness for many. The curse upon Adam is the lash wherewith an angry conscience scourgeth a sinner. The freedom from this curse is only found in the vengeance God exacted of the Redeemer for the sins of all that return to him by repentance. Both the death and resurrection of Christ concur to the same end, viz., our justification, Rom. xiv. 9, but in different manners ; his death as the meritorious cause, his resurrection as declarative of the sufficiency of his death to that end, that as the Son of God and surety of men, he had performed whatsoever he undertook in his being a sacrifice. But the first act of relying faith is about him as a bloody victim. As often as the Israelites were stung by the fiery serpents, they were to look up for health to the serpent lifted up, a type and emblem of the death of Christ. Upon every sin of a believer, the sacrifice is pleaded in heaven by the priest, and ought, in the remembrance of it, to be renewed in the repeated acts of our faith.

4. It is no true opinion that Christ died only for an example. Wounded he was for the transgressions in Isaiah's time, when his example could reach only those that came after him ; but the credit of his sufferings upon his promise to undergo them, might and did reach to the first ages of the world. The expressions in Isa. liii. sound his death higher than a bare pattern, or a testimony to the truth. The notion of expiation of sin was always implied in the notion of a sacrifice, even among the heathens. When they parted with the dearest first-born of their bodies to Moloch, it was not for an example, but for the sin of the soul, Micah vi. 6. As Christ was the Son of God sent, he was a testimony of the love of God ; as he was a sacrifice, he was our ransom from the curse of the law.

5. Comfort to every true believer. He was sacrificed *for us ;* God counted him a sinner for our sakes, that he might count us righteous for his sake.

(1.) As Christ hath been sacrificed for them, so he has been accepted for them. He is no more to be made sin, iniquity no more to be charged upon him ; his next appearance shall be without the imputation of sin, for the conferring salvation, Heb. ix. 28, with all the bonds of a believer's sins cancelled. He is pronounced God's righteous servant, and from this declaration of his righteousness, and the true and believing knowledge of it, doth our justification arise, Isa. liii. 11. Had it not been a perfect sacrifice, it could never have wrought such complete effects, and ' for ever have perfected those that are sanctified,' Heb. x. 14. He is gone with the smoke of his sacrifice to heaven, and was well entertained, which is a signification of the completeness and perfection of his righteousness for man, John xvi. 9, 10. The pure and piercing eye of divine justice could not perceive a spot in him. Had any blemish been, it could not have escaped an infinite knowledge. Nor could the justice of God, in turning over all the registers of the debts owing from the creatures, perceive one but might be cancelled upon the value of this payment, if the creature did not negligently or wilfully re-fuse his own delivery, and prefer his debts and captivity before it. It was a sacrifice offered according to God's heart, with which his soul was infinitely well pleased. The person of the Son of God made every gaping wound, every panting groan, and doleful agony, grateful to God, and profitable for us. The Godhead united to the manhood put an unexpressible value upon every pang. Not that every pang, or the least drop of blood, was sufficient for our redemption (the law required death, and death must be suffered); but all those passions preceding his death were meritorious in conjunction with his death.

(2.) This sacrifice unites all the attributes of God together for a believer's interest. The flood-gates of mercy are opened, and the fire of justice con-fined in its flames. The flames of the one centre in Christ, that the streams of the other might flow down to us ; rivers of mercy quench not the flames of justice, nor the flames of justice suck up the rivers of mercy. As the sacrificing Christ is a vengeance against sin, it is an act of justice ; as it is a means of remission of the sins of those for whom he was sacrificed, it is an act of mercy to the creature. Both justice and mercy join hands to help the fallen creature up. God is just in being merciful, and merciful in being just ; so that we may well cry aloud with the psalmist, Ps. cxvi. 5, ' Gra-cious is the Lord, and righteous.' Justice struck the sacrifice, that the streams of mercy might have a fuller scope. Compassion helped justice to a satisfaction more honourable than could have been had from creatures ; and justice helped mercy to a fuller and more illustrious exercise of itself than ever it could have had without it. Justice is now a second to mercy, of an antagonist it is become an advocate. God must ·be unjust, if he be not merciful to a believer. Since our high priest hath been faithful to God, God will not be unfaithful to him, or those for whom he offered up himself. Happy must he be that hath mercy supplicating, and justice itself pleading for him.

(3.) This sacrifice is of eternal virtue. The virtue of the sacrifice is parallel to the office of his priesthood ; a priest and a sacrifice are relatives. The immutable oath, then, that constituted him a priest for ever, settles for ever the value and virtue of the sacrifice ; for without a sacrifice he could not be a priest ; his office would expire if the virtue of his sacrifice did ; they eternally live together in conjunction. It is ' the blood of an everlasting covenant,' Heb. xiii. 20. It is an everlasting covenant, because an ever-lasting blood whereby it was settled. The ground of its prevalency is, that it was not the sacrifice of a mere man, but of God, Heb. ix. 14.

(4.) The effects of this sacrifice therefore are perfect, glorious, and eternal. It is our deliverance from wrath, the scorchings of hell, and terrors of punishment. The purity of this sacrifice expiates the impurities of our ser-vices. No sin so great but the value of this sacrifice, believed in, can answer it. The highest sin is the transgression of the law, and this is the satisfac-tion of the whole penalty of the law. Sin is an offence against God, and this sacrifice is the highest pleasure to him. None of our sins can be˜so great as those that met upon the back of this innocent lamb. It is enough to cross every book of accounts ; ' Who shall lay anything to the charge of God's elect ? It is God that justifieth,' and ' Christ that died,' Rom. viii. 33, 34. ' There is no condemnation to them that are in Christ,' because he hath as a sacrifice ' for sin condemned sin in the flesh,' Rom. viii. 1–3. Not, no desert of condemnation, that there is ; not, no condemnation because of something done by themselves; no, but because of something done by Christ, who hath obliterated the bloody roll of sin and curses by his blood. God will not refuse it to any that believingly plead it; he will not be unjust to the true value of it, nor to his own ordination. If it be unrighteous in God to 'forget the labour of a believer's love,' Heb. vi. 10, it will be so to forget the obedience of his Son, and the person interested in it. God was not so ready to bruise him for us, but he will be as ready to apply the plaster of his blood to us.

How great, then, is the happiness of a believer on the account of this sacrifice! Whatsoever is lost by the sin of the first Adam, is gained by the sacrifice of the second; with what boldness may we enter into the holiest with this blood of Jesus in our hands and hearts, Heb. x. 19.

6. We must then lay hold on this sacrifice. The people were to be sprinkled with the blood of the sacrifice, Exod. xxiv. 8, so must we with the blood of our Lamb. Thus only can it save us, 1 Peter i. 2. Thus is our Saviour described by this part of his office: Isa. lii. 15, 'He shall sprinkle many nations.' Our guilt cannot look upon a consuming fire without a propitiatory sacrifice; our services are blemished, so that they will rather provoke his justice than merit his mercy; we must have something to put a stop to a just fury, expiate an infinite guilt, and perfume our unsavoury services. Here it is in Christ, but there must be faith in us. Faith is as necessary by the ordination of God in a way of instrumentality, as the grace of God in a way of efficiency, and the blood of Christ in a way of meritoriousness of our justification. All must concur, the will of God the offended governor, the will of the sacrificing mediator, and the will of the offender. This will must be a real will, an active operative will, not a faint velleity. We must have a faith to justify our persons, and we must have an active sincerity to justify the reality of our faith. Christ was real in his sacrifice, God was real in the acceptation of it, we must be real in believing it. Rocks and mountains cannot secure them that neglect so great a sacrifice, that regard this atoning blood as an unholy thing. It is as dreadful for men to have this sacrifice smoking against them, and this blood calling for vengeance on them, as it is comfortable to have it pleaded for them and sprinkled on them. Why will any then despise and neglect a necessary sovereign remedy ready at hand? Is it excusable, that when we should have brought the sacrifice ourselves, or ourselves have been the sacrifice, we should slight him who hath voluntarily been a sacrifice for us, and cherish a hell merited by our sin, rather than accept of a righteousness purchased at no less rate than the blood of God? This sacrifice is full of all necessary virtue to save us, but the blood of it must be sprinkled upon our souls by faith. Without this we shall remain in our sins, under the wrath of God and sword of vengeance.

7. We must be enemies to sin, since Christ was a sacrifice for it. Unless sin die in us, we cannot have an evidence that this sacrifice was slain for us. He that hath an interest in Christ's blood must be planted 'into the likeness of his death,' Rom. vi. 5. We are highly unjust, if we will not sacrifice a beloved sin for him, who sacrificed a precious life, of more value than heaven and earth, for us. We should empty ourselves of our filth, since he emptied himself of his glory. The very expression, *sacrificed for us*, carries a force and a spirit in it to animate us to this. We must be friends to the duties God enjoins us. It is disingenuity to put him off with a shred of our souls, or a grain of service, who became a holocaust for us. Scanty services are fit only for a scanty sacrifice. As God shews in this sacrifice his compassions to the sinner, so he declares the certainty and terror of his penalties upon the obstinate rebel. If the Son of God, undertaking to be a sacrifice, was not preserved from death upon the account of his filiation, men cannot expect but to sink under it upon the account of their rebellion. Well, then,

let us not look upon the least sin without horror, since it is a crime not to be expiated by any lower price than an infinite blood. It should cause us to mourn also for sin. It was our unrighteousness made Christ's back and his soul to suffer ; he had never felt the wrath of his Father, if we had not broke the law of his Father. When the death of Christ, our sacrifice, comes into our thoughts, the remembrance of our sins should bear it company. We should never consider that Christ died, but we should join also with sorrow the consideration of that for which he died.

A DISCOURSE OF THE VOLUNTARINESS OF CHRIST'S DEATH.

And walk in love, as Christ also has loved us, and has given himself for us, an offering and a sacrifice to God of a sweet-smelling savour.—Eph. V. 2.

The exhortation in this verse to a mutual love, depends upon what the apostle had urged in the end of the former chapter, where he had endeavoured to persuade them to a kindness and tender-heartedness to one another, and backed it by the pattern God had set them in his pardoning grace; and in ver. 1 of this chapter, he extends that motive to all other duties, and draws a general maxim for their observance; that they ought to imitate God in all things imitable by a creature: ver. 1, 'Be ye therefore followers of God as dear children.' Consider the great example God hath set you, and as you have obligations to him, not only as your God, but your Father; so imitate him, not only as creatures, but as children, and express in your lives those admirable perfections which he hath engraven on you by regeneration, and especially his patience and meekness in bearing, and his love and kindness in pardoning, those that injure you.

Doctrine. Those that lay claim to a relation to God, without imitation of him, are not children, but bastards. They may be of his family by instruction, not by descent. There is no implantation in Christ, without an imitation both of the Creator and Redeemer.

He doth prosecute the exhortation in this verse. 'Walk in love,' let the perpetual tenor of your lives be in love; and that by the example of Christ, as before he had done it by the example of God, which indeed Christ had in person urged to his disciples before his departure from them: John xiii. 14, 15, 'I have given you an example, that you should do as I have done to you;' and amplifies this example of the love of Christ,

1. From the effect: his passion.
2. The manner of it: voluntary, *has given.*
3. The subject of it: *himself.*
4. The end of it: *a sacrifice.*
5. The event and fruit of it: *a sweet-smelling savour.* εἰς ὀσμὴν εὐωδίας. A fragrant odour, which by a *metalepsis* is put for the appeasing God, it having a wonderful force to appease the wrath of God, which was inflamed against us. The most generous example to imitate, is the person of our

Saviour ; the most efficacious motive to persuade to that imitation, is the sacrifice of our Saviour ; the course of our lives ought to be in love, not only an act, a spurt, but a walk. 'As Christ hath loved us.' An *as* of similitude, not of equality ; we cannot equal the stature of Christ's affections, but we may draw in our life lineaments like to his.

The latter words are the subject of this discourse. *Loved us.* This is the first spring of all the actions of Christ towards us, and the passion of Christ for us ; there could be no other motive as it respected us. Our misery might excite his pity, but his affection produced his passion ; he loved us as God, in common with his Father ; he loved us as man, by a participation of our nature. In this love, there is his divine will as a priest, his human will as a sacrifice ;* he pitied us while we were insensibly hurried down by the devil to a gulf of perdition : love was the only impulse, love excited him, love prepared him, love sent him, love offered him ; the highest assurance of his love was the loss of his life, the excellency of the fruit shews the goodness of the tree.

Has given himself. He was given by God, yet he offered himself, Παρέδωκεν ; there was a joint consent : 'The Son can do nothing of himself, but what he sees the Father do,' John v. 19. It is spoken after the manner of men, as sons learn of their fathers, and imitate them in their actions. Christ's giving himself, implies the Father's giving him.

Himself. He was both the priest and the sacrifice ; he offered not gold or silver, or a whole world, but himself, more precious than millions of worlds, composed only of angels and innumerable spirits, as excellent as the omnipotency of God could create.

Himself. Not only his body of flesh, not only his soul or Spirit, but himself, his whole person. His soul, his body, himself the Son of God, and the Son of man ;† he loved us as he loved himself, above what he loved himself, shall I say ? He exposed his life for us, his most holy person for us ; the act of his murderers is not regarded as a sweet-smelling savour, but his own act of obedience.

To whom did he thus give himself ? *To God.* To that God, whom by our base apostasy we had rendered ourselves obnoxious, and had fallen under his deserved wrath. Our Saviour was God's before, as he was the Son of God, but he delivers himself to God,‡ as a mediator, a victim to satisfy for our sins, and reconcile us to our injured Creator; he offered himself to God, as the judge and revenger of sin, the guardian of the law, the asserter of his truth in his threatening ; he appeared before God as sitting upon a seat of justice, that he might open to us a throne of grace.

To what end did he deliver himself ? *An offering and a sacrifice.* Not *like* an offering or *like* a sacrifice, § but an offering, a sacrifice ; not to do us a small kindness, but to offer his life for us ; he would die in our stead, that we might live by his death ; not only an offering, but a sacrifice, an incense to be consumed into smoke, a sacrifice to be stuck and bled to death ; all the offerings and sacrifices of the law were completed in Christ. All his life wherein he acted for the glory of God was an offering ;|| in his death, he bled and expired as a sacrifice ; he underwent a death, not honourable, but ignominious, and not only ignominious among men, but joined with the legal curse of God.¶ As he was the Son of God, he gave himself, having power to do it, John x. 18. Unless he had been the Son of God, he could never have been a sufficient sacrifice for us.

For a sweet-smelling savour. He gave himself with an intention to be ac-

* Cocceius.   ‡ Musculus. || Zanchius in loc.
† Zanchius.   § As Crellius in loc.   ¶ Bodius in loc.

cepted, and God received him with a choice acceptation. Sacrifices under the law were accounted by God as a sweet savour, Lev. i. 9, iii. 16, Exod. xxix. 41. This expression is first mentioned at the time of the sacrifice of Noah, Gen. viii. 21, so God is said to smell an offering, 1 Sam. xxvi. 19. God accepted Noah's sacrifice, and took an occasion from thence of declaring his counsel to Noah, that he would not destroy the world, implying, that he would in time recover it by the promised seed. A smell is here attributed to God by an ᾿Ανθρωποπαθεία. As good scents recreate and refresh the sense of a man, so did the sacrifice of Christ please and content God. Our sins had sent up an ill savour to heaven, had disturbed the rest of God. Christ expels our ill scent by the perfume of his blood, and restores a sweet savour in the heavenly places: Heb. ix. 23, 'purifying the heavenly things' himself. God being a pure Spirit, could not be taken with the smoke of the legal lambs, nor refreshed with the fumes of incense; but both God and believers under the Old Testament had a content in them, as they were shadows of this sweet sacrifice which was intended for the appeasing God, and securing the offending creature. What the legal sacrifices could not perform, as being earthy, mean, and too low for the acceptation of God, and delighted him no otherwise than as they referred to Christ, that this sweet sacrifice of the unblemished Lamb of God, possessed with a perfect love both to God's glory and man's safety, performed, and sent up such a fragrancy to the nostrils of God, that he approved both of the priest and the sacrifice, infinitely above the best sacrificers and sacrifices under the law, and changed his countenance towards the filthy creature that had raised such noisome steams in his presence.

The things observable are many.

1. The love of Christ was the spring of his passion.

2. The person of Christ was consecrated for us, and given to us.

But the only things I shall take notice of are,

1. Christ was a voluntary sacrifice.

2. Christ was an efficacious sacrifice.

Doct. 1. The sacrifice and sufferings of Christ for us were free and voluntary. His offering was a free-will offering. It is expressed in the same chapter, Eph. v. 25, 'He gave himself for the church.' His voluntariness was typified by the paschal lamb, a lamb being the mildest of all creatures, resisting neither the shearers nor butchers, Isa. liii. 7. All his work is assigned to his love, Rev. i. 5, 6. His love was antecedent to his shedding his blood, and our being washed in it. Love renders any work delightful. The Sun of righteousness hath not a less bridegroom spirit and cheerful disposition in running his humble race, than a sun in the heavens is expressed to have by the psalmist, in running his natural race in the heavens, Ps. xix. 5. He was not made poor by force, but became so, and laid aside his own riches for our sakes, 2 Cor. viii. 9. He became destitute of the advantages other men enjoy,* that from his worldly poverty we might become rich in spiritual graces. He was not emptied of his glory by another, but made himself of no reputation; he took upon him the form of a servant, it was not imposed upon him by constraint; he was not debased by others, till he had humbled himself to the lowest degree of humility. He could have resisted them when they lifted him up upon the cross, but he would be obedient to the determination of his Father to the last gasp, Philip. ii. 7, 8. The hiding the majesty of God under 'the form of a servant,' his descent not only to the earth, the lowest dregs of the world, the footstool of the divinity, but to the most abject and forlorn condition in that earth; his taking the

* Amyraut in loc.

similitude of weak flesh, and running through all the degrees of reproaches and punishment, even to the grave itself, were voluntary acts, the workings of his love, that he might rescue us from a deserved hell, to advance us to an undeserved heaven, and make us partakers of that blessedness he had voluntarily quitted for our sakes. He willingly put himself into the condition of a servant, which is to be at the beck of another, and have no will but that of his master's. He submitted his reason and affections to God, to be employed in his work according to his will. He had an absolute power over his own body, John x. 18, yet he made a free offer of it, and subjected it to the penalty to be inflicted on him. One place more: John xvii. 19, ' For their sakes I sanctify myself;' it cannot be meant of his consecration to his office of priesthood, that depended upon the call of his Father; he was constituted a priest, not by his own intrusion, but the Father's election, settled by an oath. The Father, and not himself, glorified him in this regard, Heb. v. 4, 5. Nor of his habitual and inward holiness, for so he was sanctified by the Spirit in his conception, and filled with all graces, Luke i. 35, John ili. 34. But it is meant of his offering himself a sacrifice. His Father made him a priest, the Spirit made his human nature fit to be a sacrifice, his own will made him an actual offering.

In the handling this doctrine, I shall do these four things:

I. Lay down some propositions for explaining this.

II. The evidences of this voluntariness.

III. The necessity of it.

IV. The use.

I. Propositions for explaining it.

1. The Father's appointing him to be a sacrifice, doth not impair his own willingness in undertaking. The Father is said to send him and deliver him, John iii. 34, Rom. viii. 32 ; not that the Son was over-persuaded, or came only out of obedience, without any inclination of his own. The Father being the root and fountain of the deity, all actions are originally ascribed to him, though common to all; so he is first in order of being, as he is first in order of working. The Father is said to deliver him, because the first motion of redemption is supposed to arise from the will and motion of the Father ; yet the love of Christ was the spring of all mediatory actions, and his taking our nature on him; and therefore he is no less said to give himself, than the Father is said to give him to us and for us. God is said to set him forth, Rom. iii. 25 ; yet he is said to come, Mat. xx. 28, not thrust out or forced to come. God lays our sins upon him, yet Christ is said to bear them. His engagement was an act of choice, liberty, and affection. He could not be constrained by his Father to undertake it ; his will was as free in consenting, as his Father was in proposing. The Spirit is said to be sent by the Father and the Son, to take of Christ's and shew it to us, to fit those for heaven that are given to Christ; yet his distributions are according to his own will : 1 Cor. xii. 11, ' Dividing to every man according as he will.' If you consider Christ as one God with the Father, there is but one and the same will in both.* Will belongs to essence or nature ; the essence of God being one, there are not in God divers wills, though the Godhead be in divers persons, because the power of willing is the nature, not a personal propriety. The decree of redemption was joint in Father and Son. What Christ decreed as God, he executed as man ; and what he willed from eternity, he began in time to will as man.† Christ, as God, gave himself to death with the same will and by the same action as the Father gave him ;

---

* Hooker's Polity, John x. 3 ' I and my Father are one.'

† Bodius in Eph. v. 2.

but as man he gave himself by a will inspired by the Father.* Yet for our conception's sake the Scripture represents things so as if they were distinct wills, which yet we must not imagine, any more than because the Scripture, in condescension to our weakness, represents God with eyes, and ears, and hands, we must conceive God to have a fleshly body like ours.

2. The necessity of his death impeacheth not the voluntariness of it. Many things are voluntary which yet are necessary; there are voluntary necessities. God is necessarily yet voluntarily holy; the devils are necessarily yet voluntarily evil, it is not in their power to become good, yet they are carried to evil with a complete will. Man desires to be happy by a natural, and therefore necessary, inclination, yet willingly and without constraint. This death was necessary, by a determination of God; voluntary, by a cheerful submission of Christ. The election of the good angels rendered their standing necessary, but the adherence of their wills to God made their standing also voluntary. Grace did not force them against their will, nor God's determination of Christ render him a sacrifice against his mind.

(1.) It was voluntary in the foundation. The decree was not necessary, but an act of divine liberty. Nothing can incline God to an act of grace but his own most holy will. Christ being at liberty whether he would espouse our interest or no, his undertaking to manage it was a pure voluntary act, arising from his own will. He was not bound to become a creature, and take upon him the form of a servant, but his entering into that condition was an act of free choice and condescension. No reason can possibly be supposed why the Son of God, and Lord of the creation, should make himself lower than the angels for us, by any necessity of his own condition. There was indeed a necessity for us, who could not be redeemed without him, but no necessity arising from the divine nature. If a creature ready to be famished be in a place where there is only one person of ability and sufficiency to relieve him, there is a necessity on the part of the poor creature to be relieved, and relieved by that person, since there is no other to help him, but there is no necessity on the part of the sufficient person to relieve him; the help he affords him will be a mere act of charity. This act of Christ is therefore called grace: 2 Cor. viii. 9, 'The grace of our Lord Jesus Christ, that though he were rich, yet for our sakes he became poor;' nothing could move him to become either a creature or a servant in a created state, but the yearnings of his own bowels towards fallen and miserable man.

(2.) It was necessary after this engagement. His engagement to make himself liable to punishment in our stead was free, but when he had entered into bonds to the Judge of heaven and earth, he was then in his power to be delivered up to death, according to that obligation which he subscribed and consented to; he was then legally, and by his own consent, bound to perform what he had undertaken, and could not justly detract. The promises of Christ are without repentance, as well as the gifts of God. After Christ had put himself into the state of a creature, and form of a servant, the homage due from a creature to God, and the work of a servant after his ear was bored, was necessary, and could not be refused by him. He had then broke his word passed to his Father in the covenant of redemption, had he absolutely declined it. He ought to die as Christ, Luke xxiv. 46, i. e. as clothed with our nature for such an end. He needed not to die, as he was the Son of God by eternal generation, and lay in the bosom of his Father; but it was necessary as he was made under the law, made Christ, i. e. anointed to such a purpose. It was necessary, also, in regard of the truth of God laid to pawn in several promises, prophecies, and legal representations; but still

* Aquin. sum part. iii. qu. 47, part. 3.

the fountain of all this was the free bubbling up of infinite affection to mankind. Yet this necessity was a necessity of immutability, not of constraint. The holy and unchangeable will which complied with the first proposal, remained in force till the first execution. The will of the eternal Spirit, whereby he offered himself to his Father, was immutable. It is a necessity arising from himself, and the perfection of his own nature ; from his own holy will, not from any constraint. God cannot be constrained ; liberty is so essential a property of the divine nature, that though it may determine itself, it cannot constrain itself. To be God is a term of infinite power, to be constrained is a term of impotency ; these are contradictions in the Godhead. Besides, in his human nature he could not sin, he could not be overcome by the devil, he could find nothing in him as a foundation to stand upon,* John xiv. 30. He could not do anything against the Father. But to desert his suretyship had been contrary to that law to which he had subjected himself ; the word of the oath, whereby he was constituted a priest, had been fruitless. It had been the utter ruin of all the gracious decrees of God, because all the elect were ' chosen in him,' Eph. i. 4, 5 ; the covenant with Abraham and the patriarchs had been null, the oath which he sware to them broken, Luke i. 73 ; and the foundation of their faith falling, the whole superstructure had been dissolved, and they would have believed God in vain. All this necessity is no plea against his willingness. The obligation which the truth of God lays upon him, after he hath promised, doth not diminish his first kindness and grace in making the promise. As the necessity of his death did not extenuate the Jews' sin in butchering him, so neither doth it lessen Christ's willingness in laying down his life after he had voluntarily entered into our bonds.

(3.) Though his death was violent in regard of man, yet this doth not abate the voluntariness in regard of himself. Judas betrayed him, the serjeants apprehended him, Pilate condemned him, and the soldiers crucified him. These were but instruments to execute ' the counsel of God,' Acts iv. 28 ; yet he need not have been apprehended unless he would ; he shewed his power to escape, not only the united force of the Jewish nation, but of the whole world, by striking his apprehenders to the ground with the majesty of his looks. He that can rescue himself from the hands of men, and will not, may be said to die willingly, though he die violently. They slew him as murderers, and made him a sacrifice to their revenge, not to God, ' with wicked hands,' Acts ii. 23, and with wicked minds too. He was the sole offerer of himself, as it respected God and advantaged us. Judas willingly delivered him, Pilate with an imperfect will condemned him, the Jews delightfully reproached him, but the intention of none of them was to make him a sacrifice of redemption. It was ' for our sakes he sanctified himself,' John xvii. 19, but it was not for our sakes that the Jews butchered him. Judas delivered him for the silver, and Pilate condemned him to preserve his grandeur, but he delivered himself with an excessive affection for us. His murderers had no regard to the making him an expiation for the sin of the world ; his oblation to God as a sacrifice was an act purely of his own will at the very time of his death, not of his enemies' rage. In this capacity his death was solely the fruit of his love, and the hovering of his soul over the lost sons of Adam ; it did not arise from a necessity of nature, but the will of his mercy to us ; he gave himself, and gave himself out of love, Gal. ii. 20 ; enemies did not give him, nature did not give him. The inward transports and affections of his soul, the actings of his choicest

* Cocc. de fæd. pp. 115, 116.

graces, whereby his offering was rendered acceptable to God, his murderers were not the cause of; they had not force enough to crucify him, had not a joy been set before him, which made him endure the cross, Heb. xii. 2, *i. e.* the things wherein he rejoiced, as those things are called our hope, which are the object of our hope. The joy of Christ, which made him despise the shame and ignominy of the cross, was the glorious good he should procure by his suffering, the expiation of sin, reconciliation of God, the new creation of the world ; for the producing and ripening such fruits did he hang upon the tree. This gave him contentment and pleasure in the midst of his indignities, and this was increased, not impaired, by the fury of his enemies. Though his death, in regard of men, was violent, yet, as the death of a sacrifice, it was wholly voluntary.

(4.) When our Saviour seemed unwilling to it in the time of his agony, he was then highly willing. This was when he prayed earnestly that the cup might pass from him, and begins, John xii. 27, ' Father, save me from this hour.' The strugglings of innocent nature do both times end not only in a gracious submission to the will of God, but in an ardent desire that the will and glory of God might have their full accomplishment. ' But for this cause came I unto this hour,' therefore ' Father, glorify thy name ;' do thy own work, and finish every part of thy will in me, and what thou hast appointed me to undergo. The state Christ was in must needs admit of some shrinkings in his nature, encompassed with our infirmities ; he saw the comfortable influences of God suspended, the indignation of God for our sins breaking out, the guilt of innumerable iniquities imputed to him, and the law with all its curses edged against him, and himself left to bear the weight of all this, and conflict with a wrath no creature ever bore before. The apprehensions of all these, meeting in a clear understanding, could not but raise suitable passions of fear and trouble in his human nature. If he had not known the greatness of the punishment he was to endure for our redemption, he had undertaken to ransom us from he knew not what ; if he had not feared it, he had not been a sensible man ; if he had not trembled at it, he had not been an innocent man. Suitable affections to God in his carriage towards us are the necessary duties of a creature. God is the object of fear in his vindictive justice, which Christ then was to be subject to. It had not consisted with that reverence which Christ always showed to God, not to be sensible of the sharpness of those punishments which were then providing for him as a substituted criminal in our stead. Though the person of our Saviour was but one, yet he, having two natures, had two wills, a divine and human, otherwise he were not God and man. If he had not a human soul, he were not a man ; and if he had not a human will, he had not a human soul. As he truly took our nature, so he took the laws of it, whereby it cannot affect pain, but shuns whatsoever it apprehends hurtful to it. As death was an evil against nature, he desires to decline it ; as it was to be an atonement for sin, and appeasing of wrath through the dignity of the sacrifice, he desires to undergo it ; he regarded it as man, and so had some reluctance to it ; he regarded it as a man designed for such an end, and therefore submitted to it. ' But for this cause came I unto this hour.' As it was a dissolution of nature, a fruit of God's displeasure against sin, and should for a time exclude his soul and body from the fruition of the divine favour and glory (though the personal union should not be dissolved), he startled at it ; for the more Christ loved the sense of the divine love which he enjoyed in his life, the more grievous would the apprehension of the want thereof be.* But when he considered that he was united to that nature,

* Bilson's survey, p. 398.

that he might suffer in it, and lay it down as a sacrifice to that justice which brandished a naked sword against man, that without it the world could not be freed from that misery sin had hurled it into, he then put his neck under the cross; as a patient who, considering the potion offered as bitter, abhors it, * but remembering the intention of the physician, and the beneficial qualities of the medicine, doth readily accept it. Both the abhorrency and acceptance are acts of the same will upon divers considerations, or rather the abhorrency is an act of nature regarding it as distasteful, the acceptance is an act of reason regarding it as wholesome. Now, was not the will of Christ as mediator as victorious in the issue over the reluctance as it had been in the capacity of a man desirous of the removal of the cup? The human will veils to the divine will, and conforms itself not only in a quiet posture to the resolves of God, but in an ardent desire that his will might be performed. There was more of obedience in 'Thy will be done, not mine,' and more of ardent affections in 'Father, glorify thyself,' than there was of reluctancy in 'Let this cup pass from me,' or 'Save me from this hour.' He disclaims the will of his human nature, to perform the will of his Father's mercy.

2. Wherein this voluntariness of Christ's death appears.

(1.) He willingly offered himself in the first counsel about redemption to stand in our stead. When our necks were upon the block, and the blow from justice was otherwise unavoidable, Christ steps in, diverts the blow from us to himself, and declares himself willing to suffer what we had merited, that we might escape upon that suffering. The Father proposed it, the Son consented to it. The will of God is antecedent to the consent of Christ: Ps. xl. 7, 'I come to do thy will, O my God,' which will was the will of God for our sanctification, 'through the offering of the body of Christ,' Heb. x. 10. Though he knew every thorn in the way he was to pass, the greatness of the wrath he was to undergo, yet his heart leapt into the Father's arms with a full and ready consent at the first overture. The Father proposed it not with more affection than the Son entertained it with delight: 'I delight to do thy will, O my God.' He was loath to leave expressing it: 'I come;' that is not all, 'I delight to do thy will;' nor doth it rest there, 'Thy law is within my heart.' It is so settled that it cannot be rooted out but with the utter dissolution of my heart. Thus, 'in the volume,' or the beginning 'of the book, it is written of him.' In the book of Genesis, in the first promise, the second person in the Trinity (who is supposed to appear to our first parents after the fall) represents himself a suffering Saviour, and testifies his own consent to the suffering he was to undergo, as the seed of the woman, by having his heel bruised by the serpent, and the victory he was to obtain by breaking the serpent's head. When the counsel was resolved upon, Christ is said to 'delight in the habitable parts of the earth,' Prov. viii. 31. His consent was past before the world was; it was a delight to him, because of the glory of God's grace, to be made illustrious in the sacrifice of himself. It cannot be meant of the first creation, for that is supposed, and there could be no exulting delight in that, since the defilement of it by sin presently succeeded the laying on the top-stone. It is meant, therefore, of the restoration of the world, which was to be brought by this wisdom of God. Some, to invalidate the deity of Christ, understand by Wisdom in that book and chapter, an intellectual habit, which is ridiculous. The antiquity of the Wisdom here spoken of is 'before the mountains were settled, and before there were any fountains abounding with water.' The Wisdom here described was present 'with God' when he made the world. It was entirely

* Donne, vol. i. p. 129.

familiar with him ; there was such a familiarity between God and Wisdom as between a father and a son : ver. 30, ' I was by him as one brought up with him,' and peculiarly the delight of God.

(2.) The whole course of his life manifests this willingness. His will stood right to this point of the compass all his life. He never had any defect in his understanding, nor did his memory of what was appointed for him ever fail him. In the time of his life he frequently mentioned the tragedy to be acted upon him, the manner of his death by lifting up on the cross, John iii. 14 ; and he who was intimately acquainted with the prophets knew every circumstance of his death predicted in them. Many enter the lists with difficulties out of ignorance, but the willingness of our Saviour cannot be ascribed either to ignorance or forgetfulness. He knew long before that Judas was to betray him, before such a design entered into Judas his heart, John vi. 64, yet cashiered him not from his family. He foretold the hour of his death ; his desires were strong for it ; he was straitened till he was baptized with that bloody baptism, Luke xii. 50. He had little ease in his own bowels, as though it were a kind of death to him not to be a sacrifice ; and when Peter would have dissuaded him from suffering, he useth him as smartly as he would have done the devil : Mat. xvi. 23, ' Get thee behind me, Satan,' implying that in that speech he was the same enemy, by giving him the same title. And the night before, he doth solemnly oblige himself to suffer by his deed,* as well as he had before by his word ; he makes his testament in the institution of the supper, and delivers his will into the hands of his disciples. His heart was bent to wade through it ; he gave them his blood in the sacrament, to shew how freely he would pour it forth the following day in a sacrifice. The free distribution of his body to them represented the free offering up his body for them.

(3.) At the time of his death he manifested this voluntariness in his whole carriage. When the time drew near, he declined it not ; he would enter Jerusalem with *Hosannas*, as if when he went to his death he went to his triumph ; and indeed it was so, for by that oblation of himself upon the cross, he ' triumphed over principalities and powers,' Col. ii. 15. He went into the garden, which was as it were the bringing himself to the door of the tabernacle to be offered to God.† He had at the passover bid Judas to execute quickly his traitorous intention, and now quickens the high priest's dull officers to apprehend him, when he told them twice himself was the person they sought. He summoned not one angel to take arms for his rescue, though he could have commanded legions to attend him ; but as he had rebuked Peter before for dissuading him, he now rebukes him for defending him ; moved thereto by an ardency of zeal to drink the cup : John xviii. 11, ' Shall I not drink of the cup which my Father hath given me ? ' He would not court the protection of Herod by working a miracle to please his curiosity. As he would have no relentings himself, so he would not endure them in others ; and therefore dissuades the women from expressing their natural affection in a few tears, Luke xxiii. 28. His soul was not wrung and torn from him, but he rendered his spirit into the hands of his Father, and cried with a loud voice before that last act ; so that he died not by a defect of strength, but by an ardency of will. He was more delighted with his sufferings for us than we can be with the greatest worldly pleasures and grandeurs, and valued reproaches for us above the empire of the world. To conclude, his soul was not torn from him, but he ' poured it out,' Isa. liii. 12, even that which was dearest to him, as a man doth water, freely and willingly out

* Lingend, Eucharist, p. 22.   † Dr Owen.

of the vessel, ' he poured out his soul unto death ; ' he ordered death to come and fetch it.

III. Thing.   Why this voluntariness was necessary.

1. On the part of the person.
2. On the part of justice.
3. On the part of acceptation.

1. On the part of the sacrifice itself.   He was above any obligation to that work he so freely undertook for us.   When he made himself of no reputation, it was a work of his charity, not of necessity ; and he was bound in no other bonds but those of his own love.   Nor could he be overruled to anything against his own consent ; for being ' God equal with the Father,' Philip. ii. 6, he was subject to no law, nor could be constrained to bend under the terms and penalties of it.   Christ as the second person was not under a law any more than the Father ; for he was ' in the form of God,' *i. e.* had the same essence with God.   Suppose he had been incarnate without entering into any bonds for us, though so far as he was man he was bound actively to obey the precepts of the law, yet not bound to endure the penalties of the law, unless he had been a transgressor of the precept : he was to have obeyed it as a creature, but not suffer the curse, unless he had been a guilty creature.   But he was not only made under the law, as an innocent creature, but ' in the likeness of sinful flesh,' Rom. viii. 3, as like as possible could be, sin only excepted ; and therefore observed those ceremonial precepts which concerned creatures as sinful : as circumcision, though he had no lust in his human nature to be cut off, and baptism, though he had no stain to be washed away.   And indeed, as he was not, so he could not be a transgressor, being secured by his conception from any original taint, and by the hypostatical union from any actual spot.   If he could possibly have been a transgressor, the salvation of the elect had been contingent.   Being a creature, of the seed of the woman, he may be supposed to be under the condition of the covenant of nature ; yet not violating that covenant, he could not justly die for himself.

2. Necessary on the part of justice.   The satisfaction for sin was to be made by death, because man upon his revolt from God was, by the immutable law, bound over to death.   Man could not satisfy the law but by death, and so must have lain under the bonds of that death for ever, and no convenient way could be found for his rescue, unless some one, who was not obnoxious to that penalty by nature, should suffer in his stead that death which he owed.   Now had it not been an injustice to inflict a punishment upon a person purely innocent, and unwilling to render himself in the place of the criminal ?   No man can be justly constrained to pay either a pecuniary or criminal debt for another without his own consent, either actual, at the time of paying or suffering ; or legal, when entering into the same bonds, he hath made himself legally one person with the debtor or offender.   Had not Christ voluntarily undertaken it, justice had been wronged instead of being satisfied.   It could upon no account have been just to punish one that had not been guilty upon his own score, or by substitution.   The satisfaction of justice in one kind had been an injury to it in another.   Well then, the will of Christ could not have saved us without his suffering ; because, as the law had denounced death, justice was to be satisfied by death.   Nor could the sufferings of Christ have saved us without his will, for none can be an involuntary surety ; had he not consented to have our sins imputed to him, the punishment of our sins could not have been inflicted on him.   To take from any what is not due, and when they are unwilling to part with it, is rapine.

3. Necessary in regard of acceptation.   Christ's consent was as necessary

as God's order. Had Christ suffered for us without the consent of his Father, the judge of the world, though his sufferings had been of infinite value, because of the dignity of his person, yet God had not been obliged to look upon us as concerned in him,* nor count him* to us or for us ; and had not Christ consented that they should be for us, they could not justly have been accepted for us, or applied to us. It had been an alienating the goods against the will of the donor. As God's order makes his sacrifice capable of being satisfactory, so the consent of Christ makes it capable of being accepted for us and applied to us. The heathens would not offer a beast that came struggling to the altar ; but God, under the law, regarded not the reluctance of the sacrifice, but the free will of the offerer, which was necessary to make the sacrifice a sweet savour. How much more necessary is the voluntariness of that person who was to be both sacrifice and priest ! Love belongs to the integrity of a sacrifice ; a burnt body without charity is of no value, 1 Cor. xiii. 3. The merit of his death depended, not upon the act of dying, or the penal part in that death, but upon his willing obedience in it, in conjunction with the dignity of his person ; and without this his soul might have expired without being a sacrifice. As the disobedience of Adam rendered the world obnoxious to wrath, so by the voluntary oblation of Christ, justification is conferred upon believers, Rom. v. 19. His love made his sacrifice a sweet-smelling savour. By the pouring out his soul is our redemption wrought ; Isa. liii. 12, ' He shall divide the spoil with the strong, because he poured out his soul unto death,' or he shall partake of the spoil with the strong ; he shall take us as his own spoils, who were before the devil's prey, and restore to us that blessedness which the devil rifled us of. We are restored, and himself exalted, not merely because he died, but because he died willingly. In vain had we hoped for the benefit of a forced redemption.†

IV. Use.

1. The way of redemption by a sacrifice was necessary. Why should Christ so willingly undertake this task, be a man of sorrows, lay himself down into the grave, if the atonement of our sins could have been procured at an easier rate ? He that made the world by a word would have redeemed us by a word, if it had stood with his own honour. It is at least necessary for God's greater honour and man's surer benefit. The application of it to us must be as necessary as the oblation of it for us. Think not a few tears, the heat-drops of a natural repentance, can expiate those sins for which Christ thought the best blood in his heart so necessary to be shed.

2. The death of Christ for us was most just on the part of God. What Christ did willingly submit to, God might justly charge upon him as a due debt. *Volenti non fit injuria.* That man that will enter into bond to secure the debt to the creditor, or satisfy for the criminal to the governor, may justly be sued upon default of payment by the one, and arrested for default of appearance by the other ; what he promised may justly be demanded of him.

3. How wonderful was the love of Christ ! To accept so willingly of such hard conditions for us, and die so ignominiously upon the cross we had deserved ! He knew the burden of sin, he knew the terrors of hell ; yet he did not shrink from the imputation of the one, or the sufferings of the other. It was not a willingness founded upon ignorance, but upon a clear-sighted affection. He was willing to be reproached, that we might be glorified ; he would be like to us, that we might be conformed to him ; and took our human nature, that we might in a sort partake of his divine. Oh wonderful love ! to open his breast to receive into his own heart the sharp edge of that sword which was directed against us. Had not his feet been well shod with love,

* Qu. ' them ' ?—ED.   † Hall, vol. ii. p. 246.

he would soon have turned back, and said his way was unpassable.* A courtesy is enhanced by the greater ingrediency of the will in it; our Saviour had a double will in this matter, the will of the divine, and the will of his human nature, like two streams from distant parts meeting together in conjunction. Worse than devils are we, if we are not ravished with so great an affection, which made him leave the heaven of his Father's presence for a time, to pass through our hell in the dregs of the creation.

4. How willingly then should we part with our sins for Christ, and do our duty to him! Oh that we could in our measures part as willingly with our lusts as he did with his blood! He parted with his blood when he needed not, and shall not we with our sins, when we ought to do so for our own safety, as well as for his glory? Since Christ came to redeem us from the slavery of the devil, and strike off the chains of captivity, he that will remain in them, when Christ with so much pains and affection hath shed his blood to unloose them, prefers the devil and sin before a Saviour, and will find the affront to be aggravated by the Redeemer's voluntariness in suffering for his liberty. How willingly should we obey him, who so willingly obeyed God for us! Christ did not let his enemies snatch away his life, but laid it down; our duties should not be wrung from us, but gently distil from us. The more will in sin, the blacker; the more will in obedience, the sweeter. It is in this we should imitate our great pattern.

* Gurnal's Armour, part ii. p. 444.

A DISCOURSE OF THE ACCEPTABLENESS OF CHRIST'S DEATH.

A sacrifice to God for a sweet-smelling savour.—EPH. V. 2.

HAVING despatched the first doctrine about the voluntariness of Christ's death, from those words, *hath given himself,* I proceed to speak of the acceptableness of it, from this latter clause of the verse. Allusion is made here to the perfume God commanded under the law, Exod. xxx. 34. The spices were to be pounded, and afterwards put into a censer, to be dissolved into a sweet fume in the Levitical service; Christ was bruised by his humiliation, to be rendered a sweet perfume to God.

Doct. The sacrifice of Christ was acceptable to God, and efficacious for men. There was a complete satisfaction made to God, the supreme Judge offended, pleasing to him, and effectual to free the guilty party from the obligation to the deserved punishment. Christ was white, in regard of his innocence; ruddy, in regard of his bloody passion: both put together made him the chiefest among ten thousand, Cant. v. 10. The efficacy of this sacrifice in many fruits of it is fully expressed, Dan. ix. 24. The transgression was finished, an end put to sin, the apostasy of Adam was checked, the idolatry of the Gentiles overthrown, the atonement of sin made, which could not be by the legal sacrifices; a righteousness pleasing to God, and therefore everlasting, introduced; all the predictions of him fulfilled; whereupon he is anointed, *i. e.* fully settled in all his offices, and declared by that anointing to be a complete sacrifice, and the Prince of our salvation. The last words our Saviour spake upon the cross gave us an assurance of this; he saw and knew the work completely performed, and then gave up the ghost: John xix. 30, 'When Jesus had received the vinegar, he said, It is finished; and he bowed his head, and gave up the ghost.' All the prophecies of what I was to do are accomplished; I have nothing else now to do, to render my undertaking complete, but the bowing down my head, and sending out my last breath to my Father. All the sacrifices of the law, the daily and anniversary sacrifices, were shadows and images of him, and fulfilled in their main design in and by him. It could not be otherwise than acceptable, since there was no omission of anything required of him, no commission of anything forbidden to him. The whole law, both the mediatory law and the law of nature, were within his heart; the whole law was answered by his life. He paid an obedience, not by measure, as he had received the Spirit not by measure, to prepare him to be a victim for our redemption. It was acceptable to God for us ; so must the apostle be understood. It was a sweet savour to God for those persons, and those ends for which he gave himself. As it was a sacrifice intended and offered to God for us, so it was accepted as a sweet-smelling savour by God for those persons and ends.

In handling this doctrine, I shall,

I. Premise two things for the explication of it.

II. Prove it.

III. Apply it.

I. I shall premise two things for the explication of it.

1. God was not absolutely bound to accept it for us. Though this sacrifice was infinitely valuable in itself, and had it been without a divine order, might have been counted a testimony of affection to the honour of God and the good of the creature, yet God might have refused any acceptance of it for us ; he might have rejected every sacrifice but that of the offender. If we consider it simply in itself, without any previous order, without any covenant struck between the Father and the Son concerning it, he was not obliged to have any respect to the apostate creature upon the account of it. But after a covenant struck between them, wherein it was agreed that Christ should lay down his soul as a ransom, and offer himself an unblemished sacrifice for the sons of men, and that he should see the travail of his soul, and by his righteousness justify many, after he had ' borne their iniquities in his own body on the tree,' Isa. liii. 10, 11, God could [not but accept it, unless he could have found a spot in the offering, and charged him with a non-performance of any article covenanted between them. If it were according to the tenor of the covenant of redemption, it could not be refused by God, being consequent to his decree and promise. But if we consider it in itself, God was not bound to accept it for us, though he might have had an high esteem of it ; for, according to the tenor of his law, he might have demanded a compensation from the person of the sinner, and laid the punishment upon the person upon whom he found the guilt, and exacted the life of the sinner as a sacrifice for the sin. The acceptableness of this sacrifice was from itself, in regard of the dignity of the person, the infiniteness of the sacrifice ; but the actual acceptation of it for us was from the covenant and agreement between them. When a man offers to give a thousand pound for that which is not worth a thousand pence, the sum is not only a valuable, but an over-valuable consideration for that which is desired ; but the acceptation of this sum from the other depends upon the will of the person whose propriety it is. The death of Christ was a sacrifice of a valuable consideration for the sin of the world, and sufficient to expiate the greatest crimes both for number and weight ; but the receiving of it upon such an account depended upon the will of the Law-giver, whose authority was violated in the breach of the law, and who, as the only Judge, had passed sentence on the offending creatures, and had ' concluded all under sin,' Rom. xi. 32, and sentenced the whole world (ὑπόδικον) ' under condemnation,' Rom. iii. 19. It must be accepted by him ; it had not else been of itself valid for us. In regard, therefore, of the valuableness of this sacrifice, all the beneficial fruits of it streaming upon the creature are in Scripture ascribed to the death of Christ ; but in regard of God's acceptation of it for us, they are ascribed to the grace of God ; to the grace of God, as appointing and accepting ; to the death of Christ, as procuring and purchasing. The grace of God gave a virtue to the mediation of Christ, in regard of its application to us ; but the

death of Christ had a value in itself, whether it had been accepted for us or not, or ordered by God to be applied to us. And as God respects the agreement in the promise he makes to us, so Christ doth not enter any pleas in respect of the intrinsic worth of his blood, but makes this agreement the foundation of them: John xvii. 4–6, 'I have finished the work which thou gavest me to do.' The prevalency of it for us depended upon God's order. Indeed, had he not finished the work, he could not have challenged the reward promised; there was to be merit on his part before a reward on God's. Yet the suffering on his part may be conceived without any reward on God's part, if considered separate from this agreement and divine transaction between them. We must not understand this as though, if God had not been obliged to dignify Christ for his sufferings, by the promise he had made him, he would not have rewarded those sufferings out of mere goodness; for since God in his own nature is infinitely good, he cannot but love holiness and affection to him, and testify his approbation of it by some retribution.

2. As the acceptation of it depended upon the will of the Lawgiver and Rector, so the acceptableness of it depended upon the will of the Redeemer. The apostle therefore saith, 'He gave himself for us;' the sweetness of it depended upon the will of the donor, in concurrence with the will of God. The more of will there is in any act of a creature's obedience, the more savoury it is to the divine Majesty to whom it is paid. His love both to God and us made his sacrifice a sweet-smelling savour. The merit of his death depended not upon his mere dying, or upon the penal part in that death, but upon his willing obedience in it, in conjunction with the dignity of his person; without this, he might have breathed out his soul without being a victim. Had not Christ's will been full and firm in it, that his sufferings should be for us, they could not justly have been accepted for us, or applied to us; it could not have been a payment of our debt, and the application of him to us had been an alienating the goods of another against the will of the proprietor. This sweet savour exhaled from his voluntariness; he was not dragged to his sufferings, but suffered more willingly than we had greedily sinned against God. We had conscience checking us in sinning, but Christ had no conscience checking him in suffering; it was his meat and drink to do his Father's will. As God's order makes his sacrifice capable of being satisfactory, so the free willingness of Christ makes it capable of being accepted for us, and applied to us. Involuntary services are rather passions than actions; in them we rather suffer a service than perform it. There was obedience in every preparatory act of Christ: obedience in the last act, in the suffering death; and it was his obedience in suffering, not simply the suffering itself, made it meritorious of his mediatory glory for us: Philip. ii. 8, 9, 'Wherefore God also hath highly exalted him,' viz. because of his 'obedience to the death of the cross.' His joy in performing was the incentive of God's joy in valuing, accepting, and rewarding it. God eyed his obedience in the crown he gave him, and it was in the consideration of his obedience in suffering that he advanced him to that excellent dignity.

II. Thing. That this sacrifice is acceptable to God and efficacious for us will appear in several propositions.

1. God took pleasure in the designment and expectation of it.

(1.) His eternal delights were in him, not only as his Son, but as a Redeemer. God's delight in Christ, and Christ's rejoicing in the habitable parts of the earth, and delighting in the sons of men, are coupled together, Prov. viii. 30, 31, as if God delighted in him because he delighted in the redemption of man. Hence God is introduced as speaking with a kind of joy of this ransom : Job xxxiii. 24, 'Then is he gracious to him, and saith, Deliver him from going down into the pit, I have found a ransom;' *i. e.* I have accepted a ransom, and have a price in my hand ; as Hos. xii. 8, ' I am become rich, I have found me out substance ;' *i. e.* I have got wealth enough ; so I have here price sufficient, unloose the chains of the prisoner. This finding is the same on God's part with acceptation, as finding on Christ's part is the same with obtaining : Heb. ix. 12, 'Having obtained eternal redemption,' εὐράμενος, having found. It is the speech of God ; who else but the Rector of the world, and the Judge of all flesh, hath power to order the delivery of the captive ? It is the exultation of his mercy at the appearance of a sufficient sacrifice for the forlorn sinner, whose soul was drawing near to the grave, and his life to the destroyers. It is the triumph of mercy at the thought of it.

(2.) What was the ground of his promises to him, but his pleasure in him for this undertaking ? What else can be the meaning of those words, which the apostle cites to prove the deity of Christ : Heb. i. 5, 'And again, I will be to him a Father, and he shall be to me a Son ;' that God would be always to him a Father, accepting his obedience, and he should always be a Son, offering upon the cross, or pleading upon the throne, his sacrifice and sufferings ; a Father to him as mediator, to countenance, encourage, accept him and all his undertakings ? This is a promise made to Christ. What need of any promises to Christ, considered only as the Son of God, equal with the Father ? It is a promise to Christ as the seed of David (the place the apostle cites it from is 2 Sam. vii. 14) ; and if to him as the seed of David, it is made to him as mediator, promising a kingdom to him upon his suffering, and an eternal acceptation of him as an obedient Son, the ground whereof was his purging our sins by himself, Heb. i. 3. All the promises of God to Christ respect not Christ absolutely considered as the Son of God, but in the relation of mediator, sacrifice, ransom for man ; for they are all branches issuing upon that first promise to man in paradise of the seed of the woman, whose heel was to be bruised. God promiseth to be a Father to Christ, in the same sense that Christ owns him to be his God and his Father after his resurrection, John xx. 17, which respects God's relation to him as mediator ; for as he is considered absolutely as the Son of God, God could not so properly be said to be his God. The term implies a covenant between them, in pursuance of which Christ was to be God's servant ; and in acceptance of this, God was the God of Christ, and promises to be his Father, manifesting his fatherly and gracious acceptance of his services, as a father doth the obedience of a son ; and therefore Christ pleads the righteousness of God for the obtaining the accomplishment of his grace in those that believe in him, as well as the love which God bore to him as mediator : John xvii. 25, 26, ' O righteous Father,' &c. Grace was the fountain of the promise, but justice is obliged for the performance.

(3.) Hence it was that he declared his acceptation of him at his entrance into his office, which was at his baptism : Mat. iii. 17, ' This is my beloved Son, in whom I am well pleased ;' not respecting only his eternal filiation, but the work he was entering into the exercise of, and the preparations to his being a sacrifice. With this work, wherein his Son was to glorify him, was he well pleased ; his interposition as a victim for the salvation of many brethren was grateful to God. The word רצה, the word in Isa. xlii., whence this place is cited, is often used to express God's pleasure in, and acceptance of, sacrifices offered to him ' according to his will,' as Job xxxiii. 26, Mal. i. 8 ; and here it refers to the whole work of Christ, as the whole work of redemption is called the good pleasure or *εὐδοκία* of God, Eph. i. 5. He confirms here by his own testimony what he had declared before by the angels in their hymn, Luke ii. 14, 'good will toward men,' *εὐδοκία.* So certain was God that this sacrifice would answer all his ends, that he testifies himself well pleased with him before the full performance of his work.

(4.) Hence it was that God delighted to bruise him, and in the thoughts of it he foresaw what pleasure he should take in this, as I may say, aromatic sacrifice, after it was bruised and pounded, Isa. liii. 10. Not that God did delight in the act of bruising, considered separately from the ends for which he bruised him (since all acts of justice are his strange works), but with an eye to the issue of it, which was the glory of his divine perfections, the recovery of lost man, the restoration of the health and soundness of the creation. As the physician delights not in the sharpness of the physic he administers to the patient, or a chirurgeon in lancing the body, but as it conduceth to the health of the patient.

(5.) Hence it was that he took pleasure in the representations of it before it was actually offered. Hence the very first service after the promise was probably a sacrifice, as hath been said before, and the chief part of worship in the only church God had in the world for many ages consisted in sacrifices, the representations of this grand victim in the end of the world. In all those things, which could not upon their own account satisfy God, as not being suited to his justice and wisdom, and not able to expiate the sin of a rational creature, he smelt a sweet savour as they were images of this sacrifice, whence the greatest and most pleasant fragrancy should be exhaled, Gen. viii. 20.

All this pleasure of God testified before the oblation was from the certainty of its accomplishment. God knew he 'laid help upon one that was mighty,' Ps. lxxxix. 19, mighty to please him and pleasure us. God could not have beforehand rejoiced in that which should have come short of his expectation; it is inconsistent with the Deity to have such a disappointment. The least failure in the sacrifice would have frustrated his contrivance, and rendered it as loathsome to God as the sin of Adam for which he suffered. But it was impossible for God to be disappointed, and impossible for the Redeemer, being God as well as man, to fail in the performance of his part, and thereby God come short of his satisfaction, and the sinner of the security.

2. God had a restoration of his rest, which had been disturbed by the entrance of sin, and therefore this sacrifice was highly acceptable to God. He was God's servant in whom his soul delighted or had a rest, Isa. xlii. 1; excluding all other things from contributing to the rest or delight of God. God rested in the works of creation as they were shadows of his wisdom, power, and greatness, especially as they were effluxes of his goodness, and answered his glorious ends; for the ground of his resting was a review of the goodness of them according to his own mind and idea. He saw himself and his attributes glittering in the creatures. But the rest of God was disturbed by the invasion sin made upon his rights in the world; and no sooner had he made the world and was refreshed, Exod. xxxi. 17, but disorder and confusion, by means of sin, spread itself over that frame, whereupon he cursed the earth which he had newly made, gave sentence against man, and though it was tempered with the mercy of a gracious promise, yet he left him under some outward penal evil all his days because of his revolt, and had no rest but in that seed of the woman, whose heel was to be bruised by the serpent, that the serpent's head might be shattered and bruised by him; and thereby an end put to that disorder which had entered by the serpent's breath. And therefore all the joy God hath in his church, the best part of his creation, is from this rest or acquiescence in his love or the object of his love, Zeph.

iii. 17, ' He will rest in his love, he will rejoice over thee with singing.' Hence it is that the temple, the type of Christ, is called in regard of those shadows of him, viz. sacrifices daily performed in it, ' the house of his glory,' Isa. lx. 7, ' a glorious high throne,' Jer. xvii. 12, ' the place of his rest,' Isa. lxvi. 1.   Could gold and silver, polished stones, and artificial structures, be the rest and throne of God ?   As little as the blood of bulls and goats could affect him of themselves with a fragrant smell.   His sole acquiescence was in the temple of the body of Christ, made fit to be a sacrifice, and repre- sented by those types.   Such a rest he had in him as a sacrifice, that upon that very account he gave all things into his hands ; and as by eternal gene- ration he had communicated to him the perfections of his nature, so, as he was a mediatory sacrifice, he gave him authority to execute judgment, gave him a kingdom as large as his own, and seemed to veil his own authority to increase his, and as it were stands behind the curtain, while this our Mor- decai, that saved us from death, manages all the concerns of his empire ; and all to this end, 'that men might honour the Son as they honoured the Father,' John v. 22, 23.   Such a perfect acquiescence hath God in him, that he will entertain nothing to the prejudice of the honour of Christ in his work.   He will not have the best works and sacrifices of men partners and competitors with him : he will for ever discard all those that have not the same thoughts of him, the same satisfaction and glorious rest in him, according to their mea- sures, as himself hath.   No other sacrifice shall be of value with him for the atonement of sin ; not a dram of mercy, not so much as to the quantity of the cooling virtue of a drop of water, can reasonably be expected by those that refresh not themselves with that sacrifice wherein God found so delightful a rest.   Such a rest hath God in his sacrifice, that it shall be the matter of the praises of the saints to all eternity in heaven.

3. The highest perfections of God's nature had a peculiar glory from this sacrifice.   All his perfections, not discovered before to the sons of men, are glorified punctually according to his intentions and resolves for their dis- covery.   Not a tittle of his nature which was to be made known to the sons of men, but is unveiled in this sacrifice to their view in a greater glory than the creatures were able to exhibit him.   The ' knowledge of the glory of God shines in the face' or appearance ' of Jesus Christ,' 2 Cor. iv. 6 ; i. e. all the perfections of his nature are delineated in this saving sacrifice.   In which respect some think that Col. ii. 9, of the ' fulness of the Godhead's dwelling in him bodily,' is to be taken not only that the Deity dwelt in the human nature, but the full discovery of the perfections of the Godhead was in the appearance of Christ in his body, as prepared for a sacrifice, as in a map and scheme, as clear as could possibly be represented to the view of men.   It is in the purchase of our redemption by his blood that he appears to be ' the image of the invisible God,' as well as the ' first-born' or head ' of every creature,' Col. i. 14, 15 ; the image of those perfections of the Godhead which otherwise had been utterly invisible to man ; the image not of his will, as the Socinians, but of his nature.   Hence is the glory of the Lord, as well as the salvation of his people, the name and title of Christ, Isa. xl. 5: ' The glory of the Lord shall be revealed,' Luke ii. 32.   His holiness was glorified in the discovery of the hellish filthiness of sin ; his justice in the grievous punishment of it ; his mercy to his creatures in giving the dearest thing he had a ransom for them.   In him he appeared gracious as well as righteous, transcendently merciful in the exercise of the highest justice, Ps. cxvi. 5: both shined clearly in the head of this sacrifice, being tempered for the glory of God, and the good of the creature.   The seat of justice is turned into a throne of grace, puts on the quality of an advocate instead of that of an

accuser, uttering absolutions instead of condemnations. Since justice is propitiated by the death of Christ, it steps in as an agent in the justification of a believer, Rom. iii. 25, 26. Justice, the main attribute to be dreaded by man, was so glorified and pleased by this sacrifice, that this alone would oblige him to the remission of sin, if mercy should not have any suit for itself.

4. Compare this sacrifice with the evil for which he was sacrificed, and which had invaded the rights of God, and the sweet savour of it will appear, as also the efficacy of it.

(1.) This sacrifice was as honourable for God as our sins had been a dishonour to him. As much glory accrued to him by it as injury was offered him by our sin. Our sin was the sin of a creature, and the sacrifice was the act of that person by whom God made the world. The sin was the act of his creature-image, the sacrifice was the act of the 'express image of his person,' Heb. i. 2, 3. Sin was committed by man, and expiated by him who was God. It was not only a rational sacrifice for the sin of a rational creature, but a divine. The sin was an infinite offence in regard of the person against whom it was committed, the price was of an infinite value in regard of the person by whom it was paid; the dignity of the person makes a compensation for the malice of the crime. An infinite person was not more wronged by the transgression than he is righted by the dignity of the person who made the compensation for it. It is every way proportioned to the infinite guilt of the crimes for which it is offered, and the infinite justice of God which was offended thereby. God had a price of a full value, he was fully repaired in his honour, and we delivered from our chains. In some respect the attributes of God were not so much dishonoured by the sin of Adam as they were glorified by the death of Christ. Christ glorified by his sacrifice those perfections which were not then discovered, nor discoverable to Adam in his innocence, as patience and grace, as well as those were particularly offended by the revolt of man. This sacrifice fully repairs the honour of God, which nothing else could do. The reason why the damned lie for ever under the weight of his wrath in hell is, because by all their suffering they cannot restore that honour to God, which they have robbed him of by their iniquities.

(2.) There was, therefore, a greater pleasure arose to God from this sacrifice than noisomeness from our sin. The dignity of the person suffering was equal to the dignity of the person injured, and infinitely exceeding the quality of the person offending. The sin of a creature could never be so filthy as the blood of the Son of God was holy; and the noisomeness of the first could not equal the sweetness of the latter. The stench of sin was not only balanced and tempered, but overpowered, by the sweetness of this sacrifice. Divine justice was not more incensed against the crime, than divine holiness was delighted with the offering. Sin was the sin of the human nature, the sacrifice was of the human nature in union with the divine, and offered up by an 'eternal Spirit,' Heb. ix. 14. The apostle in that text alludes to Gen. viii. 21. God smelled so sweet a savour from Noah's sacrifice, the type of this, that he resolves never more to curse the ground, or send deluge upon the new world, though he knew it would prove as bad as the old; for in the same breath wherein God's resolution is discovered to us, his sense of the evil of men's imaginations from their youth is declared also. The fragrant odour of the one was above the noisome scent of the other. Though our consciences are purged from dead works, which do morally pollute us, as the touch of a dead body did ceremonially pollute the Israelites, yet they are but partially purged here to serve the living God. There is not a service we offer but hath something mixed with it contrary to the holiness of God, yet the evil fumes that steam up with our sacrifices of duty, are overpowered by the rich perfume of the sacrifice of the Son of God; that when for the foulness of our imperfections we deserve a repulse, yet for the sweetness of his sacrifice we find an acceptation.   So much did the merit of his blood overcome the ill scent of our iniquities in the nostrils of God, that he cancels our bonds, which were due to him, and makes new ones of himself to Christ; he frees the creature from the deserved punishment, and obligeth himself to give eternal life to every one that believes in him thus sacrificed, howsoever noisome his sins were wherewith he had affronted heaven before.

(3.) Therefore it is efficacious for man, because so pleasing and sweet to God.   Sin did not so much hurt to the transgressor, as this sacrifice procures good to the believer.   Sin took away our spiritual life; Christ, by his sacrifice, procures a restoration of it in a fuller communication than before, John x. 10, a richer and more overflowing fountain than before, more abundantly than Adam in innocency, who had it mutable in his own hands, we immutable in the hands of our Head, who is our life; more abundantly than the patriarchs of the Old Testament, who had it in hope, and we in the full exhibition; a spiritual life more firm than Adam's, ending in an eternal life more durable.   Therefore the grace of Christ surmounts the effects of Adam's sin.   The apostle discourseth of the abundance of grace above the abundance of sin, Rom. v. 15–17.   As Adam's sin barred paradise against him and his posterity, the blood of Christ, as oil to the lock, makes heaven's gates open easily for the re-admission of every believer.

5. His resurrection after his bloody sacrifice is a clear evidence of the sweetness of its savour with God, and its sufficiency for us.   He was not totally swallowed up by divine justice, but surmounted all the strokes of it, and lifted up his head above the waves that surrounded him.   The fetters of death had not been unlocked, if his sacrifice had not been satisfactory. The justice of God might as well have discharged him without any sacrifice at all, as discharged him upon an insufficient one.   The freedom, therefore, of the prisoner from his chains, is an evidence of the full satisfaction of the debt, and the completeness of the sacrifice, since it is by that God, whose name hath that letter in it, 'By no means to clear the guilty,' Exod. xxxiv. 7, that the writ of execution was taken off: Isa. liii. 10, 'He was taken from prison and from judgment.'   By whom?   By him who only had authority to release him, who became a God of peace by his sacrifice, before he shewed himself a God of power in his resurrection, Heb. xiii. 20.   He was appeased as an offended lawgiver, before he gave a judicial discharge as the supreme governor, unloosed the chains of death, sent an angel as his officer to unlock the prison doors, the grave, and set him at full liberty, no more to be arrested.   There could be in this case no forcible breaking of prison, he being in the hands of the almighty God, who had as much power to keep him in the chains of death, had his sacrifice been blemished, as he had to free him when his sacrifice was spotless.   Justice, therefore, is fully satisfied, since the pains of death are unloosed, Acts ii. 24, 25, &c., for it was not possible he should be holden of them, because the truth of God was engaged that his ' holy One should not see corruption.'   This raising him was a justification of him, for when he was taken from prison he was taken from judgment also, that no suits could be brought against him, or any new actions laid upon him; and he was ' declared to be the Son of God,' Rom. i. 4, and if we take in ver. 3, that seed of David also, which was prophesied of; and he was declared to be so ' with power,' ἐν δυνάμει, not only by the power that raised him, but by the power of the government of the world, wherein he was instated upon his resurrection.   For this act of God was a testimony, that he had ordained him, and ordained him also to judge the world, Acts

xvii. 31. By this he was acquitted by God, as having done all that he did according to the articles between them. And in that act all his members have an original and fundamental discharge, to be sued out in due time in particular upon their faith. It is in this discharge he triumphs, as it was his justification before men and angels : Isa. l. 8, 'He is near that justifieth me, who will contend with me ?' This is the foundation of the apostle's *epinicion* and triumphant challenge, 1 Cor. xv. 55, 56, 'O death, where is thy sting ?' Where is sin, that ushered death into the world, and by it stung man to the heart ? It is conquered by the resurrection of Christ, which is a clear evidence of the sweetness of this sacrifice to God, and its efficacy for us. Our faith is not in vain, which it had been, according to the apostle, 1 Cor. xv. 17, if he had not risen as he died, viz., in the quality of our surety and head. Had not the sacrifice been without exception, the devil had been the victor, and Christ his triumph. He would have acquired a stronger power over men by the least blemish, as he first gained it by Adam's sin. Had he not been justified himself, he could never have justified us, nor could the mercies of David have been sure and perpetual without it, Acts xvii. 34. So mightily pleased was God with this sacrifice, that he employed his glorious power to raise him ; justice had no plea to continue him in prison, nor the devil any power to hinder the breaking of his fetters. His sacrifice was his act to propitiate God, his resurrection was God's act to comfort us.

6. The ascension and full exaltation of Christ after his bloody sacrifice is a full evidence of this doctrine. Since the promises made to Christ are accomplished, which were conditional upon the making his soul an offering for sin, it manifests he is an unexceptionable sacrifice. He had a kingdom promised him, and doth now rule in the majesty of God, Micah v. 4. Had there been the least blemish upon him, he could not have claimed the performance of any one promise, nor had justice been bound to make any good to him. Grace to man made the first promise to Christ in favour of justice, and justice would have hindered the performance of any promise had it been able to find any exception. This sacrifice of his, in pouring out his soul to death, is the foundation of all his advancement, Isa. liii. 11, 12. This being the condition on his part, could not but be followed upon the fulfilling of it with a performance of the promises on God's part. Now, Christ went first to heaven in his soul immediately after his oblation, to present his sacrifice to God, and receive his judgment about the validity of it,* for that day, the day of his sufferings, he was to be in paradise ; 'after death the judgment.' This was agreeable to the type of him in the anniversary sacrifice upon the day of expiation, when the high priest was to go with the blood into the holy place immediately after the shedding of it, and sprinkle it on the mercy-seat, for after the blood was clotted it was incapable of being sprinkled. Christ immediately after his death appears in heaven to receive the acceptation of his Father. This was in his soul, his body then lying in the grave, which the Scripture calls not an ascension till his soul and body were reunited, and both went up to heaven together. By this first entrance into heaven Christ obtained eternal redemption for us. Had not this judgment passed from God of the prevalency of his sacrifice, God had never sent an angel to unlock the grave, nor a cloud as a chariot to carry him up to heaven. This supposeth his sacrifice on earth to be already ratified in heaven. By this ascension he was again declared, as well as by his resurrection, to be without sin, without any need of repeating his sacrifice, Heb. ix. 28. His triumphant entrance into heaven assures us that his sacrifice was admitted into the bosom of God with infinite delight and pleasure. He could not have had a glory,

* Lawson's Body of Divinity, book ii. chap. iii. p. 97, much changed.

had he not punctually observed his order.   Triumph doth not precede but follow a victory.   His going to the Father was a full conviction of the righteousness of his person and his punctual discharge of his office, and the chief topic whereby the Spirit should argue men into a compliance with him, John xvi. 9, 10, is because he is gone to the Father.   Heaven had been no place for a blemished and imperfect offering.   The angels had not been commanded to be his adorers, but rather with their flaming swords have chased him out of heaven ; he could as little have continued there with a spot as Adam in paradise after his transgression.   No gift could have been poured out upon the sons of men.   The Holy Spirit could never have been the purchase of an unaccepted sacrifice.   He could not have been invested with a power to exercise any office in heaven, if he had not executed what he had undertaken upon earth ; he could not have lived to apply his sacrifice to us, if he had not been accepted in his offering himself a sacrifice for us.   But since he sits at the right hand of God, it is an infallible token of God's absolute rest in him, and his own rest from any further travel; it is an argument of special favour and dearness ; God hath given him all power in heaven and earth, ordered all the angels to worship him, and not only to give him a simple adoration, but to be at his command, his ministers and attendants in his kingdom.   He subjected his whole court to him and his service ; he bestowed upon him all the honour that was possible to be given him as Mediator, out of the complacency he had in him as a sacrifice.   It was upon the account that he ' purged our sins' by himself, that he ' sat down at the right hand of the Majesty on high,' and had all that dignity conferred upon him which is afterwards named, Heb. i. 3.   The whole prophecy of it is called *a song of loves*, Ps. xlv. (title.)   So highly pleasing it is to God, that he will not cease shooting his arrows till he hath put every enemy under his feet, that doth not agree with him in his pleasure and delight in Christ, Ps. cx. 1.   Since, therefore, he is entered into heaven, sat down at the right hand of God, and maintained the plea of his sacrifice for so many hundred years since he first entered his suit, it is a proof that the pleading his death and the sight of his sacrificed body is not wearisome and distasteful to God. It is not like a carcase that he desires to be buried out of his sight ; he joyfully hears the voice of his blood sounding in his ears to this moment. Well therefore might the apostle upon this account make so great a challenge to all : Rom. viii. 33, 34, ' Who is he that condemns ?   It is Christ that died, yea, rather that is risen again, who is even at the right hand of God, who also makes intercession for us.'   Christ by his death appeased the wrath of God ; by his resurrection he was acquitted by the justice of God; by his ascension he took possession of his regal throne ; by his sitting at the right hand of God he prevalently pleads his sacrifice for the ends for which it was offered, and by his Spirit applies his blood to them that believe in him.

7. The admirable virtue of this sacrifice evidenceth the sweetness of it in the account of God.   It had a virtue antecedent to the oblation of it, and after the oblation it hath a perpetual virtue.

(1.) It had a virtue antecedent to the oblation of it.   God, upon the foresight of this sacrifice to be made in due time, did dispense his pardon to those that rested upon this future sacrifice, and did not stay till the satisfaction should be made for the injury committed,* but imparted it to men that hoped in the merit of the sacrifice before the oblation of it, and released the captive upon the single bond of Christ before the actual payment of the

* Lessius de Perfect. Divin. p. 125.

ransom. Upon his promise to be a sacrifice, believers under the Old Testament were saved by the merit of it, as well as those under the new.
Abraham rejoiced to see his day, and was justified by faith in him. When
he appeared, his design was to ' put away sin,' Heb. ix. 25, 26. What sin?
Not only sins committed while he was in the flesh, or sins committed after
his ascension, but sins before, even those transgressions which the legal
sacrifices, from the time of their first institution, were unable to expiate ;
such sins which the high priest, entering into the holy place every year with
the blood of animals, was not able to wipe off ; and to make that perfect which
the law could not, Heb. vii. 19, and redeem from the transgressions under
the first Testament, Heb. ix. 19. As an head appointed by God, he saved
men before his coming, as Adam the first head ruined men before their birth.
It is not more efficacious now, nor will be to eternity, than it was before ;
for he is the same, in point of virtue, yesterday, in ages past, as he is to-day,
at present, and will be in the ages to come, Heb. xiii. 8. Whoever were
accepted by God in their persons and services were accepted upon the
account of the first-born or head of every creature. As in him all the elect
were chosen, so in him they were all accepted, Eph. i. 4, 6. Faith was from
the first ages of the world ; the proper object of faith is God in the Redeemer,
and he was not considered by the patriarchs but in that quality in all their
sacrifices, since he had changed the government after the fall from God as
creator to God as redeemer ; and therefore, as all his acts of government
respected the Redeemer and the redemption, so all the services of men were
to respect the Redeemer promised. What God did to them was in the name
of Christ, the angel of his covenant, and what they offered to God was with
an eye to the promised seed, which is the same thing with our doing all
things in the name of Christ, the circumstance of time only being altered,
what was future then being changed into time past now. The ground of
this was the agreement between God and Christ for the performance of
this oblation. When bonds are agreed on, and time given for the payment
of the debt, the prisoner hath his liberty till that revolution of time. Now,
not only the thing to be done, but the time when it was to be done, was
settled between them, called therefore a ' due time ' or a stated opportunity,
Rom. v. 6, and the ' fulness of time ;' and till that time there was to be a
πάρεσις, a relaxation or pretermission, a not charging the debt upon them,
which is the word used by the apostle, Rom. iii. 25, ' For the remission of
sins that are past.' Had not this sacrifice had a virtue antecedent to the
oblation of it, Christ himself in the days of his flesh could not well have
uttered those words so often, ' Thy faith hath saved thee,' before he had bowed
his head upon the cross. The removal of sin, the bar to communion with
God, upon the credit of a future sacrifice, is an undeniable evidence how
sweet the expectation of it was to God, and therefore sweet must the actual
immolation of it needs be.

(2.) After the oblation, it hath a perpetual virtue. If the virtue of it before it was offered reached to the first ages of the world, as far as Adam and
Abel, it will continue in as excellent a force to the last believer, that shall
close up the number of the elect at the end of the world. If the blood of
Abel is so efficacious as to procure a perpetual vengeance upon Cain, shall
not the blood of that person, by whom God created the world, be more efficacious to procure a perpetual blessing from the grace of God, to which he
is more inclined than to acts of vengeance ? Though this sacrifice was but
once offered, yet it works, in regard of its virtue, perpetually as a moral
cause. As the act of sin ceasing, the guilt and power of sin remains binding
over to punishment, so, though the act of Christ's offering himself ceased,

yet the virtue of it is durable. The blood of this redeeming victim is intimated to be an incorruptible blood: 1 Pet. i. 18, ' We are not redeemed with corruptible things, as gold and silver, but with the precious blood;' precious because incorruptible ; the opposition testifies it, though it be not the same expression ; precious blood is opposed to corruptible things. As his body, so likewise his blood, and the efficacy of his sacrifice, was not to see corruption ; his blood is like the rod of Aaron, always flourishing in the holy of holies before the mercy-seat. Aaron's rod flourished after Aaron's death ; the sacrifice of Christ is always fresh and smoking before the throne of God, producing the fruits it merited, and the grace we want. This blood is called ' a new and living way,'* as if it were just now shed, or had been sprinkled upon us as soon as it streamed out of his body. Since he is a priest for ever, the virtue of his death abides for ever ; he could not be a priest for ever without an everlasting sacrifice, for priest and sacrifice are relatives. If he be a priest for ever, he is a sacrifice for ever ; the same moment that the virtue of the latter ceaseth, the honour of the former would shrink away. But that is unchangeable, Heb. vii. 24. His kingdom cannot be shaken ; his sacrifice, therefore, which was the foundation of his kingdom, cannot be wasted ; he must cease sitting upon his throne, fall from being the Father's darling at his right hand, if the virtue of his merit, and the efficacy of his blood, should cease producing the true fruits of it among his people. Though the oblation was but once, yet the presentation is perpetual ; he pleads upon his throne what he offered upon the cross. If it were a wasted thing, it were not worthy of the plea of so great a person as the Redeemer, nor worthy to be pleaded before so great a person as the Judge of all the world. He is, in regard of the continued virtue, not said to have been, but to be, our propitiation : 1 John ii. 2, ' He is the propitiation for our sins ;' he is, not has been ; he is now sitting in heaven ; he was a propitiation on earth in his offering ; he is a propitiation in heaven in the presentation of that offering. While his plea is heard, his death is accepted, for his plea is only the voice of his blood, and the fumes of his sacrifice. If the gospel must be preached to the end of the world, the virtue of his sacrifice, upon which the efficacy of the gospel depends, shall endure as long as the world endures. This perpetual virtue was typified by the ashes of the red heifer burned without the camp, which were reserved for purifying from legal uncleanness, Num. xix. 9. As the power of the devil shall never be able to pull him out of his throne, so the power of sin shall never be so prevalent as to weaken the virtue of his blood. As long as he remains in a state of life, his blood will have its efficacy, because it is the blood of the everlasting covenant, Heb. xiii. 20. What greater evidence can there be of the gratefulness of it to God, than its virtue reaching to the most distant ages of the world, and running through all the revolutions of time ?

8. It is so acceptable to God, that it is a sufficient sacrifice for all, if all would accept of it, and by a fixed faith plead it. It is sufficient for the salvation of all sinners, and the expiation of all sins. The wrath of God was so fully appeased by it, his justice so fully satisfied, that there is no bar to a readmission into his favour, and the enjoyment of the privileges purchased by it, but man's unbelief. The blood of Christ is a stream, whereof all men may drink ; an ocean, wherein all men may bathe. It wants not value to remove our sins, if we want not faith to embrace and plead it. As no sickness was strong enough against the battery of his powerful word when he was in the world, so no guilt is strong enough against the power of his blood, if

* Heb. x. 20, ὁδὸν πρόσφατον, newly slain.

the terms upon which it is offered by God be accepted by us. It is absolutely sufficient in itself, so that if every son of Adam, from Adam himself to the last man that shall issue from him by natural descent, should by faith sue out the benefit of it, it would be conferred upon them. God hath no need to stretch his wisdom, to contrive another price, nor Christ any need to reassume the form of a servant, to act the part of a bloody sacrifice any more. If any perished by the biting of the fiery serpent, it was not for want of a remedy in God's institution, but from wilfulness in themselves. The antitype answers to the type, and wants no more a sufficiency to procure a spiritual good than that to effect the cure of the body. He is therefore called 'the Saviour of the world,' 1 John iv. 14. And when the apostle, upon the citation of that in the prophet, that ' whosoever believes on him shall not be ashamed,' concludes, that ' there is no difference between Jew and Gentile, but that whosoever shall call upon the name of the Lord, shall be saved,' Rom. x. 11, 13; by the same reason it may be concluded, that there is no difference between this and that man, if they believe; what is promised to one believer, as a believer, is promised to all the world upon the same condition. And when the apostle saith, ver. 9, ' If thou shalt confess with thy mouth the Lord Jesus, and believe with thy heart, thou shalt be saved,' he speaks to every man that shall hear that sentence. If any man believe, this sacrifice is sufficient for his salvation. As Adam's disobedience was sufficient to ruin all his posterity, descending from him by natural generation, so is this sacrifice sufficient to save all that are in Christ by a spiritual implantation. The apostle's comparison would not else be valid: Rom. v. 18, ' As by the offence of one judgment came upon all men to condemnation, so by the righteousness of one the free gift came upon all men unto justification of life.' And if all men in the world were united to him by faith, there could not be any more required of Christ for their salvation than what he hath already acted; for it is a sacrifice of infinite value, and *infinite* knows no limits. Since it was sufficient to satisfy an infinite justice, it is sufficient to save an inexpressible number; and the virtue of it in saving one, argues a virtue in it to save all upon the same condition. Who will question the ability of an almighty power to raise all men from death to life, that hath raised one man from death to life by the speaking of a word? If men, therefore, perish, it is not for want of value, or virtue, or acceptableness in this sacrifice, but for want of answering the terms upon which the enjoyment of the benefits of it is proposed. If a man will shut his eyes against the light of the sun, it argues an obstinacy in the person, not any defect in the sun itself.

9. The effects of this sacrifice shew the acceptableness of it to God. As the effect of Adam's disobedience demonstrates the blackness and strength of his sin, so the fruit of this sacrifice evidenceth the efficacy of it. Had it not been sweet to God, we had still been in our sins. He was to perfect his people, which had been impossible, had he not been perfect himself in his sufferings. If he hath ' perfected for ever them that are sanctified,' then that sacrifice whereby he did perfect them is fully complete, Heb. x. 14.

(1.) Remission of sin. Our lives by our rebellion were a debt to the violated law; when we transgressed the precept, we incurred the penalty. This debt is discharged to believers by Christ's offering his soul in our stead, a sacrifice for sin, a rescue for our souls. He took away sin as the Lamb of God, John i. 29; as a sacrificed lamb, for the analogy relates not to a lamb as a creature, but a lamb as a sacrifice. He took away the sin of the world;* the guilt of sin, the curse of God, whatsoever belongs to the eternal

* Chemnit. in loc.

wages of sin, he transferred upon himself. There is a perpetual virtue in its nature, *he took*, as when we say a drug purges, we signify not only the act, but the natural quality of it. The apostle concludes the efficacy of this oblation from God's remembering sin no more: Heb. x. 16–18, ' Their sins and iniquities I will remember no more ; now, where remission of those is, there is no more offering for sin.' The completeness of the fruit discovers the judgment of God for the completeness of the merit upon which it is founded. Himself, therefore, after his resurrection, gives his apostles commission to publish this as the fruit of his death, to let men know that the way to heaven, in the removal of the bar, was secured by the blood of Jesus, John xx. 22, 23 ; Luke xxiv. 27. All the sacrifices, wherein there was a daily remembrance of sin, were abrogated as useless after this offering, which surmounted the efficacy of all the legal ones put together. They expiated ceremonial uncleanness, and the pollution of the body ; this, moral iniquities and the filth of the soul. Heb. ix. 13, 14, the apostle instanceth in the most solemn offering, that of the red heifer, supposed to be of a more durable efficacy than the daily offerings, since the ashes of it were reserved for a purification for sin, Num. xix. 9. But this, much more the rest, were exceeded by this offering, that purged the conscience from those ' dead works,' that bound the soul over to eternal death. And, indeed, the ceremonial act of the high priest, in sprinkling the blood of the heifer directly before the tabernacle, ver. 4, intimated that the efficacy of it was to be derived from the flesh and blood of Christ, typified by that structure. By this we gain a plenary indulgence, so as to have ' no more conscience of sin,' Heb. x. 2. Not that there is no more sin in believers, or no more sense of sin, but no more accusations and charges of sin before God, or despairing servile thoughts for sin in their own consciences ; for in his blood we have redemption, the forgiveness of sins,' Eph. i. 7. Upon which account a challenge is made by the apostle to all the believers' adversaries to bring an effectual charge against them, Rom. viii. 33, 34. It frees us not from one or two sins, but vast numbers of them: 1 John i. 7, ' The blood of Christ cleanseth us from all sin.' So that all the powers of hell can never lay the load upon them again ; for this saves to the uttermost, covers their iniquities, and blots them out as a thick cloud. ' Death is swallowed up in victory,' the destruction and condemnation by sin ; ' O death, where is thy sting ?' *i. e.* where is sin ? that is the sting of death, 1 Cor. xv. 54, 55. And, indeed, so acceptable to God was the first undertaking of our Saviour, that God promised him this as the fruit of his suffering, that his labour should not be in vain ; that he should ' see his seed ;' that ' by his knowledge he should justify many, when he bore their iniquities,' Isa. liii. 11. And, therefore, when the apostle saith, the old man is crucified with Christ, he understands that the destruction of the body of death, and the remission of all the extravagancies of it, is purchased by Christ at the hands of God, Rom. vi. 6. And all the sense we have of remission, from any ordinance, especially by that of the supper, is not from the ordinance itself, or the remembrance of this sacrifice ; but from the perpetual and prevailing efficacy of it with God to this day. The removal of so great a weight from the soul, which we were unable to bear, so great a curse which we were unable to suffer, shews the high acceptableness of it with God.

(2.) The confirmation of the covenant. After sin had stepped into the world, and invaded the rights of God, the first covenant became utterly unprofitable for the relief of man. God makes a new one, which was not signified to be valid to any without sacrifice. It is not unlikely that the first declaration of it to Adam, in the promise of the seed, was accompanied

with the sacrifices of beasts, both to shew to him a token of that punishment he had merited at the hands of justice, and in what a bloody way his
recovery was to be accomplished. The repetition of it to Abraham was
confirmed by sacrifices, Gen. xv. 18. And the solemn covenant between
God and the Israelites was confirmed by sacrifices, and the blood of them
called by Moses, ' the blood of the covenant,' Exod. xxiv. 5, 8, *i. e.* a type
of that blood which shall be shed for the confirmation of that blessed covenant whereby the soul shall be purified from sin. And by the institution
of God this seems to be essential to a covenant with God: Ps. l. 5, ' My
saints that have made a covenant with me by sacrifice.' And this custom
was used by the heathens in their leagues and solemn contracts between
nations, and in covenants between their gods and them, which descended to
them probably by tradition from the first parents, though they had lost the
true intent of that tradition. All this respected the confirmation of the
covenant of grace (succeeding in the room of that violated covenant of
works) by the blood of the promised seed, whereby man was to be repaired,
and the devil defeated. Hence is God so mightily affected with the engagement of Christ to be our surety, that he presently establisheth the covenant
of being their God, and making them his people : Jer. xxx. 21, 22, ' Who
is this that hath engaged his heart to approach to me, saith the Lord ? Ye
shall be my people, and I will be your God.' This is the immediate issue
of this engagement. To this purpose was he given to be a witness of the
everlasting covenant, Isa. lv. 3, 4. And to this his sacrifice had an immediate respect, whence the blood that merits the striking off the chains of the
prisoners, and taking away the bars, is called ' the blood of the covenant,'
Zech. ix. 11. And Christ, in the institution of the supper, Luke xxii. 20,
calls it ' the new testament in his blood,' *i. e.* the true blood shed for the
ratification of the covenant, which was only typified by the blood of all
former sacrifices. And ' for the remission of sins;' this only is mentioned,
though other benefits besides this flowed from the covenant, because as sin
was the foundation of all evil, so pardon of sin is the fountain of all good.
Had other blessings been merited without this, a bar had been put to our
enjoyment of them by the want of this. Upon this first link all other
blessings in the chain of happiness depend. All the promises of God, which
are branches of this federal engagement, are *yea and amen* in Christ, of an
infallible certainty. He himself is ' the Amen, the faithful and true witness,'
Rev. iii. 4. And to this purpose is the sacrament of the supper appointed,
being the perpetual representation of this sacrifice, wherein God shews himself resolved to stand firm in the covenant, which was confirmed by the
cross, and make good to a believer all the branches of it. This manifests it
to be highly acceptable to God, since the covenant made just after the unprofitableness of the old is upon the account of this sacrifice ratified by God
(as the sure mercies of David) in all the parts of it, to all the indigencies
and highest satisfaction of every believer.

(3.) Restoration of peace, and intercourse with God. Man was upon
the terms of enmity with God, hating him, and being hated by him. God
hates men, not as creatures, but as sinners. Man hates God, not as God, but
as sovereign and judge. Man turned off God from being his Lord; God turned
off man from being his favourite. Therefore Christ in respect of this sacrifice is called ἱλασμός, 1 John ii. 2, our propitiation, and ἱλαστήριον, Rom. iii.
25, alluding both to the sacrifices and the place of the sprinkling the blood.
As ' he was bruised for our iniquities, the chastisement of our peace was upon
him,' Isa. lii. 5. And though he was reconciling us all his life, yet it is
principally ascribed to his sacrifice in his death, Col. i. 21, 22. All that

Christ did in his life had not been available for us, had he not added the top-stone in the shedding of his blood; and therefore in the creed there is a *transitus*, and leap from his birth to his death, all intermediate actions of his life being omitted, because that was the great work whereby it was finished. Access to God was barred up, till the way was opened by the blessed Son of God, Heb. x. 19, 20. So much is God pleased with it, that his majesty condescends to the lowest step, to solicit his apostate creatures ; and miserable man is admitted to importune God, not only with hopes, but assurance of his favour, and an happy success upon the account of this expiatory sacrifice. God hath laid aside the rigours of his justice to beseech us with the bowels of his mercy ; and tore down the partition wall that hindered his deplorable creature from an access to him, and hereby given us a full evidence what an inestimable fragrancy ascended from this sacrifice before him, since he did not only blot our sins out of the records of his justice, but restore us to his forfeited favour, and confer upon us the privilege of children, and converse with man as an object of his love, who before had rendered himself the mark of his wrath.

(4.) The mission of the Spirit. God first sent Christ to be an acceptable sacrifice to him, and to testify his high valuation of it, sent the Spirit in his name, or upon his account, to be an abiding comforter to us. Had not the sin which first drove the Spirit out of the world, been expiated according to the mind and will of God, he had not revisited the world, but left it in its original darkness. His first mission and all his consequent operations, are the fruits of this sacrifice. Though he was sent by the Father, yet sent ' in the name' of the Son, John xiv. 26, as a fruit of God's acceptation of him. His name had been of no prevalency for so great a gift, had not his death been first of a grateful savour with the Father. Had he not gone away, the Comforter could not have come to us, John xvi. 7, which refers not only to his ascension, but to his passion ; and had he gone, and his death been unapproved of, the Spirit had stayed in heaven   Nor would the Spirit have been employed to bring things to our remembrance, which were not worth our remembrance to our comfort, if they had not been first worthy of his Father's acceptation. He was not to ' speak of himself.' John xvi. 13, *i. e.* he was not to publish a new doctrine, but impress what Christ as a prophet had taught, and what Christ as a priest had acted. He would not have been sent to act upon a weak foundatic., and to propagate that which had not exactly answered the will and d sign of God   He was to glorify Christ (John xvi. 13, 14) *i. e.* to declare the efficacy of his death. Christ had not been a fit subject to be glorified in the world, had he not in the administration of his office glorified God, and been glorious in his eyes. And since he is an abiding Spirit, his perpetual inhabitation manifests the perpetual savour of this sacrifice ; for since the first acceptation of it was the cause of his coming, the perpetual fragrancy of it must be the ground of his abiding. He could no more abide, if there were an interruption of its sweetness, than he could first have come had there been a defect of sweetness in it. This sacrifice did not only procure the coming of the Spirit, but his coming with the most glorious things in the possession of God : John xvi. 15, ' All things that the Father hath are mine : therefore said I, He shall take of mine, and shew it unto you.' All the things that the Father hath ; the greatness of the Comforter, the fulness of the treasure, and his perpetual abiding with these rich gifts, are full evidences how much God is pleased with this offering. As God could not testify his good will to man in a higher manner than sending his Son to be a sacrifice for him, so he could not in a higher manner testify his delight in that sacrifice, than to send so great a person as the Holy Ghost to be a solicitor to men to accept of it, and a Comforter to those that believe in it; the third person in the blessed Trinity, to preserve the honour of the oblation of the second. God would never have been at the expense of so great a gift, to keep up the credit of a person and sacrifice wherein he had no pleasure.

(5.) The acceptance of our persons and services. His delight in this sacrifice is the ground of the acceptation of every person accepted by him; it is 'in the beloved' that every one is 'accepted,' Eph. i. 6. Not beloved simply as his Son, the second person in the glorious Trinity, but beloved as a sacrifice; for he was beloved as he was a medium for the praise of the glory of the grace of God, which was not as he was a Son by eternal generation, but as he assumed our nature by his incarnation, and offered it to God by his passion. The Trinity had been blessed, if man had not been created, and had been blessed, if revolted man had not been redeemed, and not a spark of grace shot out upon the world. Therefore, in the following verse, this, as well as the other parts of redemption, is ascribed to his blood. Had not Christ been first accepted as an oblation of infinite value, neither the persons nor services of men, abounding with guilt and filth, could have been worthy of the notice and entertainment of God. Our acceptation is the fruit of the acceptation of the offering Christ made of himself. The pleasure God takes in his obedience to death makes believers as his members, and their services as sprinkled with his blood, delightful to God; upon which account, the last time, wherein this victim was to be offered, is called 'the acceptable year of the Lord,' Isa. lxi. 2, 'and the day of vengeance of our God;' an acceptable time, when it was the day of vengeance upon sin in the suffering of the sinner's surety.

(6.) The joys and peace of conscience. By his bonds he procured our liberty, by his condemnation our absolution, and tasted of the vengeance of God, to fill us with the delights of the Spirit.* As God had a rest in his acceptation of it, so he gives us a joy and peace in our believing it, which is the acceptation on our parts, answering to the acceptation on God's part, Rom. xv. 13. This is accompanied with a repose to the conscience, a silencing our fears, and a filling with a 'joy unspeakable and full of glory.' These gifts God doth most plentifully distribute, when we are deepest in sufferings for the acknowledgment and approbation of this sacrifice; it is then Stephen shall see the heavens opened, and behold Christ at the right hand of God; have a sense how highly God values that in heaven which wicked men reproach, and believers suffer for on earth, Acts vii. 55; then it is that a 'spirit of glory and of God rests upon them,' 1 Peter iv. 14. God eats not his morsels alone; he impresseth a joy in the hearts of his people when they are either publicly witnessing to this blood, or privately acting faith in it, or celebrating the memorials of it; when we eat our spiritual meat with 'singleness of heart,' God doth accompany it with 'gladness,' Acts ii. 46. Every beam of paradise, darting into the heart at such seasons, is a token of its sweet savour with God, and an assurance of God's valuing us, for valuing that which is so much the object of his delight. Man only stands in a posture for such spiritual viands, when he is in an exercise of an estimation of Christ, in imitation of that esteem God hath of him; this is the best savour to God, next to that of the oblation of his Son.

(7.) Bestowing of the glory of heaven upon this account. The restoring men to that eternal salvation they had lost, is a certain proof of the strength of this sacrifice. As soon as Christ was 'made perfect by suffering, he became the author of eternal salvation to all that obey him,' Heb. v. 9.

* Drelincourt.

Nothing can be a higher demonstration to the sense of the creature of God's esteem of this victim, than his admission of poor creatures to reside with him for ever to behold and enjoy his glory. By this we have liberty to enter into the holy place ; not only a license or bare permission, but a right of purchase, whence it is called a 'purchased possession,' Eph. i. 14, a right of donation as a fruit of his delight in Christ : Rom. vi. 29, 'The gift of God through Jesus Christ.' Justice, that barred heaven, is satisfied, and God consented to a preparation of mansions in paradise, instead of dungeons in hell, that his enemies might become the heirs of his kingdom. So agreeable to God is the odour of this sacrifice, that God is not only content to free us from the hell we had merited, but he would also open for us the heaven we had forfeited, that we might be partakers of the glory and kingdom of his Son ; not only deliver us, but perfect us ; not only cross our debts that entitled us to prison, but impute a righteousness to entitle us to glory ; stop the mouth of hell, and open the gates of heaven. Hence we are said to be 'raised together with Christ,' viz., by the glory of the Father, as he was to 'sit in heavenly places with Christ,' by the donation of the Father, as he did, Eph. ii. 5, 6 ; the meaning of which is, that by those acts of raising up and exalting to glory his sacrificed Son, he hath sealed to every believer the perfection of regeneration in a possession of glory for ever. The satisfaction God hath in the value of this offering, cannot give forth itself in fuller expressions than in our salvation by the virtue of it, everything formidable and burdensome being removed, everything great and glorious bestowed, justice with all its vengeance appeased, the law with all its retinue of curses silenced, sin with all its demerits expiated, the covenant with all its benefits ratified, peace with its blessings restored, the Spirit with all its treasures bestowed, our services purified from their filth, our consciences pacified from their fears, whatsoever is grievous abrogated, the veil of the temple, with all the heavy weight of ceremonies, rent in twain, hell quenched, and heaven prepared and furnished for all that imitate God in his valuation of this sacrifice.

Quest. What was it that rendered this sacrifice acceptable to God, and efficacious for us ?

Ans. 1. The dignity of his person. That which is inferior cannot be the rest and satisfaction of a superior nature ; nothing but infinite, therefore, can be the rest and satisfaction of an infinite being. The holiness and goodness of any, or of all creatures, could not render a sacrifice worthy of the acceptance of God. The holiness of a creature was not infinite, to answer the infinite evil of sin, and suit the infinite holiness of God, any more than the weakness of a creature could have rendered him strong enough to endure the strokes of an infinite justice. Since the heavens are not pure in the sight of God,* and the angels, if compared with him, are not free from vanity, Job xv. 15, iv. 18, it is necessary that he in whom God doth rest should excel, not only the dignity and perfections of angels, but the condition of any finite being. If the holy angels cannot be the rest of God, because of their natural mutability abstracted from the establishing grace of God, much less can man, who is filthy, and drinks iniquity like water ; for whatsoever dignity might be considered in his person to commend the sacrifice, might be considered also in his crime to aggravate the guilt. But the dignity of this person was solely to be regarded in the offering, because he had no crime to be greatened by the consideration of it, being offered, not for any sin of his own, but for the sins of others. This sacrifice was of infinite value, and therefore worthy of the acceptance of an infinite nature ; his

* Amyrald. de Trinit. p. 245.

person was of as great a dignity as the Father's, to whom he was offered. Though there be a distinction of order between the three persons, yet not of dignity; he had no peer but God, for he was equal with him;* had equalities of perfections with God, was every way equal to the party offended; so that he is called God's fellow, one of the same nature with him; a man as stricken by the sword, yet his fellow as considered in his divine nature, Zech. xiii. 7; meant of Christ, part of the verse being applied by Christ to himself, Mat. xxvi. 31; his fellow, *though* man, yet not *as* man; in whom 'the fulness of the Godhead' dwelt, Col. ii. 9; not typically, as in the sanctuary and most holy place, nor mystically, as in believers, but personally, as his flesh was the proper flesh of the second person. Hence that name that is peculiar to the essence of God is ascribed to him: Jer. xxiii. 6, 'He shall be called the Lord our righteousness.' *Jehovah*, the incommunicable name of God; *he*, that righteous branch whom Jehovah should raise up, ver. 5, shall be called *Jehovah*; he that is raised up is Jehovah, as well as he that raised him; the glorious name of God would not have been ascribed to a simple man. He was in the form of God, before he took upon him the form of a servant, and laid not aside the form of God, when he made him-self of no reputation, and in that disreputed state became obedient to the death of the cross; upon this account, his sacrifice is more worthy of acceptance than the sacrifice of all creatures. As the mediation of a prince is far more noble than that of a peasant, and the head of a king of greater value than that of a subject, the person of one David was more worth than ten thousand of the common Israelites, 2 Sam. xviii. 3; and as the person of Christ, so the sufferings of that person, are of more worth than the souls of all men, and their bodies too, cast into the scale.

The dignity of Christ thus appearing, let us see how his sufferings are dignified by the greatness of his person.

(1.) His sufferings were partly finite, partly infinite. They were finite in regard of the time of duration; finite, in regard of the immediate subject wherein he suffered, his human nature; which, being a creature, could no more become infinite, than it could omnipotent, omniscient, or eternal. But in regard of the person who suffered, the sufferings were infinite; the deity being in conjunction with the humanity. That which is finite in regard of time, and in regard of the subject, may be infinite in regard of the object. As the sin of a short minute, and the sin of a finite creature, in regard both of the time when it is committed, and the person guilty of it, is finite; but in regard of the object, God, whose glory is eclipsed, it is an infinite evil. As the greatness of an offence is to be measured by the greatness of the person whose honour is invaded; as the striking a king is capital, when the striking an ordinary man falls under a small pecuniary mulct; so the value of a satisfaction is to be measured by the excellency of the person satisfying. As therefore an infinite sin deserves an infinite punishment, because it is committed against an infinite God, so the sacrifice of Christ deserves an infinite acceptation, because it is offered by an infinite person. The subject sacrificed makes the sacrifice infinitely grateful; as well as the person offended renders the injury infinitely heinous. This was not the sacrifice of a man or an angel, but of the head of the creation, 'the bright-ness of God's glory, and the express image of his person,' Heb. i. 3, by which his sufferings were advanced into infinity, and the merit of them an infinite odour before God. There could not have been so much honour rendered to God by the obedience of a mere creature, as there was injury offered him by the transgression of the sinner.† Though our sins were not

* Philip. ii. 6.   † Amyrald. de Trinitate, p. 265.

infinite in number, because no number can increase so vastly as to be actually infinite, since it is composed of units added to one another; yet had they been far less, they had needed an infinite virtue in the sacrifice, by reason of the infiniteness of their guilt, because the majesty of God and his perfections are infinite, which are dishonoured by sin. Such a sacrifice this is, which hath an infinite virtue of expiating.

(2.) This infiniteness ariseth from the near and strait union of the divine with the human nature. It was not the simple offering a sacrifice by the Son of God which was so acceptable. Had the Son of God offered anything else, though the offerer had been infinite, yet the offering had been finite, because not allied to, and in conjunction with, the person offering. It was infinitely valuable, not because himself was the offerer, but because himself was the offering, offering that which was in conjunction with his deity, 'purged by himself,' Heb. i. 3. 'Offered himself up through the eternal Spirit,' Heb. ix. 14. By the personal union, the dignity was conferred upon the sufferings of his human nature. If you will say, a sacrifice had been infinite, only because it was offered by an infinite person, you may as well call the meanest worm in the world infinite, because it was made by an infinite God, and in an infinite manner of operation. The dignity therefore ariseth from the unity of the same infinite person, in whom the two natures were united; so all the actions of Christ, as mediator, received their value from his person. And by reason of the unity of his person, that which was the act of one nature is attributed to the other, as when it is said, John iii. 13, 'The Son of man came down from heaven;' i.e. that person who was man, though his human nature had not been in heaven. And when his blood is called 'the blood of the Son of God,' 1 John i. 7, and 'the blood of God,' it was not the blood of the Godhead, but of that person who was God.

(3.) In regard of this near conjunction, the Godhead of Christ did influence every mediatory action. (I do not take in all the actions of the human nature, that had no respect to his meditation, any more than as they did refer to the sustentation of his human nature, as his eating, drinking, sleeping, &c.) This value was as inseparable from his sufferings, as the divine nature was inseparable from the human. In all that he did, he was the Son of God; as much upon the cross as before his descent from heaven; in the lowest pitch of his humiliation, as well as in his highest state of exaltation; the Son of God as much, when at his death he said, 'It is finished,' as after his resurrection, when he said, 'all power is given to me.' The man against whom the sword did awake, was God's fellow when he felt the piercing edge of it, Zech. xiii. 7. Indeed, he laid aside the manifestation of his glory, but could not lay aside his glory; for then he might lay aside his eternity, omnipotency, his deity, and cease from being God, which is utterly impossible. He was always the same, and as his years, so neither did his glory fail, Heb. i. 12. In all his sufferings he retained the relation and reality of the Son of God, the union of his natures remained firm in all his passions; and therefore the efficacy of the Deity mingled itself with every groan in his agony, every pang and cry upon the cross, as well as with the blood which was shed; and as his blood was the blood of God, Acts xx. 28, so his groans were the groans of God, his pangs were the pangs of God, and were therefore subjectively infinite in value. Yet did not every groan and pang procure our redemption by itself, upon the account of the infiniteness of its value in being the groans of God, because they without death did not answer the tenor of the law, nor was the curse of the law, which he was designed to endure, accomplished in any act of suffering, without shedding of blood, and that to death: Heb. ix. 22, 'Without shedding of blood there is no remission;' for as there was a necessity of the conjunction of the divine nature with the human, to make his sufferings infinite, so there was a necessity of a full conformity to the threatening of the law, and his Father's order, to make them efficacious for the honour of God and redemption of the creature. The sum is this: as what the divine nature acted was wrought instrumentally by the human, so what the human nature acted or suffered was made efficacious, and dignified by the divine.

(4.) In this respect God his deity may be accounted as it were suffering, or as if he suffered. It was not necessary his deity should suffer to make the sacrifice infinite, and indeed it was impossible. The divine nature is as impassible as it is immutable; yet in regard of the strait union of the two natures, his mediatory actions and sufferings, being the actions and sufferings of the person, may be counted as the sufferings of the Deity itself, in a moral way, and by legal estimation; as sin is called *Deicidium*, not that it is so, or can be so physically, but in a moral way, in men's doing that which puts on the nature of destroying God, were it in the power of the sinner, or possible in itself; or as sin in Scripture is called a wearying of God, when omnipotency cannot be tired, and if God were tired, he were not omnipotent. But they carry themselves so towards God, as would weary the most patient man in the world, and it is esteemed by God a wearying of him. As Christ was not guilty of sin, but in a juridical manner, by reason of his voluntary subjection to punishment in the stead of the sinner, so neither could the divine nature suffer but by way of estimation, as the person of the Son of God did voluntarily assume the human nature wherein he was to suffer. As Christ hung upon the cross as if he were guilty, so the divine nature in conjunction with it might be esteemed to suffer, as if it were passible; the Deity did suffer in an eclipse of its glory, and veiling the manifestation of it. Hence, as he had a body, his blood was the blood of a man, yet because it was the blood of his person it was the 'blood of the Son of God,' 1 John i. 7, and the 'blood of God,' Acts xx. 28 The immediate subject suffering was the human nature, but the person suffering was the Lord of glory, 1 Cor. ii. 8. In that state and condition he offered up himself, which the apostle signifies: Heb. ix. 14, 'He offered up himself through the eternal Spirit.' Διὰ, *through*, imports not only that the divine nature of Christ did offer the sacrifice, but it seems to have the same sense as the same word διὰ, Rom. iv. 11, ' The Father of them that believe, though they be not circumcised,' διὰ ἀκροβυστίας. The Father of them that believe through uncircumcision, *i.e.* in an uncircumcised state,* or Rom. ii. 27, ' who by the letter and circumcision dost transgress the law,' διὰ γράμματος, *through;* not that circumcision† was the cause of the one's faith, or uncircumcision† the cause of the other's sin, but that the one believed, and the other transgressed in those several states. So Christ here, when he offered himself, was not in the condition of a mere man, but had a divine and eternal nature in the offering himself up unto God. It is from this state and condition of his in his suffering, that the apostle draws an argument for the value of his suffering above those of the legal sacrifices, and their excellency to purge the conscience, and put the emphasis of a *how much more?* The very foundation of our redemption by his blood is his being the image of the invisible God: Col. i. 14, 15, 'In whom we have redemption through his blood, who is the image of the invisible God.'

(5.) Hence it follows, that the sufferings of this person, because of his dignity, were equivalent to an endless duration of punishment, because the infiniteness of the person did more than recompense the shortness of the

---

* Amyrald. in loc. et de Trinit. p. 268.
† Qu. ' uncircumcision,'—' circumcision '?—ED.

duration of his punishment. As the dignity of his person did outweigh the persons of all the angels, and all men in the world, had they been without spot, so the time of his sufferings, though the moments of enduring them had been fewer, in regard of his greatness, was equivalent to the eternity of the sufferings of all creatures; because it was more that God should suffer one minute, than that all creatures in heaven and earth should endure torments to an endless eternity.

(6.) Hence it follows, that in regard of the dignity of his person, he was not only equivalent, but superior to all those for whom he was a sacrifice, and to all for which he was a sacrifice. The sacrifice was as noble as the sin was vile, and offered by an hand more honourable than the persons, by whom the crime was committed, could be unworthy. The dignity of the person was greater than the meanness of the offender could be base. The sin could not be more infinitely evil than the person satisfying was infinitely excellent. What an infinite object suffered by the offence, was made up by an infinite subject expiating the crime. The dignity of his person is the reason why his righteousness hath a sufficiency in it for all 'unto justification of life,' Rom. v. 19, 20. He is superior to all that were to be redeemed by him out of every kindred and tongue, people and nation, because he is God blessed for ever. The oblation is greater than the offence, and the offerer than the transgressor. What wrath so infinite, that the blood of an infinite God cannot calm? What death so sharp and strong, that the life of God cannot remove? It should be no less a cordial to us than it is a savour to God, to think that our sacrifice is as infinite as the wrath we had merited, and more infinite than the sin whereby we had deserved it. Our sin was *objectively* infinite, as committed against God; our sacrifice was *objectively* infinite, as offered to God, proportionable to the honour he would have repaired; and *subjectively* infinite, in regard of the sacrifice offered for the reparation of it. God regarded him as the man his fellow when he struck him; we should regard him in the same relation when we plead him. To conclude, since this victim was equal with God, equal with him in essence, equal with him in nature and perfections, he could not be displeased with the sacrifice, unless he had been displeased with himself and his own nature.

2. As the dignity of the person, so the purity of the sacrifice renders it fragrant to God, and efficacious for us. His freedom from taint, and conjunction with the fulness of the Deity, are linked together in demonstrating the efficacy of it to purge our consciences from dead works: Heb. ix. 14, 'Who through the eternal Spirit offered himself without spot.' He was as free from blemish as full of an eternal Spirit. The spotlessness of his human nature was necessary to his being a sacrifice, and the union of the divine nature was necessary to his being a valuable one. As the legal lambs were to be without blemish, so was Christ a 'Lamb without spot,' 1 Peter i. 19. He had no sin naturally imputed (juridically indeed he had), no sin personally inherent; he had no sin naturally imputed, because he was not in the loins of him who introduced sin into the world, and derived it to his posterity. His extraordinary conception by the Holy Ghost in the womb of the virgin was a bar against original sin; whence by way of emphasis he is called 'that holy thing,' Luke i. 35. He was infinitely holy as he was God, habitually holy as he was man. Every faculty of his soul, every member of his body, was elevated to the highest degree of holiness. His human nature was holy by the union of the divine, holy by the effusion of the Spirit, whose office it is to sanctify. Though by reason of the divine nature united, it was impossible but that his human nature should be holy (the person of the Son of God would never have assumed a tainted nature), yet the holiness

of his human nature did flow from the stores of the Spirit, it being not the office of the second, but third person, to sanctify. But the human nature in conjunction with the divine could not but be pure. Had that been tainted while in union with the divine, making but one person, the taint might have been called the sin of God, as well as the blood of his body be called the blood of God. A thing therefore not to be imagined possible. He was holy in every action. As he was man, he was bound to all sorts of obedience; for having taken the nature, he was subject to all the duties incumbent on that nature; and he did run through every economy, he observed the law of nature, conformed to the ceremonial part of the Mosaic institutions, submitted to the baptism of John, a mid state of the church, and therein 'fulfilled all righteousness,' Mat. iii. 15, the righteousness of the positive laws of God in every state. He was holy in all his offices, harmless as a priest, faithful as a prophet; holy in his life, holy in his death, no guile was found in his mouth, no inordination of murmuring in his heart. Had there been any spot (which is impossible) his sacrifice could not have been for our sins, it must have been for his own; if his own debt could have been paid by it, ours could not; his spot had been infinitely greater than ours can be; it had been objectively infinite as ours, and subjectively infinite, which is more than ours. The rights of God had been more invaded, instead of being repaired; the guilt would have been as great in the sinner as the satisfaction could have been in the sufferer; a subjective infiniteness in the sin, as well as a subjective infiniteness in the sacrifice. But there was not, there could not be any of this; Satan could not charge him with any, but confessed him holy, Mark i. 24. The all-discerning eye of God could see nothing contrary to his honour, but justified him as holy, Heb. vii. 26. Impurity had been contrary to the dignity of his person. God could as well be unholy as the person of Christ unholy. His holiness therefore was infinite, though the holiness of his human nature was not of itself infinite, no more than his sufferings were of themselves, and in regard of the human nature, the subject suffering, infinite; yet the holiness of his human nature derived from it an infinite value, so that there was an infinite holiness in this sacrifice offered to an infinitely holy God. It had no stain to be purged by the addition of another bloody offering. It answered the design of God, terminated the rest and delight of God. Needs then must such a holiness be highly acceptable to God, who loves and is delighted with righteousness in this creature, much more with that of his only Son, the unstained and infinitely pure sacrifice for us.

8. The graces exercised in this sacrifice, rendered it fragrant in the account of God.

1. His obedience. The acceptableness of it to God did not arise simply from his dying, but his obedience in his death: Philip. ii. 8, 'Became obedient unto death ;' and not only from an obedience to the law of nature, and the precepts of God as a creature, but his obedience to the law of redeeming love as a mediator, and his delight in it, Ps. xl. 8. As the disobedience of man shook the rest of God, so the obedience of the Son of God settled the rest of the Deity. Obedience run through the whole web of his life, he submitted to a body fitted for those dreadful strokes of wrath we should have endured; a body made under the law, Gal. iv. 4. He delighted in the thoughts of performing the will of God in our flesh; he came not to do his own will; whatsoever his Father ordered him, that he spake, that he did, that he suffered, he laid down his body when the hour was come appointed by his Father. It was not a simple but an affectionate obedience: John xiv. 31, 'I love the Father, and as the Father gave me commandment, even

so do I;' where principally his obedience to the mediatory law is intended; as also, Philip. ii. 8, ' Obedient to the death of the cross,' which the law did not oblige him to ; the moral law bound over the sinner to death, but the mediatory law bound over Christ to death in our stead.   The obedience to the moral law, or law of nature, as it concerned the state of angels, was performed by him without any defect ; in this the obedience of Christ was greater than theirs, in regard of the infinite dignity of his person above all the angels in heaven ; yet the rule of their obedience was of the same nature. But in the obedience of the mediatory law, the Redeemer stood single ; as he trod the wine-press alone, so in the whole mediatory work none were in conjunction with him, none had any likeness or resemblance to him.   This was above the obedience of all creatures, not only in regard that it was the obedience of him that was God, but an obedience wherein he could not be imitated by any creature already created, or that could be created, it being a work above the strength of any created being.   It was obedience under the highest provocations to resume his glory, and come down from the cross, and declare at that moment the iniquity of those reproaches they cast upon him.   Obedience in the highest pitch of his sufferings, obedience in heaven, practising that compassionate obedience upon the throne which he learned by his sufferings on the cross, Heb. v. 8, acting according to his Father's orders, presenting his obedience on the cross, as meritorious for his members he left in the world.   If the obedience of Abraham, a sinful creature, in his willingness to offer up his son Isaac, a sinful creature also, was so pleasing to God that thereupon he makes him glorious promises, how much more grateful is the obedience of him who was God, and offered not up a son, but himself, a pure, not a spotted sacrifice !   If obedience be better than sacrifice, then sacrifice is insignificant without obedience.   The offering himself a sacrifice according to the will of God for our sanctification, was the most significant part of his obedience, Heb. x. 7, 10.   In this he did exactly answer the mediatory law as his rule, and God found the will of Christ in the performance, fully conformable to his own will in the precept, more obedient to the will of God in his offering, than Adam was disobedient to the will of God in his sinning.   Such a height and perpetuity of obedience, under all the circumstances of temptations, the strugglings of the flesh, which could not but desire the removal of penal evil, under the fear of wrath also, the sense of agonies, and reproaches of men, whereby he testified, that he preferred the glory of his Father above the safety of his own nature, obedience to his command above the contentment of his flesh, and was swayed by the form of a servant to submit, against the suggestions from his nature as a man to desire the passing it away; all this, I say, rendered his sacrifice highly acceptable.

(2.) His humility.   His humility is joined with his obedience as the cause of his exaltation, which was the evidence of its fragrancy, Philip. ii. 8. God loves to be imitated in his condescensions to his creature.   The condescension of Christ equal with God, to the ' taking upon him the form of a servant,' setting himself in the stead of the sinner, the eclipsing his own glory, shrouding it under the disguise of our flesh, submitting to an harder piece of service and a deeper humiliation than any creature in heaven or earth was capable of; to descend from heaven to earth, expose himself to the fury of men and devils without murmuring ; to bow his head to the stroke, not of an honourable, but an infamous death ; endure the wrath of a Father he loved, come down to the lowest step before he did reassume the glory which was due to him, was an unexpressible and unimitable act of humility.   Lower than this he could not humble himself.   Since humility

renders men so pleasing to God, that he heaps upon them the greatest testimonies of his favours, and richly dispenseth to them the doles of his grace,
James iv. 6 ; it must render his Son in those sufferings most acceptable to
his Father, and draw from him the greatest distribution of his favour, because it was the greatest act of humility, as well as obedience, that could
possibly be performed.

(3.) His faith.   This resolution of trust he brought with him, and this
resolution he kept : Heb. ii. 13, ' I will put my trust in him,' cited out of
Ps. xviii. 2.   He had not a spark of infidelity, or any grain of distrust in the
goodness of God.   He suffered for a time the torments of hell, without the
despair of the inhabitants of hell ; he had a working of faith under the sense
of his Father's greatest displeasure, and confided in his love while he felt the
outward and inward force of his frowns.   The sharpness of the scourge, and
the smart of his wounds, beat not off his soul from a fast adherence to him.
He had a faith of the acceptableness of his death for his elect, and gave
evidence of his confidence in the promise for a happy and glorious success,
in acting like a king while he was hanging as a malefactor on the cross, in
distributing his largesses to the poor thief, assuring him, that that day he
should be with him in paradise.   He let not his confidence in his Father
flinch ; he confided in him for the bestowing that royal power upon him,
which he signified by this promise of paradise to this criminal upon the
cross : and both his obedience to God in not turning away his back, and his
trust in God for his assistance, are put together as the ground of his justification, Isa. l. 5, 7, 8.   The height of his faith was to be discovered in opposition to the unbelief of Adam ; his humility in opposition to the pride of Adam ;
his obedience in doing all according to God's order, in opposition to the
disobedience of Adam.   By his active and passive obedience, he glorified the
holiness and justice of God ; by his humility, the sovereignty and power of
God ; by his trust, the faithfulness and veracity of God : all which must
needs render his sacrifice as a sweet-smelling savour, and efficacious for us.

4. In regard of the full compensation made to God by this sacrifice, and
the equivalency of it to all the demands of God.   His obedience was fully
answerable to the law : his active answered the preceptive part, and his passive the penalty.   As he fulfilled the righteousness of the law in his life, so he
underwent the threatenings of the law in his death ; he obeyed the commands
in our stead, and sustained the curse.   He bore the sorrows we should bear :
Isa. liii. 4, ' Surely he hath borne our griefs, and carried our sorrows,'
spiritual as well as bodily.   He took our nature, soul and body, to suffer in
that nature what was due to our souls and bodies.   Our whole nature had
sinned, and our whole nature must suffer ; Christ took our nature, that he
might suffer what was due to our nature.   He suffered in his soul, which is
the greatest part of our nature, as well as in his body, which is but the case
and sheath of the soul.   It is against the order of justice, for the principal
to sin, and the accessory only be punished.   The punishment threatened
against the first Adam was the death of the soul as well as of the body ; the
punishment borne by the second Adam was of the same nature : not a
spiritual death, a separation from God by sin, that he was incapable of, but a
moral death, a separation from God by desertion.   When he cried out, ' My
God, my God, why hast thou forsaken me ?' he was forsaken of God in regard of the sensible comforts of his presence, though not in regard of the
invisible sustentations of his soul.   The union of the two natures was not
dissolved, but the comfort of the Father's presence was eclipsed.   Though
he did not suffer eternity of torments, yet he suffered what was due to us ;
for eternity of punishment is not primarily threatened in the law, but second-

arily inferred. Death was threatened, but because man cannot satisfy by death, therefore he lies under that death for ever. He is kept in prison, because he cannot pay the debt which is due, nor repair the honour of the law which was violated. Justice would always be striking, and never contented. If the honour of the law could have been vindicated, and the justice of God satisfied by the temporary groans of a creature, not only the goodness of God, but the justice of God would release him; but because the justice of God could never have been satisfied, the person of the sinner must always have been a sufferer. Christ, therefore, suffering a cursed death, suffered what we should have suffered; death was threatened to us, and death was inflicted on him; the eternity of death was accidental. As Christ obeyed the whole law, yet not every accidental relation of the law, as it respected men in particular states, and particular callings and relations; as the duty of a parent to a child, of an husband to a wife; not for want of a principle of obedience in him, but for want of those particular relations to which those particular acts of obedience were annexed. So Christ suffered every part of the curse, but not the sins consequent upon that curse by reason of the corruption of man, nor the accidental continuance of the curse, which the impotence of man to satisfy rendered him obnoxious to, but the strength of Christ exempted him from. He endured all that the law imposed upon sinners,* whether in regard of loss by desertion or in regard of sense by malediction; hence he is said to be made a curse, Gal. iii. 13; to be made sin, 2 Cor. v. 21. And if so, he bore the punishment due to us, since the law threatened no more than a curse, and Christ bore the curse according to the threatening of the law. He suffered that which the law demanded of us, and was made such a curse as the law required. He suffered the torments of hell without the iniquities of hell, which were not possible to be committed by an infinitely holy person; he suffered those agonies which were of the nature of the torments of hell, and that desertion of God which is the sting of hell. Nothing was omitted that was demanded by divine holiness for keeping the commands, or by divine justice for violating the commands. As we were creatures, we owed God a debt of duty; as we were revolted creatures, we owed God a debt of punishment. Since our fall, sin hath made us incapable to answer the holiness of God in the performance of our duty, and our nature as creatures renders us too weak to satisfy the justice of God by enduring the penalty exacted by the law. Christ hath done both; and in answering the whole demand of the law, as to both debts, delights the holiness of God, satisfies the justice of God, and by both repairs the creature. If the creature could have satisfied justice for what was past, yet it still lay under a debt of duty for the time to come. If it had fallen short of this, it must have reassumed its suffering. What a deplorable condition had this been, to have come out of suffering one hour and return to it the next! But our Redeemer performs an obedience that reacheth to the utmost of the creature's duty, and endures a penalty that reaches to the utmost of the creature's demerits. A recompence was made by the obedience of Christ for the disobedience of Adam: Rom. v. 19, 'As by one man's disobedience many were made sinners; so by the obedience of one shall many be made righteous.' For what had the law to enjoin which he did not perform, or what had the law to inflict which he did not endure? Had he not done and suffered what the law required, how could he be called the 'end,' or perfection, 'of the law for righteousness'? Rom. x. 4. Had he not suffered what was due to sin, he could not have 'made

* Turretin. de Satisfact. p. 324.

an end' of it; and had he not done what the law commanded, he could not have 'brought in an everlasting righteousness,' Daniel ix. 24. He is λύτρον, Mat. xx. 28, ἀντίλυτρον, 1 Tim. ii. 6, a valuable price and sacrifice, commensurate to the demerit of our crimes. He suffered whatsoever was requisite to discharge our debts, and could not have been ἀντίψυχος, offering his soul instead of ours, if he had not borne in his soul what we were to bear in ours. In regard therefore of the full compensation made to God, it must needs be fragrant to God and efficacious for us.

5. In regard of the glory Christ by his sacrifice brought to God. The glory of God was that which he aimed at, and that which he perfected. It was the will of God which he came to do; but the design of God's will is to glorify himself, and declare his own name in all his acts. The glory of all the attributes of God appeared in the face or manifestation of Christ, 2 Cor. iv. 6. They all centred in him, and shone forth from him in all their brightness, and in a full combination set off one another's lustre; not only in his incarnation, but also, and that chiefly, in his sacrifice. Mercy could not be glorified unless justice had been satisfied, and justice had not been evident if the tokens of divine wrath had not been upon him. Grace had not sailed to us but in the streams of his blood : ' without blood there is no remission.' Justice had not been so fully known in the eternal groans of a world of creatures, nor could sin have appeared so odious to the holiness of God by eternal scars upon devils and men, as by the deluge of blood from the heart of this sacrifice. Wisdom in the contrivance had not been evident without the execution. The glory of the divine perfections had lain in the cabinet of the divine nature, without the discovery of their full beams; and though they were active in the designing it, yet they had not been declared to men or angels, without the bringing Christ to the altar. By the stroke upon his soul, all the glories of God flashed out in the view of the creature. When Judas went out from his company to prepare the way for his oblation, ' Now,' saith he, ' is the Son of man glorified, and God is glorified in him,' John xiii. 31. The honour of God and the glory of the Son depended upon this point, and in this last act threw off all their veils. The Father was glorified in appointing him, and the Son was glorified in submitting to be a sacrifice; the truth of God was glorified in bringing things to a period, and the obedience of his Son was glorified in his perseverance to the last act. His grace was elevated to the highest note in the songs of angels, an unsearchable depth of manifold wisdom was unfolded, a depth of wisdom more impossible to be comprehended in our minds than the whole globe of heaven and earth in our hands ; such a wisdom of God in the cross, which the angels never beheld in his face upon his throne ; wisdom to cure a desperate disease by the death of the physician, to turn the greatest evil to the greatest glory, to bring forth mercy by the shedding of blood. The ultimate design of this victim was the honour of God in our redemption ; Christ sought not his own glory, John viii. 50, but the glory of his Father in the salvation of men. Needs must that be fragrant to God that accomplished the triumph of all his attributes.

III. Use.

1. If this sacrifice be acceptable to God, it is then a perfect oblation. If it had not been perfect in itself, it could not have been accepted by an infinite justice, a justice inexorable without it. An incomplete offering could have given but an imperfect satisfaction, and that had been as good as no satisfaction at all. God would never have approved it; an all-seeing wisdom could not be deceived, a severe justice could not have acquiesced in it, a pure holiness could not have smelt a sweet savour from it. God as a

judge delivered him to be a sacrifice, God as a judge accepted him after he was offered. This sacrifice therefore answered the ends of God, both satisfied his justice and glorified his holiness. How could God else judicially glorify him, if he had not been fully glorified by him ? If he had performed an imperfect obedience, he would at the best have had but an half exaltation, or rather none; but since he hath been accepted with the highest pleasure, and hath a glory in the highest pitch, he hath performed an obedience to the utmost point, and touched the goal designed him. Though there was grace in God's appointing it, yet there was no grace given out to make it acceptable. God did not supply by his acceptation any defect in the sacrifice. There was a meritorious worthiness on Christ's part before there was an acceptation on God's part; it was not perfect by acceptation, but it was accepted because of its perfection. Infinite purity accepts nothing but what is perfect in itself, or hath a relation to that which is perfect and agreeable to its nature. He doth indeed accept the imperfect obedience of believers, but not for itself, but for this sacrifice, to which by faith it hath a relation. Had it not had a gratefulness in itself, God could have scented nothing in it; he could not have smelt a savour where none was; it would have been as little pleasing to him as the burnt-offerings under the law. This could not but be perfect in the account of God, since there was the humanity in conjunction with the divinity to be the sacrifice, and the divinity in conjunction with the humanity to be the altar for the sanctification of it; and the sequel shews that the offering hath been as valuable as the offence was provoking, since in consideration of it, justice forgets the injuries done to the Deity, and treats believers as heirs of heaven, instead of rebels. It is the inference the apostle draws from the priesthood of Christ, Heb. viii. 12; and what is the fruit of his priesthood, is the fruit likewise of his sacrifice. The righteousness of Christ is also perfect, since the all-searching eye of God sees nothing in it to give him any cause of distaste. It is perfect because everlasting, Daniel ix. 24. All the righteousness of the holy angels in heaven, had there been numberless millions of them, had not been so pleasing to God as this.

2. All popish doctrines of satisfaction, and all resting upon our own righteousness and inherent graces, are to be abandoned. There is a natural popery in the minds of men ; fallen man is desirous to stand upon his own bottom, and is as little content with God's judgments of things as his first parent was in paradise. We are studious of making God compensations, applauding ourselves in our own inventions and satisfactions of our own minting, unwilling to acquiesce in his wisdom.

(1.) This is an high presumption. If Christ were a perfect sacrifice in the esteem of God, it is a boldness and blasphemy in us not to think him so. If it be perfect, what need of anything from us to piece it out? If it were not sufficient, God was much mistaken to accept it; if it were not perfect, Christ had a want of strength and holiness to be a sacrifice, and God a want of wisdom to discern the defects of it ; he was then deceived to count that sweet which needed something else to sweeten it. Such additions are an injury to Christ; it is to make him but half a sacrifice, since he hath 'offered himself to God without spot,' Heb. ix. 14. Can we pretend to any other, without charging him with weakness and deficiency ? Is not his divinity enough to make his offering complete, without any supply from our corrupt humanity ? Can we acknowledge that perfect, that we think needs something from us to strengthen it ? It must be, then, a false assertion of the apostle, when he saith, Heb. x. 14, that 'by one offering he hath perfected for ever them that are sanctified.' To make Christ in part a Saviour is to make him in part no Saviour, and to ascribe salvation to something else as well as to him. All such satisfactions entrench upon the honour of Christ's sacrifice, and pull the crown from his head to set it upon our own; or at best, ascribe that in part to ourselves which is wholly due to him: by how much the more sufficient it is for us without any addition, so much the more glory redounds to the sacrifice. He needs no more of additions to sweeten his offering, than he needed of cordials to strengthen and support him in the time of his sufferings; they are rather gall and vinegar offered him upon his throne, as the Jews did in the time of his oblation upon the cross. It is an high presumption in us not to be content to rest in that which is the rest and pleasure of God.

(2.) It is a folly. It is as if a man should set up candles to increase the light of the sun, and eke out its beams. Can the righteousness of a man add any perfection to the blood of a God? or perfect a work which could not be done by the Deity? If God stood not in need of anything from us to perfect his work of creation, how can man be so foolish to imagine that Christ stands in need of anything from us to perfect his work of redemption? If that sacrifice wants something to render it efficacious, it must be a sacrifice of the same kind; nothing that is of an inferior nature can add an intrinsic value to that which is superior. What can man offer to God that can be in any sort equivalent to this sacrifice already accepted? All that we can offer to God is but as a few blasted ears of corn, such as Pharaoh saw in a dream, which can add nothing to the value of it. If there had been any failure in him, the defects of a redeemer could not be repaired by the offerings of the captives; and if there be no failure, all additions, all other inventions of atonement, are utterly superfluous. How foolish will it be to rest in that which God never pronounced or owned to be a sweet-smelling savour to him! If all our righteousness be as a menstruous rag, Isa. lxiv. 6, the offering it up to God is a noisome stench, not a pleasure. The best of our works and graces derive a sweetness and value from the virtue of this sacrifice, without contributing anything to the savour of it. It is a folly to leave a sure for an uncertain road. All other rests have no divine stamp and signature upon them. God never found any savour in any other offering. The Spirit of God never gave any so noble a character as this, of a sweet-smelling savour, but as they had a relation to this as the antitype of them. This one victim sends forth more grateful odours to God, and is more efficacious for the concerns of our souls, than the joint intercessions of saints and angels. Let us therefore be diligent in our duties, aim at the perfection of an inherent righteousness, but never place our confidence in them, or equal them to the sacrifice God hath so affectionately accepted. Did God ever set up his rest in the services of a creature? Can this be savoury to an infinite purity? Whatsoever is done without faith is but the offering of an enemy, whatsoever fair colours it may be outwardly adorned with. The Scripture sets an impossibility upon the head of all these: Heb. xi. 6, ' Without faith it is impossible to please God;' to gain or keep his favour. Whatsoever is done without faith, though of the highest elevation, is but a creature, and therefore not the object of trust. And whatever significancy believing works have, is from the tincture they receive from the blood of this sacrifice, wherein faith dips them, as being faith in the blood of Christ. Though Adam, while he continued in his created rectitude, might have entered his righteousness as a plea, yet, because it was mutable, it had been no fit object of trust for him. But since our revolt, all pleas of a fleshly corrupted righteousness are overruled in the court of heaven, and our pleas must run in another name; all other things have ceased to be savoury to

God, since they were tainted by sin.   Let men 'make lies their refuge,' and 'hide themselves under falsehood,' the false coverings of their own righteousness, and think to shelter themselves 'from the overflowing scourge,' Isa. xxviii. 15–17; it will be a miserable self-deceit; 'the hail will sweep away such a refuge, and the waters will overflow such a hiding-place.'   All other hiding-places, but the smoke of this sacrifice, are too weak to preserve us from the overflowing waters of divine vengeance.

3. It is a desperate thing to refuse this sacrifice, which is so sweet to God.

(1.) It is a great sin.   As faith in Christ redounds to the honour of God, as being an approbation of his mercy, justice, and wisdom in the acceptance of this sacrifice, so unbelief redounds to the contempt of God, as slighting all the pleasure the wisdom, the justice, and holiness of God took in it, as though he were delighted with a sleeveless and unworthy matter.   It is to trample upon that which is God's delight; accounting that which is sweet to the Deity loathsome to us; refusing to be guided by God's judgment of this offering; setting up our own wisdom not only equal with, but above the wisdom of God; a regarding that which God is infinitely pleased with as a frivolous thing, as though God had pleased himself with a trifle, or smelt sweetness in a weed.   God's acceptation of it owns a fragrancy in it; man's refusal calls it gall and vinegar, a rotten service.   God's language is, 'This is my beloved Son, in whom I am well pleased,' Mat. iii. 17; this is my odoriferous sacrifice, with which I am infinitely delighted.   The language of an unbeliever's heart is, This is an offering in which I can find no pleasure. The heart of God and the heart of an unbeliever, the wisdom of God and the judgment of an unbeliever, stand in direct opposition.   How inexcusable a pride is it to think that not worth our receiving which God hath entertained with the highest affection; to count that unsavoury which God hath accepted as the sweetest present can be given him in heaven or earth!   Unbelief cannot be excused without accusing God of weakness and folly.   It is a sin against his precept, as he commands us to believe; a sin against his pattern, as he directs us by his own act to an acceptance of him.   Other sins are against his sovereignty in the violations of his law.   This is against his wisdom in his gracious acceptation of a propitiating sacrifice for us.   We disown him as our Lord, and as our pattern.

(2.) It will end into a great misery.   God will not suffer that which is sweet to him to be slighted by man, without the recompence of a just indignation.   The vagabond nation of the Jews bears to this day the sad tokens of God's vengeance upon them for the unworthy refusal of so great a victim. 'Because of unbelief they are broken off' from the root, Rom. xi. 20, and are deprived of all the sweetness which God and believers taste in it.   Nothing in the world was ever the object of God's delight but this; nothing in the world can ever be pleasant to him without this.   To neglect it, is to neglect that which is the only thing God will accept, and so fall under the condemnation of law and gospel too.   It is to reject God as a satisfied judge in the flowings of his mercy, to fall under God as a provoking judge in the thunders of his wrath.   If we will not comply with divine justice in an estimation of it, we must fall under his fury for our contempt.   If this offering be not cordially, and upon God's terms, accepted by us, we must be a sacrifice ourselves; justice must have a sacrifice for every sinner, from himself or another.   God, in honour, will not pardon sin without one; in greater honour he cannot but punish sin upon the refusal of this.   Oh how fearful a thing is it to fall into the hands of the living God : * a living unpacified God, a living and reproached God, a living God who hath been

* Heb. x. 31, compared with ver. 29.

counted a ridiculous fool by a wilful sinner, in his accounting the blood of the covenant as an unholy thing! God will not have his wisdom jostled against by the folly of his creature. 'No other sacrifice remains for sin.' No other mark of distinction was appointed by God for the securing the firstborn of the Israelites from the stroke intended for the Egyptian heirs* but the blood of the paschal lamb sprinkled upon the posts of the doors; had any fed upon the lamb, and neglected the sprinkling, he had felt the sharp sword of the destroying angel; the lamb had been of no efficacy to him, not for any defect in that, but negligence or contempt in the offender. The sacrifice of Christ hath an infinite virtue to save; but it is no remedy to them that will not sprinkle their souls by faith with the blood of it; without this, we shall remain in our unatoned sins, and have the sword of vengeance doubly whetted against us.

4. It administers matter of comfort to the believer. It is some comfort to all, that they are in a fair way of being happy; the justice of God was the bar to God and man's meeting together. It was morally impossible, in regard of God's truth and holiness, for man to be restored without a vindication of that law which had been broken; but now the honour of the law is restored by this sacrifice; God hath owned it, the bar is removed, and where God hath found a sweetness man may find salvation, if he be not his own enemy, and wilfully cast away his own mercy. He 'gave himself a ransom for all,' 1 Tim. ii. 5, 6, ἀντίλυτρον, a ransom in our stead, or a counter-ransom, in opposition to the sin of Adam, the fountain of our bondage; for all upon gospel conditions. As he gave himself for all, so he was accepted for all upon the same conditions; for he was accepted as he gave himself. It is a comfort to a diseased hospital, that a physician is chosen and accepted by the governors that is able to cure every disease; it is no less a comfort to a guilty soul, that there is a sacrifice sufficient to expiate every sin. But there is a ground of sensible comfort to those that believe. If when Christ walked upon the waters, and was labouring in the floods of affliction in the days of his humiliation, he bid his disciples not to fear, how much more may we expel fear from our believing hearts, since he is sat down upon his throne, and the whole merit of his sacrifice graciously accepted! Let us represent to ourselves this crucified, but now crowned victim, lying in the bosom of his Father, represent to ourselves the Father full of delights, rejoicing in the views of this sacrificed body, drawing a perpetual stream of pleasure and sweet smells from the fumes of this sacrifice rising up continually before him; may not this calm our fears, since it smooths the frowns of divine justice? Did the people shout when the ark returned? and shall our hearts be full of fears when our sacrifice is returned to heaven, and hath found a gracious reception from that justice we had so highly provoked? A disconsolate carriage in an holy believer implies as if God had rejected it as mean and weak, rather than received it as perfect and glorious; a heavy walking is a disparagement to the greatness of the sacrifice, and the wisdom and judgment of God the accepter of it. If we should 'eat our bread with a merry heart,' because 'God hath accepted our works,' Eccles. ix. 7, much more since God hath accepted our victim, by whose merits our duties and works smell sweet, that before smelt rank by nature. We should therefore draw as much sweetness from this sacrifice for our souls, according to our measures, as God did from it for his own content and satisfaction; it appeased God's fury against us, and should banish our jealousies of God.

(1.) If once acceptable to God, then it is for ever acceptable; if once

* Daillé, sur 1 Cor. v. 7, Serm. x. pp. 394, 395.

sweet, it is always sweet. God cannot be deceived in his estimations, nor change his value of it, nor can the sacrifice ever become noisome. The strength of the divine nature, that rendered it at first grateful, preserves its savour for ever; he died to offer it, and lives to preserve the virtue of it, Rom. v. 10. The fragrancy conferred upon it by the deity in conjunction with the humanity, is as durable as the deity itself: Heb. x. 11, 'He sat down on the right hand of God,' after he had offered himself a sacrifice, to exercise the office of a priest. God would have the priest and sacrifice for ever in his sight. His priesthood is for ever, his sacrifice therefore is for ever sweet. Without a sacrifice he could not be a priest. As his priesthood hath a perpetual vigour, so his sacrifice hath a perpetual freshness and inexhaustible virtue; for the exercise of his office depends upon the continuance of the offering. The blood of this sacrifice is not compared to a pond, or water in a vessel, though of the largest capacity, but to a living and ever-running fountain: Zech. xiii. 1, 'A fountain set open for the house of David.' Repentance was hid from the eyes of Christ in offering it for a ransom from the power of the grave, and a redemption from death, Hosea xiii. 14, and no less is repentance hid from the eyes of God in accepting it. The covenant sealed by it is everlasting, and derives its duration from this blood of the victim, Heb. xiii. 20, the virtue of it endures as long as the covenant; since if that failed the covenant would expire, the superstructure not being able to stand if the foundation be rotten. And from hence an everlasting righteousness is derived, that our persons, odious by Adam, may be beautiful by Christ. At the same time that he made reconciliation for iniquity, he brought in everlasting righteousness, Dan. ix. 24; at the same time therefore that God accepted that reconciliation, he accepted that everlasting righteousness for security and justification. He hath not pacified God for a few days or years, but for ever, Heb. x. 14. If it were so sweet in the expectation as to be the ground of the justification of those that hoped for it, it is much more sweet since the oblation, and of a stronger efficacy. He is the captain of the salvation of all the sons that are brought to glory, and that believe. Himself was 'made perfect through sufferings,' Heb. ii. 10. The twenty-four elders confessed themselves 'redeemed by this blood,' Rev. v. 8, 9; the patriarchs that died before him, as well as the apostles who expired after him; he was a lamb, a sacrifice, 'slain from the foundation of the world,' Rev. xiii. 8. Not in regard of decree * (that were a jejune sense of the place, as it would be to say, a man were dead from the foundation of the world, because it was appointed for him once to die), but in regard of efficacy and a mystical sprinkling of his blood upon those that lived at the beginning, as well as those that shall live at the end of the world. If it had a savour with God for those that lived before him, it hath much more a savour for those that have lived since his actual offering and acceptation.

(2.) From this ariseth pardon of sin. He was a sweet savour as he offered himself, and in the ends for which he offered himself. He was a sacrifice for sin; for so those words περὶ ἁμαρτίας, Rom. viii. 3, which we translate *and for sin*, must be understood and read thus, 'And by a sacrifice for sin condemned sin in the flesh.' If offered for sin, and accepted as an offering for sin, the consequent of this must be remission. Through the blood of that beloved whom he accepted, 'we have redemption, even the forgiveness of sins,' Eph. i. 6, 7; not of one, or two, or a few sins, but all; he was made sin indefinitely, all kind of sin in the extent, as much made sin as he was made accursed; as he bore all the curse, so he satisfied for all sin, the greatest as well as the least; so that the blood of this sacrifice

* Daillé, Serm. sur Ps. cx. 1, p. 409.

' cleanseth from all sin,' 1 John i. 7, where gospel dispositions are found ; from all that from which the law of Moses could not justify ; Acts xiii. 39, ' And by him all that believe are justified from all things, from which you could not be justified by the law of Moses.' What was impossible to be done by the sacrifices of the law, is completely done by the offering of the Redeemer. The strength of this is directly opposite to the weakness of the other ; that could not really justify from any, and this is able to justify from all. As it was not over-valued by God, so it cannot be overbalanced by sin ; since the judgment of God hath passed upon it with an approbation, the monstrousness of guilt is not too great for an expiation. Whatsoever our sins are, yet they have their limits ; but God's infinite pleasure in the sacrifice speaks the merit of it infinite, and the efficacy of it eternal. All sins were at once laid upon the head of this offering, Isa. liii. 7 ; he suffered but once, and therefore at one time all sins by one act were laid upon his shoulders, 1 Peter ii. 24, ' he bore them his own self,' and God accepted him his own self, and accepted him as he bore them, and glorified him, because he purged them, Heb. i. 3. So that though he did but once offer himself, and that for all sins in the bulk, he was received with a welcome, as if he had offered in particular for every sin ; and therefore there is no more need of an offering, but a recourse to that one price. To think it is not able to expiate all sin, is to undervalue the judgment God hath given of his Son, to charge him with a mistake, and to imagine that there is more in sin to ruin than in this sacrifice to repair.

(3.) Hence then there can be no condemnation to them that are in Christ. The apostle lays down this conclusion, and confirms it by the reason of his being a sacrifice, Rom. viii. 1, 3. They who are presented by Christ, quickened by the virtue of this sacrifice, cannot fall under the stroke of divine justice. If it was offered for those that should believe, it was accepted for such as should believe, it being accepted for the same persons, and the same ends for which it was offered, and therefore those persons fundamentally accepted in the acceptation of it, and the ends for which it was offered, granted, and concluded on in the act of acceptation. The apostle upon this score breathes out a challenge to all to bring a condemning charge against him ; the justice of God, the curse of the law, the charges of conscience, and the accusations of devils may be all answered by this : Rom. viii. 33, 34, ' It is Christ that died, it is God that justifies.' It is Christ that is offered, and God that accepts. Justice cannot condemn ; for though his sacrifice was sweet and pleasant to all the perfections of the divine nature, yet justice was the peculiar object of it. God as a judge delivered him, God as a judge accepted him : justice required it, and justice is disarmed by it ; justice only was to be contented ; mercy required no blood ; wisdom stepped in to decide the controversy, and make an agreement. If the condemning attribute be satisfied, there is no condemnation to be expected. If it be sweet to justice, justice cannot refrain its former frowns ; justice cannot be pleased with that, and displeased with those for whom it was offered and accepted, and by whom it is received. It is part of our happiness that we come not only to God as gracious, but God as a judge, ' To God the judge of all,' Heb. xii. 23. As Christ was made sin for us, so are we made righteous by him. He was made sin to undergo a condemnation, that we might be made righteous and be above a condemnation. It is more efficacious to divert the sword of divine justice from the believing offender, than the blood of the paschal lamb was to turn the edge of the angel's sword from the house of an Israelite. The blood of Christ sprinkled cannot be of less force than the blood of a silly lamb, since the efficacy of it was not as it was the blood of a lamb, but the blood of a type, deriving its virtue not from the subject whence the blood was drawn, but from the person signified, and the sacrifice prefigured by it. Well then, his condemnation hath procured our absolution, and God's acceptation of him hath insured our liberty; the sweet savour of the sacrifice hath overcome the stench of our sins. Though God forsook him for a time, he hath now accepted him, that he may not abandon us for ever; neither the wrath of God nor the malediction of the law is to be feared. God by this one act hath stopped the course of his vengeance, and laid aside the thunders of Sinai. The flames we have deserved are quenched by the blood flowing from the wounds of this victim ; the smoke of our sacrifice shadows us, and in God's acceptance of him every believer finds his infallible absolution.

(4.) Here is a sufficient ground for peace of conscience. This only can give a repose to our spirits, turn our fears into hopes, and our sorrows into songs. If it were a sweet savour to God, whose infinite knowledge was acquainted with the least mite, as well as the greatest mountain, in the number of our sins, and whose holiness found an infinite loathsomeness in our iniquities ; if it thus contented God, it may settle the agitation of our spirits ; and because it stilled fury in God, it may silence troubles in us; if it gave God a delight, who in the knowledge of our sins, loathing of them, and condemning of them, is ' greater than our hearts,' 1 John iii. 20, it is a ground of peace to us, who come infinitely short of God in knowing our charge, infinitely short of his holiness in loathing our guilt, and infinitely short of his justice in condemning ourselves. That which hath been a sweet savour to pacify God, wants not a savour to appease our consciences. Our great inquiry is, in troubles of spirit, how shall we appear before God ? The answer from this doctrine is, in the smoke of this sacrifice ; the impurities of our natures, the sin of our souls, and the mixture in our services are purified by this. The sweetness of this sacrifice hath sweetened the terrors of the Lord, and rendered man a welcome supplicant to that God, before whom he durst not formerly appear.

(5.) Here is a full ground of expectation of all necessary blessings. God accepted it as it was offered ; it was offered not only as a propitiating, but a purchasing sacrifice, and the acceptance of it was in the same quality wherein it was offered, Acts xx. 28. His blood was a purchasing blood ; he purchased a people for heaven, and purchased heaven for his people ; he did not only silence justice with its wrath, but merited heaven with its riches, and shed his blood as a price for the pleasures of paradise. God judged this sacrifice not only enough to free man from misery, but instate him in happiness ; not only to deliver our souls from the pit, but to enlighten us with the light of the living. It was valued by him as a full compensation for the wrongs he had sustained, and a full merit for the blessings we wanted. When he found this ransom, his voice was not only ' Deliver him from going down into the pit,' but ' I will make his flesh fresher than a child's ; ' a strength and vigour of grace shall be restored in him, as the radical moisture in a child ; ' He shall return to the days of his youth, he shall pray to God, and God will be favourable to him, and he shall see his face with joy,' Job xxxiii. 24–26. The Israelites addressed to the propitiatory, not only for the pardon of their sins, but the conferring of other blessings ; this is the blood of the covenant, and therefore procures for us the blessings of the covenant. The blessings we want are often in the gospel ascribed to the merit of this sacrifice, and not simply to the grace of God. The grace of God appointed the sacrifice, but the blessings we receive were merited by it ; our victim was so pleasing to God, and the obedience in it so full of an infinite love to him, that he gained by it the affections of God, and a grant of whatsoever was most precious, to be bestowed upon those for whom he offered himself, that thereby the pleasure he took in it might be fully evidenced.

5. *Use.* Let us lay hold of it and plead this sacrifice.

(1.) Let natural men imitate God in an acceptance of this sacrifice. No man perisheth for want of God's pleasure in it, but for want of his own acceptance of it upon the gospel conditions. No bitten Israelite perished for want of a brazen serpent, but for want of a look to it. Cast not an aspersion upon God by undervaluing that which he doth so highly prize; be guided by his infallible judgment, rather than by the errors of your own; think not of it coldly, as if you were indifferent whether you had a share in it or no, since God received it not with an indifferent, but an unconceivable affection. Let that which is sweet to God be so to us; that which is savoury to that infinite Spirit, cannot justly be unsavoury to our contracted souls. God found no sweetness in the blood of goats, or smoke of incense, Ps. l., but only in this sacrifice; nor should any of us rest on the transitory pleasures of this life, and sing a *requiem* to our souls from perishing enjoyments, but from the blood of the Lamb that endures for ever. There is no likelihood for a creature to find rest in that wherein God finds none; we are not sure of our lives, but we are sure we are guilty; and shall any of us be unconcerned about a powerful sacrifice? Let a self-abhorrency possess our souls, without which we can have no esteem of this offering. As God's loathing of sin made him value this for expiation, so our sense of sin will make us value this for our atonement. Let no man think that unworthy of him which God thinks not unworthy of himself; he commanded the angels to adore him for it, either when he brought him into the world to be a sacrifice, or brought him into the world above, after he had ' by his blood purged our sins,' Heb. i. 6. God would have men and angels concur with him in the magnificent acceptation of our Saviour.

(2.) Let those that believe, continually apply and plead it. This is so sweet to God, that there is no need of a new sacrifice, but there is need of a daily application; there was no need of a new serpent to be erected upon every sting, but there was need of a new looking up to the serpent upon every wound. We can be no more without this one day to comfort our souls, than we can be without bread to nourish our bodies; the remembrance of it must come up with the remembrance of every sin in our consciences. In this only shall we find mercy for our iniquities, and comfort for our sorrows. What was sweet to God in the acceptance, will be sweet to him in the pleas of it; it hath not lost its savour, nor hath God changed his judgment. Christ is in the fragrancy of his sacrifice with God, as well as in his divinity, ' the same yesterday, to-day, and for ever.' We contract a daily guilt, and we stand in need of a daily application to this. God will not make us perfect in this life, to keep up the continual credit of this sacrifice, that we may live by faith, and have every day sensible thoughts of the power of this oblation. Let all our pleas with God be founded in his acceptance of this; it is always to be pleaded by us, as it is always eyed by the Father. No pardon is granted but upon the account of it: in every pardoning act, God looks first with pleasure upon this victim, and dips his pen in the blood of it to blot out the iniquity. No blessing is poured upon us, on which the merit of this sacrifice is not stamped; and no petition must be presented by us, but in the virtue of it.

A DISCOURSE OF THE NECESSITY OF CHRIST'S DEATH.

Ought not Christ to have suffered these things, and to enter into his glory?
—LUKE XXIV. 26.

THE words are an answer of our Saviour's to the discourse of two of the disciples who were going to Emmaus, ver. 13. He came *incognito* to them while they were discoursing together of the great news of that time, viz., the death of their master, whom they acknowledge ' a prophet mighty in deed and word before God and all the people,' ver. 19 ; confirmed by God to be so by miracles, and confessed to be so by the people. Yet they questioned whether he were the Messiah that should redeem Israel,. and erect the kingdom so much promised and predicted in the Scripture. They could not tell how to reconcile the ignominy of his death with the grandeur of his office, and glory of a king. And though they had heard by the women of ' a vision of angels' that assured them ' he was alive,' yet they do not seem in their discourse to give any credit to the report, but relate it as they heard it; though both by what they said before, ver. 21, that they had ' trusted that it was he that should have redeemed Israel,' and also by the sharp reproof Christ gives them, ver. 25, ' O fools, and slow of heart to believe all that the prophets have spoken !' we may conclude that they thought it a mere illusion, or a groundless imagination of the women. Christ, to rectify their minds, begins with a reproof, and follows it with an instruction, that what they thought a ground to question the truth of his office, and the reality of his being the Messiah, was rather an argument to confirm and establish it, since that person characterised in the Old Testament to be the Messiah was to wade to his glory through a sea of blood, and such sufferings in every kind as cruel and shameful as that person in whom they thought they had been deceived, had suffered three days before ; and afterwards discourseth from the Scripture that his death, and such a kind of death, did well agree with the predictions of the prophets; and therefore, ' beginning at Moses and all the prophets, he expounded unto them in all the scriptures the things concerning himself.' He might well sum up in two or three hours' time (wherein we may suppose he was with them) most of those testimonies which did foretell his sufferings for the expiation of sin. The proposition which he maintains from Moses and the prophets, is in the text, ' Ought not Christ

89

to have suffered those things ?' which is laid down by way of interrogation, but equivalent to an affirmation ; and he backed, without question, his discourse with many reasonings for the confirmation of it, to reduce them from the distrust they had to a full assent to the necessity of his death, in order to his own glory, and consequently theirs; the foundation of his own exaltation, and the redemption of mankind, being laid in his being a sacrifice.

Ought not ?

1. It is not said, it is convenient or becoming. As it was said of his baptism, Matt. iii. 15, ' It becomes us to fulfil all righteousness.' His baptism had more of a convenience than necessity.* He might have been the Messiah without subjecting himself to the ceremonial law, or passing under the baptism of John. But it was impossible he should be a redeeming Christ without undergoing an accursed death. No sin was expiated merely by his submission to the yoke of legal rites, or the baptismal water of John ; all expiation of sin was founded only in his bloody baptism.

2. It is said, *he ought*. Not an absolute, but a conditional *ought ;* not his original duty as the Son of God, but a voluntary duty as the redeemer of man. He voluntarily engaged at first in it, and voluntarily proceeded to the utmost execution, yet necessarily after his first engagement. Necessity there was, but not compulsion. All necessity doth not imply constraint, and exclude will. Paul must necessarily die by the law appointed to all men, but willingly he ' desires to be dissolved, and to be with Christ.' God is necessarily holy and true, yet not unwillingly so. Angels and glorified souls are necessarily holy by their confirmation in a gracious and glorious state, yet voluntarily so by a full and free inclination ; necessary by the decree and counsel of God, necessary by the engagement and promise of Christ, necessary by the predictions and prophecies of Scripture.† All which causes of necessity are linked together, because the restoration of man required such a suffering ; therefore it was from eternity decreed by God, embraced by Christ, published in Scripture. It was ordained in heaven, and set out in the *manifesto* of the Old Testament ; so that if this death had not been suffered, the counsel of God concerning redemption had been defeated, the word and promises of Christ violated, and the truth of God in the predictions of the prophets had fallen to the ground. The decree of God was declared in many prophecies before the execution ; and this will of God is an evidence of the necessity of it. ‡ Why did he ordain it, if it were not necessary to so great an end ? Though the end, the redemption of man, was not necessary, yet, when the end was resolved on, this, as the means, was found necessary in the counsel of God. The natural inclination and will of Christ, as man, did startle at it, when he desired that this cup might pass from him. It was contrary to the reason and common sense of men. How, then, should that infinite Wisdom, that wills nothing but what is unquestionably reasonable, have determined such a means, if it had not been necessary for his own glory and man's recovery ? But both the Father and the Son were moved to it by the height of that good which they bore to the fallen creature.

These things, ταῦτα. Every one of those severe and sharp circumstances. The whole system of those sufferings, not a dart that pierced him, not a reproach that grated upon him, but was ordained ; every step he took in blood and suffering was marked out to him. Since Christ was to die for the reparation of man, for the expiation of sin, it was necessary that his death should be attended with those particular sharpnesses that might render his love more admirable, the justice of God more dreadful, the evil of sin more abominable,

---

* Daillé, Serm. de Resurrect. de Christ, p. 226.   † Gerhard in loc.
‡ Daillé, Serm. de Resurrect. de Christ, p. 226.

and the satisfaction itself more valuable. The intenseness of his love had not been set off so amiably in a light and easy death, as in a painful and shameful suffering; and though the greatness of his merit and the fulness of his satisfaction did principally arise from the dignity of the suffering person, yet some consideration might be also had of the greatness of his suffering. Not only his death, as he was considered equal with God, but his shameful death in the circumstance of the cross, is a mark of his obedience and a cause of his exaltation, Philip. ii. 8. Both were regarded in the crown of glory, and that high dignity wherein he was instated, so that the sum of Christ's speech amounts to this much: be not doubtful whether the person so lately suffering, whom you account so great a prophet, were the Messiah. You clearly may see in the prophets that nothing hath been inflicted on him but what was predicted of him; so that it is not merely the malice of man that hath caused those sufferings; that was only a means God in his infinite wisdom used to bring about his own counsel. He was not forced to what he suffered, but willingly delivered up himself to perform the charge and office of a Redeemer, which could not else have been accomplished by him; and that glory which you expected, was not by the order of God to be conferred upon him till he abased himself to such a passion. He will have a glory to your comfort, though not answering your carnal expectations. Be not dejected, but recover your hopes of redemption which you seem to have lost, and let them be rectified in the expectation, not of an earthly, but an heavenly, glory.

Observe,

1. The nature of Christ's sufferings, *these things.*
2. The necessity, *Ought not Christ to suffer?*
3. The consequence, *and to enter into his glory.*

There are two doctrines to be insisted on from these words:

1. There was a necessity of Christ's death.
2. Christ's exaltation was as necessary as his passion.

For the first, there was a necessity of the death of Christ. It was necessary by the counsel of God, Acts ii. 23; 'Him being delivered by the determinate counsel and foreknowledge of God, Acts iv. 28. It was not a fruit of second causes, which God only suffered by a bare permission, but it was a decree of his will fixed and determined, and that before the world began, an irrevocable decree God made to deliver his Son to death for the sins of men, and according to this counsel he was in time delivered, and by the merit of his death hath reconciled to God all those that believe in him.

In handling this doctrine, I shall shew,

(1.) What kind of necessity this was.
(2.) That it was necessary.
(3.) The use.

1. What kind of necessity this was.

Prop. 1. His death was not absolutely necessary, but conditionally.

(1.) It supposeth, first, the entrance of sin. There was no necessity that sin should enter into the world. There was no necessity on man's part to sin. Though he was created with a possibility of sinning, yet not with a necessity; he was created mutable, but not corruptible: 'God made man upright,' Eccles. vii. 29. His faculties, as bestowed upon him, stood right to God. He had an understanding to know what of God was fit for him to know, a will without any wrong bias to embrace him, and affections to love him. God permitted him to fall, the devil allured him to sin, but neither the one nor the other did immediately influence his will to the commission of his crime. There was no necessity on God's part that sin should enter ; though his wisdom thought good to permit it, yet there was no absolute necessity that it should step up in the world.   He might have fixed man, as well as the holy angels, in an eternal purity ; he might have enlightened the mind of man by a particular act of grace at the first proposal of the temptation by the devil, to discern his deceit and stratagem, and so might have prevented man's sin as well as permitted it.   Had not sin entered, there had been no occasion for the death of the creature, much less for the death of Christ.   The honour of God had not been invaded ; there had been no provoked justice to satisfy, nor any violated law to vindicate.   Some indeed there are* that think the incarnation of Christ had been necessary without the entrance of sin, because they consider God of so holy a nature that it had been impossible for him to be pleased with any creature, though the work of his own hands, so that neither angels nor men could have stood one moment in his sight without beholding him in the face of a mediator.   Several had anciently imagined† that if man had continued in obedience till the time appointed for his confirmation, then Christ would have been incarnate, and man have become one mystical person with him for his confirmation, as the angels were confirmed by him ; but none assert the death of Christ but upon supposition of sin.   All sacrifices for sin imply the guilt of sin antecedent to them ; but after man had transgressed the rule by his disobedience, and thereby made himself incapable of answering the terms of that righteous law which God had set him, the death of Christ became as necessary as his incarnation, for the righting the injured law and satisfying offended justice, and the conveyance of mercy to the creature, with the honour of God and preservation of his rights.   As Christ's rejoicing from eternity, 'in the habitable parts of the earth,' supposeth the creation of the world in the order of God's decree, Prov. viii. 31, so the eternal counsel of God, for the making his Son a sacrifice, supposeth the rise of sin and iniquity in the world.   Had not man run cross to the preceptive will of God, he had enjoyed the presence of God without a sacrificed mediator, and would have had an everlasting communion with him in happiness ; but after sin entered upon the world, there was need of a propitiation for sin.   An infinitely pure God could not have communion with an impure creature.   It was not fit a sovereign majesty should make himself savingly known to his creature without a propitiatory.

(2.) It supposeth death to be settled by God as the punishment of sin. Some question whether it were absolutely necessary that death should have been threatened upon the breach of the law.   It is true, as the law depends upon the will of the lawgiver, so doth the punishment.   And it is in his liberty, if you consider him as an absolute sovereign, to annex what penalty he pleaseth ; yet, as all laws are to spring from righteousness, so all punishments are to be regulated by righteousness and equity, that a punishment deserved by the greatest crime should not be ordered as the recompense of offences of a lighter nature.   But in the case of transgressions against God, no penalty less than death, and eternal death, could, according to the rules of justice, have been appointed.   It is certain sin doth naturally oblige to punishment: it is senseless to imagine that a law should be transgressed without some penalty incurred.   A law is utterly insignificant without it, and it is inconsistent with the wisdom of a lawgiver to enact a precept without adding a penalty.   If, therefore, a punishment be due to sin, it is requisite, according to the rules of justice and wisdom, to proportion the punishment to the greatness of the offence.   I say this is the rule that

---

* Bacon's Confession of Faith, at the end of his Remains, pp. 117, 118.
† Jackson, vol. ii. quart. p. 191.

righteousness requires. And it is as natural that a crime should be punished suitably to its demerit as that it should be punished at all. Why doth any fault deserve punishment, but because there is an unreasonableness in it, something against the nature of man, against the nature of a subject, against the authority of the lawgiver, against the order and good of a community? The punishment therefore ought to be as great as the damage to authority by the crime. To order a punishment greater than the crime is tyranny; to order it less than the crime is folly in the government: unrighteousness in both, because there is an inequality between the sin and the penalty. Now, such is the excellency of God's nature, and so inviolable with his creature ought his authority to be, that the least offence against him deserves the highest punishment, because it is against the best and most sovereign being. It seems therefore to us that God had not acted like a righteous governor if he had not denounced death for the sins against him; the offence being the highest, the punishment in the order of justice ought to be the highest. What could be supposed more just and reasonable than for God to deprive man of that life which he had given him, that life which man had received from the goodness of his Creator, and had employed against his authority and glory? As his sin was against the supreme good, so the punishment ought to be the depriving man of his highest good. The vileness of the person offending, and the dignity of the person offended, always communicate an aggravation to the crime. The sin of man, being infinite, did, in the justice of God, merit an infinite punishment. And this is not only written upon the hearts of men by nature, that it is so, but that it is deservedly so, Rom. i. 32, 'that they are worthy of death.' The justice of God in inflicting death for sin is as well known as his power and Godhead, and the justice of it is universally owned in the consciences of men when they are awakened. Adam, when he sinned, did not think the offence of so great a weight, but his roused conscience presented him with those natural notions of the justice of God, and sunk him under the sense of it, till God had revived him by a promise.

(3.) It supposeth that, after man's transgression, and thereby the demerit of death, God would recover and redeem man. There was no necessity incumbent upon God to restore man after his defection from him and rebellion against him. As God was not obliged to prevent man's fall, so he was not obliged to recover man fallen. When he did permit him to offend, he might have let him sink under the weight of his own crimes, and left him buried in the ruins of his fall. He might for ever have reserved him in those chains he had merited, and have let him feed upon the fruit of his own doings, without one thought of his delivery, or employing one finger of that power for his restoration, whereby he had brought him into being; for the restoration of man was no more necessary in itself than the first creation of him was. As God might have left him in his nothing without producing him into being, so he might have left him in his contracted misery without restoring him to happiness. Nor was it any ways more necessary than the reducing the fallen angels to their primitive obedience and felicity. The blessedness and happiness of God had no more been infringed by the eternal destruction of man, than it was by the everlasting ruin of devils. Upon the supposition that God would save sinners after his justice was so fully engaged to punish them, no way in the understanding of man can be thought of, but the sufferings of the creature, or some one for him, to preserve the justice of God from being injured. Though the thoughts of some differ in other things, yet not in this. All say it was not simply necessary that man should be freed from his fallen state. But since God would not hurl all men into the damnation they had deserved, and treat them as he did the devils in the rigours of his justice, this way of the death of his Son was the most convenient way ; * and indeed necessary, not necessary by an antecedent necessity (for there is no such necessity in God respecting created things), but a consequent necessity upon a decree of his will, which being settled, something else must necessarily follow as a means for the execution of that decree ; as supposing God would create man to be Lord of the creature, and return him the glory of his works, it were then consequently necessary that he should create him with rational faculties, and fit for those ends for which he created him ; but the creation of man in such a frame is not of absolute necessity, but depends upon the antecedent decree of his will, of creating such a creature as should render him the tribute of his works. So it is not necessary that God should free man from the spot of sin, and the misery contracted thereby, and reduce him from damnation to felicity ; but since he determined the redemption of him after the violation of the law, which he had confirmed by the penalty of death, God could not without wrong to his justice and truth freely pardon man, because he is immutably righteous and true, and cannot lie ; and since he is so righteous a judge that he can no more absolve the guilty than he can condemn the innocent, Exod. xxxiv. 7, his justice was an invincible obstacle to the pardon of sin, though men had implored his mercy with the greatest ardency and affection, unless this justice had been satisfied with a satisfaction suitable to it, *i. e.* infinite as the divine justice is infinite ; and since neither man nor any other creature, being all of a finite nature, were able to give a full content to the justice of God, a necessity is then introduced of some infinite person to put himself in the place of the fallen creatures, clothe himself with their nature, and suffer in it the penalty they had merited, that they might be exempted from that which, by the transgression of the law, they had incurred.

(4.) It supposeth Christ's voluntary engagement and undertaking of this affair first. There could be no necessity upon God to redeem, nor any necessity upon Christ to be the Redeemer ; but after his consent, which was wholly free, his promise engaged him to performance. He was free from all bonds till he entered into bond ; he was at liberty whether he would be our surety ; no compulsion could be used to him : John x. 18, he had ' power to lay down his life.' It implies a liberty either of laying down his life or not ; a liberty of choice whether he would die for man or no. He had power if he pleased to avoid the cross, but he undertook it, ' despising the shame,' Heb. xii. 2. And after having once undertaken this charge, it was necessary for him to suffer. As it is in the liberty of a man's choice whether he will engage himself in bonds for an insolvent debtor, yet when he is entered into suretyship, both his own honesty and the equity of the law necessitates him to stand to his engagements, and pay the money he is bound for, if the debtor be still insolvent ;† so after Christ hath promised payment for bankrupt man, he could not retract both in regard of his truth, and in regard of the tenderness which first moved him to it. He could not violate his promise, nor deny his contract ; both the order of his Father and his own righteousness did not permit him to cast off this resolution. Though it was naturally voluntary, yet it was morally necessary ; and therefore often when he speaks of his sufferings to his disciples, he puts a *must* to them : Mat. xvi. 21, John iii. 14 ' *must* suffer many things,' ' *must* be lifted up.' And his prayer from a natural inclination of the human nature, that this cup might pass from him, *if it were possible*, not being granted, shews it to be morally impossible,

* Petav. Theol. tom. iv. lib. ii. cap. 13, sect. 10.
† Daillé, Serm. de Resurrect. de Christ, p. 226.

after it was determined, that we could be saved any other way. God's not answering his own Son, manifests an impossibility to divert his death without our eternal loss. Had not that promise been past, if Christ had been incarnate, he might have lived in the world with glory and honour ; he might have come, not as a surety, but as a lawgiver and judge ; but after that promise made by him to his Father, and that the Father had by the covenant of redemption 'laid upon him the iniquities of us all,' and Christ on his part had covenanted to ' take upon him the form of a servant,' Philip. ii. 7, and to be ' made under the law,' Gal. iv. 4, he did owe to God an obedience as our surety according to the law of redemption, as well as an obedience to the moral law as a creature, by virtue of his incarnation.   Had he been incarnate without such a promise of suffering, he had not been bound to suffer unless he had sinned ; for, having no spot, neither original nor actual, he had stood firm upon the basis of the first covenant. But the obligation to the obedience of suffering was incumbent upon him by virtue of the compact between the Father and himself.   Had he been incarnate without that precedent compact, he had owed an obedience to God in his humanity as a creature ; but as he was incarnate for such an end, and was, pursuant to the law of redemption, made under the moral law, he owed an obedience to both those laws, an obedience as a creature, an obedience as mediator, as a son owes obedience to a father by virtue of his relation of a son ; but if this son be bound apprentice to his father, he owes another obedience to him as a servant by virtue of the covenant between them ; the duty of obedience as a servant is superadded to that of a son ; so the necessity of obedience as a surety was added to the necessity of obedience as a creature in regard of Christ's humanity, so that this necessity is only consequent, and supposeth at first the voluntary engagement of Christ.   For indeed his sufferings could not be of infinite merit for us except they had been voluntarily undertaken by him.* If his sufferings took their worth and value from his person, they must likewise have their freedom and election from his person.   Whatsoever punishment, reproach, and trouble the fury of wicked men brought upon him, was not suffered by an absolute necessity, but conditional, after the engagement of his will.

Prop. 2. All things preceding his death, and all circumstances in his death, did not fall under a necessity of the same kind. Upon the former supposition, his death was necessary, and could not be avoided. Death was threatened by God as a sovereign ; it was merited by man as a malefactor, and was necessary to be inflicted by God as a judge and governor. And by virtue of this threatening, and his engagement in suretyship, it was necessary that he should suffer, not as an innocent person, but under the imputation of a sinner ; a reputed sinner, though he were perfectly innocent in his own nature : 1 Cor. v. 21, he was ' made sin for us.'   Yet Christ, in his humiliation, did undergo some things which were not immediately necessary to our redemption.   We might have been redeemed by him without his being hungry and weary. But this was mediately necessary to our redemption, in manifesting the truth and reality of his human nature.   We might have been redeemed without the piercing of his side, and the letting out the water in the *pericardium*. But this was convenient to shew the truth of his death. These were necessary by virtue of God's decree, manifested in the prediction of the prophets, to be done unto him. But his incarnation and passion to death were immediately necessary to our recovery and the atonement of sin. We could not have been redeemed unless he had satisfied justice ; justice could not be satisfied but by suffering ; suffering could not have been under-

* Bilson on Christ's sufferings, p. 286.

gone unless he had been incarnate. A body he must have prepared for suffering; nor could he have suffered for us unless he had been incarnate in our nature.

2. Thing. To demonstrate this necessity. Having declared what kind of necessity this is, wé may now demonstrate this necessity.

1. To suffer death was the immediate end of the interposition of Christ. The principal end of his undertaking was to right the honour of God, and glorify his attributes in the recovery of the creature; but the immediate end was to suffer, because this was the only way to bring about that end which was principally aimed at in Christ's interposition, and God's determination concerning him. Death being denounced as the punishment of sin, Christ interposeth himself for our security, with a promise to bear that punishment in our stead for the procuring our exemption from it; therefore, what punishment was of right to be inflicted on man for the breach of the law, was, by a gracious act of God, the governor of the world and guardian of his laws, transferred upon Christ, as putting himself in our stead. His first interposition was for the same end with his death, but his death was evidently for our sins. It was for them 'he gave himself,' Gal. i. 4; they were our sins which 'he bare in his own body on the tree,' 1 Peter ii. 24; 'for our iniquities he was wounded, and for our transgressions he was bruised,' Isa. liii. 5; our health was procured by his stripes, and therefore intended by him in his first engagement. He offered his person in our stead, which was able to bear our sin, and afford us a righteousness which was able to justify our persons; he offered himself to endure the curse of the law in his own body, and fulfil the righteousness of the law in his own person; he would be united with us in our nature, that he might make the sins of our nature his own in suffering for them, and give to us what was his, by taking to himself what was ours; he took our stripes that we might receive his medicine. This, therefore, being the end of his first undertaking, was necessary to be performed; for Christ is not yea and nay, 2 Cor. i. 19, one time of one mind, and another time of another, but firm and uniform in all his proceedings, without any contradiction between his promise and performance.

That this was the end of his first interposition is evident,

(1.) By the terms of the covenant of redemption incumbent on his part. What God demanded was complied with on the part of Christ. The demand of God was the offering of the soul, because upon that condition depends the promise of his exaltation and seeing his seed: Isa. liii. 10, 'When thou shalt make his soul an offering for sin, he shall see his seed;' or as others, 'When his soul is put an offering for sin.' The word אשם is properly a sin-offering, and his soul is the matter of this offering, as well as the spring and principle of the offering himself to God. It was upon this condition only he was to see his seed; he had had no seed, i. e. none had been saved by him according to this covenant, unless his soul had made itself an offering for sin. This death of Christ was the main article to be performed by him; this was the eye of Christ fixed upon in the offering himself in the first transaction to do the will of God: Ps. xl. 6–8, 'Burnt-offering and sin-offering hast thou not required. Lo, I come; I delight to do thy will,' Heb. x. 7, 8. The will of God for a satisfaction by sacrifice. The will of God was the demand of something above all legal sacrifices; for he had no pleasure in those which were offered by the law, wherein Christ complies with God; and it was something which was not to fall short of, but surmount those legal offerings. The denial of any pleasure or content in them implies a demand of a higher pleasure and content than all or any of them could afford. To this Christ gives his full consent, and offers himself, according to the will of God, to be a sacrifice, and puts himself in the place of those sin-offerings wherein God had no pleasure ; as if he should have said, A sin-offering, Lord, thou wilt have, and one proportionable to the greatness of the offence ; since none else can be suitable to an infinite majesty, I will be the sin-offering, and answer thy will in this ; and therefore the apostle infers, Heb. x. 10, that the offering the body of Christ for our sanctification, our restoration, was the particular will of God in this affair, which will Christ particularly promises in that eternal transaction to perform : Gal. i. 4, 'Who hath given himself for our sins, according to the will of God.' And, indeed, God could not have been said to enter into his rest at the foundation of the world without this transaction, as he is said to do, Heb. iv. ; for foreseeing that an universal stain and disorder would overspread the world by sin, that the glory which would naturally issue to him from the creatures would meet with an obstacle from it, and no way be left for the glorifying of any other attributes after sin but his power and justice in the due and righteous punishment of the creature, he could not take any pleasure in the works of his hands, had not the second person stood up as a sacrifice of atonement to purify the bespotted world, rectify the disorder, and render a content to the justice of God, that all the other attributes of God in the creation might have their due glory perpetuated and elevated. It was in this one person, and that by his blood, that God found the best way and method to gather together those things which sin had scattered, Eph. i. 7, 10. And the first promise in paradise after the fall, of the bruising the serpent's head, in having the seed of the woman's heel bruised by the serpent, intending thereby his death (as is cleared up by considering the revelations of God afterwards), shews that this was fixed in him, since it is most likely it was the second person appeared to Adam and made that promise. This was the first promise to man, founded upon this covenant of redemption.

(2.) The command that Christ received to die, manifests his interposition for this end. He was made under the law, and his death is called 'obedience,' Philip. ii. 8.* Obedience implies a command as the rule of it. Obedience to the moral law engaged him not to die for us ; it had bound him over to death, had he been a transgressor of it ; but considered in itself, it obliged him not, being innocent, to suffer death for those that were delinquents. Obedience, therefore, in regard of his death, must answer to a particular command of God, flowing from some other act of his will than what was formally expressed in the moral law. Such a command he received from his Father, to lay down his life, John x. 18 ; which supposeth the free proffer of himself to a state of humiliation for such an end as dying. Had it not been obedience to a command, God had not been bound to accept his offering. Though in itself, and its own nature, upon the trial of God it would have been found sufficient, yet it had been a just exception, 'Who hath required this at your hands ?' If he had not offered himself to this purpose, he had not been God's voluntary servant ; and if he had not received a law in order to the performance of what he offered, he had not been God's 'righteous servant,' as he is called, Isa. liii. 11, there being no rule whereby to measure his righteousness in this act. The concurrence of both these made his death necessary and acceptable. Though, as I said before, this command of dying for us was not formally any command of the moral law, yet after once he had received this order, and obliged himself to the performance of it, the moral law obliged him to the highest manner of performing this, i. e. with the highest love to God and his neighbour, whose nature he had taken, and thereby became our kinsman. Since God was

* Cocc. de Fœd. cap. v. p. 117.

dishonoured and man damaged by sin, his love to the glory of God and the salvation of man were to be with the greatest intenseness; and this the moral law enjoins in all acts we undertake for God.

(3.) If he had not interposed himself for this end, he could not have suffered. Since God passed such a judgment on him, and laid upon him the iniquities of us all, there must be some precedent act of Christ for this end ; for it was not just with God to force any to bear the punishment of another's sin. The justice of God, in his dealings with man, is regulated by his own law ; he inflicts nothing but what his law hath enjoined. To punish without law, and a transgression of it, is injustice. No law of God ever threatened punishment to one in every respect innocent. Christ, by a free act of his own, put himself into the state of a reputed nocent, and by his interposition for us, as a surety, was counted by God as one person with us ; as a surety and a debtor are, in a legal and juridical account, as one person, and what the debtor is liable to in regard of that debt for which the surety is bound, whether it be a pecuniary or a criminal debt, the surety being considered as one person with him, is to undergo. Christ's substituting himself in our stead was to this end, that the sins of those that God had given him might be imputed to him ; for he proffered himself to make his soul an offering for sin. It could be no sin of his own ; sin he did not, sin he could not. It must be another's sin, transferred upon him in a juridical manner; transferred, I say, upon him, not by any transfusion of our sins into Christ by way of inherency, but by imputation, without which he could not be a sufferer. For what reason, what justice had there been to expose one to suffering, that was wholly innocent, and had no sin, neither by inherency nor imputation ? How could any be liable to punishment, that could not in any manner be regarded as guilty ? To be under judgment, supposeth a man's own crime, or the crimes of others. Since God, therefore, ' made him to be sin for us,' 2 Cor. v. 21, and could not in justice make him so without his own consent; his consent, then, in the first offer of his mediation, was to be made sin for us, *i..e.* to bear our sins. He offered himself for the same end for which God accepted him, and for which God used him. Pursuant to this offer of himself, he was made under the law, and put into such a state and condition, by his investing himself with the human nature, as that the law might make its demands of him, and receive the penalties which were due by it for the offence.

Add to this, the giving of some to Christ to save, John xvii. 18, vi. 89, which presupposeth the obligation of Christ to death ; for after sin, the law being to be vindicated, and justice glorified, God's committing some to him to save, presupposeth his engagement to satisfy the law and justice on their behalf.* It was for this end also he came to the hour of his death, John xii. 27 ; and his prayer to his Father, to ' save him from this hour,' had been groundless, if he had not passed his word to his Father to enter upon that hour. What need he have prayed to his Father to save him, who might have saved himself, if there had been no antecedent obligation to undertake this task ?

He thus interposing himself for this end, it was necessary he should die. For,

[1.] Else none could have been saved from the foundation of the world. Some were saved before his actual death upon the cross. God was the God of Abraham, Isaac, and Jacob ; but ' God is the God of the living, not of the dead,' Mat. xxii. 82. They therefore lived in his sight before the actual oblation of Christ upon the cross ; but they could no more have been saved

* Cocc. de Fœd. cap. v. pp. 118. 119.

without the credit of this death of Christ in our nature, than the fallen angels could have been saved. The reason they are not saved, is rendered by the apostle, Heb. ii. 16, because Christ took not their nature ; his taking our nature therefore, and dying in it, is the cause of any man's salvation that lived after his coming ; his promise of taking our nature, and dying in it, is the cause of the salvation of any that lived before. The apostle's reasoning would not else stand good ; had Christ assumed the angels' nature, they would have been saved ; had not Christ then assumed our nature, we could not have been saved ; and had he not promised to assume our nature, none could have been saved. He could not have been called the Captain of the salvation of all the sons that are brought to glory, whereof many were before his coming, Heb. ii. 10. They must have been saved upon the account of that future death, or else there must be some other name besides that of Christ whereby they were saved ; but that there is not, Acts iv. 12. Faith had not always been the way of salvation. Christ had begun to be a mediator and redeemer at the time of his death, and not before ; and so had not been in that relation ' the same yesterday, to-day, and for ever.' Had he not died, he could not have been set out with any good ground before his coming as an object of faith. The promises of him had wanted their due foundation, the predictions of him had been groundlesss ; and, consequently, the faith and hope of the ancient believers had been in vain. It is certain, all that were saved, were saved upon the account of his death ; for the merit of his death might have an influence before it was suffered, it being a moral, not a natural, cause of salvation ; as many times a prisoner is delivered upon the promise of a ransom before the actual payment of it.

[2.] Since some were saved before upon the account of his future death, had he not died, God had been highly dishonoured. Had not Christ performed his promise of suffering, and thereby satisfying the justice of God, God, having saved many before his incarnation upon the credit of this promise, had received a manifest wrong. It would have argued a weakness in him to lay such stress upon that which would not be full and secure, which would never have been accomplished. God had not been omniscient, but had been deceived in his foreknowledge, had his expectations been frustrated. For what was the reason God saved any before, but upon the credit of this ransom, which was promised to be paid in time, and his foreknowledge, that when the term came, the surety would not be wanting to discharge himself of his promise ? Had not, then, Christ really suffered, and accomplished what he had promised, God had suffered in his honour, and all things could not have been said to be present to him ; he would have been deceived. As if a prisoner be delivered upon the promise of a ransom, and the ransom be not paid according to agreement, the person that hath delivered the prisoner suffers in point of wisdom in trusting a person that hath not been as good as his word, and is defeated of that which is in justice due to him. Again, since God had admitted some to happiness before the actual suffering of Christ, had not Christ performed what he had actually undertaken, God must have renounced either his justice or his mercy ; his justice, had he let sinners go unpunished, and then he had denied in part his own name, which is ' by no means to clear the guilty,' Exodus xxxiv. 7 ; or else he must have punished sin in the persons of those whom he had already brought to happiness ; and had he done so, how had the honour of his mercy suffered, in turning them out of that felicity wherein he had always* placed them ! Some, therefore, make the remission of the sins past before the coming of Christ not to be properly a full pardon, but a passing by, the full remission not

* Qu. ' already '?—ED.

being to be given till the actual payment was made ; and indeed the word the apostle useth in that place, Rom. iii. 25, is different, πάρεσις, a passing by, a word not used for pardon in all the New Testament, but ἄφεσις. Had not Christ suffered, there had been nothing of the righteousness of God manifested in the remission of sins which were past ; the end of God had been frustrated, it being his end, in the death of Christ, ' to declare his righteousness for the remission of sins that are past, to declare at this time his righteousness,' *i.e.* what his righteousness was in passing by sins before committed, to declare that he pardoned no sins before, without an eye to this satisfactory death of his Son ; but that in all his former proceedings he kept close to the rules of his infinite justice. Now, had not Christ died according to his engagement, God had highly suffered in his honour, his omniscience had been defeated ; God had been deceived in the credit he gave, his righteousness had not been manifested, his justice had suffered, or his mercy to his poor creatures had been dammed up for ever from flowing out upon them.

2. The veracity of God, in settling the penalty of death upon transgression, made it necessary for redemption. God passed his word that death should be the punishment of sin, Gen. ii. 17 ; the veracity of God stood engaged to make this word good upon the conditions expressed. The sentence was immutable, and the word that went out of God's mouth must stand ; had it been revoked without inflicting the punishment, the faithfulness and righteousness of God, in regard of his word, could not have been justified : ' God cannot lie, or deny himself,' Titus i. 2, 2 Tim. ii. 13 ; his truth is not a quality in him, but himself, his essence. Had he, then, after so solemnly pronouncing, without any reverse, that the wages of sin should be no less than death, been careless of his own word, and left sin unpunished, God had made a breach upon his own nature, and had infringed his own happiness ; for a lie or falsity is the fountain and original of all evil and misery. Supposing God had other ways to deal with man (though it is beyond the capacity of man to imagine any other way of God's government of him, or any intellectual and rational creatures, than by a law, and a penalty annexed to that law, which otherwise would have proved insignificant), yet after his wisdom had settled this law, and the threatening had passed his royal and immutable word, it was no longer arbitrary, but necessary by the sovereign authority, that either the sinner himself, or some surety in his stead, should suffer the death the sinner had incurred by the violation of the precept ; we must either pay ourselves, or some other pay for us, what we stand bound in to the justice of God. Impunity had been an invasion of God's veracity, which is as immutable as his nature ; since, therefore, the inflicting of death upon transgression was the real intent of God, upon the commission of sin death must enter upon man, otherwise God would be a disregarder of himself, and his threatenings a mere scarecrow.

(1.) Had God violated his word, he had rendered himself an unfit object of trust. He had exposed all the promises or threatenings he should have made after man's impunity to the mockery and contempt of the offender, and excluded his word from any credit with man. Had God set man right again by a mere act of mercy, without any regard to his word past, and inflicting any punishment upon the offender, though he had made man more glorious promises than at the first, he would have had little reason to trust God. If he had found God unfaithful to himself in the word of his threatening, he could not have concluded that he would have been true to the word of his promise, but might reasonably have suspected that he would falsify in that as he had done him in the other. Had his truth failed in the concerns of his justice, it had been of little value in those of his mercy. He might be as careless of the honour of the one as of that of the other. If a man fail of his word in one thing, there is little reason to believe him in another. The righteousness of God would as little have engaged him to fulfil his promise, as it did engage him to fulfil his threatening. God would have declared himself by such an act, not willing to be believed, not worthy to be trusted, feared, loved, because regardless of his truth and righteousness. And by the same reason that he denied himself fit to be trusted, he would deny himself to be a God, because he would thereby have acknowledged a weakness incompatible to the nature of the Deity. How could any trust him who had denied himself, by restoring a life to him, without righteousness and truth on his part ? It had rather been an encouragement to them to disown him to be any fit object for their confidence, since the great ground of trust among men is their faithfulness to their word. Upon the supposition of God's restoring the creature, the doing it by the intervention of a satisfaction was very necessary to fix the creature's confidence in God ; for when he sees God so righteous and true that he will not do anything against the rules of his truth and justice, he hath the more ground to believe God after a satisfaction made, that he will preserve the honour of his wisdom in approving and accepting that satisfaction, and his truth in promising, declared upon it.

(2.) Had God violated his word, he had justified the devil in his argument for man's rebellion. The devil's argument is a plain contradiction to God's threatening. God affirms the certainty of death, the devil affirms the certainty of life : Gen. iii. 4, ' Ye shall not surely die.' Had no punishment been inflicted, the devil had not been a liar from the beginning. God would have honoured the tempter, and justified the charge he brought against him, and owned the envy the devil accused him of, and thereby have rendered the devil the fittest object for love and trust. As the devil charged God with a lie, so, had no punishment been inflicted, God would have condemned himself, and declared Satan, instead of a lying tempter, to be the truest counseller. He had exposed himself to contempt, and advanced the credit of his enemy, and so set up the devil as a God instead of himself. It concerned God, therefore, to manifest himself true, and the devil a liar ; and acquaint the world that not himself, but the evil spirit, was their deceiver, and that he meant as he spake.

(3.) Suppose God might have altered his word, yet would it consist with his wisdom to do it at that time ? It was the first word of threatening that ever went out of his lips to man ; and had he wholly dispensed with it, after he had fenced his precept with such a penalty, and seen such a contradiction in his new created subject to his truth, authority, and righteousness, such a daring contempt of his rich and manifested goodness, he had emboldened the apostate creature in his sin, and encouraged him to a fresh rebellion as soon as ever he had been set right again by an infinite mercy, without any mark of his justice. Men would have thought God had either been mistaken in the reason of his threatening, and had settled a penalty too great for the offence, or had wanted power to maintain his authority in inflicting the due punishment, had he indulged man in this sin. What influence could any of his precepts have had upon the souls of men, if he had so lightly passed by the transgression of his law ? Would he not have been less secured in the rights of his authority for the future, than he had been for the time past ? Would not man have been encouraged to have run the same risk of disobedience, in hopes of an easy pardon, and continued the attempt which he had begun in his first apostasy, to have freed himself from all the orders of the divine law, to have been his own rule ? How could a just sense and awe of

God have been preserved in the minds of men, when they should have thought
God like one of themselves, and as false to his own righteousness as they
had been to his authority? Ps. l. 21.   This certainly would have been the
issue, had man been set up in his former state without inflicting that punishment upon the human nature, which had been so righteously denounced, and
so highly merited, by the disingenuity of man.   Man had been more tempted
by this to sin than he could have been by the devil, and when he had been
brought to an account for his second transgression, he would have excused
himself by God's indulgence to him for the first; and, indeed, God's denial
of his truth in this, wou.ld seem to be a sufficient apology for after offences.

(4.) Therefore God, for the preservation of his truth and righteousness,
accepts of a surety to bear the just punishment for man.   Since God had
enacted, that if man sinned he should die, upon man's apostasy God must
either eternally punish him to preserve his truth and justice, or neglect his
own law, and change it to discover his mercy.   These things were impossible
to the nature of God; he must be true to his nature, and true to his word.
If justice should destroy, what way was there to discover his mercy?   If
mercy should absolutely pardon, without the due punishment, what way was
there to preserve the honour of his truth?   The wisdom of God finds out a
means to preserve the honour of his truth in the punishment, and discover
the glory of his mercy in a pardon, not by changing the sentence against sin,
but the person; and laying that upon his Son, as a surety, which we in our
own persons must have endured, had the rigour of the law been executed
upon us, whereby his righteousness and veracity are preserved by the punishment due to the sinner, and the honour of mercy established by the merit of
our Saviour.   Death was threatened by the law, but there was no exclusion
of a person by that law, that should offer himself to stand in man's stead
under the punishment.   Man had been for ever irrecoverably miserable, had
such a clause been inserted, and would have been without hope as much as
the devils.   And therefore, saith a learned author of our own,* this acceptance of a surety for us was not an abrogation of the law, for then there could
be no execution of the sentence upon wicked men and unbelievers for their
sins against it (where no law is, there is no transgression; and where no
transgression, no just execution); but it was a merciful relaxation or condescension of the sovereign lawgiver, by his infinite goodness and wisdom, to
find out an expedient for the good of the fallen creature, with the preservation of the rights of those divine perfections engaged in the threatening.
God was not prejudiced, or his immutability impaired, by a change of the
person. suffering, as long as the penalty threatened was inflicted.   Though
there was a translation of the penalty, yet there was not a nulling of the
penalty; the person was changed, not the punishment; death was threatened,
death was inflicted.   Death was threatened, not so much to the person of
Adam, as the human nature, whereof he was the head, and regarded the
descendants from him; death was suffered by the human nature, though in
another person; death was threatened to Adam as the root of all in him;
death was suffered by Christ, as the mystical head of all in him by faith, so
that, as in Adam sinning, all sinned that were in his loins as in their root,
Rom. v. 12, 14, 18, so it may be said, that in Christ suffering all believers
suffered, his sufferings being imputed to them by virtue of that union they
have with him.   Besides, God having created the world for the displaying
his divine perfections in Christ, 'for whom all things were created,' Col.
i. 16, had in his eternal counsel decreed the death of Christ as a surety for
man; and this threatening, as well as the creation, being pursuant to this

* Burges of Justificat. part ii. p. 84.

eternal counsel, did not exclude, but rather include, the surety, though it be not expressed.

3. The justice of God made the death of Christ necessary for our redemption. Christ, in his coming, respected the glory of God's righteousness, for he substituted himself as a sin-offering, instead of those insufficient ones under the law : Heb. x. 8, ' Sin-offering thou wouldst not ; lo, I come to do thy will,' *i. e.* the will of the divine justice as well as divine mercy, for in the legal sacrifices both were expressed; justice in the death of the beast, whereby man was taught what he had merited, and mercy in substituting the beast in his room. Christ came to do that in the room of a sin-offering, which the legal sin-offerings were not able to effect. The command of the Father did chiefly respect this satisfaction of justice. It principally required of him the laying down his life, and making his soul an offering for sin, John x. 18. And this it was which his obedience did principally respect, whence it is called an ' obedience to death,' Philip. ii. 8. Death is an act of justice. After the command was given, with the sanction of it, the authority of God in enacting it, and the justice of God in adding the penalty to it, were contemned, and man could not well be reduced to his order without a reparation of the damage done to the authority and justice of God. How could God be the judge of all the earth, doing right, Gen. xviii. 25, had he suffered such a manifest wrong to himself to go unpunished ? Justice had as loud a cry for condemnation, as mercy could have for any stream of compassion. The sanction of the law was irrevocable, unless God had ceased to be immutable in his justice as well as his truth. God can do whatsoever he will, but he can will nothing against his goodness and righteousness.* God had derogated from his own righteousness, if he had not recompensed the sin of man. For as justice requires punishment, so it requires the greatest punishment for the greatest offence. Satisfaction must then be given in such a manner as the justice of God in the law required. It must be then by suffering that death it exacted as due to the crime, which must be done by the person sinning, or some other capable to do it in his stead, and answer the terms of the law, between whom and the sinner there might be such a strait union, as that there might be a mutual imputation of our sins to him, and his sufferings to us. That he might suffer, justice was to impute our sins to him ; that his sufferings might be advantageous, mercy and justice were to impute his sufferings to us.

I shall lay down under this three propositions.

(1.) It seems to be impossible but that justice should flame out against sin. There is the same reason of all God's attributes. It is impossible that the goodness of God should not embrace and kindly entertain an innocent creature, for then he would not be good. It is impossible his mercy in Christ should refuse a penitent believer ; then he would not be compassionate. It is impossible he should look upon sin with a pleasing† countenance ; then he would not be holy. It is impossible that he can be false to his word ; then he could not be true. It is impossible that he should not act wisely in what he doth ; then he would be foolish. Shall we deny the same rights to his justice, that we acknowledge to belong to the other perfections of his nature ? Why should not his justice be as unchangeable and inflexible as his goodness, mercy, truth, and wisdom ? Shall we acknowledge him firm in the rest, and wavering in this ? Justice is as necessary a perfection pertaining to him as the governor of the world, as his wisdom, or any other glory of his nature. Had God acted the part of a just governor, if he had suffered

* Dr Jackson.   † Qu. ' pleased' ?—ED.

those laws to be broken with impunity, whereof he was the guardian as well as the enactor ? Is there not a double reason of punishment accruing to him, both as he is the offended party and the rector of the world ? And what is justice, but a giving to every one his due, reward to whom reward belongs, and punishment to whom punishment is due ? If God had pardoned where punishment was due, it had been an act of mercy, but what had become of his justice ? If God be not just in everything he doth, he is unjust in something, and then doth iniquity, which is utterly impossible for the divine nature ; he neither will nor can do iniquity, Zeph. iii. 5. This is an insepa- rable property of the divine nature. What should his creatures judge of him, if he were utterly careless of vindicating his law, and did totally abstain from evidencing his holiness to his rational creatures ? Is his holiness only to be manifested in precepts, and not demonstrated in punishments ? If his love to righteousness be essential to him, the exercise of that righteous- ness upon suitable objects is necessary. His love of righteousness flows from his nature as righteous : Ps. xi. 7, 'The righteous Lord loveth right- eousness.' It is not only an act of his will, but of his nature ; it is not *so* natural to him as heat is to the fire, that doth necessarily scorch and burn, without any influence of a free and rational principle. There is a liberty of the divine will to order those acts of his justice in convenient seasons. God acts in all things according to his own nature, and cannot act below himself and the rectitude of it. The first foundation of all his actings towards his creatures is in his will. As upon the supposition that God would create man (which it was free for him to do or not to do, and so depended only upon his will), he could not, according to the rectitude of his own nature, but create him upright, otherwise he had denied his own holiness ; so, upon the supposition of man's sinning (the prevention or permission of which de- pended upon his will), he cannot but punish him, because otherwise he had denied his justice, and seemed to have approved of the disorder man had introduced into the world ; and if he had not punished it in the degree it merited, there had seemed to be some abatement of that hatred which was due to the unrighteousness of it ; for so much as a punishment is lessened, so much less doth the detestation of the crime appear. The power of God is not limited hereby ; his own holiness and truth, and the righteousness of his nature, bound him.* Doth any man deny the power of God, in saying he cannot forget his creature ? Would it not be a weakness in him to be ca- pable of lying ? Is it not an imperfection to be capable of doing any thing unjust ? And what would it be but injustice in the Judge of all the earth to let sin go unrevenged ? It is rather an argument of strength and virtue, whereby he cannot renounce the rectitude of his nature.†

[1.] This seems to be a general and a natural notion in the minds of men. God hath settled it as an immutable and eternal law, and engraven it upon the hearts of men, that sin is to be punished with death. What other sen- timent could be expressed by the universal practice of sacrificing beasts, and, in some places, men, for the expiation of their sins, implying thereby a ne- cessity of vindictive justice, that God would not leave sin unpunished, without a compensation from the sinner himself, or some other in his stead ? And therefore they thought the blood of man, the best of the creatures, a means to avert the stroke they had merited from him themselves. What other foundation could there be of all those sacrifices than a conscience of sin, and a settled notion of the vengeance of God ? For that which they principally, or only, respected in those sacrifices, was the justice of God. Upon this account it was probably that the apostle so positively asserts, Rom. i. 32,

* Daillé, de la Resurrect. de Christ, p. 358.　　† Turretin, de Satisfac. p. 300.

that they ' knew that they were worthy of death.' They sufficiently expressed it in subjecting other creatures to the stroke of death in their stead, to pacify the offended deity, acknowledging thereby, that he could not pardon sin without a satisfaction.   This was learned by them in the school of nature, not by the revealed will of God ; or if it were handed to them by tradition from Adam, it had so near an alliance with an universal principle in their own consciences, that it met with no opposition or dispute, the practice of it being almost as universally spread, as the notion of the being of a God, since we scarce find a nation without the sacrificing animals for the appeasing the divinity they adored.

[2.] The holiness of God seems necessarily to infer it.   Since justice is nothing else but the testimony or expression of God's hatred of sin, it must be by consequence unavoidable, unless the sin committed can be wholly undone, which is impossible ; or his justice be appeased some way or other. If God did not punish sin, how could his hatred of it be manifest ?   His creature could not discern any aversion in him from it, without the interposition of vindictive justice ; for that perfection of God's nature, which requires that he should have an implacable detestation of sin, requires also that the sinner, remaining under guilt, should be perpetually punished.   If God cannot but hate all the workers of iniquity (Ps. v. 5, ' Thou hatest all the workers of iniquity '), he cannot but punish them.   The holiness of God is not only voluntary, but by necessity of nature ; were it only an act of his will, he might love iniquity if he pleased, as well as hate it.   How could it be said of him by the prophet, Hab. i. 13, that he is ' of purer eyes than to behold evil, and cannot look upon iniquity,' if his purity had been only from choice, and a determination of the indifferency of his will, and not from his nature? It is not said, He *will not* look on iniquity, *i. e.* with affection, but he *cannot.* God cannot but be holy, and therefore cannot but be just ; because injustice is a part of unholiness.   And upon the holiness of God, Joshua asserts the Israelites' sins in themselves unpardonable: Josh. xxiv. 19, ' He is a holy God, he is a jealous God, he will not forgive your transgressions, nor your sins.'   He is jealous of the honour of his perfections ; his holiness and jealousy stand as bars against forgiveness, without some means for preserving the honour of them ; his holiness and jealousy, whereby his justice and wrath are sometimes expressed, are linked together, and are nothing else but the contrariety in the nature of God, which is infinitely good and righteous, to the nature of sin, which is evil and unrighteous, whereby he is inclined to detest it.*   All hatred is a desire of revenge ; and the stronger the hatred, the more vehement the inclination to revenge.   The loathing of sin being infinite in God, as he is the rector of the world, and so necessary a perfection of his nature, that without it he would not be God ; the inclination to punish it, and thereby highly manifest his hatred of it, necessarily follows that perfection.   A will to punish sin is always included in an hatred of it.   Now, if the hatred of sin be as essential to God as his love to his glory, punishment must follow it.   There is a certain connection between the one and the other. This hatred must necessarily be evidenced by some acts, according to the greatness of the evil.   How shall it be testified, but by punishment ?   If he doth not punish, how shall we certainly know but that it pleaseth him ?   By his bare precept we cannot, if he suffers it to be violated at the pleasure of men without rebuke ; we may then judge him to be a negligent governor, and one that hath no regard to his own command, and cares not whether his creature observes it or no.   Hatred cannot be discovered without some expressions of aversion.   What signs can those be, unless God's denying his

* Amyraut, des Religions, p. 309.

communications to his creature, and a positive inflicting of evil ? If a governor hates a disorder never so much, if he expresseth it not, whereby the offending person may be sensible of his hatred, it is as much as no hatred ; for, *Idem est non esse, et non apparere.* What would all his prohibitions of sin amount to, if he did not punish the commission of it ? He that cannot but prohibit sin, cannot but punish sin. God cannot but prohibit sin, because he cannot but hate it, it being contrary to his holy nature. The commands of God are not bare acts of his will, but of his wisdom and righteousness. If they proceeded from bare will, without any regulation by his wisdom and righteousness, he might command things contrary to the law of nature, and the necessary relation of a creature to himself. So neither is his hatred of sin only a free act of his will, but necessarily results from the rectitude of his nature. If it were only an act of his will, as the creation of the world, he might as well love sin as hate it ; as he might as well have neglected the creation of the world as performed it, and let the several creatures remain in their nothing, as well as have brought them into being. But it flows from the righteousness of his nature (Prov. xv. 9, ' The way of the wicked is an abomination to the Lord '), and consequently so doth his justice, which is an expression of this hatred, otherwise God would be unjust to his own holiness.

(2.) Hence it follows, that this justice must be satisfied before man could be restored. The justice of God was the bar in the way, and must be removed by punishment. Christ could not have brought one son to glory, had he not first been ' made perfect by suffering,' Heb. ii. 10. The wrath of God for the violations of the law, was the flaming sword that guarded paradise from being entered into by guilty man. This was becoming God as the governor of the world, in which capacity he is considered in punishment. It became not God to do anything unjustly or inordinately. It was an intolerable thing that the creature should despoil God of his honour, and withdraw itself from that indispensable subjection it owed to its creator. It became God to restore that order by punishment, which had been broken by sin.

Let us consider,

[1.] Justice had at least an equal plea with mercy. If mercy pleaded for pardon, justice as strongly solicited the punishment of the sinner. The remission of the offence would appear more charitable ; but the vindicating the public laws, and punishing the offence, would appear more righteous. It was not convenient the creature should be utterly ruined as soon as ever God had displayed his power in creating it, nor was it convenient the creature should be emboldened in sin by a free act of pardon, after so high and base an act of disingenuity. What could mercy plead on the behalf of the creature, that justice could not as strongly plead on the behalf of God ? If the ruin of the creature be argued to move compassion, the dishonour of God on the other side would be argued to excite indignation. If the nature of God, as love, 1 John iv. 8, be pleaded by mercy, the nature of God, as righteous and a consuming fire, Heb. xii. 29, would be opposed to it by justice. His mercy would plead, It were not for his honour to let his enemy run away, just after the creation, with the spoil of the best of his works. His justice would reply, It was fit the judge of the world should do right, and be the protector of his righteous law. If his mercy inclines him to will our salvation, justice would not permit him to leave sin unpunished, and his laws trampled in the dust. Had mercy been discovered without preserving the rights of justice, when the whole nature of man fell, God had been but a half governor of the world, and exercised but one part of government.

[2.] Justice seems to have a stronger plea. (1.) The highest right falls on the side of justice. That had been declared and backed by his truth, when mercy was not yet published upon the stage of the creation. The righteous and just nature of God had been signified to man, and his veracity brought in to second it, Gen. ii. 17. No notion of pardoning mercy had yet been imprinted upon the mind of man, or revealed to him; so that God was not so much concerned in honour to shew mercy, which stood single, as I may say, and lay hid in the nature of God, without the appearance of any perfection to back and support it. Had man stood, the veracity of God had stood on the side of his goodness (for we may suppose a promise of life implied, if man continued in obedience, as well as a threatening expressed, if he fell into rebellion). But when men broke the precept, the whole force of God's truth fell on the side of justice. There being not a syllable of pardoning grace uttered in any promise before the sin of man, the truth of God had no part at that time to take with mercy; so that there were greater engagements at that time, from the manifestation of God's nature, for the making good his justice, than for the demonstration of his mercy.

(2.) Mercy could principally plead the good of the creature, justice principally insisted on the honour of God. Mercy might solicit the liberty of God's will, but justice might strongly challenge the holiness and rectitude of God's nature to support it. The creature was fallen under the hatred of God and penalty of the law, and rendered itself an unfit object of love by its rebellion and filthiness.

(3.) Besides, the wits and consciences of men cannot frame so many arguments for the necessity of mercy, in regard of God, as for the necessity of his justice. Mercy is wholly a free act, but justice is a debt due to a sinful creature. The necessity of mercy to a fallen creature, in regard of God, cannot possibly be asserted with any reason. For it would then be asserted on the behalf of devils more than men. I say, the necessity, for perhaps something may be said for the congruity of God's shewing mercy to man rather than to devils. Justice respects merit caused by the righteousness or unrighteousness of men,* according to which God immutably carries himself in rewarding or punishing of them, and never doth reward or punish any but according to their merit; but the mercy of God doth not at all respect merit, or any work done by man, but is busied wholly in giving freely, and offering graciously to man those things he hath not deserved.

(4.) Again, justice had stronger arguments from the rectitude of God's nature. Justice might argue, If God did righteously judge sinners to everlasting death, then if he had not judged them to everlasting death, he had done unjustly, being unmindful of the rectitude of his own nature. And if he should not now, after sin, inflict eternal death, but wholly lay aside his threatening, he would do unjustly; for those being contrary acts, one of them must needs be unjust. Who could call that a righteous government, wherein laws should be made with the greatest wisdom, and be broken with the greatest impunity?

(5.) Again, consider, though mercy be essential to God, yet mercy must not be unjustly exercised. The fallen creature, indeed, was an object of both : as *miserable*, he was an object of mercy ; as *criminal*, he was an object of justice. But being first criminal before he was miserable, he was first the object of justice by his crime, before he was an object of mercy by his misery. Had he been miserable without being culpable (which was impossible, in regard of the goodness of God), he had then been an object of com-

---

* Zarnov. de satisfact. Christi, part i. cap. ii.

passion only. But falling under justice first, it was not fit mercy should wholly despoil justice of its rights.

(6.) Again. Man, as miserable by the fall, is not the object of mercy. For what mercy could pardon an obstinate rebel? And how could man have been otherwise, without some supernatural operation upon him? Mercy could not challenge any footing to exercise itself about man, till he had confessed and bewailed his crime, and been sensible, not only of his misery, but of his offence. It is not honourable for God to exercise mercy upon those that continue in their enmity; this seems to be clearly against the rectitude of the divine nature; this had been a favouring of the crime as well as the criminal. Had he been sensible of and sorrowful for his misery, without a true grief for his offence, this had been an act of love to himself, but had had in it nothing of a true affection to God. After man had contracted in his nature an enmity against God, how could he have acquired a true repentance flowing from an affection to God? Repentance for a fault against a prince, and enmity against a prince, are inconsistent. How should man have attained this quality of himself, any more than the devils have done, of whose repentance we read not one syllable in the Scripture, who are left to those habits of malice and aversion from God, which they had superinduced upon themselves? And if devils, who were creatures of greater understanding, and more sensible of their misery, because they fell from a greater happiness than man, were morally impotent to this, can we think that man had a stronger bias in his will after the revolt from God, to return again to God? Besides, repentance is made a gift of God, 2 Tim. ii. 25; and the Spirit that gives repentance, is a fruit of Christ's death; and the repentance itself is made a fruit of Christ's exaltation, due to him upon his death, Acts v. 32. To strengthen this, it may be considered that when God came to examine Adam, as a judge, about his crime, there is not a syllable that savours of any true repentance issues from him, Gen. iii. 8–10, &c., whatsoever he might exercise after the promulgation of the gospel-promise.

[3.] Consider, if there had not been a tempering of these two perfections towards man, one of them had remained undiscovered to the world. Justice only could have appeared in the creature's suffering, mercy only could have appeared in the creature's restoration. Mercy could not have been discovered by the condemnation of the creature, nor justice by the mere salvation of the creature. Had there been no punishment, or a light one below the demerit of the creature, there had been no demonstration of the highest glory of his holiness in the hatred of sin, or of the highest glory of his justice in the punishment of sin. Had the punishment due to the creature been inflicted upon him, the creature had been utterly destroyed, and mercy had been for ever obscured; and had mercy solely acted about the creature, justice had been wronged. Justice therefore must be one way or other righted, that the streams of his grace might flow out to man, since, after man's fall, justice had stopped all commerce of God with man, because sin had rendered him unfit for the communications of God. As the nature of compassion must be satisfied in acting about a miserable creature, and the love God bore to man as his creature manifested; so the nature of justice must be satisfied for the injury done, and the hatred of God to man as a sinner discovered. And this must be satisfied either by the creature's bearing the punishment, or compensating the injury, for that properly is satisfaction. God's justice could not have come off with honour without it; for since he was engaged by his word to have sin punished, would not God have been unjust had he laid by all consideration of his justice and holiness in this case? Had justice been glorified upon the person of the sinner, mercy would have lost the manifestation of itself, and have had no objects to exercise itself about; had mercy been glorified in bringing man to a happy state, without any punishment, after so base a breach of his law, where had been the demonstration of the unchangeable holiness of God, and the exactness of his justice? God therefore appointed a Mediator, in whom he might act as a righteous judge for the punishment of sin, according to his law, that his dreadful majesty might be more feared; and a tender father according to the necessity of his creatures, that his love might be commended, as a wise governor tempering both together. And therefore God, foreseeing the fall of man, elected some to eternal glory, but in Christ as the means, Eph. i. 4, not as the meritorious cause of election, but as the means and foundation of the execution of it, that the glory of his grace might issue out in the preservation of the rights of his justice, maintained by the blood of his Son, in whom we have redemption, ver. 6, 7, and without this way we cannot see how the glory of God had been preserved. God had made the world for his glory, and the communication of his goodness. After the world was polluted and disordered by sin, the justice of God, by annexing such a penalty to the law, stood as a bar in the way of any kindness to the creature, unless some way might be found out to preserve the honour of that justice. Shall God in a moment lose all the glory of his creation? Did he make the creatures, whose fall he did foresee, only to punish and damn them; and that the glory of his other perfections, save that of his justice and holiness, should be spoiled by it? His glory therefore must be preserved; that could not be if the glory of his justice or mercy were wholly lost. To preserve it, therefore, Christ is substituted in our room, and the Captain of salvation made perfect through sufferings, which was most becoming God, as he was Lord of all, and his glory the end of all, Heb. ii. 10. His love not permitting him to leave the world under the curse, nor his justice to leave sin without punishment, both those necessities are provided for by the wisdom of God; a wonderful temperament wrought, whereby sin is punished in the surety, and impunity secured to the believing sinner.*

[4.] This satisfaction must be by death, because death was threatened. Since it was the judgment of God that sin was worthy of death, God had contradicted his own judgment and holy wisdom, if he had remitted it without death, or punished it with less than death. God established our propitiation in the blood of Christ, 'to declare his justice,' Rom. iii. 25.† If justice had required less than death, it had been unjust to have demanded so much as death, for then he had demanded more than was due. Sin could not be expiated by a less punishment than it had merited, but that was death. Besides, the love of God to his Son would not have permitted him to expose him to a cursed and cruel death, merely to shew his justice implacable, had it not really been in itself implacable without it, as the most transcendent means to discover the incomprehensible purity of his nature. Certainly, that God who would not do the least injustice to the meanest of his creatures, would not have delivered up his Son to so shameful a death, and took so many counsels about it, and made it the principal work of his wisdom in all ages of the world, to order all things for the execution of it, if justice could have been contented with less than death, and remission of sin could have been granted by the pure mercy and bounty of God, at least after the threatening. Could justice have been satisfied at a lower rate than death, the Father would have answered the request of his Son when he prayed so earnestly that this cup might pass from him; nor would death have been exacted of him, if a drop of his blood had been a sufficient payment to the demands

* Daillé sur iii. Jean, p. 330. † εἰς ἔνδειξιν, for a demonstration of his justice.

of justice. The suffering death had been superfluous, and the imposing death upon him had been an unrighteousness in God; and his giving himself up to death, without any necessity, had been an injustice to himself. Could a few drops of blood have satisfied justice, it might have been satisfied without any blood at all, as well as with a punishment beneath what the law demanded. The effusion of one drop of blood cannot pass for a punishment of sin. when death for it was required by the law, so that it could be no less than death.

Prop. 3. None could satisfy the justice of God but the Son of God incarnate.

[1.] Let us remove those things that might be supposed capable to do it. Nether could man do it for himself, nor any intellectual or rational creature do it for him, nor any observances of God's institutions do it, so that it must necessarily fall upon some one above the rank of creatures. Some divine person only was capable to undertake it and effect it. There is a necessity of satisfaction to the law, both by paying obedience to every tittle of it, and by enduring the penalty for the transgression of it. God stands so much upon the honour of his law, that the heavens shall be folded up, and the earth shaken out of its place, before one point of the law shall be disregarded, Mat. v. 18. Some one therefore must repair the breach made upon it, and restore the honour of it. Let us see if anything else could.

(1.) Man was unable to do it for himself. It must be done either by active or passive obedience, by doing or suffering; but was man capable of either as a full compensation to God? Man by sin fell in his person, and with all that he had, under the curse of the law, Gal. iii. 10; and what was under the curse, and by sin was forfeited, could not remove the curse. Man may be considered as a sinful creature or a gracious creature. A sinful creature cannot satisfy; for being a sinner in that satisfaction, he doth offend the holiness of God, and heap new provocations before the eyes of his justice instead of pacifying it. A gracious creature cannot, for that supposeth satisfaction first, whereby justice is moved to take away the bar that locks up the treasures of grace from being dispensed to man. A man might be gracious after a satisfaction, but not before; besides, grace is finite, for whatsoever is in a finite creature is finite; its effects therefore cannot be of an infinite value.

(1.) Man could not effect it by offering something to God, or by doing something equivalent to the offence.

1. Man had nothing to give. What was there he could call his own, since he was a creature, especially since as an offender he had forfeited what was his by right of creation? Had man the world to give? How came he by it? Was it created by him or for him? If not by him, it was none of his own; he was but a steward to manage all for the use of his Lord and true proprietor. Can a steward recompense his lord for the wrong done to his honour, by offering to his master those goods which are his own already, and which the steward was only entrusted with? The world was none of man's to give; he never had it as an absolute lord by right of an independent propriety, nor was it possible he should, since he was not either the creator or preserver of it; and neither man, nor any other creature in the world, could possibly be brought into a state independent on God, so that man held as a feudatory *in capite* of God. But suppose it had been his own, he had forfeited all by his rebellion; for his sake, for his sin, the earth was cursed by the sovereign Lord of it, Gen. iii. 17; and a thing cursed in all the parts of it could not be fit for an oblation to the divine Majesty.

2. Nor could his repentance be a compensation. Bare grief for an offence

is not a compensation for an injury done to man, much less for an affront of
so high a nature offered to God. But we find no such thing in man at the
time wherein he fell from the top of his felicity to the gulf of misery. If he
who had a sense of the happy state he had lost, and the miserable condition
he had contracted, was more for excuses than relentings, how can a penitent
posture be found by nature in any of his descendants? Gen. iii. 9–13. If
there were any blushes in him, they were occasioned more by the discovery
of his crime than by the sense of the crime itself; and he was troubled more
at his loss than at his offence, and so might relent that he was miserable,
not that he was criminal; and so it was a repentance as it respected himself,
not as it respected the honour of his Lord; and such a repentance is to be
found in hell, but is unable to break those chains wherein they are held.
How should man come by a repentance? Can he break himself into a true
contrition? What stone was ever heard to melt itself? Is not captive man
fond of his sin, in love with his chains? And how can he by nature attain
that which is so contrary to what he is by nature mightily delighted with?
The least spark of grace is above the power of corrupted nature. How should
man, then, come by this repentance? Must it not be a melting spark from
heaven lighting upon his soul, that must produce so kindly a work in a forsaken creature? Would it have consisted with the wisdom of divine justice
to seize upon the forfeiture, to withdraw from man supernatural grace, and
presently to restore it without any regard to the vindication of the honour of
that justice? Besides, suppose man had been able to repent of himself, and
had actually performed a repentance of the right stamp, what would this have
signified, since no such thing was required as the condition the righteousness of God exacted in the law? That demanded not repentance, because
it gave not liberty to any crime. It challenged an exact and perfect obedience,
complete in all circumstances, of man in his uprightness; and, in case of
failure, left man to the severity of the penalty he had incurred   Not a drop
of repentance was allowed as any part of legal obedience. That was introduced upon a change of the dispensation from legal to evangelical. 'The
law is not of faith,' and as little of repentance, 'but the man that doth them
shall live in them,' Gal. iii. 12. Besides, if repentance and faith in the
mercy of God could have razed out the sin of Adam, and broken in pieces
the chains of eternal death, could we think that God should be at the expense
of the blood of the promised seed? What need had there been of a sacrifice
to appease God, if he had been already appeased by the relentings of man?
What a vanity had that been, to go about the taking away that which the
faith and repentance of Adam had already removed!* The wisdom of God
would not do anything useless and in vain. Faith and repentance could
never change the nature of God's righteousness, but must first suppose some
satisfaction made to justice, and then step in as conditions; and the one as
an instrument apprehending and applying mercy obtained by some other
means, not the efficient or meritorious cause, no more than the looking upon
the brazen serpent was the efficient or meritorious cause of the cure, but only
the means. But how can we think man after his fall should have either faith
in the mercy of God, or repentance, which flows from a sense of mercy, when
no mercy had been revealed to him? He found nothing of it in the law;
and though he might apprehend such a perfection in God by the consideration of his own nature, yet since he had never seen any miserable object to
draw out such a perfection, it is a question whether he knew any such quality
to be in himself or no, and therefore could not conclude any such perfection
to be in God, since there was not the least revelation of it, and therefore could

* Zarnov. de Satisfact. part i. cap. iv. pp. 14, 15.

have no footing for any such exercise of faith and repentance till the discovery of mercy in the promised seed.

3. Nor could any after obedience to the law be a compensation for the offence. For,

(1.) Man had not power of himself after his fall to obey. He had by his revolt lost that original righteousness which enabled him to a conformity to the law: Gen. iii. 10, ' I was afraid, because I was naked.' His corporeal nakedness could be no more the cause of fear after, than it was before, his sin ; but he was naked, *i. e.* stripped of the image of God, and his primitive integrity. Man cannot now do any work commensurate to the precepts of the law. In everything he comes short of his duty; and therefore, being defective in what he ought to do by the law of creation, cannot satisfy for the injury done to God in the state of corruption : ' How shall a man be just with God ? If he will contend with him, he cannot answer him one of a thousand,' Job ix. 2, 3. God requires an obedience to the law, not according to our measure, but according to his own righteousness, which is perfect; and this no sinful creature can arise to of himself. If any man were able to offer God a spotless obedience, free from any defect the law could find in it ; by whose strength would he do it ? Not by his own; for since he was a sinner, he hath been without strength. To be *sinners*, and to be *without strength*, are one and the same, Rom. v. 6, 8. From whom, then, should he have this strength ? From the Creator ? How can he then satisfy God by that which is God's already ? It is as if when a man had wronged a prince, he should satisfy him for the injury by a sum taken out of the prince's exchequer. Indeed, man is not willing to obey any command of God ; there is nothing in his nature but an enmity against God and his law, Rom. viii. 7, and therefore no complete will to give God any satisfaction, or pay him any obedience. The will is naturally enslaved to sin, and under the power of vicious habits, sins always, never obeys perfectly, but in the moment of a material obedience offends God, comes short of what the law requires. Till the will of man be changed, he cannot be willing with a complete will to obey God; and the will cannot be changed before a satisfaction be made, because it is not reasonable that the punishment of sin, which was a spiritual as well as eternal death, and consisted in leaving the soul under the power of those ill habits it had contracted, which are indeed the death of the soul, as diseases are the death of the body, should be taken off till some satisfaction were made. Man can no more free himself from this spiritual death, than he can free himself from the death of the body ; and we have no reason to think God would do it before a satisfaction, for then the law he had enacted would be wronged by himself. Well, then, man hath not power to obey God: Job xiv. 4, ' Who can bring a clean thing out of an unclean ? not one ;' *i. e.* saith Cocceius, Who can change an unclean thing into a clean ? Is there not one ? Yea, and but one ; Christ only can do it.

(2.) Supposing man had power to obey the law, and that perfectly, yet this was due to God before the sin of man, and therefore cannot be a compensation for the sin of man. After obedience will not make amends for past crimes ; for obedience is a debt due of itself, and what is a debt of itself cannot be a compensation for another. What is a compensation, must be something that doth not fall under the notion or relation of a debt due before, but contracted by the injury done. Obedience was due from man if he had not sinned, and therefore is a debt as much due after sin as before it ; but a new debt cannot be satisfied by paying an old. As suppose you owe a man money upon a bond, and also abuse him in his reputation, or some other concern ; is there not a new debt contracted upon that trespass, a debt of reparation of him in what you have wronged him? The paying him the money you owe him upon bond, is not an amends for the injury you did him otherwise. They both in law fall under a different consideration. Or when a man rebels against a prince of whom he holds some land, will the payment of his quit-rent be satisfactory for the crime of his rebellion? So obedience to the law in our whole course was a debt upon us by our creation; and this hath relation to the preceptive part of the law, and to God as a sovereign: but upon sin a new debt of punishment was contracted, and the penalty of the law was to be satisfied by suffering, as well as the precepts of the law satisfied by observing them. And this was a debt relating to the justice of God, as well as the other to the sovereignty of God. Now, how can it be imagined that man, by paying the debt he was obliged to before, should satisfy the debt he hath newly contracted? The debts are different: the one is a debt of observance, the other a debt of suffering, and contracted in two different states; the debt of obedience in the state of creation, the debt of suffering in the state of corruption; so that the payment of what was due from us as creatures, cannot satisfy for what was due from us as criminals. All satisfaction is to be made in some way to which a person was not obliged before the offence was committed; as men wronged in their honour, are satisfied by some acts not due to them before they were injured. So that all men taken together, yea, the creatures of ten thousand worlds, cannot, by obedience to the preceptive part of the law, satisfy for one transgression of it; because, whatsoever they can do, is a debt due from themselves before. When men fell from God, and entered into league with the devil, they laid themselves at the foot of God's righteous wrath, and sunk themselves into the desert of eternal death, and so stood in another relation to God than as subjects; and God might require a reparation for the past disobedience, and security for obedience for the future; unless man could perform this, he must lie bound in chains of darkness. What compensation could man make for what was past, or what security could he give for time to come? Some other, therefore, must interpose, whose suretyship God would accept; who could give a satisfaction to God, as pleasing to him as sin had been displeasing, and offer to God what was not due to him before; who was able to perform what he undertook, and whose security for what was due for the future, might be esteemed valid; and therefore it must be some divine person, that was not bound in his own nature to those terms of obedience, which were necessary to this satisfaction.

(3.) Supposing man had power after his fall to obey, and that obedience were not due before, yet could not his obedience be compensatory for the injury by sin. Because being a finite creature, whatsoever obedience he could pay could not be infinite, and so not proportioned to an infinite majesty. Since the sin of man is infinite, in regard of the person offended, who is an infinite and eternal Being, and thereby debased below the meanest of his creatures, in the reflection that every sin casts upon him, as being not worthy to be beloved and obeyed; and that which doth satisfy must be as great as the demerit of the crime (for it must be proportionable to the disgrace and damage accruing to God by sin); this a finite creature cannot do: for though obedience is an honour paid to an infinite person, as well as sin a contempt of an infinite person, yet the offence is always aggravated by the person offended, as an injury done to a prince is by the dignity of his person and the greatness of his authority; but the satisfaction is measured from the capacity of the subject offending, which is finite, and not commensurate to the greatness of a wronged God. Nor can our obedience and holiness be counted infinite, because they are the fruits of an infinite Spirit in us ;* for by the same reason all creatures should be accounted infinite, because they are the works of an infinite power. The Spirit infuseth the habits of obedience and holiness, and excites them ; but the creature, and not the Spirit, exerciseth them, the soul doth obey and believe, &c., so that though they are the Spirit's *efficiently*, yet they are the creature's *subjectively*. Besides, though the Spirit dwells in believers, yet he is not hypostatically united to them, as the divine nature of the second person was to the human. The Holy Ghost and the soul do not make one person ; if so, the acts of the new creature would be subjectively infinite, as the mediatory acts of Christ were, because his person, which was the subject of them, was infinite. So that our obedience cannot be infinite ; and, indeed, the best obedience any mere creature is able to pay, cannot be so honourable to God as sin is debasing, because by our obedience we honour him according to his nature, as far as our capacity reacheth, and give him no more than his due, and acknowledge him as he is the most excellent Being, the most rightful sovereign ; but in sin we prefer every thing before him, do what we can to ungod him, fight against his sovereignty, snarl at his holiness, dare his justice, and render him so vile, as if he were not fit to be ranked above, or with any of his creatures in our hearts ; and what rate of obedience is able to render God a satisfaction for so great a contempt and audaciousness ? All the obedience a subject can pay to a prince, can never be esteemed in value equal to the contempt, which an endeavour to destroy his person, and pull down his statues, and trample his picture in the dirt, doth cast upon him. Sin is of a higher order in the rank of evils, than the works of righteousness are in the rank of good.†

2. Nor could man give a full satisfaction by suffering, so as to obtain a restoration to happiness. He is as unable to suffer out his restoration, as he is to work it out. His sufferings would be as finite, in regard of the subject, as his obedience ; but the glory he had stained, and the justice he had wronged, were the glory of an infinite God ; and the sufferings of a finite creature, though lengthened out to eternity, could not be a compensation to an infinite glory disgraced by sin. Alas ! the wrath of an incensed God is too fierce and heavy for the strength of a feeble man to break through. But suppose it were possible for a man that had committed but one crime against God, and afterwards repented of it, and retained no more affection to that sin or any other, by suffering torments for some millions of years, to make a compensation for that one sin ; yet how is it possible for men, whose natures are depraved, and have nothing of a divine purity in them, to satisfy by suffering, since they suffer, not only for sin, but in a sinful state, and are increasing their sins while they are paying their satisfactions. No suffering of any that retain their rebellious nature can be a satisfaction to the majesty of God, so as to free such a creature from suffering, while that nature remains, and he loves that sin for which he is punished, though he hath not opportunity to commit it. Besides, since man by nature is ' enmity against God,' Rom. viii. 7, God's judicial power would not render him amiable to the sinner, nor suffering inspire him with a love to his judge ; if he should therefore suffer multitudes of years, without any certain hope of recovery, could he be without a hatred of God ? So, then, all the time he would be suffering he would be highly sinning ; and still sinning would increase the debt of suffering instead of diminishing it. A creature, while a creature, in every state is bound to love God ; but no fallen creature can do it without a change of nature. Besides, if a man be not able to satisfy by suffering for one sin, how is he able to satisfy for numberless ? Every

* Polhill of the Decrees, p. 188.   † Lessius.

new sin increaseth our obnoxiousness to God, both in its own nature, and as it is a virtual approbation of all former sins, at least of the same kind; now he that cannot pay a farthing, or a shilling, or make satisfaction for a small sum, is not able to make a recompence for millions. And though a man might begin his satisfaction by suffering, where would he end? Since he cannot give one infinite in value, he must give one infinite in time, and then he would be always paying, and never coming to a period of payment; for when you have in your thoughts run along the line of eternity, you would have further to go than you have gone; for in looking back you may find a beginning, but in looking forward you will never find an end; the further you look, still more remains to come than is past.

To conclude this. The church of old saw her utter inability any way to make a propitiation for sin but by God himself: Ps. lxv. 3, 'Iniquities prevail against me; as for our transgressions, thou shalt purge them away,' תכפרם. Our iniquities are too strong for us, we cannot make an atonement for them; but thou shalt be the Messiah, thou shalt propitiate by the Messiah, who is typified by the legal propitiatory, and therefore the same name is given to Christ: Rom. iii. 25, 'a propitiation,' or the propitiatory for our sins. Since the first age of the world to this day, wherein so many ages are run out, there is not one man to be found that ever was his own ransomer, or paid a price for his own redemption.

(2.) No creature is able to do it for us. All creatures are nothing in their original; there could be then nothing of dignity in a mere creature to answer the dignity of the person offended. The plaster would be too narrow for the wound. The whole creation of creatures was of a finite goodness, and nothing to the honour due to so great a majesty. If a creature could satisfy, it could not be by his own strength, but by a great deal of grace conferred upon him, so that he had not paid what was his own to God, but what was God's own already. No creature but must be sustained by the grace of God, that he may not fall into utter ruin while he is satisfying. Angels themselves could not do it but by grace; and the more any creature should do by the grace of God, the more he would be obliged by God, and the less compensate him. Again, it must be one creature, or a multitude of creatures. How one mere creature could satisfy for a numberless number of men, every one of them foully polluted, cannot well be conceived by common reason. One creature can only be supposed to be a sufficient ransom for one of the same kind. There could not be a dignity in any creature to answer the dignity and equal the value of all mankind. If a multitude of creatures were necessary, there must be as many creatures satisfying as were creatures sinning; so God would lose one species of creature to restore another, or an equal number of creatures to them that were redeemed. But indeed no creature could satisfy if the wrong was infinite; and by the rights of justice the satisfaction is to be proportioned to the greatness of the injury and the majesty of the person injured. Those being infinite, no creature was able to manage this affair and bring it to a happy period, because no creature but is finite, and cannot be otherwise than finite, infiniteness being the incommunicable property of the Deity; therefore neither man nor any angel was able to effect it.

1. Not man. This is clear. All men were sunk into the gulf of misery, and he that was unable to redeem himself, could not pretend to an ability to redeem another: Ps. xlvii. 7, 'None of them can by any means redeem his brother, nor give to God a ransom for him.' All that a man hath is not of so much worth as the soul of man; so that no man can pay a sufficient price for the redemption of his captive brother. All human nature could not have shewn a valuable sacrifice. Consider him as man, he is worse than

nothing and vanity. How shall God have a satisfaction for an unexpressible evil, from that which is worse than nothing? Can the drop of a bucket repair an infinite damage? But consider him in a state of rupture with God, and you find him, by his uncleanness, much more unfit for so great a task. It had been too much a debasing the majesty of God, had one mere man been sacrificed for others as a sufficient price of redemption, as if he had been equal in dignity to the offended majesty of God. And what advantage could it have been to the rest of mankind, since the sacrifice would be as corrupt and unclean as those that needed it? No such thing as an innocent mere man can be found, since Adam's revolt, in all those ages which have run out since; all were sunk into the common gulf, all come short of the glory of God, Rom. iii. 23. All were destitute of the image of God, and become filthy; every one without exception, Ps. xiv. 8. And could the sacrifice of rebels redeem rebellious creatures? Could anything morally impure content God, when a maimed beast was not thought fit for his altar? A polluted sacrifice, overgrown with uncleanness and corrupt imaginations, would rather have provoked than pacified him. But suppose an innocent man could be found out, stored with all the holiness of men and angels; yet how can we conceive that the holiness of that man should please God, as much as the sin of Adam displeased him? Such a person in his obedience would only have given God his due; whereas by sin, man robbed God of his holiness, more dear than many worlds, and unconceivable numbers of men and angels.

2. Nor could angels be a sacrifice for us; because they were not of the same nature with the offending person. And the apostle intimates that the redemption is to be made in the same nature that transgressed, when he excludes the fallen angels from the happiness of redemption, because Christ took not upon him the angelical nature, Heb. ii. 17. Though the angels were innocent, yet they were creatures and finite; nor were they the offending nature. And though they transcend man, both in the dignity and holiness of their nature, yet they come infinitely short of the dignity of God, who was injured. They are not pure in his sight, with such a purity as is commensurate with the infinite holiness of their Creator: Job iv. 18, 'He chargeth his angels with folly.' They would fall and vanish from their glory if they were not supported by the grace of God. By angels is not meant prophets, messengers God sends to men; for he speaks of persons distinct from them that dwell in houses of clay: but the prophets were of this latter number. And that he means the good angels is evident, by giving them the title of his angels, his servants, as peculiarly belonging to his service. He proves man not to be just and pure in God's sight, à majori, because he chargeth the angels with folly. There had been nothing in the argument to say, man is not more pure than his Maker, because the devils are not. Angels were creatures, and therefore had not a holiness adequate to the holiness of God. What proportion was there between a finite, mutable holiness, and that which is immutable? Though angels were innocent, yet in their own nature they might cease to be so. They had not strength enough to bear and break through an infinite wrath; they could not satisfy, so as to effect redemption, till their satisfaction had been completed, which could not have been even in an endless eternity. What is finite in nature, can never become infinite in nature; one cannot pass into another. If one sunk a number of them into hell, how could one angel, or a number of them, answer for the multitude of sins charged upon the world? So great also is the malignity of sin, and so great an injury to the majesty of God, that it cannot be compensated by all the services and sufferings of saints and angels. But suppose angels had

been capable to be sacrifices for us, and so our redeemers, it had not been agreeable to the wisdom of God to confer that honour upon a creature, to be the redeemer of souls, which would mount a step higher than the bare title of creator, and thereby glorify a creature above himself.

To conclude this. The most excellent satisfaction and sacrifice becomes the dignity of an injured God, and such a satisfaction, that there cannot be imagined a greater by a creature ; but whatsoever satisfaction can be given by men or angels, is not so great as may be imagined and apprehended by a creature ; for such an one may be imagined as may proceed absolutely holy from the person offering, and be attended with an immutable innocence, without any possibility of a charge of folly, which is a condition above a created state. God was made lower than any creature by sin; and therefore such a satisfaction was suitable, as might render God infinitely higher than any creature, and demonstrate the highest and most glorious perfections of his nature. This was wrought by the death of the Son of God, and could not have been evidenced in that height by the death of any creature.

3. Ceremonial sacrifices, under the law, could not be sufficient for this affair. The Jews, indeed, did rest upon them ; thought that, if not by their own virtue, yet by the virtue of God's institution, they purged away their sin, Isa. i. 13, 14. But,

[1.] This was against common reason. Common reason would conclude, that the sin of a soul could never be expiated by the blood of a beast, and that a nature so inferior could not be a compensation for the crime of a nature so much superior to it. The prophet spake but the true reason of mankind, when he asserted, that the Lord would not be pleased with thousands of rams, or ten thousands of rivers of oil, nor the first-born of the body be a satisfaction for the sin of the soul, Micah vi. 6, 7. The first-born and fruit of a man's own body was too low, much more the first-born of a beast. The soul was the principal in sin, and what fitness had a corporeal blood to make amends for the crime of a spiritual nature ? A rational sacrifice only was fit to be an atonement for the sin of a rational being. The brutish nature was not the human, there was no agreement between the nature of man and that of a bullock. The transgressing nature was to suffer, the soul that sins, that shall die, Ezek. xviii. A beast had no communion in nature with man, whereby it might respect the sinner, nor any worth in itself, whereby it might respect God, nor any willingness or intention for such an end. Can any think sin so light, as to be expiated by such pitiful mean blood ? The remedy ought to be suited to the disease and the party afflicted.* The sin consisted in rebellion and hatred of God ; the remedy then must consist in perfect righteousness, exact obedience, and intense love to God ; all which beasts were uncapable of. A man must put off his own reason, and have very debasing apprehensions of the perfections of God, if he thinks infinite holiness scorned, infinite justice provoked, infinite glory rifled, can put up all upon the offering brutish blood, that knows not why and to what end it is offered. It was too base a thing to be thought to bear a proportion to an infinite offended nature. What should the flesh and blood of goats signify to a spiritual nature, with which it had no agreement ? Ps. l. 13. It was not agreeable to the wisdom of God. A wise earthly lawgiver would not think the life of a beast to be a fit recompence for the capital crime of a malefactor. The wisdom of God knew that they were unproportioned to the end of an expiatory sacrifice. And was it not inconsistent with this perfection, for God to be contented with so vile a thing, after such terrible thunderings from mount Sinai, and giving the law with so much solemnity ? What

* Turretin. de Satisfact., pp. 240, 241.

a ridiculous thing would all that ado appear to be, if a beast's blood were
powerful enough to quench the force of those flames, and put to silence the
thunders of the divine fury, if the transgression of any part of it might be
washed away by so cheap an offering ?   Besides, the same wisdom surely
would not let man, the most excellent creature, be beholden to brutes for
the merit of righteousness, nor could they be agreeable to the justice of God
in the law, which required the death of the party offending.   If all the
beasts of Lebanon were sacrificed, and the cedars cut down for wood for the
burnt-offerings, all could not be a sweet-smelling savour before God.   There
is an infinite disproportion between this kind of satisfaction and the divine
majesty.   With God only is plenteous redemption, Ps. cxxx. 7, 8 ; with God,
not in the blood of beasts, but in the true sacrifice, and ransomer ; yet with
God, and not then manifested to the world.

[2.] The repetition of those sacrifices shewed their imperfection and
insufficiency.   It is from this head the apostle argues their weakness and
impossibility to take away sin, Heb. x. 1-4.   There was after them a remembrance of sin ; the offerer was not so bettered by them, but still he had need
of new ones to keep him right with God.   Had any thing been perfected by
them, they had ceased, only the new application of an old sacrifice had been
required ; but there was no ground for an after application of a past sacrifice
upon new sins, because the efficacy of the blood ceased as soon as it was
shed and sprinkled, so that multitudes of them could not constitute an inexhaustible treasure of reconciliation and merit.   The variety of them manifested that there was nothing firm in them.   As many medicines shew their
own inefficacy, so the many sacrifices and purifications did evidence that a
firm and efficacious propitiation was to be sought elsewhere.   If the great
annual sacrifice, the most solemn one in that whole institution (of which
you may read, Levit. xvi. 29, xxiii. 27), could not effect it, much less could
sacrifices of a lower dignity.   It is from the repetition of this great sacrifice
Paul argues the insufficiency of it.   This was the most solemn sacrifice,
because it was offered by the high priest himself, and for all the people, and
the blood sprinkled in the holy of holies.   A less sacrifice could not have a
larger virtue than the greatest, yet the repetition of this shewed its imperfection.

[3.] God never intended them for the expiation of sin by any virtue of
their own.   The majesty of God, that sin fought against, was infinite ; the
sacrifice then must be infinite ; but none of those sacrifices under the law
were so.   Why then did God constitute them ?   Not with any intention to
purge away the sin of the soul, but the ceremonial uncleanness of the flesh :
Heb. ix. 13, 14, 'The blood of bulls sanctifies to the purifying the flesh.'   The
apostle compares those and the sacrifice of Christ together, shewing that
one purified only the flesh, the other the conscience.   It was not a moral
guilt they were intended to remove, but a ceremonial, as when one was
defiled by touching a dead carcase or a leprous body, which was in estimation a defilement of the body, not of the soul.   It was a guilt judged so by
God, not by any law of nature, but a positive law, an arbitrary constitution,
which punished it not with death, but with a suspension from communion
till it were expiated by a sacrifice ; and therefore God might settle what compensation he pleased of a lower nature, for that which was not a moral
guilt, for there was nothing in those ceremonial impurities which might waste
the conscience, or be accounted a dead work, ver. 14, or infect the soul.*
But as to moral crimes, they were rather the confessions than expiations of
them.   And, indeed, God often discovered their weakness, and that they

* Turretin. de Satisfac., pp. 237, 238.

could not give him rest, or recompense the injury received by sin : Isa. lxvi. 1, ' Where is the house that you build me, and where is the place of my rest ?   For all those things have my hands made, and all those things have been, saith the Lord.'   By the house or temple, is meant all the Jewish economy, and the lump of sacrifices ; all those things, though God appointed them, and though they had been used and performed, God had no rest in. They neither satisfied his justice, nor vindicated the honour of his law, nor could they ever take away sin, Heb. x. 11.   And, therefore, the only wise God never instituted them for that end, unless we will say he was deceived in his expectations, and mistaken in the end of his appointments.   God therefore rejected them, not only upon the hypocrisy of the offerers (as sometimes he did), but upon the account of their own nature, being unable to attain the end of a propitiatory sacrifice, Heb. vii. 18.   They were disannulled for the weakness and unprofitableness of them.   Though they had been practised for so many ages, yet not one sin had been expiated by them in that long tract of time.

[4.] God did therefore appoint them to prefigure a more excellent sacrifice, able to do it.   The vileness and poorness of a beast appointed for sacrifice might admonish the Jews that such light things were insufficient for so great a work as the taking away of sin, the wrath of God, and eternal punishment, and redeeming the soul of man (more precious than all the beasts of the field or birds of the air) ; they must needs conceive sin was too foul to be washed away with such blood ; and this would naturally lead them to conceive that they prefigured a sacrifice more excellent and sufficient for those ends.   They were but shadows, Heb. x. 1, and did typically respect a crucified, dying Christ as the substance ; and what virtue they had was not in and from themselves, but from their typical relation to that which they shadowed.   They signified the sacrifice of Christ, by whose blood, in the fulness of time, the sins that were past were to be expiated, Rom. iii. 25 ; and as shadows received what value they had from their substance.   They did not as shadows purge away any sin, but represent that which should.   The shadow of a man shews like a man, but hath not the virtue and power of a man, whose shadow it is, to act what he doth.   They easily might collect from them that they were not able to expiate their sins themselves, that it must be done by death, and by the death of some other, not the offender, but of one too that was innocent, and whose sacrifice might be of perpetual virtue ; and this those shadows signified to any inquisitive mind.*   And the Scripture evidenceth this, the will of God was the reparation of mankind ; and when those were insufficient for it, Christ steps in as the great sacrifice wherein God had pleasure, to do this will of God, viz., man's restoration in a way congruous to the honour of God, Heb. x. 6-8.   So that what pleasure God had in the institution of legal sacrifices, did not arise from anything in themselves, nor was terminated in them, but in this sacrifice, more excellent than the sacrifice of worlds of creatures.

[2.] Since all these were insufficient, some other must be found. out to effect it.   And this was Christ only, the Son of God.   To fancy a satisfaction below the demerit of the offence, and disproportioned to the injury committed, is to wrong the wisdom and justice of God, and to vilify God in such low thoughts of his nature.   That only can be properly called a satisfaction, which is suited to the majesty of God, and is equivalent to the sin of man.   Now, since none else were able to offer to God anything for the reparation of his glory, there must be something offered to God, which is greater

* Mornæ, Cont. Inst. p. 168, &c.

than everything that was not God.   There was therefore a necessity of some
divine person to give that satisfaction which was necessary for the honour of
God; that, as a father saith, there might be as much humiliation in the expiation as there was presumption in the transgression.   If God would have
accepted a satisfaction less than infinite, he might as well have pardoned sin
without a satisfaction at all.

(1.) Christ was the fittest, and only capable of effecting it.   He was more
excellent than all the creatures of the lowest and highest rank put together.
There was none whose merit and dignity could equal the greatness and infiniteness of the injury done to God by sin.   None could compensate the
blackness of the offence with such a greatness of satisfaction.   And indeed
we cannot imagine that God would expose his Son to so cruel a death, were
it not necessary or highly convenient for his honour, or that the Son himself
would have taken such a task upon his shoulders, to redeem man in a way
of perfect justice.   The death of Christ was necessary, our redemption could
not else have been in the most perfect manner.   None but a divine person
could offer a price of redemption worthy of God.   His person was infinite,
and therefore was able to compensate an infinite injury.   He was the prime
male in the world, and therefore called the first-born of every creature, Col.
i. 15, *i.e.* the basis and foundation of the whole creation.*   He was innocent;
he was free from everything that might render him an unsavoury sacrifice.
He was like us, and in that had what was necessary for a sacrifice, but sin
excepted; and in that he wanted what would have made him incapable of
effecting our redemption.   It was necessary that we should have such a
surety and satisfier as was not only innocent, but immutably so, that could
not by any means be bespotted by sin; and that the apostle intimates, Heb.
vii. 26, 'holy, harmless, undefiled, separate from sinners,' and from sin.   Had
he only been holy, without being immutably so, the election of God had not
stood firm; for since God chose some to bring to glory, and that in Christ,
it had been a tottering and uncertain resolution, had the perfecting the redemption of his chosen ones depended upon the transactions of a mutable
person, that could not eternally secure himself from offending.   Had it been
possible for the Redeemer to sin, it had been possible for the absolute decree
of God to become vain, and of no effect.   He had also strength to do it; his
own arm brought salvation, Isa. lxiii. 5.   He paid God that which he was
not bound to pay; he paid an obedience as man, which was not due from
him as God.   He was made subject to the law, Gal. iv. 4; not, he was subject to the law by his nature, but made so by his incarnation.   He was the
fittest, in regard of his being the second person in the Trinity.†   It was not
fit the Father should suffer, he is regarded as the Governor of the world;
who should then have been judge of the satisfaction, whether it had been sufficient or no?   Was it fit the Father should have appeared before the tribunal
of the Son?   Nor was it so fit that the Spirit of God should undertake it;
because, as there was a necessity of satisfaction to content the justice of God,
so there was a necessity of applying this satisfaction, and quickening the
hearts of men to believe and accept it, that they might enjoy the fruits of
this sacrifice.   The order of the three persons had then been disturbed; and
that person whereby the Father and the Son execute all other things, had
changed his operation.

He was fit, in regard of both natures in union.‡   Since neither man nor
angel could do this business, and there is no nature above theirs but the

---

* Davenant *in loc.*
† Amyrald. sur Heb. vi. p. 156, 158, much changed.
‡ Ferii Orthod. Scholast. cap. xxii. sect. 3, p. 223.

divine, it must be the divine nature and human together: human, because man had sinned; divine, because the satisfaction should equal the offence. Here they are both in conjunction; the substance of the satisfaction is made in the human nature suffering, and the value of the satisfaction is from the divine. Had he not been mortal, he could not have undergone the punishment sin had merited; and had he not been divine, he could not have given a reparation equivalent to the damage by sin; he was man to perform it, and God to be sufficient for it.

(2.) The honour of God was most preserved and elevated thereby. This way mercy did not invade the rights of justice, nor justice trespass upon the bowels of mercy; both contain themselves in their own spheres. Mercy was preserved from being injured by seeing man solely punished, and justice was preserved from being wronged by seeing man solely pardoned. Thus was the nature of God glorified, without one attribute clashing against the other. Justice could not so well have been declared without the death of Christ, he was therefore set forth εἰς ἔνδειξιν, Rom. iii. 25. To declare his righteousness, as an index of justice, to point to every head and part of it in the nature of God. In this way God saved us as a judge, a lawgiver, and a king, Isa. xxxiii. 22; as a judge in the manifestation of his righteousness, as a lawgiver in the vindication of his holiness, as a king in the demonstration of his sovereignty, in such a way as that his justice is cleared, his law righted, and his sovereignty acknowledged. His hatred of sin was more clearly manifested, and his truth in his threatenings made good and established, and sinners more obliged to God, and engaged upon the account of ingenuity to a greater abhorrency of sin, and a fear and love of God, which, by the suffering of any creature, could not have had so strong a foundation in them. God set a high value upon his law; it was his royal law; and had it been wholly neglected, the royalty of God had not only been violated, but his holiness and righteousness had been disparaged, which shone forth in the law, and made up the whole frame of it; and since death was required by the law, death must be suffered, that there might be an agreement between the threatening and the suffering, the punishment and the justice of God, which required it. We may reasonably think it had been a greater act of wisdom to make no law, than to let it be violated always, without preserving the honour of it.

The doctrine of the death of Christ is the substance of the gospel.* Though there be many doctrines in it besides that, there is no comfort from any of them without the consideration of the cross of Christ; for, though God be merciful in his own nature, yet since sin hath made a separation between God and his creature, it is impossible to renew any communion with him, without a propitiation for the offence. We see, then, Christ is the only meritorious cause of our justification; nothing that we can do can satisfy God, we must be wholly off from ourselves and our own righteousness, as to any dependence on it, and act faith in the death of the Son of God, if we would be secure here in our consciences, or happy hereafter.

As to suffer death was the immediate end of the interposition of Christ; and the veracity of God in settling the penalty of death did require it; and the justice of God made the death of Christ necessary for our redemption; so,

4. It was necessary in regard of the offices of Christ.

(1.) For his priestly office. The reason that he was to be made like his brethren, subject to the law, and the penalties and curse of it, with an exception of sin in his own person, was, that he might be a faithful and merciful high priest. Heb. ii. 17, 18, 'Wherefore in all things it behoved him to

* Amyraut, Sermons sur l'Evangile, Sermon 3.

be made like unto his brethren, that he might be a merciful and faithful high priest in things pertaining to God, to make reconciliation for the sins of the people;' faithful to God for the expiation of the guilt of sin, merciful to men for the succouring them in their miseries by sin; faithful to God in that trust committed to him, to satisfy God for the guilt of sin, that his anger might be averted, and the sinner received into favour, and therefore he was made like to them in the curse, though not in the sin; which was necessary for his being a merciful high priest. This qualification of compassion could not result in such a high manner from anything so well as from an experimental knowledge of the miseries we had contracted; and this must be by a sense and feeling of them. No man is so affected with the wretched state of men in a shipwreck by beholding it in a picture, as when he sees the ship dashed against the rocks, and hears the cries, and beholds the strugglings of the passengers for life; nor is any man so deeply affected with them upon sight, as upon feeling the same miseries in his own person. That makes a man's compassions more readily excited upon seeing or hearing of others in the like state. Now, had not Christ run through the chief miseries of human life, and the punishment of death, he had not had that experimental compassion which was necessary to qualify him for this priesthood. It was by being made perfect through sufferings that he became the author of eternal salvation, Heb. v. 10. It was a thing becoming God as a just and righteous sovereign, in bringing many sons in glory, to make the Captain of their salvation perfect through sufferings, Heb. ii. 10; 'it became him, by whom and for whom are all things.' It became God, as the sovereign of all things, to have his justice vindicated, and, as the end of all things, to have the glory of his attributes exalted. Had not Christ suffered, he had not been a perfect Saviour, neither faithful to God nor merciful to man, because without blood justice had not been satisfied, and so sin, the great hindrance of salvation, had not been expiated. If he were a priest, he must have a sacrifice. A priest and a sacrifice are relatives. A priest is not properly a priest without a sacrifice, nor a sacrifice properly a sacrifice without a priest. Being settled a perpetual priest, Ps. cx. 4, he must have a perpetual sacrifice. Now, having nothing worthy of God's regard but himself, he sacrificed himself. No other sacrifice could have been perpetual in its efficacy, and consequently without a perpetual sacrifice he could not have been a perpetual priest. He as a priest purged our sins, but by himself as a sacrifice: Heb. i. 9, by his own blood as an offering, he entered into the holiest as a priest, Heb. ix. 12. He could not have entered into heaven to act as a priest there without blood, and no blood was fit to be brought in there but his own. There had been else no analogy between him and the legal priests, who were to enter into the most holy place with blood, and never without it. He could not have been an interceding priest unless he had been a sacrificing priest, because his sacrifice is the ground of his intercession. His intercession is not a bare supplication, but a supplication with unanswerable arguments, a presenting his atoning blood, which he carried with him into the holy place when he went to appear in the presence of God for us; whence the apostle, speaking of his advocacy, joins it with his propitiation, 1 John ii. 1, 2. His propitiation on earth and his advocacy in heaven complete him a priest for ever. The one is the foundation of the other. Without it, Christ had been a bare petitioner in heaven, and would have had no ground for any plea against the demands of justice.

(2.) For his kingly office. The first thing he was to do for our reconciliation, was the offering his soul for sin, Isa. liii. 10. Upon this article did all the promises of his mediatory exaltation depend; so that nothing of the dignity promised could be rightly claimed, or reasonably expected, by him, without the performance of this main and necessary condition, which himself had consented to in the first agreement. For consenting to this undertaking, upon the condition of the promise of his exaltation, he implied that he would not expect any exaltation, unless he performed the condition required on his part, of making his soul an offering for sin ; and therefore, without such an oblation, could not justly demand the making good the promise to him. There was an *ought to die*, and then *to enter into glory* by the way of death, as a price to be paid for the restoration of our nature to that happiness from whence it fell; his obedience to death was to precede, his exaltation to a throne and dominion was to follow; he was not to sit down on the right hand of the Majesty on high till he had purged our sins by himself, Heb. i. 3 ; nor had he been Lord of the dead and living unless he had died, Rom. xiv. 9. The royalty, not only over those whom he had redeemed from sin, but over the good angels, was granted him as a recompence for his sufferings, Philip. ii. 8, 9, and the conquest of the evil angels was by his death ; for in his cross he triumphed over principalities and powers, Col. ii. 15. The change of laws in the church, which is a part of royalty, was to follow this sacrifice of himself, which is understood in Cant. iv. 6, ' Until the day break, and the shadows fly away, I will get me to the mountains of myrrh.' The removing the shadows of the law was to follow his being upon the mount Moriah, the place of his sufferings, there being an allusion in the word מּוֹר, *myrrh,* or *Moriah.* Nor had the Spirit been sent into the world, unless his death had preceded : John vii. 39, ' The Holy Ghost was not yet given, because Jesus was not yet glorified.' This rich treasure could not be dispensed till the acceptation of this sacrifice, till his glorification ; and he could not have a mediatory glory till he had offered his mediatory sacrifice. It is the Lamb slain that hath seven eyes and seven spirits, Rev. v. 6; power to prefer his people, and power to send the Spirit to them for their supply. Besides, the Spirit could not have come as a comforter without it, because the consolations he shoots into the soul are drawn out of this quiver. Without his death, we had not had a propitiation for sin, the mysteries of divine love had lain undiscerned in darkness ; since we cannot be renewed without the Spirit (because the nature of man was depraved by his fall, whereupon justice denied the restoration of original righteousness), justice must be satisfied, and God reconciled, before mercy could restore it. Justice must be appeased, before it would consent to the return of that favour which had devolved into its hands by forfeiture ; so great a gift as the Spirit, the author of renewing grace, was not like to be bestowed upon us by God, while he remained an enemy. The gift of the Spirit is therefore ascribed to the purchase of Christ's death.

(3.) There was some necessity of it for his prophetical office. His death was the highest confirmation of his doctrine. This was not indeed the only cause, nor the principal cause, of his death ; if it were, his death would differ little in the end of it from the death of martyrs. Besides, if he had suffered death chiefly for this, what need was there of his undergoing the curse, and groaning under the desertion of his Father ? There was no absolute necessity of his death for the confirmation of his doctrine, since the miracles he performed were a divine seal to assure us of its heavenly original ; therefore he directs the Jews to his works, as a means of believing him to be from heaven, John x. 38. Yet in his death he set forth a perpetual pattern of that obedience, meekness, love to God and man, and trust in his Father, above what any creature had ever been able to propose to us. He taught us in his life by the words of his mouth, and in his death instructed us by the exemplary exercise of his graces, and the voice of his blood, 1 Peter ii. 21. He taught us the highest part of obedience to the utmost, by performing the exactest and sublimest part of obedience to his Father ; and, therefore, after he had discoursed to his disciples of his death and departure, he adds the reason of it, ' That the world may know that I love the Father ; and as the Father gave me commandment, even so I do,' John xiv. 31 ; that the world might know that he loved the glory of the Father, who was so merciful as to be willing to remit sin, yet so just, as not to remit it without a sacrifice.

5. The death of Christ was necessary upon the account of the predictions and types of it in the Scripture. Had not Christ suffered, all the predictions had been false, and the types to no purpose. In this the veracity of God was engaged, not only in making good the threatening of death discovered to the first man, in inflicting what was threatened, but in the way of redemption by his Son. This was not only truth to his own resolve, as he had determined it, but truth to his word, as he had published it. God having decreed and declared the redemption of mankind, and the death of the Messiah as the medium, could not appoint then another way, because his counsel had not only pitched upon redemption as the end, but the death of Christ as the means ; and there could be no change in God. Had there been a change in the end, and had God altered his purpose for man's redemption, he had obscured and lost the glory of all those attributes which sparkled in it. There could be none in the means ; if so, it must have been for the better or worse. The better it could not be ; for no way of so great a sufficiency could be found out as this, nor could any sacrifice of a higher value be thought of. Nor could it be worse ; for he could not have pitched upon any deficient way but he would have testified himself weary of, and changed in, his end for which he appointed those means. This necessity of his death, Christ, in his discourse with his staggering disciples, confirms by the exposition of all the Scriptures, which contained the things concerning himself, beginning at Moses, i. e. at the books of Moses, and all the prophets, Luke xxiv. 27 ; which he testifies again, ver. 43, naming the Psalms also as particularly containing things that concerned his person and death. Moses discovered it by types, as he was the minister of settling them, and by prophecies, as he was the amanuensis to write some of them. The prophets declared it in express words, they spake it all with one mouth ; and their chief prophecies centred in this, that Christ should suffer : Acts xxvi. 22, 23, ' Saying none other things than what Moses and the prophets did say should come ; that Christ should suffer.' And the apostle Peter excludes none of the prophets from speaking of those things which were to be done in the latter days, Acts iii. 21 ; and that this was the design of the Spirit in them, to testify of the sufferings of Christ, 1 Peter i. 11.

(1.) Predictions. We shall speak of a few.

[1.] The first promise : Gen. iii. 15, ' It shall bruise thy head, and thou shalt bruise his heel ;' speaking to the serpent of the seed of the woman, which was to defeat all his devices. The Messiah here, as the seed of the woman, was promised to Adam to break the serpent's head, i. e. to take away sin and eternal death from man, which the devil had introduced, by the subtle contrivances of his head, into the world ; for he was to take away the strength, power, and wisdom of the devil, signified by the head. The way whereby he was to do it was by having his heel bruised, viz., the heel of his humanity, by suffering. For as he was the seed of the woman, having human nature, he was to be bruised, he was to feel the power of the devil (now, the power of the devil was the power of death, Heb. ii. 14), yet so to feel the power of the devil as not utterly to sink under it ; for not his head, but his heel, was to be bruised, *i. e.* his flesh, not his wisdom and chief design for the redemption of man. He was only to be bruised, not destroyed, or to see corruption; so that his death and resurrection are here predicted. And by suffering his heel to be bruised by the serpent, he was to break the serpent's head, *i. e.* through death to destroy him that had the power of death, Heb. ii. 14. And we know the death of Christ was the conquest of the devil. Sufferings are necessary ;* for there can be no conquest of the devil but by a satisfaction performed to the righteousness of the law ; for his whole empire consisted in the curse of the law ; and the law, after sin, required death, called therefore a 'law of sin and death,' Rom. viii. 2. The devil was the jailor, having the power of death ; the law must be satisfied before the prisoner be freed from the jailor's power. The value of those sufferings is declared,† because his bruise cannot wholly destroy the seed, nor hinder him from bruising the serpent's head. He could not by suffering bruise the serpent's head, unless he had been innocent, and from his innocence derived a dignity and worth to his sufferings ; and this no fallen creature could do. Again, he must be innocent ; for if he had been under the power of the devil, he could not have bruised his head. And since he was to overcome the devil by having his heel bruised, it signifies his suffering for those sins which were the foundation of the empire and dominion of the devil. Adam might well understand this conquest of the devil to be the death of the seed, because after this promise he was taught to sacrifice ; and the sacrifices, he was presently taught (as may be well conjectured by the skins of beasts, viz., of sacrificed beasts, wherewith God clothed him), as a comment upon this promise, shewed him in their death what he had deserved, and in what manner he was to expect his redemption, so lately promised him. And surely the wisdom and goodness of God would not teach him the way of sacrificing, without acquainting him with the reason and end of sacrifices, which the Scripture mentions as a means to make man accepted with God, Gen. iv. 7; to purge away sin, 1 Sam. iii. 14; and to make reconciliation for it, Ezek. xlv. 17. And Adam, having more natural knowledge after his fall than all his posterity have had since, might easily know by reason that the blood of beasts was too weak and vile to make an atonement for his late offence, which had brought so much misery upon him, and thereby was manifested to be infinitely offensive to God, and therefore more offensive to him than the blood of beasts could be pleasing. This he could not but know, that those sacrifices 'could not make him that did the service perfect as pertaining to the conscience,' as the expression is in Heb. ix. 9. And Adam, being the high priest, as head of all, could not but know that those sacrifices were offered for sin ; because this was the end of the appointment of a priest, and the chief part of his office, as well as the end of the sacrifice : Heb. v. 1, ' Every high priest is ordained for men in things pertaining to God, that he may offer sacrifices for sin.' Let us further consider. The end of this promise was to defeat the devil, and to comfort Adam after his revolt from God, and thereby his falling under the vindictive justice of God, and to cheer him up before he should hear his own sentence, which was pronounced, Gen. iii. 17–19. So that Adam could not reasonably understand this promise any other way for his comfort, than that this promised seed should take away sin and the death threatened for it ; otherwise it had been but little comfort to Adam to see himself ruined beyond any hopes of recovery, and to hear only of the destruction of his enemy. But in this promise Adam saw the sentence of death respited, because the seed of the woman was promised, which necessarily included the continuance of his life, else there could have been no seed of the woman. This also signifies

* Cocc. in Gen. iii. 15.   † Cocc. in Gen. iii. 15.

to us that the sufferings of Christ were intended for a satisfaction of the violated law and provoked justice; for if sin and death were to be taken away by Adam's imitation of this promised seed when he should appear, Adam could take no comfort in the promise, unless he had been sure to live to see this promised seed in the flesh. How could he imitate as an example the promised seed whom he was never to see in the world, but was to return to dust long before the appearance of it in the world? And it was necessary Adam should behold this seed in the flesh, if the breaking of the fetters of sin and hell were to be brought about only by his imitation of this seed. Again, to bruise the serpent's head cannot reasonably be understood of a confirmation only of the promised mercy (which some make the end of the death of Christ). There was no need of bruising the heel barely for a confirmation of this mercy; for that was confirmed by the unalterable promise and will of God. And no question but Adam thought it sufficiently valid, since he received it from the mouth of God himself, and had so late an experience how true God was to the word of threatening. There is no other thing left, then, as the end of this bruising the heel, but to render mercy triumphant without any wrong to justice, and to vindicate the honour of the law, and, in a way of righteousness, not only of sovereign dominion, to defeat the serpent and restore the fallen creature.

[2.] Another prediction is Psalm xxii. All the circumstances of his passion are here enumerated: sufferings, revilings, contempt by men, the desertion of God, his agonies, the parting his garments; and, at last, the propagation of the gospel and the calling of the gentiles are here predicted. The Jews understood it of the body of the Jewish nation;[*] but the design of the psalmist is to set forth a particular person, who is distinguished from the wicked crew that oppressed him, and from those that favoured him, whom he calls his brethren, and distinguisheth himself from the congregation wherein he would praise God, ver. 23; and upon the death of this person the world was to be gathered in to God: ver. 27, 'All the ends of the world shall remember, and turn unto the Lord;' agreeable to the prediction of our Saviour, that when he should be lifted up, he would draw all men after him. Here is the prediction of the very words he spake upon the cross, when he lay under the imputation of our sins, and cried out, under the sense of his Father's wrath, ver. 1, 'My God, my God,' &c. The miserable condition he was brought to, ver. 6, as a worm and no man, exposed to such a state of misery, and to be of no more account than the most contemptible animal, a worm. The word *worm*[†] comes of עלו, which signifies the grain which gave a scarlet dye, because the colour proceeded from a worm enclosed in that grain. Our Saviour was as a worm crushed to tincture others with his blood. The very gesture of the people when they reviled him, wagging their heads, ver. 7, and Mat. xxvii. 29; the reproaches they belched out against him, ver. 8, Mat. xxvii. 43, 'He trusted in God, let him deliver him;' the sharpness of his death, ver. 14, 'I am poured out like water, all my bones are out of joint;' a distortion and racking of all his bones, effusion of his blood, dissolution of his vital vigour (like wax melted) under the sense of God's wrath, an expression used, Ps. lxviii. 2, to shew the greatness of God's wrath against sin and sinners; his extreme thirst, ver. 15, 'My tongue cleaveth to my jaws;' the manner of his death by crucifixion, ver. 16, by piercing his hands and his feet, shewing it to be a lingering and painful death, which manner of death is also prophesied, Zech. xii. 10, 'They shall look upon me whom they have pierced,' which the ancient Jews understood of the Messiah,

---

* Dr. Owen on Heb., vol. i. Exercit. pp. 217, 218.

† תולעת. Vermillion colour is derived of *vermis*.

and is a proof that the Messiah was to be pierced or digged into.   And this place is cited as a prediction of the death of Christ, John xix. 37, Rev. i. 7 ; and as the manner of his death, so the excellency of his person is described there.   The same person is a God to pour out the Spirit, and a man to be pierced ; he works wonders as God, and suffers wonders as man.

[3.] The whole 53d of Isaiah is a prediction of this. He was to be rejected of men, wounded for our transgressions, to have our sins laid upon him by God, to bear iniquity, to be led as a sheep to the slaughter, to make his soul an offering for sin.   This is so plain that the Jews anciently understood it of the Messiah ;* but the latter Jews, to evade it, have fancied a double Messiah, one a sufferer, another a triumpher, the sufferer of the tribe of Ephraim, the triumpher of the tribe of Judah; but where doth the Scripture mention a Messiah of the tribe of Ephraim ?   It always fixeth his descent from the house of David, of the tribe of Judah.

Many other prophecies there are of this : Zech. xiii. 7, ' I will smite the shepherd,' and Dan. ix. 24, the ' Messiah shall be cut off, but not for himself;' he shall be counted the wickedest man, and put to death as the greatest malefactor, who hath no crime of his own to merit death, but his death shall be for the good of mankind.   And the ends of it are expressed, ver. 24, to finish transgression, and make an end of sin, and to make reconciliation for iniquity, and to bring in everlasting righteousness, and to seal up the vision and prophecy; to finish transgression, or restrain it; to abolish sin in regard of the guilt of it, and restrain it from accusing us before God, and procuring the condemnation of us ; to make an end of sin, or seal up sin, covering it, that it shall no more appear against us, as the writings of the Jews were rolled up, and sealed on the back side, that the writing could no more be seen ; to make reconciliation for iniquity, to expiate iniquity (a word belonging to sacrifices), to take away the obligation of sin (and it is observable, that all the words used in Scripture to signify sin, are here put in, פשע, חטאה, עון, to shew the universal removal of them, as to any guilt, by the death of Christ), and to bring in everlasting righteousness.   As righteousness was lost by the first Adam, so it was to be restored by the second, to make us for ever accepted before God.   And to seal up the vision and prophecy, to accomplish all the visions and prophecies in the appearance of his person, and performance of his work.   All prophecies pointed to him, and centered in him ; and the end of his coming and excision was to deliver us from sin, and introduce such a righteousness as might be valuable for us before God.   And then he was to be a prince, when he had been a sacrifice, and cut off for the sins of the people.   As the time approached for the coming of this promised seed, God made clearer revelations of the death of the Messiah, and his chief design in it.   And this is such a testimony of a dying Messiah, by the hands of violence, and for those great ends which the Christian religion affirms, that the Jews, with all their evasions and obstinacy, know not how to get over it.

(2.) The second thing is the types.   There were several types of Christ in the Old Testament, both in the persons of men and the ceremonies of the law.   No one type, no, nor all together, could fully signify this great sacrifice.   The figure hath not what the truth hath.†   The image of a king represents not all that the king hath or is.   Moses was a type of the Messiah, who was to be raised up like to Moses, Deut. xviii. 15.   Moses, put into an ark, was exposed to the mercy of the Egyptians on the land, and the crocodiles in the river, and after that advanced to be chief governor of Israel ; Jonah,

---

* Pugio fidei. part iii. distinct. i. cap. x. § 4, 5, and distinct. iii. cap. xvi.
† Theodoret.

buried three days in the belly of the whale ; Noah, penned up in an ark, to become the father of a second generation ; Joseph, cruelly put into a pit, and sold by his brethren, and afterwards lifted up to a throne, to be the preserver of his spiteful brethren,—these, it is likely, had all some relation, as types, to Christ. It would be endless to mention all ; let us consider in general.

[1.] Sacrifices. These were practised by all nations, as well Gentiles as Jews, and from a notion that they did pacify their offended deities. Heathen authors give us a full account of their sentiments in this case ; and the Philistines, neighbours to the Jews, declare this as their sense in their trespass offering, they would return to God after they had felt his hand, 1 Sam. vi. 3–5. The common notion of all heathens was, that they were offered to God for a propitiation for sin, and either for preventing the judgments they feared, or removing the judgments they felt.

(1.) These sacrifices could not arise from the light of nature. Being universally practised, they must arise from the light of nature, common to all men, or from some particular institution derived to all men by tradition. The light of nature could not be any ground for the framing such an imagination in men's minds, that God should be appeased by the blood of irrational creatures. The disproportion of them both to the offence, the offender, and the offended person, hath been seen and spoken of by the wiser sort of the heathens themselves. Natural light would rather have dictated to them that their devout prayers, deep repentance, and hearty reformation would have been more efficacious to avert the anger of God than the cutting the throat of a bullock or lamb, and pouring out the blood at the foot of their altars. They could no more suppose that such offerings should appease an offended God, than the cutting off a dog's neck, or the crushing a fly before the statue of a prince would have appeased the anger of their injured sovereign. And none could think but the killing a worm, and offering it to the prince, had been as well or more sufficient to have mitigated his wrath, than the killing a thousand cattle had been to allay the wrath of God, in regard of the proportionableness of a worm to the one, greater than that of all the beasts in the world to the other. The light of nature would not instruct the heathens barbarously to take away the lives of men, and offer them for the expiation of their sins. For that teacheth us to love one another, as being descended from one root, and being of the same stamp. Besides, had any law of nature obliged men at any time to bloody sacrifices in such a nature, it would have obliged them still. No law of nature is razed out by the gospel, but more cleared ; and whatsoever is due to God by the law of nature is more improved by the Christian religion. Natural light would be able to make more objections for the forbearance of such a practice, than arguments for the preserving it in the world.

(2.) They must be therefore from institution. And since the practice hath been so universal, and the head of it can less be traced than the head of the river Nilus, it must be supposed to descend from the first man by tradition, and carried by his posterity to all the places which they first peopled, and so continued by their descendants. Bloody sacrifices seem to be instituted just after the fall. How should Adam be clothed with the skins of beasts ? Gen. iii. 21. If it be meant that God only taught him to clothe himself with the skins of beasts, it implies a giving him order to slay beasts, and most probably first in sacrifice, and ordering him to take the skins for clothing, which in the Levitical service were appropriated to the priests. For food it is probable they were not killed ; the food then appointed was the herb of the field, even after the fall, Gen. iii. 18. And the objection against this, that there were but two of a kind, male and female, created, and therefore if two beasts of the same kind had been slain, a species had been destroyed, is of no validity. For the story of the creation mentions not such a parsimonious creation, nay, it is more probable there were more than two of a sort created. However, sacrifices began early. Abel is the first we plainly read of, Gen. iv. 4. He brought of the firstlings of his flock, and Cain brought of the fruit of the ground, an offering to the Lord. They may not be out of the way who think that there was a crime in the matter of Cain's sacrifice, it not being a bloody one. No doubt but he had seen his father offer to God the fruits of the earth, as well as the bodies of beasts, and might think that the offering those fruits of the ground (the tilling whereof was his proper employment) was sufficient, that there was no need of blood for the expiation of his sin. He seems to stand upon his own righteousness, and offer only what was an acknowledgment of God's dominion and lordship over the whole world, as if he had only been his creature, and not an offending creature. It was not inconsistent with a state of innocence for a man to make such acknowledgments to God, as the Lord of creation and the Benefactor of man. But after the fall there was not only the dominion of God, but his justice, to be acknowledged, which was best signified in a way that might represent to man the demerit of his offence and the justice due to him, which could not be by the offering of fruits, but by the shedding of blood, without which there is no remission.

(3.) If then they were from the special institution of God, they must be figures of something else intended. For since we find an universal sentiment in the practisers of them among the Gentiles, that they were for expiation, and that common reason could not find ground enough to fortify such an opinion in them ; and that the Scripture, the ancientest book in the world, gives us an account of their ancient practice and divine institution ; they could not be instituted by God, as the prime means of appeasing him, for that could not be congruous to the nature of God. There was no proportion between the justice of God and them, nor between them and the sin of man. But the most reasonable conclusion would be, that they were ordained to signify some other thing or sacrifice intended for the expiation of sin ; that they were typical of the death of some one able to bear the punishment and purge the transgression. Since they could not purge the conscience, they must be concluded to be types of something that should have a sufficiency and an actual efficacy to this end. And this the heathens might have guessed from reason and the universal practice, that they were shadows of something else, though they could not have imagined the true person they were shadows of.

To sum up, therefore, the account the Scripture gives us of them, we must consider * that after Adam's revolt, and contracting death and the curses of the law by that apostasy, there was a necessity of maintaining the honour of the law, and God's own veracity in the commination, and satisfying his provoked justice, which must be done by that nature which had offended. Upon this account, and for this end, the second person, the Son of God, voluntarily exposed himself, and stood as a screen between the consuming fire and the combustible creature. Hereupon the sufferings of the Son of God were mutually agreed upon, the particular sufferings appointed and determined, and the time when he should be incarnate, and expose himself to that which the criminal should have endured, was settled, and the redemption, the design of those sufferings, declared by promise ; and because the time would be long before his coming to suffer, and the faith of men might

* Owen, Heb. vol. ii. Exercit. p. 61.

languish, God kept it up by lively representations of those sufferings, and the end of them, in the death of sacrificed beasts. Not that they should rest upon them, but use those shadows as props to their faith in the promised seed, till the fulness of time should come. All those sacrifices were a rude draught, or initial elements or rudiments, to teach the world what was to be done with a full efficacy by the person appointed to it. Whence the apostle calls them 'the rudiments of the world,' Col. ii: 20. And so they were a copy of what was resolved in heaven from eternity, to be fulfilled in time, for the expiation of sin. They all had relation to Christ. They were to be without blemish, and dedicated wholly to God, as things that were to perish for his glory ; and being burnt, and the smoke ascending to heaven, God might, as it were, partake of the oblation, as the Scripture testifies : Gen. viii. 21, ' And God smelled a sweet savour,' viz., from Noah's sacrifice. So Christ offered himself as a holocaust to the Father, as the antitype of those victims that were wholly to be consumed by fire. And this blood speaks better things than the blood of Abel's sacrifice, or the blood of all the sacrifices shed from the very first ; for this pacifies an angry God, purges a guilty conscience, and breaks the chains of hell and damnation. There is no question to be made, but the believers among the Jews did apprehend the heel of the promised seed bruised in every sacrifice ; they could not else offer them in faith. As mathematicians measure the greatness of the stars, which are above their reach, by the shadows of the earth, which are within their compass, so did they, upon the view of those sacrifice-shadows, apprehend the virtue and efficacy of the grand oblation.* As those that did understand Christ in the manna did also eat Christ in the manna, 1 Cor. x. 3, 4, so those that did apprehend Christ in the legal sacrifices, were also sprinkled with the blood of Christ. Thus was Christ a lamb slain from the foundation of the world, not only by purpose and decree, but significatively and typically in all the ancient sacrifices. I might here instance in the two anniversary goats, Levit. xvi., one offered, the other devoted to the wilderness ; in the red heifer, Num. xix., burnt upon the day of expiations, both eminent types of the death of Christ ; as also in the passover or paschal lamb, the blood whereof sprinkled upon the posts was of no necessity in itself for the Israelites' preservation from the destroying angel, nor had any intrinsic virtue in it to procure their security. The angel, no doubt, had acuteness of sight enough to discern the houses and persons of the Israelites from those of the Egyptians.† We cannot justify the wisdom of God in this conduct, if we refer it not to Christ, as a representation of that great miracle of redemption to be wrought by him for the true Israelites, when he should come to free man from a bondage worse than Egyptian. This is the true Lamb of God, that hath the virtue and vigour of all that whereof the paschal lambs had but the image and shadow. Let me add the observation of one,‡ the command of God, that the bones of the paschal lamb should not be broken, signified that the redeemer of the world should die such a death wherein the breaking of bones was usual. Yet that that circumstance should not be used in his death, and therefore that that order of not breaking the bones of the paschal lamb, is cited by John, as if it had been literally meant of him and not of the lamb : John xix. 36, ' That the Scripture should be fulfilled, a bone of him shall not be broken.' I might also instance in that eminent type of the blood of Christ, the blood of the sacrifice sprinkled upon the altar, book of the law, vessels of the sanctuary ; after which the elders of Israel ate and

* Mares. contra Volkcl. lib iii. cap. xxxiii. p. 389.
† Daillé sur 1 Cor. v. 7. Serm. xx. p. 381.
‡ Pearson on the Creed, p. 408.

drunk in the presence of God, no longer exposed unto his anger, Exod. xxiv.; commented upon by the apostle, Heb. ix. 19, 20.

[2.] Isaac's death was a type of the death of Christ. Of his death ; for he was, in the purpose of his Father, upon the command of God, cut off. And Isaac, bearing the wood, did prefigure the manner of the death of Christ, viz., such a death wherein the bearing the wood was customary.* As in crucifying, the offenders bore the cross to the place of execution, and Christ did his. And a type also of the resurrection of Christ ; for it was the third day from the command of offering him that Abraham received him to life as new born, and raised from the dead, Gen. xxii. 4, and that in a figure of some nobler sacrifice and resurrection, Heb. xi. 19. Moriah was the place appointed by God where Abraham was to offer his son, Gen. xxii. 2, in one part whereof was the temple and the tower of David; another part of the mount was without Jerusalem, and was called Calvary, upon which Isaac was to be sacrificed, as Jerome tells us from the Jewish tradition. Now, upon Abraham's readiness to offer his son Isaac, God binds himself by an oath, that in his seed all the nations of the earth shall be blessed, Gen. xxii. 16–18. In his seed, as dying, and to be offered up, and rising again, as Isaac did in figure. God now binds himself by an oath to do that to Abraham which he had before promised to Adam ; the intent of which oath the apostle, Heb. vi. 13, 19, 20, refers to the settling of Christ as redeemer, and more positively affirms this seed to be Christ, Gal. iii. 10. This oath to Abraham was pursuant to that promise to Adam, which expressed the bruising of the seed of the woman ; and now God by oath appropriates this seed to Abraham (as being singled out from the rest of the world), from whom the Messiah should descend. God obliged himself to bless the world by one of the seed of Abraham to be offered up really, as Isaac was in figure. And by his hindering him from sacrificing Isaac, and shewing him a ram, he intimates that there would be some interval of time before the blessed seed should be offered. And the words which Abraham speaks, Gen. xxii. 8, ' God will provide himself a lamb for a burnt-offering,' seem to be a prophetic speech of the death of this great sacrifice, though Abraham might not at that time know the true meaning of that speech, no more than many of the prophets knew what they prophesied of, 1 Peter i. 11 ; and the mount Moriah is concluded by that prophecy, ver. 14, ' In the mount of the Lord it shall be seen,' to be the place of the appearance of this seed : in the mount the Lord Jehovah shall be seen, the particle *of* not being in the Hebrew text, which was the place afterwards of the sufferings of Christ.

1. Let us here see the evil of sin. Nothing more fit to shew the baseness of sin, and the greatness of the misery by it, than the satisfaction due for it ; as the greatness of a distemper is seen by the force of the medicine, and the value of the commodity by the greatness of the price it cost.† The sufferings of Christ express the evil of sin, far above the severest judgments upon any creature, both in regard of the greatness of the person, and the bitterness of the suffering. The dying groans of Christ shew the horrible nature of sin in the eye of God ; as he was greater than the world, so his sufferings declare sin to be the greatest evil in the world. How evil is that sin that must make God bleed to cure it ! To see the Son of God haled to death for sin, is the greatest piece of justice that ever God executed. The earth trembled under the weight of God's wrath when he punished Christ, and the heavens were dark as though they were shut to him, and he cries and groans, and no relief appears ; nothing but sin was the procuring meritorious cause of this. The Son of God was slain by the sin of the lapsed

* Pearson on the Creed, p. 416.   † Charron.

creature; had there been any other way to expiate so great an evil, had it stood with the honour of God, who is inclined to pardon, to remit sin without a compensation by death, we cannot think he would have consented that his Son should undergo so great a suffering. Not all the powers in heaven and earth could bring us into favour again, without the death of some great sacrifice to preserve the honour of God's veracity and justice; not the gracious interposition of Christ, without becoming mortal, and drinking in the vials of wrath, could allay divine justice; not his intercessions, without enduring the strokes due to us, could remove the misery of the fallen creature. All the holiness of Christ's life, his innocence and good works, did not redeem us without death. It was by this he made an atonement for our sins, satisfied the revenging justice of his Father, and recovered us from a spiritual and inevitable death. How great were our crimes, that could not be wiped off by the works of a pure creature, or the holiness of Christ's life, but required the effusion of the blood of the Son of God for the discharge of them! Christ in his dying was dealt with by God as a sinner, as one standing in our stead, otherwise he could not have been subject to death. For he had no sin of his own, and 'death is the wages of sin,' Rom. vi. 23. It had not consisted with the goodness and righteousness of God as Creator, to afflict any creature without a cause, nor with his infinite love to his Son to bruise him for nothing. Some moral evil must therefore be the cause; for no physical evil is inflicted without some moral evil preceding. Death, being a punishment, supposeth a fault. Christ, having no crime of his own, must then be a sufferer for ours: 'Our sins were laid upon him,' Isa. liii. 6, or transferred upon him. We see then how hateful sin is to God, and therefore it should be abominable to us. We should view sin in the sufferings of the Redeemer, and then think it amiable if we can. Shall we then nourish sin in our hearts? This is to make much of the nails that pierced his hands, and the thorns that pricked his head, and make his dying groans the matter of our pleasure. It is to pull down a Christ that hath suffered, to suffer again; a Christ that is raised, and ascended, sitting at the right hand of God, again to the earth; to lift him upon another cross, and overwhelm him in a second grave. Our hearts should break at the consideration of the necessity of his death. We should open the heart of our sins by repentance, as the heart of Christ was opened by the spear. This doth an *Ought not Christ to die?* teach us.

2. Let us not set up our rest in anything in ourselves, not in anything below a dying Christ; not in repentance or reformation. Repentance is a condition of pardon, not a satisfaction of justice; it sometimes moves the divine goodness to turn away judgment, but it is no compensation to divine justice. There is not that good in repentance as there is wrong in the sin repented of, and satisfaction must have something of equality, both to the injury and the person injured; the satisfaction that is enough for a private person wronged is not enough for a justly offended prince; for the greatness of the wrong mounts by the dignity of the person. None can be greater than God, and therefore no offence can be so full of evil as offences against God; and shall a few tears be sufficient in any one's thoughts to wipe them off? The wrong done to God by sin is of a higher degree than to be compensated by all the good works of creatures, though of the highest elevation. Is the repentance of any soul so perfect as to be able to answer the punishment the justice of God requires in the law? And what if the grace of God help us in our repentance? It cannot be concluded from thence that our pardon is formally procured by repentance, but that we are disposed by it to receive and value a pardon. It is not congruous to the wisdom and righteousness

of God to bestow pardons upon obstinate rebels.   Repentance is nowhere said to expiate sin; a ' broken heart is called a sacrifice,' Ps. li. 17, but not a propitiatory one.   David's sin was expiated before he penned that psalm, 2 Sam. xii. 13.   Though a man could weep as many tears as there are drops of water contained in the ocean, send up as many volleys of prayers as there have been groans issuing from any creature since the foundation of the world; though he could bleed as many drops from his heart as have been poured out from the veins of sacrificed beasts, both in Judea and all other parts of the world ; though he were able, and did actually bestow in charity all the metals in the mines of Peru: yet could not this absolve him from the least guilt, nor cleanse him from the least filth, nor procure the pardon of the least crime by any intrinsic value in the acts themselves ; the very acts, as well as the persons, might fall under the censure of consuming justice.   The death of Christ only procures us life.   The blood of Christ only doth quench that just fire sin had kindled in the breast of God against us.   To aim at any other way for the appeasing of God, than the death of Christ, is to make the cross of Christ of no effect.   This we are to learn from an *Ought not Christ to die?*

3. Therefore, let us be sensible of the necessity of an interest in the Redeemer's death.   Let us not think to drink the waters of salvation out of our own cisterns, but out of Christ's wounds.   Not to draw life out of our own dead duties, but Christ's dying groans.   We have guilt, can we expiate it ourselves ?   We are under justice.   Can we appease it by any thing we can do ?   There is an enmity between God and us.   Can we offer him anything worthy to gain his friendship ?   Our natures are corrupted, can we heal them ?   Our services are polluted, can we cleanse them ?   There is as great a necessity for us to apply the death of Christ for all those, as there was for him to undergo it.   The leper was not cleansed and cured by the shedding the blood of the sacrifice for him, but the sprinkling the blood of the sacrifice upon him, Lev. xiv. 7.   As the death of Christ was foretold as the meritorious cause, so the sprinkling of his blood was foretold as the formal cause of our happiness, Isa. lii. 15.   By his own blood he entered into heaven and glory, and by nothing but his blood can we have the boldness to expect it, or the confidence to attain it, Heb. x. 19.   The whole doctrine of the gospel is Christ crucified, 1 Cor. i. 23, and the whole confidence of a Christian should be Christ crucified.   God would not have mercy exercised with a neglect of justice by man, though to a miserable client: Lev. xix. 15, ' Thou shalt not respect the person of the poor in judgment.'   Shall God, who is infinitely just, neglect the rule himself ?   No man is an object of mercy till he presents a satisfaction to justice.   As there is a perfection in God, which we call mercy, which exacts faith and repentance of his creature before he will bestow a pardon, so there is another perfection of vindictive justice that requires a satisfaction.   If the creature thinks its own misery a motive to the displaying the perfection of mercy, it must consider that the honour of God requires also the content of his justice.   The fallen angels, therefore, have no mercy granted to them, because none ever satisfied the justice of God for them.   Let us not, therefore, coin new ways of procuring pardon, and false modes of appeasing the justice of God.   What can we find besides this, able to contend against everlasting burnings ?   What refuge can there be besides this to shelter us from the fierceness of divine wrath ?   Can our tears and prayers be more prevalent than the cries and tears of Christ, who could not, by all the strength of them, divert death from himself, without our eternal loss ?   No way but faith in his blood.   God in the gospel sends us to Christ, and Christ by the gospel brings us to God.

4. Let us value this Redeemer, and redemption by his death.   Since God

was resolved to see his Son plunged into an estate of disgraceful emptiness, clothed with the form of a servant, and exposed to the sufferings of a painful cross, rather than leave sin unpunished, we should never think of it without thankful returns, both to the judge and the sacrifice. What was he afflicted for, but to procure our peace ? bruised for, but to heal our wounds ? brought before an earthly judge to be condemned, but that we might be brought before a heavenly judge to be absolved ? fell under the pains of death, but to knock off from us the shackles of hell ? and became accursed in death, but that we might be blessed with eternal life ? Without this our misery had been irreparable, our distance from God perpetual. What commerce could we have had with God, while we were separated from him by crimes on our part, and justice on his ? The wall must be broken down, death must be suffered, that justice might be silenced, and the goodness of God be again communicative to us. This was the wonder of divine love, to be pleased with the sufferings of his only Son, that he might be pleased with us upon the account of those sufferings. Our redemption in such a way, as by the death and blood of Christ, was not a bare grace. It had been so, had it been only redemption ; but being a redemption by the blood of God, it deserves from the apostle no less a title than riches of grace, Eph. i. 7. And it deserves and expects no less from us than such high acknowledgments. This we may learn from *Ought not Christ to die ?*

A DISCOURSE OF THE NECESSITY OF CHRIST'S EXALTATION.

Ought not Christ to have suffered these things, and to enter into his glory?—
LUKE XXIV. 26.

WE have already spoken to the first part of this scripture, and from thence declared the necessity of Christ's death; the next is his exaltation. His sufferings were necessary for the expiation of our sin, and his exaltation necessary for the application of the merits of his death. Some add the particle *so*, and so to enter into his glory; but that is not in the Greek, though it may be implied, for the entrance of Christ into his glory was to be by the way of suffering.

Observe by the way, the great· grace of God, that makes often the diffidence of his people an occasion of a further clearing up of the choicest truths to them. Never did those disciples hear so excellent an exposition of the Scriptures concerning the Messiah from the mouth of their Master, as when their distrust of him had prevailed so far. Glory he was to enter into. By this glory is not meant only his resurrection; that was not his glory, but the beginning of his exaltation, a *causa sine qua non;* it freed him from mortality, and invested him with immortality, but was not the term, but a necessary means of his glory (as the fetching Joseph from prison was a necessary antecedent to his elevation on a throne; he could not be a governor while he was a prisoner). By his resurrection, he was prepared for it; by his ascension, he was possessed of it; his resurrection was an entrance into his glory, but not the consummation of his felicity. *His glory.* It is called his as distinguished from the glory belonging to any other; thus he distinguisheth a glory peculiarly his own from the glory of his Father, and the glory of the holy angels, when he mentions his coming to judgment in all those glories : Luke ix. 26, 'When he shall come in his own glory, and in his Father's, and of the holy angels ;'* in the mediatory glory, in the glory of the Father, the glory of his Godhead, as he is equal with God; in the glory of the whole creation, the angels being the top of it; or in the glory of all the administrations of God, the glory of God as Creator, creation being attributed to the Father ; the glory of the holy angels, by whose disposition the law

  * Sterry of the Will, p. 244.

135

was given, in the glory of the legal administration; in his own glory, the glory of the gospel administration, as judging men according to those several degrees of light they were under, the light of nature, that of the law, and the more glorious of the gospel, his glory.

(1.) As having a peculiar right to it.

[1.] In regard of his designation to it by his Father. He calls it a glory given by God, John xvii. 24. His glory, as promised him by the Father, and covenanted for by himself. He was to be the first-born, higher than the kings. of the earth, Ps. lxxxix. 29. His glory, as by gift he was to have 'dominion from sea to sea, and from the river to the ends of the earth. They that dwell in the wilderness shall bow before him; and his enemies shall lick the dust. For he shall redeem the soul of the needy from deceit and violence. His name shall endure for ever: men shall be blessed in him; and the whole earth was to be filled with his glory,' Ps. lxxii. 8, 9, 14, 17, 19.

[2.] In regard of his purchase of it, all this was his glory. It is generally said that Christ had a title to glory, by virtue of the union of the divine nature to the human. It is true, had Christ been only incarnate for no other end but to take our flesh, glory had of right belonged to him from the beginning, by virtue of that union; but in regard of that economy of God for redemption by blood, and the covenant passed between them consisting of such articles, it was not his incarnation, but his passion invested him with a right to claim it; he was to fulfil his charge before he was to have the fruition of his reward. His glory was promised to him, not as assuming our flesh, but as suffering in our flesh, and making his soul an offering for sin, and being incarnate for this end. Glory belonged not to him till his death had been actually suffered, and declared valid in the sight of God. The satisfaction of his Father by him was to precede his Father's satisfaction of him, Isa. liii. 11. His obedience to death gave a *wherefore* to his exaltation: Philip. ii. 9, 'Wherefore God also hath highly exalted him.' The right to it may be measured by the order of conferring it; it was not conferred till he 'had purged our sins,' Heb. i. 3, and therefore the right to claim it was not till he had performed what was due to his Father.

(2.) As being the first subject of glory, as being the spring of glory to all that were to be glorified. As Adam, the head of mankind, was the first subject of God's rich gifts to his reasonable creature, so was Christ the first subject of God's glorious grace, and gifts to and for his redeemed creature. Others have a glory from him as private persons, Christ hath this glory as a public person, as a second Adam, and so it is his glory peculiar to him, and incommunicable to any else, as being the only and singular head, the one and only public person in the charge of redemption. As his sufferings were peculiarly his, wherein neither men nor angels could be partners with him, so is the glory peculiarly his. As he trod the wine-press alone, so he alone hath right to the crown, and whoever else wears a laurel wears it as his member, not as a head.

Let us consider the connection: 'Ought not Christ to suffer those things, and to enter into his glory?' It is argued whether there was a meritorious connection between the sufferings of Christ, and his glory, *i. e.* whether this glory was merited by his suffering.

1. Some say his sufferings were not meritorious of his own glory; though his exaltation followed upon his passion, yet it was not merited by it. His cross was the way to his crown, but not the deserving cause of his crown; he merited by his sufferings a glory for us, but not for himself; and the act of God whereby it was conferred, is expressed by a word, ἐχαρίσατο, Philip. ii. 9, 'given him,' or freely given him, 'a name which is above every name,'

which signifies an act of grace and not of debt. As he did not fulfil the law for himself, but for us, that he might redeem us from under the curse of the law, by being made a curse for us; and therefore is said to be given to us, Isa. ix. 6, or for our sakes, not to himself or for his own sake; so he acquired nothing for himself by his death but what he had possession of before, *quoad divinitatem* and *quoad humanitatem;* for all power both in heaven and earth was conferred upon him before his death, Mat. xi. 27. All glory,* say they, would have flowed down upon his humanity at the instant of his conception, as the glory of the husband is conferred upon the spouse at the first moment of marriage; but God, by a special dispensation, detained it till he had accomplished his work in the lowest degree of his humiliation; God suspended his concourse, as he did to the fire, which hindered it from exercising its proper quality of burning upon the three children; but this work being performed, and the suspension taken off, his glory could not but naturally fill his humanity, as the quality of fire would return to its natural course upon removing the stops; and therefore, to assert any merit for himself, is a disparagement of, and an impeachment to, his glorious union; and for those places which are alleged for his merit of it, as Philip. ii. 8, 9, Heb. i. 9, and also the text, they shew the order of conferring it, rather than the merit of it, that his glory followed his passion, not that his passion merited his glory;† his glory rather seemed to be a necessary consequent of God's acceptation of his death, and a testimony of heaven's approbation of it. As the occasion of his death was the fall of man, so the moving cause of his death was the redemption of man, not the exaltation of the name of Christ primarily and immediately. For our sakes he slid down from heaven into our nature; for our sakes he bore that burden the law and wrath of God had cast upon him; it was for us that he combated with death, and forced our enemies out of their fortresses. And so by this voluntary submission and humiliation, he came to his former dignity; for if he came to an higher dignity than he had before, it had been evident that he was obedient for himself, not for others.

2. Others say, Christ did merit this glory for himself. The oil of gladness was poured upon his humanity, wherein he had fellows, because he had loved righteousness, Heb. i. 9. *Therefore* is a causal particle, not only of the final cause, but the moral, efficient, or meritorious cause. He did by this merit an exaltation at the right hand of God, above all the choirs of angels. It was indeed due upon his suffering, yet called grace,‡ because the whole design of redemption, in the pitching upon Christ, and the sending him, was an act of free grace in God to us; as it was grace to accept his interposition for us, so it was grace to promise him this glory, and set this joy before him for his encouragement in his sufferings;§ and as it was free grace to unite the flesh to the person of the Son of God, so it was of grace that there was a continuation of demonstrating the glory of the Deity in the same flesh. Yet, after his sufferings, the glory of Christ may be said to be a merited reward, because his glory was not improportionable to his sufferings; he merited the dispossession of the devil, and merited therefore the transferring that power upon himself, to manage for the honour of God, which the devil had usurped over man in rebellion against God. A man may have a double title to an inheritance, by birth and by some signal services done, whereby what was due to him by birth may be due to him by merit; as when a province flies into rebellion against the lawful prince, he

---

* Donn, vol. i. p. 108. Alvarez de Incarnat.   † Suarez.
‡ As was noted before in the word ἐχαρίσατο, Philip ii. 9.
§ Coccei. de Fœdere, sect. cvi.

sends his eldest son with an army to quell those tumults ; his arms prove successful, and the rebels are reduced to obedience. Doth he not merit a title to that inheritance by his sword, which was due to him by his birth ? Indeed, Christ did not merit his first mission, no more than the prince's son merited his being sent for the reduction of the rebels; nor did he merit his first unction and habitual grace. This belonged to the perfection of the soul of Christ, and fitted him for his mediatory work in our nature ; he could not have wanted this without prejudice to the work of redemption, and to our salvation, which was the end of it, though this was necessarily consequent upon an admission of Christ's mediation, and a necessary article in the covenant of redemption, yet it was the act of God's free grace. Nor must we think that this glory was the motive to Christ to engage him first in this undertaking, but pure grace to us ; for what attractives could there be in our nature to make this divine person assume it ? Or what glory could be conferred upon the humanity, that could allure the Deity to embody itself in it ? Could the promise of an honour to be conferred upon an angel, if he would enclose himself in the body of a fly or other insect, move him to link his own nature with that for ever, since he enjoyed before a higher honour in his own nature than could be conferred upon him upon such a conjunction ? It was the grace of Christ that moved him when he was rich to become poor, not that he might be the richer by that poverty, but we : 2 Cor. viii. 9, 'For you know the grace of our Lord Jesus Christ, that, though he was rich, for our sakes he became poor, that we through his poverty might be rich.' Yet Christ may be said to merit this mediatory glory for himself; the Holy Ghost was a meritorious fruit of the sufferings of Christ, and why not that glory then which was necessary to the sending the Holy Ghost, whose coming he had purchased ? The very sending the Holy Ghost was a great part of his glory ; and we must remember, that whatsoever was merited by Christ, was not merited by virtue of his humanity singly considered, but as having the Deity in conjunction with it ; and why might not so great a person merit at the hands of God ?

3. Let this be as it will, yet the sufferings of Christ were a cause of his glory, or a way to his glory, by mediatory compact. For as he was by that bound to pay an obedience he was not obliged to before, so was the Father by that obliged to give him a glory proportionable to his work, and a glory distinct from the glory of the Deity. The waters were to come into his soul, Ps. lxix. 2 ; he was to drink of the brook in the way, therefore should he lift up his head, Ps. cx. 7. This order did God require for the exalting of him, combat before triumph. This glory could not be conferred upon him before his suffering. If he had enjoyed it from the beginning, by virtue of the hypostatical union, his body had been impassible, incapable of suffering, and so could not have been a sacrifice for our sins. His triumphant laurel grew upon the thorns of his cross, and received a verdure from his dying tears. The palms spread in his way at his entrance into Jerusalem, a little before his suffering, are by some regarded as an emblem of this, it being the nature of that plant to grow higher by the weights which are hung upon it, for so did our Saviour rise more glorious by his pressures. There was a worthiness in his death to entitle him to the fruition of glory : Rev. v. 12, ' Worthy is the Lamb that was slain to receive power, and riches, and wisdom, and strength, and honour, and glory, and blessing.' Worthy to receive power for silencing the oracles of the devil, power to conquer his enemies ; riches, to pour out upon his friends ; wisdom, to govern his empire ; strength, to execute his orders ; worthy to be honoured, adored, blessed by all. And this glory he challenged as due by virtue of his sufferings, John xvii. 1. It was fit he

should be lifted up above death after he had so obediently suffered, and be instated in the empire of the world after he had so magnificently redeemed it. The necessity of his sufferings is here described, and also the necessity of his glory. *Ought not* is to be referred to both,—ought he not to suffer, ought he not upon those sufferings to enter into glory? How did he suffer? As man. He entered into glory as man; as man he suffered, as man he was glorified. His divine nature was impassible, and also unglorifiable by any addition of glory to it. His death was necessary for us, so was his glory. He died in a public capacity as a surety for mankind; he was exalted in a public capacity as the head of those he died for. As he offered himself to God for us upon the cross, so he entered into heaven to appear in the presence of God for us upon his throne, Heb. ix. 24.

The doctrine to be hence observed is this,

Doct. The exaltation of Christ was as necessary as his passion.

As it was necessary for him to reconcile us by his death, so it was necessary for him to reinstate us in happiness by his life, Rom. v. 10. Reconciliation is ascribed to his death, salvation to his life in glory. He could not have been a Saviour without being a sacrifice; he could not have applied that salvation without being a king; he was to descend from heaven clothed with our infirmities, to suffer for our crimes. He was to ascend to heaven, invested with immortality, to present our persons before God, and prepare a glory for every believer.

In the handling this doctrine I shall shew,

I. The necessity of this glory.

II. The nature of it.

III. The ends of it.

IV. The use.

I. The necessity of this glory.

First, Upon the account of God.

1. In regard of his truth, the truth of his promise; his promise *to* him, his promises *of* him.

(1.) His promise to him, to Christ. God's truth was engaged for his glory, as the Mediator's truth was engaged for his suffering; and therefore that was as necessarily to be conferred upon him, as the other was to be endured by him. As the ignominy of the cross was an article on his part, so the honour of a crown was an article on God's part. Upon the making his soul an offering for sin, did depend all the promises made to him of his headship over the church, dominion over the world, manifestation of his Deity, propagation of his kingdom, and subjection of his enemies. Without the performance of what he promised, he could not claim one; and upon the performance of what he promised, he could claim all, and his claim could meet with no demur in the court of heaven, so long as God was true to his word. Christ was to surrender himself as a surety for man to the wrath of God, and God was to surrender the government of the world into the hands of Christ. His visage was to be marred, and he was to sprinkle many nations by his blood, Isa. lii. 14, 15; and then kings should shut their mouths at him. Kings in power, kings in wisdom, should be astonished at his growth, and submit to his sceptre. As he was to suffer for many nations, so he was to judge among many nations, Micah iv. 3. He was not to see corruption, his soul was not to be left in hell, Ps. xvi. 10, 11; 'Thou wilt not leave my soul in hell, neither wilt thou suffer thine Holy One to see corruption,' &c., Acts ii. 27, 28. Christ articled with God to go into the state of the dead, but not to be left there; he was to pass into the grave, but not to be invaded by the rottenness of it; he was to be shewn the paths of life, *i. e.* to be restored to another life, to be possessed of a fulness of joy, that was to follow his resurrection, after the ignominy of his death and the agonies of his spirit. As he was to have a fulness of spirit in the world, so he was to have a fulness of joy in his glory. As his grace was to be so great as not to be measured, so his glory was to be so great as not to be bounded; and as his death was to be of a short duration, not fully the term of three days, so his pleasures were to be of an endless duration, pleasures for evermore. And all this glory was to flow from the presence of God, whom his human soul was for ever to behold and converse with, with infinite pleasure: 'In thy presence is fulness of joy.' His whole exaltation, which consisted principally in a manifestion of his Deity and Sonship, was passed by a decree of God, and published to him as Mediator: Ps. ii. 7, 'I will declare the decree, the Lord hath said unto me, Thou art my Son, this day have I begotten thee;' which is interpreted of his resurrection, Acts xiii. 33, which was the first powerful declaration God issued out to the world of his being his Son, Rom. i. 4. Upon which account Peter tells us he was foreordained, both to his sufferings and glory, before the foundation of the world, 1 Peter i. 20, 21; he was to inherit the spoils of his enemies, and take for his own what was before Satan's prey as a reward; and that for the pouring out his soul to death, Isa. liii. 12, he was to see his seed upon the making his soul an offering for sin, Isa. liii. 10; then also his days were to be prolonged. What! to a miserable and infirm life? No, but to such a one as should endure to eternity, wherein is included, not only his resurrection, but his glorious state. How could he see his seed, if he remained in the fetters of death? or behold them with comfort, if he should enjoy an immortality in as infirm a body as he had in the time of his humiliation? The sight of his seed was to follow his investiture in glory, and was a part of it; then it was that nations should run unto him, Isa. lv. 5. All those promises were made to him as incarnate, and making himself an oblation; for, as God, he was not the subject of any promise. He was to bear our iniquities on the cross, and then to live triumphantly upon a throne. Christ pleads this, John xvii. 1, 'The hour is come; Father, glorify thy Son;' the hour of my passion, the hour of thy promise. I am willing to undergo the one, and just now ready to drink of the brook in the way; be thou ready, O Father, according to thy promise and oath, wherein thou stoodest obliged to perform the other part, my glorification; and particularly the manifestation of my deity, upon which all the other parts of my exaltation depend. Ver. 5, 'And now, O Father, glorify me with thy own self, with the glory which I had with thee before the world was;' which was not the glory of his humanity (which was not in being before the world was), but the glory of his divinity in the full unveiling of it, that it might shine brighter before the eyes of men. It had indeed before been obscured in the form of a servant in the time of his life, in the repute of a criminal at the time of his death; but now he prays that he might be manifested to be what he really was, a person that had a glorious existence before the world was, and that had no need to come down and take the nature of man for any advantage to himself. Now, as God promised him a glory, and Christ pleads the promise, so God performed it; and therefore his ascension is expressed by God's receiving him up into glory, as well as by his own act of entering into it: 1 Tim. iii. 16, 'received up into glory,' Ἀνελήφθη, recovered again unto glory; for it was impossible God should be false to his eternal purpose, and his repeated promise.

(2.) His promises or predictions of him. So that his exaltation was necessary to justify the prophecies of it, which were not the predictions of one or two of the most eminent of the prophets, but that which all of them,

one way or other, spake of ever since the world began, Acts iii. 21.   Isaiah
is the plainest of all, and many things to this purpose are inserted in his
prophecy : Isa. iv. 2, ' In that day shall the branch of the Lord be beautiful
and glorious, and the fruit of the earth shall be excellent and comely.'   As
he is the fruit of the earth, he shall be excellent in his humanity ; and as he
is the branch of the Lord, he shall be acknowledged in his divinity ; or, as
he is the branch of the Lord in his conception by the Holy Ghost, and the
fruit of the earth in his birth of the virgin, he shall be glorious in the world.
And this was to be for his service, and as the servant of God : Isa. lii. 13,
' My servant shall be exalted and extolled, and be very high ;' which relation of service he had not in the divine nature, but his mediatory function ;
and so glorious was his life to be, and so long the duration of it, after he
should be taken from prison and from judgment, that it should be past the
declaration of any creature : Isa. liii. 8, ' Who shall declare his generation ?'
And it is very clear, in Ezek. xvii. 22, ' I will also take of the highest branch
of the high cedar, and will set it ; I will crop off from the top of his young
twigs a tender one, and will plant it upon a high mountain and eminent,'
&c.   This is not meant of Zerubbabel, under whom the people had not such
a signal rest, nor did his empire extend so far as to shadow the fowl of every
wing, the people of every nation.   Christ was a plant of his Father's setting,
a young twig in his humbled, a tall cedar in his exalted, state ; planted in
the highest mountains, eminent above all the rest ; i.e. even he was to be
cut off, but not for himself, Dan. ix. 26 ; not to himself, say some ;* his
cutting off shall not be without a second springing up in a resurrection.   And
when he is the Son of man, he was to be brought with the clouds of heaven,
with the angels which attended him at his ascension, before the Ancient of days,
and that near to him ; and so welcome he was to be upon his approach, as
to be presented with the dominion of the whole world, Dan. vii. 13, 14,
which is not to be understood of his coming at the day of judgment, but his
coming after his oblation.   He comes not here to judge man, but to be
judged by his Father ; and upon being found to have performed the part of
the Son of man, he hath a kingdom both extensive and everlasting bestowed
upon him, which should not be destroyed by the subtleties or force of his
enemies ; a present only worthy of the Son of God.   Again, he received not
his power at the day of judgment, but upon his resurrection and ascension
after his death ; but this expresseth the first investiture of this power in him.
This glory was prophesied of a thousand years before the accomplishment :†
Ps. lxviii. 17, 18, ' Thou hast ascended on high.'   The whole design of the
psalm manifests it, as well as the citation of it by the apostle, Eph. iv. 8.
Joseph was not taken from prison to live his former life of slavery, but a
princely life upon a throne, and rule the whole kingdom next to the sovereign
prince ; so Christ was not to live the same life after his resurrection that he
had done before in his sweats and combats, and to endure the contradictions
of sinners against himself ; but was to be advanced to a place suitable to his
greatness, upon the right hand and throne of his Father.

2. Upon the account of righteousness and goodness.

(1.) In regard of his innocence, he was a real innocent, though a reputed
criminal ; innocent in himself, guilty only as standing in our stead ; holy,
harmless, undefiled, separate from sinners, Heb. vii. 26, as if there were not
words enough to express his purity, he being most holy and undefiled.   It
doth not seem to consist with the justice of God for him so to give his life for
us as never to reassume it.   He was a person more excellent than the whole

* Sennert. de Idiotis. linguar. orient., canon xxviii. p. 25.
† Daillé de l'Ascension, p. 431.

world of men and angels. He being a divine person, his life was incomparably more excellent than the lives of all mankind. Surely God, that loved him so dearly, would not have given so glorious a life for the salvation of men, to be swallowed up in the grave without a happy restoration of it. It doth not seem to consist with the wisdom, love, or justice of God to give so excellent a life for the saving ours, if it were not again to spring up to a glorious state out of the ashes of mortality. Was not his death the fruit of his innocence? Was it equal that he should be held in the bands of that, or walk in the world under the load and burden of a mortal body, any longer than the expiation of our sins required?* If this had been, had not a fundamental law of God, which orders immortality and happiness to perfect holiness, been violated, which is impossible?

(2.) In regard of the near alliance to himself. Did it consist with equity to let that person who was equal with himself in regard of the divine nature; that person who was in the form of God, as well as in the form of a servant, Philip. ii. 6, 7; that nature which was so gloriously united to a nature infinitely above the angelical, to corrupt in the grave and crumble to dirt and filth? to be a banquet for worms that had been a fragrant sacrifice to God? Or could it be counted equity to have raised him to no better a life than that miserable one he led before, his agonies in the garden, and his gaspings on the cross? Had it not been an unrighteousness to himself, as well as to his Son? Surely that a flesh which had the honour to be the temple of God, a branch of the Lord, the powerful conception of the Holy Ghost, that had the glory to be personally united to the Son of God, to live and subsist in him, should not be glorified after it was raised again, seems to be against all the laws and rules of goodness and righteousness.

(3.) In regard of the work he had performed. How could justice forbear to deliver the surety, after he had paid so much that it was impossible, upon an exact scrutiny, to find a farthing wanting? How could it be agreeable to goodness to continue a person under the chains of death, or the lighter fetters of an infirm and earthly life, who was not liable to more punishment, nor capable of performing a greater service in this world than what he had already done? It was the interest of satisfied justice to raise him from death; and was it not as well the interest of remunerative righteousness to exalt him to be the head of that church he had so dearly purchased? Could goodness continue him a little lower than the angels, who had performed a task that would have broke the back and cracked the heart of the whole angelical nature to accomplish? If God rewards as a righteous judge, 2 Tim. iv., a reward below an exaltation above all the angels had been disproportioned to so deep a humiliation, to so punctual, and in all respects a voluntary and unconstrained, obedience. Was it congruous to the goodness of God to let so signal an obedience, more excellent than the obedience of millions of worlds of angels, pass away without as signal a reward? That so sharp a cross, endured by an innocent with so much affliction and freeness, should not be succeeded by a crown as glorious as the cross was ignominious? In equity he was to be placed far above principalities and powers, the revolted rabble of devils, and their companions bad men, since he had so gloriously conquered and routed those armies of hell, Col. ii. 15, and above the corporations of the standing angels, since he had so graciously confirmed them, Eph. i. 10, by whom those blessed spirits commenced masters of a greater knowledge of the perfections of God than they had by the whole creation for four thousand years. There was all the reason that so incomparable a victory should be attended with as glorious a triumph.

* Daillé sur Resurrect. de Christ. p. 361.

(4.) In regard of the glory which redounded to God from this work. All that was done tended to the restoring of God's honour in the casting out the prince of the world from his usurpation, demolishing idolatry, and restoring the worship of God upon pure and spiritual principles. God received more glory by his mediation than by all the works of his hands, the glory of his grace in his mission, the glory of his justice in his sufferings, and the glory of his wisdom in the whole dispensation, which was a new glory that never accrued to him before, nor could ever be brought into his exchequer by any other way than this. By this the bar to God's resting and rejoicing in his work was removed, the bands of sin were broken off, a carnal Adam changed into a spiritual, the defaced image of God restored, the world formed into a second and more noble creation, and the kingdom of God established in the world by the conquest and spoiling of the revolted spirits. If God were glorious by creating a world, he was more glorious in the redemption of the world. It was reasonable Christ should be advanced to the highest pitch of glory, suitable to that degree of emptiness to which he had abased himself for this end,* that he should triumphantly be settled in the most glorious and majestic place of the empire of God, and have not only the highest place of residence, but the greatest height of authority over men and angels, having made peace between God and the creation, and between one part of the creation and another; that as he died once with a pure zeal for the glory of God, he might live in a new state to a further exaltation of him; for so he doth: Rom. vi. 10, ' In that he lives, he lives unto God,' to gather his people, to glorify them, and be glorified by them. As there was a glory brought to God by Christ in his low estate, so there was a further glory to be brought to him in his exalted estate, according to the voice of the Father to him: John xii. 28, ' I have both glorified my name, and will glorify it again.' As he had glorified it in the doctrine and miracles of Christ, so he would glorify it again by his passion and resurrection, sending the Spirit, propagating the gospel, and setting him upon the throne as the judge of the world. This glorifying God was the argument Christ pleaded for his assistance and exaltation in the prophet (Ps. lxix. 7, ' Because for thy sake I have borne reproach, shame hath covered my face '), that the faith of the saints in the divine promises might not be enfeebled by any carelessness of God towards him, ver. 6. And near the time of his death he pleads it in his own person, that he might be in a state to carry on that glory he had begun to bring to God, to the highest degree : John i. 17, ' Glorify thy Son, that thy Son also may glorify thee.' Christ was to do more service for God in heaven than he did on earth, and glorify his Father after his Father had glorified him, *i. e.* by a particular application of his death to men, by the virtue of his intercession, though indeed the foundation of all that glory was laid upon the cross by his satisfaction. Had God been good to the Redeemer, if he had given him less than a crown for a cross, a reward for the work effected by his suffering ? And had he been righteous and good to himself, if he had put Christ into a state below that which should capacitate him to perfect the remains of that honour of his name, which were further to be extant in the world ? What capacity could we imagine him to have if he had lain under the feet of death, or sat languishing on the footstool of the earth in a feeble immortality ? A throne was due for the glory he had gained, and a throne was fit for the glory he was yet to effect.

3. Upon the account of love to Christ. His paternal affection to his Son required not only a deliverance of him from the jaws of death, but the putting such a crown upon his head, by which he might be known by all to be his

* Faucheur, in Acts ii. 9, p. 109.

Son, whom he embraced with an ardent affection.* God would not love his Son according to his own greatness, if he did not manifest it to the world with the most signal marks and ensigns of authority. And surely after he had vanquished his Father's wrath, and triumphed over the enemies of his honour, he could expect no other than the strong effluxes of his Father's love in the highest expressions of it. What could hinder him from resting in his bosom, when all the wrath excited by the transgressions of the law was calmed, and the Redeemer came out victorious from that furnace of wrath wherein he had been enclosed. Wrath thus being quenched by his sufferings, there was no room for the exercise of any other affection to him than that of love; and no testimony could be given proportionably to such an affection, but the highest degree of honour conferred upon him. The Father loved him because he laid down his life, John x. 17; and the same affections would be more strongly manifested after he had laid it down, and prompt him to shew him greater works than those which had been wrought in the world, that the world might marvel, John v. 20. He would manifest him to be the partaker of all his counsels, that nothing of authority should be denied him, nothing of knowledge concealed from him. These were the signal demonstrations of the Father's love, expected by our Saviour.

Secondly, It was necessary on the account of Christ himself.

(1.) In regard of his nature.

[1.] As it was of an heavenly original : He came down from heaven, Job iii. 13. He was that holy thing born of the virgin, but as overshadowed by the power of the highest, Luke i. 35. He was not born by the force of flesh and blood, according to the law of creation settled in old Adam; he was an heavenly man, or the Lord from heaven, 1 Cor. xv. 47, and therefore was immortal in the true and original constitution of his nature.† And though he lived in a veiled condition to fulfil the charge which he undertook, and which could not otherwise be accomplished, yet, after the completing of it, he could not be retained in the bands of death, but must necessarily return by the law of his own nature to his true and original condition, and lead an heavenly and glorious life, suitable to the principle whereby he was formed.‡ All things are ordered by God in places suitable to their nature; heavy things are placed lowest, lighter things highest; and if for the good of the universe they remove out of their proper place contrary to their natures, as soon as ever the occasion which obliged them to such a motion is over, they return to the place of their former settlement proportionable to their nature. As air, whose place is above the earth, when it is enclosed in the bowels of the earth, and there increased by vapours, will find its way out by an earthquake, to that place which God hath settled for it; stones descend, and water flows down to its proper place, as soon as the let is removed ; so, though Christ, for the good of mankind, stepped into the world, yet when he had effected that business, he must necessarily take his flight to heaven, his proper place. When that which obliged him to come upon the earth was ceased, and he had no more to do here, upon that occasion of the expiation of our sin, heaven, that was the principle of his original, was to be that of his rest and abode. As earth was assigned to the first man, who was earthly, for an habitation, so heaven was the proper element of repose for the second man, who was heavenly. It was most convenient that an earthly man should be lodged in the earth, and the Son of God have his seat where the throne of his Father was. § It was not fit that any creature should be above the person of the

* Amyrald, Symbol. Apostol. p. 169.   † Daillé, Melan. part ii. p. 631.
‡ Daillé sur l'Ascens. de Christ. p. 434, somewhat changed.
Faucheur, in Act. i. 9, p. 109.

Son of God, what nature soever he had assumed, and therefore his exaltation above the angels was due also upon that account.

[2.] As his body was changed by the resurrection.   Since after his resurrection his body was made immortal, and had new qualities conferred upon it, whereby it had acquired an incorruptible life ;* as our bodies shall at the resurrection be incorruptible and spiritual, 1 Cor. xv. 42, 44 ; it was not fit it should make any long stay in a place of corruption and misery ; and that so excellent a person should have an habitation in a world of men and beasts. A corrupted place was not convenient for an immortal body; nor an earth, cursed by God, suitable to an unstained nature, that had nothing further to do here by himself.   But seeing it was the most perfect body, it was convenient it should be taken up into the most perfect place, and ascend above all bodies.†   Indeed, while he had a body of such a mould as ours, and furnished with the same earthly qualities and infirmities with ours, his abode in the world was somewhat suited to his body as well as to his work ; but when he had put off his grave-clothes, and was stripped of that old furniture, and enriched with new and heavenly qualities, heaven was the most proper place for his residence.   Again, had the earth been a proper place for him, it was not fit the Divinity should stoop to reside in the proper place of the humanity, but the humanity be fetched up to the proper place of the Deity, where the Deity doth manifest itself in the glory of its nature.   The lesser should wait upon the greater, and the younger serve the elder.

[3.] As the greatest part of his exaltation consisted in the manifestation of his Deity.   It was not fit so great a conqueror and Redeemer, who was God as well as man, should have his deity still under the veil of our flesh, after he had accomplished so great a work.   Indeed, he hath our flesh united in heaven to his divine nature, but his divine nature is not veiled by it, as it was here.   Now, had his deity been manifested here below in that vast brightness and splendour which was proper for it, the sons of men had been undone, and met with their ruin instead of their recovery; for who can see God and live ? Exod. xxxiii. 20, ' No man can see my face and live.'   Heaven was therefore the only place where this could be manifested in that illustrious manner which it ought to be, though earth was the place for the powerful effects of it.   I say, then, it was not fit the glory of his deity should have been longer overshadowed by the veil of his humanity ; and it could not have broken out in its clearness without not only dazzling our eyes, but consuming our beings, in that state we are.   The brightness of an angel is too great an object for weak man, without the shadow of some assumed body, much more the brightness of the Son of God ; and what need was there of his being veiled for us still, when he had done all that was necessary to be effected in that veil of infirmity he had wrapped himself in ?

(2.) It was necessary upon the account of Christ, in regard of his offices. Had not Christ been glorified, the offices conferred upon him by his Father could not have been executed ; his prophetical, priestly, and royal functions could not have been exercised, to which he was chosen by God, and without which he could not have been a Saviour to us.   He had been a sacrifice, without being a priest ; a king, without possessing a throne ; a prophet, without a chair to teach in ; at least none of these offices could have been managed in a way worthy of himself, unless he had been in a glorious condition, and his humanity in a glorious place.

[1.] It was necessary for his prophetical office.   As he did but begin to exercise his priestly office in his death, and began to execute his royal func-

* Faucheur, in Act. i. 9, p. 109.
† Savonarola, Triumph. cruc. lib. iii. cap. 19.

tion in his miracles, so he did but begin to manage his prophetical office in his life: Heb. ii. 3, ' Salvation began to be spoken by the Lord.' His death was a consecration to a further exercise of his priestly office, his signs and wonders the first essays of his kingly, and his own teachings the first rudiments of prophecy. After his ascension he did, as the Sun of righteousness, spread the wings of his grace, and flew about the world in the illuminations of hearts, Mal. iv. 2. As it is with the sun, so was it with Christ, the nearer the earth in the winter of his humiliation, the less force he had for the production of fruits, but the higher he mounted in heaven the more vigorous. The beams of the sun shot from heaven make us distinguish those things which we mistook in the dark, and the rays of Christ, after his ascension, manifested the difference between truth and error. Then the living waters of the sanctuary grew high, Ezek. xlvii. 3–5, and what was before but a drop of knowledge in Christ's beginning to teach, became an unfathomable sea of knowledge in Christ's effusion of the Spirit at his ascension.

[1.] Without this ascension, his doctrine had not had a perfect confirmation. As his divine Sonship was declared in part in his resurrection, Rom. i. 4, so his doctrine met with a confirmation in that manifestation of him to be the Son of God; but as that was but the first step to a manifestation of his person, so it was but the first degree of the manifestation of his doctrine. The more complete justification of his doctrine was cleared by his elevation to heaven; it then appeared that he did (as he said himself) declare the words of God; that as his humiliation discovered him to be a man, his exaltation and the fruits of it discovered him to be a divine prophet of a greater dignity and richer influence than all that went before him. He had been unjustly charged, in the delivery of his doctrine, with the crime of blasphemy, and very few were persuaded either of the divinity of his person or the heavenliness of his doctrine. By his ascension God declared him to be a prophet sent by him, and that prophet whereof Moses spake, Acts xxi. 22; he acknowledged him to be really what he reported himself to be, one with the Father, having a perfect knowledge of the Father, one speaking the words of God, and acting according to the order of God. Had what he asserted of himself been false, he had been so far from being advanced to heaven, that he had been hurled down to the bottomless pit for his imposture. God would not by any act, much less by the conferring so great a glory, have contributed credit to a lie. But God hath decided the controversy between him and the Jews, his accusers, and cast them by, owning him in the quality of his Son, and the great prophet, whereby he had entitled himself among them. What greater testimony can there be than God's putting all power into his hands, giving him the keys of death and hell, the power of opening the seals, and slaying by the words of his mouth? Thus God recommended his doctrine, and by lifting him up to heaven, set him there as a Sun to free the world from the blackness of error, wherewith the night had filled it.

[2.] Without this the apostles could not have been furnished with gifts for the propagation of his doctrine. Those weak men could not have gone about so great a work without a mighty furniture and magazine of divine eloquence and vigorous courage; to give this was not his immediate work as Mediator, and in the economy of the divine persons pertained to the Holy Ghost. It was necessary, therefore, that he should, as high priest, enter into the holy place, and appear before God with the blood of his eternal sacrifice, that the treasures of the Spirit might be opened, and that that divine flame might issue out from thence to inspire them with abilities for so great an undertaking. This he had not had power to do, unless he had been glorified, John vii. 34, ' The Holy Ghost was not yet given, because Jesus was not yet glorified.' He could not before invest his officers with a transcendent power, because he was not mounted to a full execution of his own office. It was after this he erected the Christian church among the Gentiles as well as Jews, completed the rule of faith in the writings of the apostles, which was to endure to the end of the world. Without this glorification, he had not been the universal teacher of the mysteries of salvation, nor qualified the apostles for the propagation of his doctrine. But by this means he exercised his office, not only among the Jews, as the minister of the circumcision, but among all nations of the Gentiles, as the chief doctor and prophet of the world, by the publication of the gospel and the grace of the Spirit.

[3.] Nor could the apostles without this have had any success. They had nothing of a worldly stamp and beauty that could persuade people to an entertainment of their doctrine. They had not the wealth and grandeurs of the world to offer them, nor could allure them by earthly empires and conquests, as Mahomet did his followers. To preach a crucified God would be justly thought an extravagance and the fruits of a frenzy; but when they should hear not only of his resurrection, but the possession of a glory, from so many witnesses upon whom they could fasten nothing of distemper, an end would be put to their astonishment.* His crucifixion could not appear so irrational to them, as the news of an exaltation, whereby the ignominy of the cross was changed into the glory of a crown, would appear amazing. Since the Spirit could not come unless Christ were glorified, it was impossible that without this glorification of the Redeemer, and consequently the effusion of the Spirit, that those delegates of Christ could publish the gospel with such power, resist such violences, triumph over such oppositions; and impossible for men to have believed or regarded what they said, since their doctrines were so contrary to the common maxims of the world, which had been so long strengthened by education and custom, the strongest chains next to corrupt nature. As the ascension of Christ gave the apostles (the spectators of it) courage to publish the greatness of our Saviour with boldness, as before they had denied him with cowardice in his humiliation, so it made way for the entrance of his doctrine into the belief of the hearers, which otherwise they would have been ashamed to entertain, had it not been backed with so great an argument, and testified by such witnesses, and seconded by such miracles, against which they could have no exception. Without this, those main truths of the gospel upon which the Christian religion depended, and which are the life and soul of it, as the redemption of man, the justification of believers by the blood of his sacrifice, had wanted a ground for the manifestation of them, and all the comforts of the gospel been frustrate. Men could have had no apprehension of such things without an accomplishment of his glory. Hence it was that so often Christ assured his disciples while he was instructing them, in the time of his life, of the great works they should perform, and the success they should meet with after his departure. His doctrine had been more obscure, and lost much of its clearness, had he stayed below.

[4.] Heaven alone was a fit seat for him wherein to exercise this office. It was no more convenient for him to be placed on earth, who was to disperse his light into the understandings of men, and scatter ignorance in all parts of the world, than for the sun to have been placed on the earth for the spreading its beams into all climates of the world. An earthly seat was fit for an earthly prophet; but was it fit for him who was constituted by God, not only a prophet to the Jews, but to all the nations and tribes of mankind; whose doctrine was not to be confined to the narrow limits of Jerusalem or Judea,

* Amyraut. in Tim. p. 224.

but extend to all parts of the world?* What though the dusty earth bore his body in the days of his humiliation, while he was laying the foundation of those truths which were to sound in every quarter! Yet when he came to be installed the sole doctor and teacher of the whole world, it was not fit he should be placed in any sphere lower than that of heaven, whence he might make his voice known both to heaven and earth, to men and angels, and convey his instructions to those blessed spirits who were yet to learn more of the mysteries of divine wisdom, Eph. iii. 10, and also to the multitudes of the Gentiles, as well as to the small number of the lost sheep of the house of Israel.

(2.) Necessary it was for his priestly office. Though he was a priest by authority in the days of his humiliation, yet he was not fully installed in the perpetual exercise of this office, till his 'sitting at the right hand of God,' Ps. cx. 1, 4; and when he was declared harmless, and undefiled, and separate from sinners, though sacrificed for them, and thereupon made higher than the heavens, and by that declared to be the Son of God, then he was as his Son consecrated a 'priest for evermore,' Heb. vii. 26, 28.

[1.] He had not done the whole work of a priest had he remained upon the earth. As the legal high priest had not been a complete high priest, and fulfilled every part of his office, had he not entered into the holy of holies, so neither had Christ performed the whole work of a priest had he remained upon earth and not entered into the heavenly sanctuary, to appear or be manifested in the presence of God for us, Heb. ix. 24. It was not enough for the legal high priest to cut the throat and pour out the blood of the sacrifice in the outward tabernacle, and offer it upon the altar on the day of the annual expiation,† but he was to pass within the veil, to present the blood of the victim to the Lord, and sprinkle it towards the propitiatory, Lev. xvi., and upon his return to publish the atonement and reconciliation to the people; so that there had been no analogy between the type and antitype, if our Saviour after his oblation on earth had not in the quality of a priest passed into the heavens, as through the veil which separated the heavenly sanctuary from the outward court. It was necessary therefore that the true high priest should advance into the true sanctuary, into heaven itself (figured by that legal place), where God hath his residence among the true cherubims and angels of glory; that he should sprinkle this mercy-seat, and present before the throne that blood which he had shed upon the cross, till the time that, the number of his elect being completed, he is to return out of the sanctuary, *i. e.* descend from heaven to earth to pronounce the sentence of their general absolution, and gather them to himself in the glory of his kingdom. By his own blood he entered into the holy place, having obtained eternal redemption for us, Heb. ix. 12. This entering into the holy place with the blood of the sacrifice was the main end of the sacrifice, and a necessary act of the high priest, and appropriate to him alone. The end why it was offered in the temple was, that it might be presented in the sanctuary; so while Christ disposed himself to those sufferings which he was to undergo for the expiation of our sins, it was necessary he should be upon the earth; but after he had offered himself a sacrifice upon the cross, it was no less necessary for him to ascend in person, and carry the treasures of his blood with him, to be laid up in that repository, to be sprinkled in the heavenly places, and remain for ever as a mark in the true sanctuary, as a treasure of perpetual merit. The legal priest was also to burn incense in the holy place. By incense in Scripture is frequently meant prayer. If Christ be not then an intercessor in heaven,

* Daillé sur l'Ascension de Christ, p. 435, somewhat changed.
† Faucheur in Acts, vol. i. p 111.

there is no analogy between the type and the antitype.   This intercession, a great part of his priestly office, could no more have been managed but in heaven than the oblation, the first part of his office, could have been performed anywhere but on earth.   Had he therefore remained upon the earth after the shedding of his blood, he had not fully executed his office, but had performed it by halves, and that which he had performed on earth had been without strength, without performing the other in heaven; for then it was that he was made an high priest for ever after the order of Melchisedec, Heb. vi. 20 and a minister of the sanctuary, Heb. viii. 1, 2.   He is hence called the high priest of our profession, Heb. iii. 1, as performing all the duties, and enjoying all the privileges really, which the legal high priest did perform and enjoy figuratively.   Without this glorious translation, he could not really in his own person have carried his blood into the sanctuary, nor appeared in the presence of God for us, nor have opened heaven for those that are his followers.

[2.] Heaven only was fit to be the residence of so great a priest.   As he was a priest, it was fit he should have a sanctuary ; as he was the great priest, it was fit he should have the highest sanctuary ; as he was the everlasting priest, it was fit he should have an everlasting sanctuary ; as he was an undefiled priest, it was fit he should have an undefiled sanctuary ; as he was a priest constituted and consecrated in a special manner by God, and not by man, as Aaron and his posterity were, it was fit he should have a special sanctuary, which Aaron and his posterity had not ; as he was to appear in the presence of God for us, it was fit it should be in a place where God doth manifest himself in the glory of his deity.   Now, no place but heaven can challenge all those qualities.   It was very convenient and necessary that he who was the high priest according to the order of Melchisedec, a blessing as well as a sacrificing priest, distributing spiritual and heavenly blessings to his people, should not be seated in an orb inferior to that place whence those blessings were to receive their original, and flow down upon the world.   And since he was a priest not designed for one particular nation, nor consecrated only for such a spot of land as Judea, but for the whole world, it was necessary that he should be in such a place where all may address themselves to him that stand in need of the exercise of his office, and from whence he may behold all with those compassions which are annexed to his priesthood.   It was necessary also that he that made the reconciliation for men should reside with God (who had been offended, and now was reconciled) to preserve it firm and stedfast, since while the world doth last there are daily so many breaches made to forfeit it.

[3.] It was necessary for his kingly office.   It was fit that he that had done so great a work, and had merited so great a crown, that was exalted to be a prince and a saviour, and had received an heavenly authority and power to give repentance and forgiveness of sins, Acts viii. 31, should also be received into heaven till the time of the restitution of all things, Acts iii. 31, till all things be restored to their due order.

[1.] It was necessary for his triumph.   Indeed, for the beginning of the exercise of his prophetical charge, there was a necessity of his residence among men for the divulging some truths and counsels of his Father ; and while he was to conflict with his enemies with sweat and blood, it could not well be but in the field of battle wherein the enemies were ; but when he came off with victory, he could not conveniently triumph in the place of battle, or reign as a king suitably to his grandeur upon the dunghill of the earth.* It was fit he should sit in triumph at the right hand of his Father, to end

* Amyraut. in Tim. p. 213.

and complete the fruits of his victory : Ps. cx. 1, ' Sit thou at my right hand, till I make thine enemies thy footstool.' As he had not been in a capacity to reign had he continued as a subject under the dominion of death, so he could not exercise the office of a king so commendably as upon the throne of his Father. Heaven only was a palace fit for the residence of the King of kings.

[2.] It was necessary for his government. As heaven is the fountain of providence, so it was fit that the king, into whose hands God committed all judgment, the power and government of the world, should sit upon a throne in heaven; and it was not congruous that he that was made the head of principalities and powers, the governor of the angelical spirits, should have a meaner dwelling than the greatest of his subjects, and as low as the vilest of his vassals. The wisdom of God hath disposed all causes in an order superior to those effects which depend upon them;* the heavens are above the earth, because the earth is influenced by them; and the sun above the earth, because the earth is enlightened by it. It was no less necessary, according to the order of God's wisdom, that he who was made by God his viceroy both in heaven and earth, and had the management of all things conferred upon him, should be lodged in a place superior to those things he was to govern, from whence he might send forth his directions to all his subjects. And though he had by his death given his enemies a mortal wound, and stripped the devil of the right he had acquired by the sin of man, yet, in the order of divine wisdom, the possession he had of the world was not to be taken away, and men reduced to the sceptre of this great king, but in a way convenient to the nature of man. Those gifts, therefore, which were necessary for the reduction of him, could only be dispensed from heaven; it was therefore necessary for Christ in person to ascend thither, to give out his commission, and enable his servants with gifts, whereby to ' wound the head of his enemy,' Ps. lxviii. 18, 21. It was fit that an eternal King should have an everlasting palace; that a King constituted in a special manner by God, should have a palace not made with hands; that he who was put into the possession of all nations, Ps. ii. 8, and had a grant of all the kingdoms of the world to be his own, Rev. xi. 15, that was not to rule in a corner of the earth, and sway the sceptre in places that could be included in a map, should have his throne fixed in any part of the world but the glorious heaven. An earth defiled by that sin he hated, and an earth yet too much filled with those enemies he had conquered, was not a place convenient for the perpetual residence of so great a monarch. It was most fit also that he who was ordained the Judge of the whole world, and confirmed in that office by his being raised from the dead, Acts xvii. 31, should be taken up into that sovereign court of heaven, and come in majesty from thence to execute that charge. All the ends of his government and triumph could not have been answered without this glory; he could not have reigned in the midst of his enemies unless he had been placed above them, nor conducted his church to an happy immortality, unless he had had a possession of that heaven he was to conduct them to.

3. As this glory was necessary on the account of God, and on the account of Christ, so it was necessary on our account also,

(1.) That God's choice acceptance of his sacrifice for us might be manifested. The acceptance of it by God was in part manifested by his resurrection; but the infinite pleasure he took in it, and the fragrancy of that savour he smelt from it, had not been testified to the world had he given him only the recompence of an earthly life and glory. Indeed, his resurrection

* Daillé, vingt Serm. p. 435.

is an attestation of the truth and fulness of his satisfaction, for he rose again for our justification, Rom. iv. 24. He cannot be considered as our propitiation but in the state of his resurrection. No man is freed legally and justly from prison till he hath paid his debts ; so then the resurrection of Christ is an argument that his payment was commensurate to the debt; but the glorious exaltation of Christ is an argument of the high acceptableness of it to God. Who can doubt of his satisfaction after his resurrection ? and who can doubt of the infinite content God took in his obedience after he had crowned him with so immense a glory, and established him a prince and a priest for ever at his right hand ? God hath not only declared himself satisfied, but satisfied with an incomparable pleasure. God made a diligent search into him, to see whether he was without spot, and perfect in his person and works : Dan. vii. 13, ' And they brought him near before him,' *i. e.* the Son of man before the Ancient of days. As persons and things are brought near to be tried and diligently inspected, so was Christ brought near to God in a judicial way, that God may pass a judgment upon him and his work ; and upon a strict view he was so ravished with his obedience, that he conferred upon him a dominion, glory, kingdom, that all people, nations, and languages should serve him, an everlasting dominion, a dominion that passes not away, &c., ver. 14. Such a multitude of expressions used in this donation do signify the mighty pleasure of God in him, as if (to speak after the manner of men) God had been grieved that there was not more to confer upon him. As by the resurrection of Christ God declared himself by the title of a God of peace, Heb. xiii. 20, so in the ascension of Christ he declared himself a God of all grace to us, 1 Pet. v. 10. He declared himself reconciled to us by raising Christ from the dead, and he hath declared himself a God of all grace in calling us to an eternal glory by Christ, because the glory Christ hath is a pledge of that glory believers shall have as a fruit of God's high acceptance of him. This is the cordial Christ gives his disciples, and assures them they had reason to rejoice in the midst of their worldly calamities at his going to his Father, if they well understood it, John xiv. 28. It is indeed a clear evidence that God hath an inconceivable pleasure in him ; he would not otherwise have suffered him to enter heaven, but would have thrust him back again upon the earth. In his death there is a satisfaction, and in his glory the highest testimony of it. Without a glorious entrance into heaven, his resurrection with his continuance upon earth had not been so clear a witness of God's high value of his sufferings ; but now by his glorified state it must be concluded that his death was not the common fate of mankind, but highly meritorious, since God hath rewarded him with so great an honour as the government of men and angels ; I say it must be concluded, not only that it was a death proportionable to what the justice of God required, but an infinite purchase of whatsoever happiness the creature wanted.

(2.) That the Spirit might have a ground to comfort us. Since the end of the Spirit's coming is to comfort us, and the principal argument whereby he comforts us is the high value of his death with God, and the acceptance he meets with in heaven, there had been little or no ground for him to build his comfort upon without the ascension of Christ to glory. How doth the Spirit demonstrate the sufficiency of Christ's righteousness ? Not because he was raised, but because he goes to his Father, and is seen no more here : John xvi. 10, ' He shall convince the world of righteousness, because I go to the Father, and you see me no more.' His resurrection is the first corner stone of comfort, because it was a necessary antecedent to his glory. But had he been only raised to an earthly life, our joy had been but a twilight mixed with darkness, and the arguings of the Spirit for our cheering been somewhat disputable, and wanted much of that efficacy which now they have. This going to the Father, which includes a glory, was the spring whence the Spirit was to draw those waters of consolations he was to pour into our souls. Had Christ remained upon the earth, the Spirit had not come; but if he had, the breasts of consolation had been very lank, and little could have been drawn out by us. Some jealousies would have remained, we could not have fully answered the accusations of our sins, our own consciences would have had some racks, and we should have felt sometimes some griping doubts. If God had appeared reconciled by the raising him, yet he would not have appeared highly pleased with us without his glorious translation. We might have had some comfort in peace with him, but seen no appearance of favourable and gracious smiles in his countenance. Our Saviour lays a stress upon that of seeing him no more here, viz., in that state wherein he was before, or in a state without a glory. This, in his account, was a sufficient argument of the value of his death with God. Could we behold him here in the flesh, we might discard all our hopes of standing before God in a glorious eternity as vain imaginations; but when ye shall see me go to my Father, and maintain my interest in his favour, you may conclude that God is not only pacified, but hath lofty thoughts of grace towards you. Without this his going to the Father, the cordials of the Spirit would have wanted their due temper, and had not found any relish in our guilty consciences.

(3.) That there might be an irresistible ground of faith. If the Spirit had wanted a ground of comfort, our faith had wanted a ground of reliance. As faith respects the person of Christ, it had been subject to staggering; it could have had no assurance that he had truly the dignity of the Son of God if he had remained in the condition of a man upon the earth.* As faith respects the death of Christ, though it might have concluded an expiation of the crimes, yet not a fulness of merit to procure a complete felicity, if he had had no other sphere but the rude earth to spend his immortal life in. And less confidence still had belonged to faith as it respects the word and promise of Christ; for how could we imagine he could prepare mansions for us in heaven, if he had never stepped from the earth? or restore us to paradise, a place of bliss, that could not find the way back to that heaven from whence he said he descended to redeem us? We could not have concluded that his death had been a ransom if his word had been false; and his word had had no credit with us if he had not returned to that heaven to which he affirmed he always had a right. He could never bring us to that place to which he could not restore himself. Had he not risen, we should have thought him no higher than a mere man; nay, an impostor, and his death a punishment of his own crime. Had he not risen, we should have regarded him as no other than a conquered captive of death among the rest of mankind; and had he, after his resurrection, resided in the corrupted earth with our flesh, could we have imagined it to be the flesh of God, any more than we could have conceived it so had it remained under the power of death? His glory hath given assurance and courage to our faith, which had been very languishing, or rather nothing at all, had he stayed on earth; nor could we have had any hopes ever to have attained the happy vision of God in heaven. Had the Redeemer abode on this side that place of glory, we had been without a pledge of so great a felicity; nor could our souls have been carried out with those noble affections suitable to the extraction of them. Our love to Christ had been directed by a knowledge of him after the flesh, 1 Cor. v. 16, and therefore had mounted no higher than a carnal affection.

* Daillé, Melan. part i. p. 143, &c.

We should have had no ground for those refined and spiritual affections, and lifting our hearts to heaven, which are the ennoblement of our spiritual natures. Without this entrance into glory, there had been no foundation for the superstructure and exercise of any grace in a lively and delightful manner ; and without it, and the acknowledgment of it, all falls to the ground.

But now there is a ground for all, since,

[1.] Satisfaction is declared to be full. The validity of the price is not to be scrupled, since we are assured of the weight of his glory. Shall we doubt of the sufficiency of that, after the assurance of so many jewels in his crown ? What is all his glory but a return of his blood, and an approbation of the value of it for the ends for which it was shed ? His appearance in heaven could not have been glorious, had not his oblation on earth been satisfactory. For our sins being in the nature of debts, Mat. vi. 12, and the justice of God in the law in the nature of a creditor, to which we are responsible, Gal. iii. 10, his death was the payment, his resurrection the acquittance, but his glory the fullest testimony that God can give that he is satisfied, and remains so. So that there is no room for any doubt of eternal redemption purchased, since his entrance into the holy place, with the blood of his sacrifice, Heb. ix. 12. His exaltation assures man that he hath appeased God.

[2.] And therefore all enemies are removed out of the way. His triumph had not been just if his victory had not been full. The law would have resisted his elevation, and stopped his way to the throne, if it had anything to object against him. This glory manifests that all the enemies which stood with drawn weapons between him and his throne are removed out of the way, the obligation against us cancelled, the devil disarmed by the taking away sin, upon which his power was founded ; ' principalities and powers' spoiled of their prey, Col. ii. 14, 15 ; justice appeased, the law fulfilled, sin expiated, death vanquished ; all those are sealed to us by his entrance into glory, and God's hanging ' the keys of death and hell' at his girdle, Rev. i. 18.

[3.] Heaven is assured. As our bond against us is evidenced to be cancelled, so God hath entered into a bond by this act towards Christ, whereby he doth acknowledge that he, as it were, owes heaven to every believer upon the account of the surety, and hath manifested his reality by beginning the payment of it in the glory of his person. For in setting Christ ' at his right hand in heavenly places,' all believers were virtually set there, Eph. ii. 6. As his resurrection assures us of the fulness of the payment of our debt, so his glory assures us of the fulness of the merit of our happiness. Had he lain in the grave, our hopes would have remained wrapped up with him, and mouldered to dust with his body ; or, after his resurrection, had he remained on the earth, our hopes had aspired no higher than the place of his residence.* But when we do not only see him rising victoriously from the horrors and corruptions of the grave, but mounted into an incorruptible glory, we have reason to believe we shall, by his power, enjoy that glory we believers breathe after. For as he did not rise to live for himself, and expose his members to a perpetual captivity under death, so he hath not received his glory to reign for himself, and leave his members grovelling in the mire of the earth ; but both the intention of God in conferring it, and the design of Christ in receiving it, was, that all united to him in grace might be joined with him in glory, to see and enjoy, according to their measures, the glory God hath given him, John xvii. 24. Now had Christ stayed in a miserable world, though he had not lain in a corrupting grave, we could not have concluded our debt to have been paid to divine justice, nor expected the benefits he had promised, nor upon any ground elevated our hopes, hearts, or affec-

* Faucher in Act. vol. i. p. 62.

tions to heaven; there had not been those comfortable encouragements to duty, nor those delightful motives to any acts of religion. But now his admission into glory spirits our faith, erects our hopes, expels our fears, stifles our jealousies and doubts, and fixes wings to a spiritual love, by giving us not only a demonstration of the fulness of his satisfaction, but the overflowing redundancy of his merits for our happiness, and a pledge of an eternal and glorious life.

To sum up all, and in that the whole scheme of the Christian religion and doctrine in short, let us consider, since it was the common condition of the sons of Adam to have rebelled against God, and, after that revolt, were no more able to stand in the presence of God's consuming justice than straw and stubble before the fury of a flame, there was a necessity for some other person to make way for our return by appeasing that justice which was exasperated against us. Though this person were found out, and kindly and courageously undertook, and as faithfully, and to a full content of justice, performed it in the most perfect manner, yet there could be no assurance of it without some signal testimony of the gratefulness of the person and the accomplishment of the undertaking. His continuance in the world would have nourished rather some jealousies of the imperfection of his person and passion, than assurances of their acceptation with God. His exaltation, therefore, was a necessary sign that he had fulfilled righteousness and disarmed justice, conquered death and hell, and opened the gates of heaven. Since he suffered as our surety, his glory would manifestly be conferred on him because he so suffered, and therefore it would respect our interest; and though by the efficacy of his death, had he only risen again, we had been freed from those torments that remain after death, yet had he not been glorified in heaven, we could not have been restored to the happiness of that paradise we had lost, no more than our bodies could have been delivered from the darkness of the grave, had he himself remained under the chains of death. We should have wandered about the earth without a supreme felicity, though without a smarting punishment. But by his glory we have a certain evidence that we are not only freed from the dominion of death, but made heirs of life, and have a pledge in our hands that we shall enjoy it. If we have a union with him by faith, and a communion with him in the power of his death, there is no doubt but we shall have a communion with him in the felicities of his heavenly glory; and to such a confirmation of our faith and hope was an entrance into his glory necessary. This doctrine is the highest comfort in the Christian religion; and without this, and a share in it, what comfort can we expect in the deplorable, and, I may say, stupefying dispensation we are now under?

Second thing. The nature of this glory. It was a great glory. As he was filled with the Spirit without measure above all the prophets, for the performing his mediatory function, so he was instated in a glory without stint above all the angels for the application of the fruits of his mediation; as great a glory as a creature united to the person of the Son of God was capable of receiving. As he had the Spirit without measure, so he had a glory without end. God did *super-exalt* him, as the word signifies, Philip. ii. 9, ὑπερύψωσε, as he was set at the right hand of God, which was granted to no mere creature, and had a name above every name. Christ consisted of two natures, divine and human; let us see how these were glorified.

1. His deity was glorified.

(1.) This could not properly have any addition of intrinsecal glory. To enter into glory doth suppose a temporary exclusion or absence from glory,

as to be advanced supposeth some meaner state, as the term from whence
that advancement is. Now, the Deity was never empty of any essential
glory ; nor could that be advanced, because it, being infinite, was not capable
of any higher degree, but was above all alteration. The substance and pro-
perties of that nature, which always remain the same, are incapable of
abasement and elevation. We may as well conclude a diminution of the
essence of God, as a decrease of the essential glory of God. The divine
nature cannot ascend, any more than it can descend, because of its filling all
places by its immensity ; so neither can it be humbled or exalted ; but the
person that consists of both natures may be said to descend and ascend, to
be humbled and exalted, because that person which was glorious in heaven
manifested himself on earth by the assumption of our nature, and ascended
to manifest himself in heaven in our nature, which he had assumed on earth.
The Deity then had no new glory by the entrance of Christ into heaven, as
it had no essential disgrace by his humiliation on earth ; for that nature is
immutable and infinite, free from any change. If the divine nature might
be essentially less than it was, it might wholly cease to be what it was ; all
diminution is a degree of destruction.

(2.) There was a manifestation of the glory of this divine nature of Christ.
The divine nature, while it was wrapped up in the rags of our infirm flesh, wanted
that reputation which was due to it from man ; and in this respect Christ is
said to ' empty himself,' as the word ἐκένωσε, which we render ' made himself of no reputation,' signifies, Philip. ii. 7. He that was sovereign became a
subject, as the seed of the woman, to the law of nature, subject as an Israelite
to the law of Moses, subject as a man and our surety to the penal infirmities
belonging to the human nature, as weariness, hunger, thirst, death. And as
the divine nature seemed to be humbled in being obscured under the veil of
our flesh, so it is glorified in breaking out with most resplendent rays in the
Son. As he was humbled in the form of a servant, so he was exalted in
appearing in the form of God. ' In the same sense that we say Christ as
God was humbled, in the same sense we may say Christ as God is glorified ;
but it is certain that Christ, who was equal in regard of his deity with his
Father, did humble himself to the form of a servant', Philip. ii. 7, 8.* As
the divine nature may be said to be humbled by suffering an eclipse, so it
may be said to be glorified by emerging out of it, as the sun may in a sort
be said to enter into a glory, or reassume its glory, when it scatters a dark
cloud which muffled it, and strikes its warm and clear beams through the air.
There is nothing here of a glory added to the sun, but a glory exerted by the
sun, which before lay in obscurity, under a thick mist ; and when God is said
to be glorified by men, we must not conceive any addition of intrinsic glory
to God, but an acknowledgment of that glory he displays in his works of
creation, providence, and redemption. So the exaltation of Christ was not
the conferring a new glory upon the divine nature, but the outshinings of it
in the sacred vessel of his humanity, and surmounting those mists wherewith before it had been clouded. It was then a manifestation of him as the
Son of God, and a discovery of that relation he had to the Father from
eternity, which was not only clouded in the days of his flesh, but all the time
of the Old Testament, and was not known, at least in such a measure and
clearness, as in the discovery of the gospel. Therefore he prays, John xvii. 1,
' Father, glorify thy Son ;' discover this prerogative of Sonship, that I am the
only begotten of the Father, of the same essence with thee, and not a mere
man, as the world accounts me. Therefore the resurrection of Christ, which
was the first step to his glory, is called a new nativity of him as the Son of

* Jackson, vol. iii. fol. 314.

God in regard of his manifestation: Acts iii. 33, 'In that he hath raised Christ from the dead, as it is also written in the second psalm, Thou art my Son, this day have I begotten thee ;' as his resurrection was a confirmation of his eternal generation, and consequently of his deity, and therefore Christ adds in his prayer, John xvii. 5, 'Glorify me with thy own self,' *i. e.* in a way of equality with thyself. As the Father did not in the [time of his humiliation treat him as a son, but as a servant, as a sinner, as one he was angry with, he was exposed to the violences of men, as if he had been utterly neglected and abandoned by his Father ; he desires therefore that he might have that glory he had with God before the world was, that he might be treated and declared to be the Son of God, equal to the Father in power and majesty ; and that this might be manifested both in heaven and earth, in heaven to the angels, and in earth to Jews and Gentiles. And thus he 'sat down on the right hand of the Majesty on high,' as 'the brightness of the Father's glory, and the express image of his person,'* all which is not an addition of glory, but a manifestation of glory ; for Christ, John xvii. 1, desires the Father to glorify himself as his Son, that he might glorify him as his Father. Now the glory Christ brought to God was not a new accession of any glory to the nature of God, but a displaying the glorious perfections of his nature to the sons of men. So the glory of Christ's deity is the springing of it out of that obscurity wherewith it was masked, and a breaking out from under the cloud of his humanity in a glorious lustre. And after he was clothed with ' a vesture dipped in blood,' his name was manifested to be 'the Word of God,' Rev. xix. 13, *i. e.* he was manifested to be the Word of God, after and upon the account of his death, and his glory was sensible as the glory of the only begotten Son of God.

(3.) There was a manifestation of the glory of his deity in and through his humanity. As it had been obscured in the humanity while he was humbled, so it breaks out in the humanity when that nature is glorified, as a candle in a dark lantern doth through the transparent horn or crystal, when the obscuring plate is drawn aside. This glory he prayed for: John xvii. 5, 'Glorify me with the glory I had with thee before the world was.' The glory he had as God before the world was, was not impaired, and therefore is not that which he here desires ; his humanity was not glorified before the world was, that had no existence till it was formed in the womb of a virgin. We must therefore understand it of the glory of his deity, to be extended to his humanity, to capacitate it for those offices which were to be performed in it. He was to be the guardian of his church as Mediator, and the Judge of the world ; but his humanity could not know the names of all his people he was to guide, unless informed by his divinity. As man, he is to execute judgment, John v. 27, which he could not do unless he knew the inwards of men, and viewed their thoughts ; nor could his humanity do this, unless instructed by his divinity. This knowledge is not originally from the human nature, but by revelation from the divine ; the government of the world, of angels, and men, could not be managed by him as the Son of man, unless his humanity were enlivened, and thoroughly influenced by the divinity as he was the Son of God ; so that Christ here desires another manner of glory in regard of manifestation than was before, a derivation of that glory to his humanity. He doth not say, *Glorify me with that glory which my humanity had with thee before the world was ;* but which *I, my divine person,* had with thee : that that glory which I had with thee from eternity, according to my divine nature, may be derived upon the human nature, to fashion it for those great ends for which it is designed. I see no reason to understand

* For so Camero refers the word *sat down* to the ἀπαύγασμα, Heb. i. 3.

it of the glory of his humanity, which he had before the world was, by the predestinating decree of God; for then there would be no peculiarity in Christ's prayer to himself, for every assured believer may pray the same, Lord, give me that glory which I had with thee before the world was, viz., in thy decree. But no such expression fell from the lips of Moses, David, Paul, or any of those most triumphant in the assurances of everlasting happiness. It must be some expression of glory peculiar to the Son of God, and therefore a manifestation of the glory of the deity in his humanity in another manner than before, since that person that was the Son of God was now also the Son of man. Now this was no addition of glory to his deity, but a new mode of manifesting that glory which the human nature had before the world was, which never was exerted in such a manner before. It was a real addition of glory to his humanity, but a new way, or manner of manifestation of his divinity.

2. His humanity was really and intrinsecally glorified. There was a glory conferred upon his humanity by the grace of union with the second person in the blessed trinity ; this was at the first conception in the womb of the blessed virgin. A greater glory than this can no creature have, to be ' called the Son of God,' Luke i. 35. There was also a glory bestowed upon it by the communication of unmatchable perfections to his soul, a fulness of the Spirit, a spotless sanctification, and an infallible knowledge of God, and of those truths he was to reveal. But now his humanity did ascend up where his person was before, and our nature was carried up to sit with him in the same court, where he had been glorious before in his deity. ' He ascended far above the highest heavens,' Eph. iv. 10, into that place where God represents himself in the greatest majesty to angels and glorified spirits. He descended to assume our nature, he ascended to glorify our nature. The humanity was taken into perpetual society and conjunction with the deity at the first assumption of it ; but by his exaltation the eternal subsistence of it in the deity was confirmed ; and by the translating it to heaven, assurance was given that it should never be laid aside, but be for ever preserved in that marriage knot with the divinity. It was so enlarged and spiritualised, as to be a convenient habitation for the fulness of his deity to reside in, and exert its proper operations : Col. ii. 9, ' In him dwells all the fulness of the Godhead bodily ;' not dwelling as if imprisoned, but to break forth in all its glories and graces ; not formerly dwelling in it, but now dwells. There is a way of the presence of the deity with the humanity above all those manners of the presence of God with angels and men ; it dwells in it, and acts in it, as a soul in its own body it is clothed with, so that the humanity is the humanity of the Son of God, and heightened to be the sacred vessel of the fulness of the Godhead. That nature wherein the person of the Son of God was ' made lower than the angels, was crowned with glory and honour,' Heb. ii. 7. That nature wherein he was raised, was set ' at God's right hand in heavenly places,' Eph. i. 20, and in that nature, as well as in the divine, the person of the Son of God had a sovereign authority granted to him. Thus the humanity was glorified above all the reach of any human understanding. The glory of the saints is not to be fathomed by the conceptions of men, much less the glory of Christ, the exemplar of all the glory they are to have.

The humanity of Christ, consisting of two principal parts, body and soul; both were glorified.

(1.) His body. As his sufferings were in order to his glory, so the part wherein he suffered was to enjoy a glory. ' Enter into his glory,' i. e. a glory due to him for his sufferings, therefore due to every part wherein he suffered.

This being an essential part of the human nature, is not laid aside; the knot between this and his deity remains for ever indissoluble; it remains still as to its substance, though enriched with new qualities, being stripped of the mutability and mortality to which it was subject on earth.   As in his descent the deity was emptied of the manifestation of its glory, so in his exaltation, his body of its natural infirmities.   The image of the first Adam, except the substance, was razed out, and was actually framed in the second Adam; there was not a destruction of the body, but a transfiguration of it, and his body is no more changed in regard of the substance by its translation into heaven, than it was in his transfiguration on the mount; nor changed in its lineaments, but in its qualities: Mat. xvii. 2, 'His face did shine as the sun;' the substance remained, but changed into a glorious appearance; he had the same lineaments in Tabor as he had at the foot of the mount.   Peter could not else have distinguished him from Moses and Elias.   Had he not been stripped of his infirmities, he had still, even in heaven, been in some sort lower than the angels, which he was designed to be only for a time, Heb. ii. 7, βραχύ τι, 'a little while,' a short space, in the time of his humiliation.

[1.] His body is therefore of a spiritual nature, in opposition to infirm flesh. Flesh in Scripture is sometimes taken so: Ps. lxxviii. 39, 'He remembered that they were but flesh,' i. e. infirm and perishing flesh.   The natural bodies of the saints shall, at the resurrection, be changed into spiritual, 1 Cor. xv. 44; much more is the body of Christ in glory, since it is the pattern according to which the body of the saints shall be copied and fashioned, Philip. iii. 21.   His state in the world is called 'the day of his flesh,' Heb. v. 7; his state above is a spiritual state, as being free from the infirmities and clogs of the flesh.   Flesh he hath still, but more suited to that heaven which was his original; an heavenly, no longer an earthly, image, 1 Cor. xv. 48, 49; like turf or wood, that loses its drossy and foggy qualities, when heightened into a pure flame, or minerals heightened into spirits.   His body was spiritual after his resurrection, it could pass in a short moment from one place to another, Luke xxiv. 31.   As his body rose, so it ascended, and remains a spiritual body, or as one calls it, organized light.

[2.] It is therefore bright and glorious.   If the righteous are to 'shine as the sun in the kingdom of their Father,' Mat. xiii. 43, the head of the righteous shines with a splendour above that of the sun, for he hath a glory upon his body, not only from the glory of his soul (as the saints shall have), but from the glory of his divinity in conjunction with it.   The glory of his divinity redounds upon his humanity, like a beam of the sun, that conveys a dazzling brightness to a piece of crystal.   There was an interruption of this glory while he was in the world, though the human nature then was united with the divine.   But this interruption was necessary for those acts which he was to perform in our stead, for the satisfaction of God and the discharge of his office.   Had the glory of the divinity broke out upon his body, he had not been capable of suffering.   What mortal could have stood before him, much less laid hands on him?   What mortal durst have accounted him a blasphemer, an impostor, and have exercised any violence against him, had his divinity so fashioned his humanity?   But now it is, as it was in his transfiguration, Mat. xvii. 2; the glory he had then in transitu wrought an alteration not only in his body, but in his garments, which could not be of the most splendid, as not suiting his present state of humiliation, yet they 'became shining, exceeding white as snow, so as no fuller upon earth can white them,' Mark ix. 3; much more must that firm and perpetual glory in heaven have the same influence upon his refined body, that hath cast off those corruptible qualities which hung upon it on earth, and doth more excel in glory that body be had on earth, than the glory of the sun surpasseth that of a glow-worm. It is such a glory as would dazzle mortals to behold it; for if his glory upon mount Tabor cast Peter into an ecstasy, what effect would his glory upon his throne work upon a moral nature? Whence it follows that there must be a mighty change of the bodies of the glorified saints, to capacitate them for the beholding this glory of Christ, the intent views whereof are part of their happiness, John xvii. 24.

[3.] His body is immortal. His body now lives, and shall live for evermore: Rev. i. 18, ' I am he that lives, and was dead ; and behold, I am alive for evermore, Amen;' which is confirmed by him with a solemn *Amen*. A corruptible body is not fit to be admitted to sit down upon the throne of the Father in heaven. The promise that secured to him, in the state of his humiliation, a speedy resurrection from the grave, and an impossibility of seeing corruption, Ps. xvi. 10, is as valid as ever. That body that was not dissolved to dust by the power of the grave, cannot sink into nothing in the glories of heaven. The union of the Godhead to it preserved it here, and the perpetual confirmation of that union preserves it for ever above. His body lives an indissoluble life, death shall never more lay hands on it; he hath no more sufferings to endure, or satisfactions to make to the demands of the law. Men and devils cannot touch him in his person, though they do in his mystical body. He is above the reach of all temptations, all wrath from his Father, all violences from men, and therefore his glorious body is not in such a state as to be ground between the teeth of communicants, or eaten by rats and mice, or in any part of it dropped upon the ground, and buried again in the dust or mire, as the bread in the supper may. If that were really the body of Christ, the body of Christ would be then so treated, as consisted not with the glory it is now possessed of.

(2.) As his body, so his soul, the principal part of the humanity, was glorified. That suffered in agonies and sorrows: ' His soul was sorrowful, even to the death,' Mat. xxvi. 38. That also enters into glory; and indeed the body cannot be rightly glorified without the glory of the soul; for the glory of the body is but the reflection of the glory of the soul in any creature.

[1.] He hath an unspeakable joy in his soul. Ps. xvi. 11, ' Thou wilt shew me the path of life: in thy presence is fulness of joy; at thy right hand are pleasures for evermore.' It is Christ's triumphing in the consideration of his exaltation, and taking pleasure in the fruits of his sufferings; ' thou wilt shew me the paths of life.' God hath now opened the way to paradise, which was stopped up by a flaming sword, and made the path plain by admitting into heaven the head of the believing world. This is a part of the joy of the soul of Christ; he hath now a fulness of joy, a satisfying delight instead of an overwhelming sorrow; a 'fulness of joy,' not only some sparks and drops, as he had now and then in his debased condition; and that in the presence of his Father. His soul is fed and nourished with a perpetual vision of God, in whose face he beholds no more frowns, no more designs of treating him as a servant, but such smiles that shall give a perpetual succession of joy to him, and fill his soul with fresh and pure flames. Pleasures they are, pleasantness in comparison whereof the greatest joys in this life are anguish and horrors. His soul hath joys without mixture, pleasures without number, a fulness without want, a constancy without interruption, and a perpetuity without end. And having a fulness of joy, he hath a fulness of knowledge in his soul; he increased in wisdom in his soul, as he did in stature, and that as really in the one as he did in the other, Luke ii. 40; his humanity had not the knowledge of all things in his humiliation, his soul had one thing revealed to it after another. But in his exaltation his soul is endowed with all the treasures of wisdom and knowledge. He knows now the time of judgment, since he is constituted the Judge of the world, whereof his resurrection was an assurance to men, and no less an assurance to himself, Acts xvii. 31, since by his resurrection, the first step of his exaltation, God judged him a righteous person, and acknowledged him his Son with power, that had redeemed a world, whereby there was an evidence also that by him he would judge the world. Among other infirmities of his nature, his soul hath put off that of ignorance. Nothing that is a treasure of knowledge is concealed from it; he hath the knowledge of God's decrees concerning his people: Rev. i. 1, God gave the revelation of all to him; no other person opens the book, or is acquainted with the counsel of it, Rev. v. 5–7. This knowledge he hath in his humanity, as he is the lion of the tribe of Judah, and the root of David. This revelation is to him as Mediator, in his human nature, distinct from that knowledge he had as God. As his mediatory glory is distinct from that essential glory he had as God, so there is a revealed knowledge to him, distinct from that knowledge he had as God. There was a necessity that Christ, in his human nature, should understand the secrets of God, since he was in that nature to be the executor of the counsels of God; and this is another part of the glory of his soul.

(3.) His person was glorified. His divine nature being glorified in a manifestation, and a new manner of manifestation, and his human nature being glorified by an accession of new qualities to it, his person then was glorified. As his person was the prime subject of humiliation in taking upon him the form a servant, so it was the prime subject of exaltation and glory. His person was the *subjectum quod*, and his human nature the *subjectum quo*. In regard of his person he is glorified, as in regard of his person he was humbled; the same person 'that was rich became poor,' 2 Cor. viii. 9. He that was rich and he that was poor was one and the same person. Howsoever riches and poverty were distinct conditions, and divinity and humanity were distinct natures, yet they were the conditions and they were the natures of one and the same person, who is both rich and poor in regard of different states, as well as immortal and mortal, existing from eternity and born in time in regard of different natures, eternal as God and born as man, above all suffering and violence as God, exposed to suffering and violence as man. The person that was crucified was the Lord of glory, 1 Cor. ii. 8; the person that was crucified and suffered entered into glory; it was the person of Christ therefore wherein this glorious exaltation did terminate. As the deity was not emptied, nor could be, but obscured in the assuming our flesh and investing himself in the form of a servant for the performance of those mediatory acts in his humiliation which were necessary for our redemption, so the deity could not be exalted but by displaying itself, and discharging that disguise of infirmities wherewith it was clouded. Nor could the exaltation of his human nature, simply considered, be for the happiness and comfort of his people, for as man barely considered he could not be the king of angels and governor of the church; he could not, as man barely considered, direct the angels in their needful messages, or relieve the church in her great distresses; for the humanity was neither omniscient nor omnipotent, nor could be. It is impossible humanity can become a deity, and a creature inherit the incommunicable perfections of the Creator; but as the deity is in conjunction with the humanity, and doth make use of the humanity, and act in and by it, he is capable of performing those things which were necessary, as Lord of the world and head of the church. The actions Christ doth perform, as sitting at the right hand of God, are the acts of him as man; but the principle of those acts is his divine nature as he is God. The glorious exaltation of Christ is therefore the exaltation of his person, for those ends which were necessary for the good of the believing world.

(4.) This glory which Christ entered into was a mediatory glory. The glory Christ was advanced to was not the essential glory of God, for this he always possessed ; this was communicated to him in the communication of the essence, and inseparable from him. As being God, he had all the prerogatives of God ; but it was a mediatory glory conferred upon his person, as the first-born of every creature ; such a glory as the humanity, so dignified by the divine nature's assumption of it, was capable of. The humanity being a creature, was not capable of a divine and uncreated glory. The glory Christ hath as God is the same with the glory of the Father, but the glory Christ hath as mediator is peculiar to him as a person consisting of a divine and a human nature ; therefore it is in the text called *his glory*, in a way of peculiarity belonging to him as a sufferer ; for the divine nature was not capable of an addition of glory, nor the human nature capable of the infinite perfections of the divine. In regard of his essential glory, he was the Son begotten ; in regard of his mediatory glory, he was the heir appointed, Heb. i. 2. He is appointed heir in order after his sufferings, as he was appointed mediator in order to his sufferings, Heb. iii. 2. He was mediator by a voluntary designation, so he was heir by a voluntary donation. His glory was given to him upon condition of suffering, and conferred upon him after his suffering ; but he was from eternity the Lord of glory, and Son of God by a natural generation. The one belonged to him by birth, the mediatory by office ; the one is natural to his person, the other is the reward of his sufferings : Philip. ii. 8, 9, ' Wherefore God hath exalted him,' viz., because of his obedience to death. In the essential glory, he is one with the Father ; in his mediatory glory, he is lower than the Father, as being his deputy and substitute. His essential glory is absolute, his mediatory glory is delegated, judgment is committed to him, John v. 22. The essential glory is altogether free, and hath no obligation upon it ; the mediatory glory hath a charge annexed to it (for he is ' ascended far above the heavens, that he may fill all things,' Ephes. iv. 10), an office of priesthood to intercede, and a royal office to gather and govern those that are given to him by his Father. His essential glory he would have enjoyed, if he had never undertaken to be our ransom ; yet without his sufferings for us, he had never had the glorious title of the Redeemer of the world. As God had been essentially glorious in himself, if he had never created a world; but he had not then been so manifest under the title of Creator. This glory was, nevertheless, properly neither divine nor human ; not divine, because, considered as man [he] was a creature, and a divine glory is incommunicable to any creature ; considered as God, there could be no addition of glory to him.* This is said to be given him as that which he had not before ; not a human glory, for as man only he was below it, and was not a subject capable of it. A mere man was unable to govern and judge the world. To be head of the church, and judge of the universe, are titles that belong to God, and none else ; but it was a mediatory glory proper to the person of Christ, and both natures as joined by the grace of union for the work of mediation. Now though Christ, in regard of his divine nature, was ' equal with his Father,' Philip. ii. 6, yet in the state of mediator and surety for man, his Father was ' greater than he,' John xiv. 28 ; and in this state he was capable of a gift and glory from the Father, as from one that was superior to him in that condition ; as it hath been recorded in history, that a king equal, nay, superior, to another prince, hath put himself under the ensigns of that prince inferior to him, and received his pay ; as he puts himself in such a

* Rivet in Ps. cx. p. 300, col. 1 changed.

military state, he is inferior to that prince he serves as his general. And what military honour may be conferred upon him for his valour and service, is an honour distinct from that royal dignity he had before as a sovereign in his own territories. So is this name given to Christ ' above every name,' Philip. ii. 9, *i. e:* a glory surpassing that of all creatures, the potentates of the earth, or seraphims of heaven, which was a distinct glory from that which he had, as one with the Father, before his incarnation and passion, and had possessed if he had never suffered. But this glory mentioned by the apostle was given him upon his sufferings. It was not therefore a name in regard of his eternal generation, as some interpret it;* for the particle *wherefore*, in the beginning of ver. 9, puts a par to any such interpretation, it referring this glory as a consequent upon his humiliation to the death of the cross. It was therefore a mediatory glory, whereby the authority of God was conferred upon him, not absolutely and formally, as though he were then made God, but as to the exercise of it as mediator in that human nature which he had so obediently subjected to the cross for the glory of the Father and the good of the creature.

(5.) This mediatory glory consisted in a power over all creatures; for it was such a ' name as was above every name, so that at the name of Jesus every knee shall bow, and that every tongue shall confess that Jesus Christ is Lord, to the glory of God the Father,' Philip. ii. 10, 11. He had the same power committed to him which the Father hath; his throne is the highest, being the same with that whereon the Father sat, Rev. iii. 21, a throne of government and dominion. His commission is extensive, a power as large as the confines of heaven and earth: Mat. xxviii. 18, ' All power is given me both in heaven and earth. A power over hell is also put into the patent: Rev. i. 18, ' And have the keys of hell and death.' His right to this was conditionally conferred upon him at the first striking of the agreement between the Father and himself, Isa. liii. 10–12. He promised upon his oblation for sin, to ' divide him a portion with the great,' and he should ' divide the spoil with the strong.' This was acknowledged due to him upon his resurrection, which, being an owning of the validity of his performance, was an acknowledgment of the justice of his claim; and to this that in Mat. xxviii. 18, refers, ' All power is given to me.' But the solemn investiture was not given him till his ascension. God put the sceptre in his hands when he used that form of words, Ps. cx. 1, ' Sit thou at my right hand till I make thy enemies thy footstool;' for in the apostle's sense, to sit at the right hand of God and to reign, are one and the same; for what is ' sitting at the right hand of God till his enemies be made his footstool,' is ' reigning till all enemies be put under his feet,' 1 Cor. xv. 25. At his resurrection he was stripped of his servile garb, at his ascension he put on his royal robes, at his session on the right hand of God he was crowned, and began the exercise of his royal dignity.

[1.] He hath all power in heaven. Power in the treasures of heaven, power over the inhabitants of heaven.

(1.) Power in the treasures of heaven, of sending the Comforter: John xv. 26, ' The Comforter whom I will send,' which was sent in his name, John xiv. 26. His power was first in heaven, then in earth; his power on earth could not have been manifested without a power first in heaven; by his power in heaven he gathered his people on earth. When God had given us the greatest gift, his Son, for the honour of his mercy, he gives the greatest gift next to him, viz., that of the Spirit, for the honour of his Son's mediation. As Christ, in the evangelic economy, acted for the honour of the

* *Ambrose.*

Father, so doth the Spirit in the same economy for the honour of Christ:
John xvi. 14, 'He shall glorify me.' He is therefore called the Spirit of
Christ. He is also said to have 'the seven spirits of God,' Rev. iii. 1.
Seven is a scriptural number of perfection; he hath the full power of the
gifts and graces of the Spirit to bestow upon the church, and fill his mystical
body with. By this it was evident that as a mediator he had a mighty power
with God, since the first fruits of his exaltation was the effusion of a comforter
for us, a second advocate on earth. This being the fruit of his mediation,
and given to him as mediator, was a full confirmation not only of the virtue
of his death, but the powerful continuance of it still in heaven, not only that
it was accepted for us, but that the virtues and fruits of it should be perpetually distributed to us. This power of the Spirit was given to Christ immediately upon his ascension, as the purchase of his sufferings, and the
reward of his conquests: Ps. lxviii. 18, 'Thou hast ascended on high, thou
hast led captivity captive, thou hast received gifts for men.' By his solemn
investiture, he was settled in a power over the treasures of God, and gave out
that in abundance which before was communicated in some few drops; the
heavens are opened, and a golden shower comes down upon the world. In
a sensible and apparent manner, he received this Spirit before for himself, for
he had it without measure, he received it before, when he entered upon his
office, to fit him for his mediation, he now receives this power as mediator
upon his ascension, and as a steward for his people, to distribute this rich
revenue of God for the greatening of his church; upon his ascension he received it to give out to those he had left behind him in the world, Ps. lxviii.
18. 'Received gifts for men,' Eph. iv. 8; it was then the donative of the
Father to Christ, that it might be Christ's donative to us.

By the way, we may take notice of another argument for the necessity of
the exaltation of Christ in heaven, since the Spirit being an heavenly gift, it
was not fit he should be sent by a person that was not possessed of heaven;
and it being the purchase of the mediator, and to be sent in his name, it was
convenient the mediator should be in heaven, and have a more glorious
residence than in the earth, before the mission of so great a gift.

(2.) Power over the inhabitants of heaven. In his incarnation, in the
days of his flesh, he was lower than the angels; in his ascension, he is made
higher by the shoulders than the loftiest of them, and this in regard of his
office as mediator, for as God he had an essential superiority above them before; the superiority over them as he was God he had by nature, the superiority over them after his humiliation he had upon the execution of his
mediatory office. The angels that had their residence in heaven were to
bow to him, yield obedience to him, as he was God-man, for so he was
exalted as *Jesus*, as one that had 'suffered death,' Philip. ii. 9. They were
to give him an adoration which pertained to God, and, according to this
divine order, they pay him actual adorations before his throne as 'the Lamb
of God,' Rev. v. 11–13, and they are put in subjection to him as their head,
not only for a time but for ever, in this world and that which is to come,
Eph. i. 21, to order, direct, and commission them for the ends of his mediation, according to that compassionate sense he hath in his glory, of the infirmities and distresses of his people. He is Lord of all of them to this
purpose; one hath not the privilege to stand before God, and another subject to run upon his errands in the world, but all are subjected to the sceptre
of Christ, to be used by him at his pleasure in his service. And in this respect he received all power, first in heaven, then in earth; 'things in heaven'
are first gathered, after that 'things on earth,' Eph. i. 10. The holy angels
were all subjected to him upon his exaltation by one entire donation, the

promise of making him their head was fully accomplished; whereas there is to be a revolution of time to the end of the world, before things in earth shall be gathered to him, before all his elect shall submit to his sceptre, and his enemies be debased to his footstool. But upon his advancement, as there was an actual donation of them by his Father, so there was an entire submission of them in one body to him. The whole corporation of those blessed spirits waited upon him in his entrance into heaven to his coronation, according to the will of their God, and his God, who had given them a precept to 'worship him,' Ps. lxviii. 17, 18, and that in a military posture as their general, noted by the word *chariots*, which were used chiefly in war and warlike triumphs.

[2.] Power in earth over all creatures: 'There is nothing left that is not put under him,' Heb. ii. 8. All things are given him by God, to be in subjection either voluntary or constrained. He is Lord of all the creatures as God-man, because all the creatures were made for man; and Christ being the Lord of all mankind, is also the Lord of all the creatures that were made for the use and benefit of man.* He is therefore 'the first-born of every creature,' Col. i. 15; the right of primogeniture is conferred upon him, and so he became Lord of all; as Adam, in regard of his dominion over all earthly creatures, might be said to be the first-born of them, though himself is created after them. His power upon earth consisteth in this, that all the worship of God is to be done in his name; our supplications for the supply of our wants, our acknowledgments for the receipt of his blessings, must be presented 'in his name,' John xvi. 26, Eph. v. 20. He is made a priest to offer our sacrifices and incense of prayers; he is the channel through which God conveys all the marks of his kindness to us; he hath power as a prince 'to give repentance' as the means, and 'remission of sin' as the privilege of those that are given to him, Acts v. 31. He hath a name above every name in the earth; no person was ever so famous, none ever was adored by so many worshippers, none worshipped with so much fervency, none ever had so many lives sacrificed for his glory, and acknowledgment of his mediation and person. His glory hath extended one time or other over the whole world. It is a power that hath given check to the power of kings, and silenced the reason of philosophers; it hath put to flight the armies of hell, and been celebrated by the songs of angels; no name was ever so glorious, no power ever so great.

The third thing I should come to is,

III. The end of his glory. As his sufferings were necessary for us, so was his glory; as it was needful he should die to redeem us, so it was needful he should enter into glory to bless us. There are two great things accrue to us by Christ, *acquisition* of redemption, and *application* of redemption; the one is wrought by his death, the other by his life; the one by his elevation on the cross, the other by his advancement on his throne. It is there he hears us, and from thence he purifies us; had not Christ entered into glory, we had wanted the application of the fruits of his death, and so his incarnation and passion had been fruitless.

I shall name only two, one consequent upon the other.

1. The sending the Spirit. Indeed, since there could be no grace and sanctification without the Spirit, we must suppose that the Spirit was given before the coming of Christ. In the old world, the Spirit did strive with men, and the Spirit of God was in and upon the prophets, and the holy men in the Old Testament; but it was communicated in weaker measures, in

* Sabund. Tit. 263, 550.

scanty drops, not in that abundance till the instalment of Christ; it was then shed abundantly through Jesus Christ, Titus iii. 6, whence our Saviour is said, after his ascension, not to drop upon persons, but to ' fill all things,' viz., by his Spirit, Eph. iv. 10. The Spirit was in the world before, as light was upon the face of the creation the three first days, but not so sparkling and darting out full beams till the fourth day of the creation of the world. The full effusion of the Holy Ghost was reserved for the time and honour of Christ. He was communicated to the Jews anciently for working miracles and uttering prophecies; but the Jews tell us, that after the death of Zechariah and Malachi, the Spirit of God departed from Israel, and went up. So that afterwards miracles were very rare among them, and therefore, when the disciples at Ephesus, of the Jewish race, Acts ix. 2, said they had not heard whether there were any Holy Ghost or no, it is not to be understood that they had not heard that there was such a person, for that they believed, but they knew not whether the Holy Ghost, which departed away after the death of Malachi, was restored again in the gift of prophecy and miracles. The golden shower of the Spirit for grace and gifts was not to be rained down upon the world in so full and sensible a manner till the coronation of Christ, as only at some public solemnities of princes the conduits use to run with wine. Hence Christ flatly tells his disciples, that it was expedient for him to go, that the Comforter might come, which was not to come till after his departure; and particularly by his mission: John xvi. 7, ' Nevertheless, I tell you the truth, it is expedient for you that I go away; for if I go not away, the Comforter will not come unto you; but if I depart, I will send him to you;' and this he avers as a certain truth. Indeed, Christ received the Spirit for himself at the first inauguration and entrance into the exercise of his office at his baptism, but not fully to convey it to his people, but upon his coronation, and full investiture with all power. Then he received ' the promise of the Spirit,' Acts ii. 33, i. e. he obtained the full execution of the promise in the full effusion of the Holy Ghost, when he had entered into the sanctuary not made with hands. The purchase of it was a fruit of his death, but the mission of it was consequent upon his exaltation; by his death, in satisfying the justice of God, he removed that bar which had been upon those treasures, and broke the seal from the fountain, that the waters of divine grace might be poured out upon men; by his death he merited it, by his glory he possessed it, and then made the effusion of it, and that for the good of his people.* ' It is expedient for you:' it was not only for his honour that he went to heaven, but for our advantage, that our faith might be perfected, our hope elevated, and every grace strengthened and refined. Now the Spirit was sent to this end, to carry on the work of Christ in the world, and to apply the redemption he had wrought. He was to ' bring things to remembrance, whatsoever Christ had said to them,' John xiv. 26; he was ' not to speak of himself,' John xvi. 13. He was not to be the author of a new doctrine in the church, but to impress upon men what Christ had taught, and what he had wrought by his passion. He is therefore called ' the Spirit of truth,' i. e. teaching and clearing up to the minds of men, that truth which Christ had taught and confirmed by his blood, and to raise the superstructure upon that foundation Christ had already laid. He was to declare only what he heard, John xvi. 13, 14; to act the part of a minister to Christ, as Christ had acted the part of a minister to his Father; to glorify Christ, i. e. to manifest the fulness of his merit, and the benefits of his purchase; for he was to receive of Christ's, i. e. the things of Christ, his truth and grace, and manifest them to their souls, and imprint upon them the comfort of both. This Spirit being

* Pont. part v. Medit. xvii. p. 324.

then a fruit of the glory of Christ, is an abiding Spirit for those ends for which he was first sent, John xiv. 16. The permanency of the Spirit is as durable as his glory. Christ must be degraded from his exaltation, before the Spirit shall cease from performing the acts of a comforter and advocate on earth.

2. Consequent upon this was the communication of gifts for the propagation and preservation of the gospel. Christ was to raise a gospel church among the Gentiles, to apply the fruits of his death. This he could not do without receiving gifts to bestow upon men. These gifts were not to be received by him, till his finishing his work; and this work could not be declared to be completely finished without his advancement to the right hand of his Father, Ps. lxviii. 17. He received them with one hand, and distributed them with the other; he handed them to the world, as they were conveyed to him by his Father in his glory. 'He ascended up far above all heavens, that he might fill all things,' Eph. iv. 10; all the world with the knowledge of himself, all kinds of men with gifts; officers with abilities; private Christians with graces. His glory is the foundation of all Christianity; by those gifts of the Spirit to men, he rescues men from a spiritual death, and plants them as living trees in the garden of God. By those we find our hearts linked to him in love, panting after him with desires, and aspiring to the happiness of heaven, where he is. All the channels through which he pours the waters of life upon the world, were cut and framed by his hands. The Spirit is called the seven spirits in the hand of Christ, and joined with the seven stars, Rev. iii. 1, as being distributed by him in the seven states and periods of the church, to the end of the world.

There might be more named, but they may come in in the Use, to which we may now proceed.

IV. *Use.*
I. Of information.
1. How groundless is the doctrine of transubstantiation. 'And to enter into his glory,' after his suffering. Had there been such a thing as his daily descent to earth in the sacrifice of the mass, it had been a very proper season to have intimated such a notion to his disciples in this discourse; he might have had a very fair occasion to say, Wonder not at the sufferings of your Redeemer; he ought not only to suffer those things, but you shall see him every day a sufferer in the sacramental wafer. As often as a priest shall be the consecrator, you shall crush his body between your teeth, and see him suffer a thousand times, not by the hands of violent men, but between the teeth, and in the stomachs of impure creatures. No such thing is here spoken of; it is 'enter into his glory.' He was to be a sufferer but once, and then be received into glory; his glory was to follow his sufferings. By this doctrine his daily sufferings would follow his glory, would be together with his glory. He would be a sufferer on earth, while he were glorified in heaven; and while he sits at the right hand of his Father, his body would be corrupted in the foul stomachs of some men, as bad as devils, at one and the same time. Is this a glory his human body entered into, to be frequently degraded to a lodging in an impure stomach, among the dregs of the last nourishment which was taken in, to pass from thence to the draught, and be condemned to the dungeon of putrefying jakes? Would not this be worse than his sufferings on the cross, which were but temporary, and more loathsome and ignominious than all the reproaches he suffered on earth? This is a dealing with the Mediator as the heathens did with God, in changing his glory into a corruptible image. This is inconsistent with that glory he

is entered into after his sufferings ; there is a repugnancy between his sitting upon a throne, and being subject to the accidents of material things on earth.   As Christ was silent in any such doctrine, so were the angels at his ascension (Acts i. 10, 11, 'This same Jesus, which is taken up from you into heaven, shall so come in like manner as you have seen him taken up into heaven'), when they had a fit occasion to mention it; especially when they mention his coming so again for the comfort of the disciples that were spectators of it.   They mention, not a coming every day in body and soul in the wafer, into their mouths, but only of a visible and glorious coming again in the same manner as he ascended.   As he hath entered into glory, so the heavens receive him, and contain him, till the time of the restitution of all things.   His body is too glorious to pass into the mouths and stomachs of man, and undergo those various changes with their nourishments.

2. How greatly is our nature dignified !   He is entered into glory with our nature, and hath lifted up our flesh above the heavens, and hath in this glorified our very dust.   In that nature wherein he suffered, in the same nature he hath ascended into the most glorious part of the creation of God, above the highest heavens.   The humanity of Christ, and in that our nature, was not taken up for a time, but for ever.   It was debased for a short space : Heb. ii. 7, 'Thou madest him a little lower than the angels ;' or, 'Thou hast made him lower than the angels for a short time.'   But he is advanced for ever : 'Thou hast crowned him with glory and honour.'   The Redeemer is always to wear our nature ; it is never to be out of fashion with him.   How glorious is this for us, that the Son of God should take our nature, our dusty humanity, all our infirmities except sinful, to clear our natures from all penal infirmities, to transform our clay (if I may so say) into virgin wax, and wear it as a pledge that the members of his body shall at length be brought to him !   Our nature now hath, by Christ's assumption of it, an affinity with the divine, which that of the glorious angels hath not in such a manner.   Our nature, not theirs, was assumed, and remains united to the person of the Son of God.   It is advanced to the right hand of God, sits upon the throne with God.   The angelical nature is below the throne, stands about it, but is not advanced to sit upon it.   Our nature hath not only now a dominion over the beasts, as at the first creation, but a principality above and over the angels, Eph. i. 21.   By creation we were made a little lower than the angels ; by this union of the divine, and the exaltation of the human nature of the Son of God, our nature is mounted above theirs.   It was then made as low as earth, it is now advanced as high as heaven ; yea, above the heavens.   Our nature was before at the foot of the world, the world is now at the foot of our nature.

3. How pleasing to God is the redemption of man !   Christ's glorious advancement speaks a fragrancy in his satisfaction to God, as well as a fulness of merit for men.   There was a good pleasure in his mission, there was a sweet savour in his passion ; for since he is crowned with glory upon a throne, that so lately suffered ignominiously upon a cross, what can the consequence be but that his obedience to death was highly agreeable to the mind of God, and afforded him a ravishing delight !   For without his receiving an infinite content by it, it is not possible to imagine he should bestow so glorious a recompence for it.   We have his word for a testimony of his delight in the service he designed : Isa. xlii. 1, 'Behold my servant, in whom my soul delights.'   We have his deed for an evidence of the pleasure he took in the service he performed, by putting the government into the hands of the Mediator, and giving him power over the angels, and setting him at his right hand as his Son.   He hath testified what a ravishing sense he hath of the

redemption he wrought, and of that death whereby he completed it. He took more pleasure in him as the Redeemer than in all the angels in heaven. The apostle challengeth all to produce any one angel to whom God spake so magnificent a word, 'Sit thou at my right hand, till I make thy enemies thy footstool,' Heb. i. 13. 'To which of the angels said he so at any time?' He is proclaimed to the angels as an object of worship as he is brought into the world, Heb. i. 6, as he is the heir appointed as well as he is the heir begotten; as 'he hath by inheritance obtained a more excellent name than they.' He hath now a glorious empire over the angels, as Mediator in his humanity, which he had before in his deity, as God blessed for ever. He enters into his glory as Adam into the possession of a world, with a dominion over all the works of God. Had not every part of his work in the world administered a mighty pleasure to God, there had not been a hand reached out to have lifted him to glory; but he went up 'with a shout,' Ps. xlvii. 5,— with the applause of God and acclamations of angels. No shouting had been in heaven, no chariot sent from thence to fetch him, no attribute of God had bid him welcome, had any been disgraced by him. There had been a gloominess and disorder instead of a jubilee, nor could he ever have sat down upon the throne of the divine holiness, had not the holiness of God, the most estimable perfection of his nature, been highly glorified by him.

4. How terrible should the consideration of the glory of Christ be to the unregenerate and unbelievers! The greatness of God's pleasure in the redemption performed by our Saviour, testified by this his exaltation, argues a wrath as terrible against those that lightly esteem him. What greater provocation than to set our judgment against the judgment of God, and to think him not worth glory by our disesteem, who hath deservedly entered into a glory above all creatures. It is far worse to despise a Saviour in his robes than to crucify him in his rags. An affront is more criminal to a prince upon his throne, than when he is disguised like a subject and masked in the clothes of his servant. Christ is entered into glory after his sufferings; all that are his enemies must enter into misery after their prosperity. As there is the greatest contrariety in their affections, so there will be the greatest distance in their conditions. Such cannot be with him where he is in glory, because they are contrary to him. What prince upon his throne and in his majesty would admit into his presence base and unworthy criminals, but to punish them, not to cherish them? Impure persons are not fit to stand before a prince's throne. The sight of Christ in glory is the happiness of believers, not to be communicated to the wicked. Those that will not bow to him must bend to him; if they will not bend to him in his glory, they must fall under his wrath, and be parts of his conquest in his anger, if they will not surrender to him upon his summons from his throne of grace. What a folly is it to kick against that person, before whom, one time or other, all knees must bow, either voluntarily or by constraint, and render him an active or a passive honour! Philip. ii. 10, 11. Since he had a power joined with his glory, that power will as much be exercised against his enemies as for his friends. As the one are to sit upon his throne, so the other are to be made his footstool; and whosoever will not be ruled by his golden sceptre, shall be crushed by his iron rod.

Use 2 is of comfort. The great ground of almost all discomfort is a wrong and imperfect notion of the death, and especially of the exaltation, of Christ, and his sitting at the right hand of God. Sorrow filled the disciples' hearts, because they apprehended not the reason and ends of Christ's departure from them, John xvi. 5, 6. Had they considered whither he was to go, and for what, they would not have been dejected.

(1.) By his glory the justification of believers is secured. As all believers did make a satisfaction to God in the death of Christ, so they are all discharged by God in the resurrection and ascension of Christ. Christ having a full discharge by his entering into glory as a common person, all those whose sins he bore have a fundamental discharge in that security of his person from any more suffering. As he bore the sins of many as a common person in the offering himself, and thereby satisfied for their guilt, so he receives an absolution as a common Head for all those whose guilt he bore in his sufferings. The glory he entered into secures him from any further lying under the burden of our sins, or enduring any more the penalties of the law for them; for as he suffered, so he was acquitted, and entered into glory as our surety and representative: Heb. ix. 27, 'As it is appointed unto all men once to die, and after that the judgment, so Christ was once offered for the sins of many; and unto them that look for him, shall he appear without sin unto salvation.' As judgment is appointed for all men as well as death, and they receive their final and irreversible judgment after death, so Christ, by his exaltation, is judged perfect, fully answering the will and ends of God; and shall not appear any more as a sacrifice in a weak and mangled body, but in a glorious body, as a manifestation of his justification, fitted for the comfort of those that look for him. Upon the score of this judgment passed upon him by God in our behalf, he is to appear at length for salvation. If he suffered for us, his sufferings are imputed to us; and if his exaltation be an approbation of his sufferings for us, then the validity of his sufferings for our justification is acknowledged by God's receiving him into glory; for as in his death all believers were virtually crucified, so in his justification (whereof his exaltation is an assurance) all believers have a fundamental justification. It was for the purging, not his own but our sins, that he 'sat down at the right hand of the throne of the Majesty on high,' Heb. i. 3; and therefore he sat down as justified for us. The reason of his advancement was the expiation performed by him. As long therefore as the glory of Christ holds, the reason of that glory holds, i. e. the stability of his expiation, and consequently the security of our justification upon faith. The glory Christ is dignified with adds no value to his sufferings, but declares the value of them; as the stamp on bullion declares it to be of such a current value, but adds no intrinsic value to what it had before. In Christ's death, the nature of his sacrifice is declared; in his resurrection, the validity and perfection of his sacrifice is manifested; in his glorious ascension, the everlasting virtue of that sacrifice is testified. All three, eyed by faith in conjunction, secure our justification, and render a perpetual repose to the conscience. His throne being for ever and ever, the virtue of his sacrifice, upon the account of which he was placed in that throne, is incorruptible; and therefore there is no room for dejection and jealousies of the sufficiency of the ransom, after so illustrious a recompence received by him. Had he not indeed entered into glory, we had but a weak assurance of a discharge from the Judge.

(2.) Hence there is a perpetual bar against the charge our sins and Satan may bring against us. As Christ suffered for us, so he entered into glory for us. He suffered in the notion of a redeemer, and he is ascended up into heaven under the notion of an advocate. He sits not there as a useless spectator, but as an industrious and powerful intercessor. The end of his being with the Father is to be an advocate: 1 John ii. 1, 'We have an advocate with the Father;' and the office of an advocate is to plead the cause of a client against a false and unjust suit. He drew up the answer upon the cross to the bill sin had put in against us, and in his glory he pleads and makes good that answer. He merited on the cross, and improves that merit on his throne, and diffuseth his righteousness to shame the accusations of sin. It was through the blood of the covenant he rose ; it was through and with the blood of the covenant he entered into the holy place, to carry the merit of his death as a standing monument into heaven. He fixes the sight of it always in the eye of God, and the savour of it is in his nostrils, so that as the world, after the savour of Noah's sacrifice, should no more sink under the deluge, so a believer in Christ should no more groan under the curses of the law, though he may smart in this world under the correction of a Father. We have great enemies : the devil tempts us, and corruptions haunt us, and both accuse us. To whom do they present their accusations, but to that Majesty, at whose right hand the Redeemer hath his residence ? Whence must the vengeance they call for ensue, but from that Majesty, upon whose throne a suffering Saviour sits in triumph to answer the charge, and stop the revenge ? Since he suffered to tear the indictment, hath he entered into glory to have it pieced together again and renewed ? As he bowed down his head upon the cross to expiate our sins, so he hath lifted it up upon the throne to obviate any charge they can bring against us. This is a mighty comfort to a good and clear conscience in the midst of infirmities, that Christ is ascended into heaven, and is on the right hand of God, angels, authorities, and powers, evil ones as well as good, being made subject to him ; evil ones by force, and good ones voluntarily ; and therefore secures those from any charge of evil angels that are baptized into his death, and have ' the stipulation of a good conscience towards God,' which is the apostle's reasoning, 1 Peter iii. 21, 22.

(3.) The destruction of sin in a perfect sanctification is hereby assured, since his glory is a pledge of the glory of believers. It is an earnest also of all the preparations necessary to the enjoyment of that glory, but a perfect holiness is the only highway to happiness. A Redeemer in glory will at length ' present to himself a glorious church,' Eph. v. 27 ; glorious without spot, smooth without wrinkles, sound, without blemish, like to himself. The resurrection of Christ, the beginning of his exaltation, is the foundation of the sanctification of every believer. The power which raised him, and set him in heaven, was an earnest of the power that was to be exerted to raise and work in those that were to be his members, and fix them in the like condition, Eph. i. 19, 20. Christ being risen and exalted for their justification, was an assurance that the same power should be employed for doing all works necessary in a justified person. As in his death they were crucified with him, and by virtue of his resurrection raised from their spiritual death, so by virtue of his exaltation they shall at last cast off their grave-clothes, and, like Elijah, be wholly separated from a dusty mantle. All that are chosen by God shall pass into a conformity to the image of his Son, Rom. viii. 29. What did Christ enter into glory for, and receive a power, but to destroy the strength of that in the heart, the guilt whereof he expiated by his blood, that as he appeased the anger of God and vindicated the honour of the law by removing the guilt, he might fully content the holiness of God by cleansing away the filth ? As he had a body prepared him to accomplish the one, so he hath a glory conferred upon him to perfect the other, that as there is no guilt shall be left to provoke the justice of God, so there shall be no defilement left to offend his holiness. The first-fruits of this glory therefore was the mission of the Holy Ghost, whose proper title is a ' Spirit of holiness,' in regard of his operation as well as his nature, and whose proper work is to quicken the soul to a newness of life, and mortify by his grace the enemies of our nature. He is not entered into glory to be unfaithful in his office, unmindful of his honour, negligent of improving the virtue of his blood in

that were to follow him, and was crowned with glory as he is the Captain of salvation, Heb. ii. 9; so that this glory was not possessed by him merely for himself (for he was glorious in his deity before), but to communicate to our nature which he bore in his exaltation. As immortality was given to Adam, not only for himself, but to derive to his posterity, had he persisted in a state of innocence; so the second Adam is clothed with a glorious immortality, as the communicative principle to all believers. As God, in creating Adam the root of mankind, did virtually create us all, so in raising and glorifying Christ, the root of spiritual generation, he did virtually raise and glorify all that were his seed, though their actual appearances in the world, either as men or believers, were afterwards. As the resurrection of Christ was an acquittance of the principal debtors in their surety, so the advancement of Christ was the glorification of his seed in the root. When the head is crowned with a triumphant laurel, the whole body partakes of the honour of the head; and a whole kingdom has a share in a new succession of honour to the prince. As those that believe in Christ shall sit with him upon his throne, Rev. iii. 21, so they shall be crowned with his glory; not that they shall possess the same glory that Christ hath (for his personal glory as the Son of God, and his mediatory glory as the head of the church, are incommunicable, it hath an authority to govern joined with it, which the highest believer is uncapable of), but they shall partake of his glory according to their capacity, which he signifies by his desire and will: John xvii. 24, 'That they may be with him where he is, and behold his glory;' not only *with him* where he is, for so in a sense devils are, because, as God, he is everywhere, but in a fellowship and communion with him in glory. He is exalted as our head, whereby we have an assurance upon faith of being glorified with him. Had he stayed upon earth, we could have had no higher hopes than of an earthly felicity, but his advancement to heaven is a pledge that his members shall mount to the same place, and follow their Captain; in which sense his people are said to 'sit together with him,' Eph. ii. 6. And herein is the difference between the translation of Enoch into heaven, the rapture of Elias in a fiery chariot, and the ascension of Christ: they were taken as single persons, he as a common person. Those translations might give men occasion to aspire to the same felicity, and some hopes to attain it upon an holy life, but no assurance to enjoy it upon faith, as the ascension of Christ affords to his members. And further, the glory of Christ seems not to be complete till the glorification of his members; his absolute will is not perfectly contented, till his desire of having his people with him be satisfied, John xvii. 24. The departed saints are happy, yet they have their desires as well as fruitions, they long for the full perfection of that part of the family which is upon earth. Christ himself is happy in his glory, yet the same desires he had upon earth to see his believing people with him in glory, very probably do mount up in his soul in heaven; and though he fills all in all, and hath himself a fulness of the beatific vision, yet there is the fulness of the body mystical, which he still wants, and still desires. The church, which is his body, is called 'his fulness,' Eph. i. 23. It is then his glory is in a meridian height, when he 'comes to be glorified in all his saints' about him, 2 Thes. i. 10. The elevation then of the Head, is a pledge of the advancement of believers in their persons, and a transporting them from this vale of misery to the heavenly sanctuary. His death opened heaven, and his exaltation prepares a mansion in it; his death purchased the right, and his glory assures the possession.

Use 3. Of exhortation.

Meditate upon the glory of Christ. Without a due and frequent reflection upon it, we can never have a spirit of thankfulness for our great redemption, because we cannot else have sound impressions of the magnificent grace of God in Christ. It is the least we can do, to give him a room in our thoughts, who hath been a forerunner in glory, to make room for us in an happy world.* As the ancient Israelites linked their devotion to the temple and ark at Jerusalem, the visible sign God had given them of his presence, ought we not also to fix our eyes and hearts on the holy place which contains our ark, the body of the Lord Jesus? The meditation on this glory will keep us in acts of faith on him, obedience to him, 'lively hope' of enjoying blessedness by him, 1 Peter i. 21. If we did believe him dignified with power at the right hand of his Father, it would be the strongest motive to encourage and quicken our obedience, and fill us with hopes of being with him, since he is gone up in triumph as our head; it would make us highly bless God for the glory of Christ, since it is the day of our triumph, and the assurance of our liberty.

(1.) It will establish our faith. We shall esteem Christ fit to be relied upon, and never question that righteousness, which hath so great an advancement to bear witness to the sufficiency of it. Since his obedience to death was to precede the possession of his glory, that being now conferred, evidenceth his obedience to be unblemished. It gives us also a prospect of that glory which shall follow our sufferings for him, which is very necessary for the support and perfection of our faith.

(2.) It will inspire us not only with a patience, but a courage, in suffering for the gospel. By this the apostle encourageth Timothy to endure hardness: 2 Tim. ii. 8, 'Remember that Jesus Christ, of the seed of David, was raised from the dead.' The elevation of Christ is a full confirmation of the gospel, and all the doctrines contained therein. Who can faint under sufferings for that, that seriously reflects, and sees the ignominy of the cross turned into the honour of a crown? If his humiliation was succeeded by an exaltation, the members may expect the same methods God used to the head. What shame can it be to confess, yea, and die, for one that is so highly advanced, especially when, in that advancement, we have a communion with him? A conformity to him in suffering, will issue in an honour in the same place. If he entered as a forerunner, then all that are to follow him must go the same way, to mount to a like honour.

(3.) It will encourage us in prayer. From this topic Christ himself raised the disciples' hopes of speeding in their petitions: John xiv. 12, 13, 'Because I go to the Father, whatsoever you ask in my name, that will I do;' for so some join the words. He was glorified as a priest, not only because he was one, but that he might be in a better capacity to exercise the remaining part of his office. The perpetuity of his priesthood is a great part of his glory; and it is a part of this office to receive and present the prayers of his people, Rev. viii. 3. How cheerfully may we come to him, who is entered into the holy of holies for us, if we had sensible apprehensions of his present state! A dull frame is neither fit for that God that hath glorified Christ, nor fit for that Christ that is glorified by him.

(4.) It would form us to obedience. Since the humanity is in authority next to the deity, it would engage our obedience to him, to whom the angels are subject. The angels, in beholding his glory, eye him to receive his commands; and we, in meditation on it, should be framed to the same posture. Christ, by his death, acquired over us a right of lordship, and hath laid upon us the strongest obligation to serve him. He made himself

---

* Daillé vingt serm. p. 443.

a sacrifice, that we might perform a service to him : Rom. xiv. 9, 'He both died, and rose, and revived, that he might be Lord both of the dead and living.' By his reviving to a new state and condition of life, his right to our obedience is strengthened. There is no creature exempt from his authority, and therefore no creature can be exempt from obedience to him. Who would not be loyal to him who hath already received a power to protect them, and a glory to reward them ?

(5.) It would alienate our affections from the world, and pitch them upon heaven. The thoughts of his glory would put our low and sordid souls to the blush, and shame our base and unworthy affections, so unsuitable to the glory of our head. If we looked upon Christ in heaven, our 'conversation' would be more there, Philip. iii. 20, 21 ; our hearts would 'seek' more 'the things which are above,' Col. iii. 1 ; we should loathe everything where we do not find him, and think on that heaven where only we can fully enjoy him. It would make us have heavenly pantings after the glory of another world, and disjoint our affections from the mud and dirt of this. This would elevate our hearts from the cross to the throne, from the grave to his glory, from his winding-sheet to his robes. If we think on him mounted to heaven, why should we have affections grovelling upon the earth? It is not fit our hearts should be where Christ would not vouchsafe to reside himself after his work was done. If he would have had our souls tied to the earth, he would have made earth his habitation ; but going up to the higher world, he taught us that we should follow him in heart, till he fetched our souls and bodies thither to be with him in person.

(6.) It would quicken our desires to be with Christ. How did the apostle long to be a stranger to the body, that he might be in the arms of his triumphant Lord ! Philip. i. 23. How did Jacob ardently desire to see Joseph, when he heard he was not only living, but in honour in Egypt ! And should not we, upon the meditation of this glory, be enflamed with a longing to behold it, since we have the prayer of Christ himself to encourage our belief that it shall be so ? What spouse would not desire to be with her husband in that glory she hears he is in ? What loving member hath not an appetite to be joined to the head ? There is a natural appetite in the several parts of some animals, as serpents, &c., to join themselves together again. No nature so strongly desirous to join the several parts, as the same spirit of glory in Christ, and of grace in his members, is to join head and members together. The thoughts of his glory would blow up desires for this conjunction, that we may be free from that sin which hinders his full communications to us, and by pure crystal glasses receive the reflections of his glory upon us.

(7.) It would encourage those at a distance from him to come to him, and believe in him. What need we fear, since he is entered into glory, and sat down upon a throne of grace ? If our sins are great, shall we despair, if we do believe in him, and endeavour to obey him ? This is not only to set light by his blood, but to think him unworthy of the glory he is possessed of, in imagining any guilt so great that it cannot be expiated, or any stain so deep that it cannot be purified by him. A nation should run to him because he is glorified, Isa. lv. 5. The most condescending affections that ever he discovered, the most gracious invitations that ever he made, were at those times when he had a sense of this glory in a particular manner, to shew his intention in his possessing it. When he spake of all things delivered to him by his Father, an invitation of men to come unto him is the use he makes of it, Mat. xi. 27, 28. If this be the use he makes of his glory to invite us, it should be the use we should make of the thoughts of it to accept his proffer. Well, then, let us be frequent in the believing reviews of it. When Elisha fixed his eyes upon his master, Elijah, ascending into heaven, he had a double portion of his spirit. If we would exercise our understandings by faith on the ascension and glory of the Redeemer, and our hearts accompany him in his sitting down upon the throne of his Father, we might receive from him fuller showers, be revived with more fresh and vigorous communications of the Spirit; for thus he bestows grace and gifts upon men.

A DISCOURSE OF THE END OF THE LORD'S SUPPER.

For as often as ye eat this bread, and drink this cup, ye do shew the Lord's death till he come.—1 Cor. XI. 26.

THE Corinthians were a church planted by Paul, watered by a long preaching among them ; but notwithstanding all his pains, he receives news of some corruptions crept in and overspreading that church. Some that minded the welfare of the Corinthian church, had stirred it up to write to Paul for the decision of several cases, which were controverted among them. In this chapter the fifth case comes to be handled, about the ordering their public assemblies.

(1.) Concerning the carriage of men and women in the church. (2.) The celebration of the Lord's Supper. (3.) The use and exercise of spiritual gifts, chap. xii. In ver. 17, the apostle makes a transition from the first to the second, and taxeth them with their divisions, which were the ground of their other miscarriages.

Observe, Divisions in a church are usually attended with sad consequences. They despoil the church of its beauty and ornaments, and many times are an occasion of sullying the beauty of divine institutions ; they here hindered a communion one with another. All communion is founded upon union. Divisions shook that, and brought in gross miscarriages about the Lord's Supper ; a disorderly meeting, one taking before another, and making the Lord's Supper a scrambling feast ; discovering more passion one against another than a mindfulness of the sufferings of Christ ; and their unworthy receivings provoked God to send among them deadly diseases, ver. 30. For the reformation of those abuses, the apostle reduceth them to the consideration of the first institution.

Observe, In all reformations, we are not so much to mind what this or that custom of the church is, when there is a clear word to walk by. Christ overthrows polygamy by reducing the number of persons married to the first institution : Mat. xix. 4, 9, ' God created male and female.' This miscarriage was chiefly in their ἀγάπαι, or banquets which they had before the supper, which were set up in imitation of Christ, who kept his last supper with his disciples, at the end whereof he instituted this sacrament. Now, in the eating of this, the rich brought their dainties, and ate to gluttony and excess, before the poor were met together, and left the scraps for the meaner sort, and thereby did shame them, ver. 22 ; *i. e.* did upbraid them with their poverty. Whence observe,

1. The community of goods, or a voluntary levelling, was not a standing institution in Paul's time ; among the Corinthians you find it not in use. There were rich, and there were poor ; distinctions among men ; men were proprietors of their own goods.

2. How soon will corruptions creep into the best church ! This mighty corruption, an epicurean carriage, crept into this knowing and well-gifted church betimes, while the great apostle was living, who had the conduct of them, and of all the churches of the Gentiles. The devil will sow his tares where God sows his wheat. As he opposed Christ at the very entrance into his office, to make his mediation insignificant, so he will endeavour to corrupt a church at the first entrance of the gospel, to make it altogether fruitless.

3. Human ceremonies are not to be urged, especially when they by abuse degenerate into superstition, carnality, and profaneness.* The apostle, when he explains what he had ' received from the Lord,' and ' delivered to' the Corinthians, makes no mention of a divine institution of those ἀγάπαι, love-feasts, which they used in those days, in imitation of the supper which preceded the first institution of this ordinance. He speaks nothing in the defence of this custom, nor urgeth it upon them, but only presseth the institution. Divine institutions, because of God's sanction, are not to be laid aside, though abuses creep in. What is man's must be discarded, what is God's must be preserved. Tares ought to be separated from the wheat. This human ceremony might claim precedency of all others that wanted the stamp of divine authority, and that by reason of its seniority, more ancient than all those of a later date in the church ; yet it being but human in its original, is laid aside, and not practised (that I know of) in any church in the world. Paul proves here the divine institution, not any superaddition by the prudence of man.

The Apostle,

1. Shews the end of the institution of this ordinance. In the repetition of the words of institution, ver. 23–25, ' This do in remembrance of me.'

2. He shews the duty of communicants, in the text, ' Ye shew the Lord's death till he come.' This is rendered as a reason why Christ commanded them to eat and drink in remembrance of him, because in that action he would have them shew his death, and celebrate his praise for his sufferings in our stead.

'Οσάκις, *as often.* The Lord's supper ought to be *often* administered. The frequency is implied, though how often is not declared. Christ's death is to be every day fixed in our thoughts ; and to help our weakness, there should be a frequent representation of it to our sense, *i. e.* in such a way as Christ hath instituted, not as man may prescribe.

Ye. It is the duty of every particular person who communicates in this ordinance to shew Christ's death.

As often as ye eat this bread, and drink this cup. ' Eat,' not ' see.' This ordinance is not celebrated for the eye only, or for the ear ; there must be union, there must be communicating.

Bread, cup. There is no transmutation, no transubstantiation ; *bread* still, *cup* still ; the subject for the adjunct, *cup* for the *wine* contained in it. It is the same bread and cup after the consecration in regard of their nature, not of their use, dignity, and efficacy. *Bread, cup ;* the one eaten, the other

* Slichting. in loc.

drank. Both must be communicated; bread and cup are not to be separated; Christians have a right to both. Papists have deprived the people of the cup, by the juggle of a concomitancy; because by partaking of the bread, which is the body of Christ, they partake of the blood too which is in it. Christ plainly obviates this error at the time of the institution, when he adds, in giving the cup, emphatically, Mat. xxvi. 27, ' drink ye all of it;' and Mark, chap. xiv. 23, expressly adds, ' They all drank of it,' which is in neither place expressed of the bread. As if our Saviour, foreseeing this error introduced into the world, as he did, would, by a particular note *all*, leave the authors of it without excuse. The most lively representation of his death, the comfort and end of it would be lost, which is signified by his blood.

Καταγγέλλετε, *shew*. Some take it in the *indicative* mood, as our translators, *ye shew*. It notes to us that by this ceremony the death of Christ is represented. Some take it in the *imperative* mood, and then the words are to be read thus, ' Shew you the death of Christ;' intimating that it is an indispensable duty, that as often as we eat this bread, and drink of this cup, we should have our thoughts and hearts full of the sufferings of Christ, meditations of him, and thanksgivings for him. It is not only a bare declaration of Christ's death, but of the benefits of it.

Till he come. It is a perpetual ordinance in the church. ' Till he come;' till he shew himself in his perfect majesty, that we may enjoy perfect glory with him. Till he come to judgment, when he ' shall come in that manner as he was taken up into heaven,' Acts i. 11. When remembrance of his death shall be swallowed up in the vision of his person, and fruition of the highest fruits of his sufferings, when remembrance shall be removed by sense. In the meantime, it is a standing monument and memorial of the sufferings of our Saviour.

And by the way, we may observe, that the church shall continue to the end of the world, because these mysteries are to be kept up till Christ put a period to this form of the creation. And the church only is the seat and subject of these institutions; they were appointed for the church, not for the world, *i.e.* the unbelieving world.

In the verse observe:

1. The action, *eating, drinking*.
2. The object, *bread, this bread, this cup*.
3. The end of the action, expressed by a command, *shewing the Lord's death*.
4. The *frequency* of it implied.
5. The durableness of it, *till he come*.

Doctrine.

1. The Lord's Supper is chiefly instituted for the remembering and shewing forth the death of Christ.
2. The Lord's Supper ought frequently to be celebrated.
3. The Lord's Supper is a lasting and continuing institution, not to be put down at the pleasure of any men.

For the first;

Doctrine. The Lord's Supper is chiefly instituted for the remembering and shewing forth the death of Christ.

It is not a bare historical remembrance of the death of Christ; for then

1. Every profane man who assents to the history of Christ's death, and believes the acting of this tragedy on the cross, and hath a notional belief of the ends of it, might be partaker of this ordinance. But the apostle puts a

bar to that: ver. 28, 'Let a man examine himself, and so let him eat of that bread;' *so*, not otherwise.   There would be no need of self-examination if it were only an historical remembrance.

2. A man could not then receive more unworthily, or incur a greater damnation in this than in other acts.   But here the apostle fixeth a particular guilt of the body and blood of Christ when received unworthily, vers. 27, 29.

As Christ's death was not a bare dying, but a death with high and glorious ends, so our remembrance of it is not to be a bare historical, but a practical remembrance and declaration.   As Christ's remembrance of the promises of his Father was not only an assent to the truth of them, but a recumbency on him for the performance, so our remembrance of the death of Christ ought to be.   It is not a speculative remembrance only, as when a man sees a picture of a prince, but such a remembrance as a man hath when he sees the picture of a dear friend absent from him at that time; he remembers not only his person, but the mutual love between them, the actions his friend hath done for him, which stirs up a sense of gratitude at that time.   In the handling this doctrine, I shall shew,

I. This is the end of the institution.

II. What it is in the death of Christ that is here remembered and shewn forth.

III. How we should shew forth this death.

I. The remembrance and declaration of the death of Christ is chiefly intended hereby.   The Scripture declares this in the time of institution, the night wherein he was betrayed.   The words of institution, ' This is my body, which is broken for you,' ver. 24 ; 'This cup is the new testament in my blood, which is shed for you,' Luke xxii. 20 ;* and the command, ' Do this in remembrance of me,' evidenceth that all the preceding actions of breaking, taking, eating, are commemorative signs of Christ, to excite and confirm our faith in the apprehension of him and his merits.

For the explication consider,

1. God was always careful of appointing and preserving memorials of his favour.   The pot of manna and Aaron's budding rod were to be preserved in the ark as standing memorials of God's kindness; stones were appointed to be set up for a memorial of the division of the waters of Jordan to give the Israelites passage to the conquest of Canaan, Josh. iv. 5 ; the passover was instituted as a memorial of the Israelites' affliction,† and God's gracious protection of them from the plagues of Egypt, their security from the destroying angel, who was commissioned to take away the lives of the Egyptians' first-born, and indeed of all the wonders performed by God in their behalf in that memorable deliverance, as appears by the command for the celebration of it, Exod. xiii. 8, 9.   At this passover it is supposed by some that they sang the song of Moses, Exod. xv., for the deliverance at the Red Sea, and after David's time the lxxviii. Psalm, composed by Asaph, treating of the whole deliverance from Egypt and conduct to Canaan, and their own unworthy carriage towards God.   And is there not much more reason for a standing memorial of that mercy of which all those were but the types ?   It hath been the custom of all nations to have an anniversary commemoration of those heroes who have been the instruments of some public happiness to them, and of all societies to commemorate their benefactors.   And is there any reason to deny that to the great benefactor of mankind, the Redeemer of the world, Emmanuel, God with us ?   Shall poor temporary deliverances among the heathen be remembered (deliverance of the capitol by geese, as it was among the Romans),

* Illyric. in 1· Cor. xi. 22.   † Kellet's Threefold Supper, p. 136.

and shall not the great work of redemption, the contrivance of God, the business of heaven, the admiration of angels, the conquest of devils, and the delight of God, have special commemorations?

2. These memorials are necessary,

(1.) Because of the nature of our affections, which rather follow the orders of our sense than the commands of our souls, and are more excited by sensible than invisible objects. Therefore the Jews had Christ in the swaddling-bands of types as well as in the womb of a promise, something manifested to the eye as well as sounded in the ear. Most things we cannot understand but under sensible representations; we understand not God's power, goodness, justice, but by the objects we see those attributes conversant about. Hence are those frequent metaphorical resemblances of spiritual things in the Scripture; and our Saviour sets himself forth to us under the notions of bread, wine, bridegroom. Where there is also such a distance between our heads and our hearts that we can roll the most saving truths in the one without transmitting any part of them to the other, there is need of something to quicken our affections: seasonable memorials renew seasonable thoughts and affections.

(2.) In regard of the inconstancy of our affections. We admire anything at the first notice and arrival, we adore it at the first sight, which by continuance grows more familiar. What our affections rouse themselves up to receive at the first approach, they afterwards, being glutted with the presence of, begin to flag, like the strings of an instrument, that sound well at the first tuning, but quickly slack and need a watchful ear and careful hand to wind them up. We want, therefore, those memorials to keep up our hearts in a warm and glowing temper. In things that concern God's glory and our own salvation, we are all like table-books, quickly worn out; every intruding thought, like a sponge, dasheth out what was written. When we see things acted before our eyes, then we remember what was acted upon the cross. When Christ was risen from the dead, then the disciples 'remembered the word Christ had spoken to them,' John ii. 22. We are naturally dull, and want actual excitements to awaken our sleepiness, and balance our unsteadiness.

(3.) In regard to the natural ingratitude and enmity we have to a crucified Christ, and the weakness of faith. What the world did, that doth every man's heart naturally, account the cross foolishness. It is a matter of difficulty to raze out our jealousies of God, and bring God and the heart together. The trembling believer is apt to look upon God as an enemy rather than a Father, and thinks Christ too glorious to entertain such a wretch. We need these memorials of the bounty of God and kindness of a Redeemer, to stifle our suspicions of him. Who can cherish unworthy reflections on God, when he hath represented to his eyes the strokes God inflicted on the Redeemer? Who can resolve not to love Christ, who sees him bleeding, breaking, dying for them? Gal. iii. 1. The disciples were afraid to perish, Mat viii. 25, 26, when they had Christ in the same vessel with them; they betrayed a weakness of faith when they had Christ present with them, and had frequently beheld his miracles. How is our faith weak when Christ is absent from us? He hath therefore instituted a symbol of his spiritual presence, about which our minds might exercise themselves, as well as the eyes of men did behold his body; that we might urge our hearts to believe his kindness, and settle it upon our affections, and chide ourselves for our unbelief at the sight of bleeding love.

II. What it is in the death of Christ that is here set forth.

1. The painfulness of his death. It is the picture of him as he hung upon the cross, a man of sorrows, broken and bruised by his Father in the day of

his great wrath and great love, when his body was torn, his soul in a dreadful agony, his side pierced, his blood shed. The substance of these, by the breaking of bread and pouring out of wine, is represented; the burden of God's wrath lying upon him, and his groanings under it, are here shadowed. A picture represents the lineaments, looks, and sorrows expressed in the face, which help the fancy, and guide it into more lively apprehensions. The mind of man can conceive more than the eye of man can see. This doth not of itself express the sorrows, cries, groans, agonies, strugglings of Christ; but nothing can be more auxiliary to our souls in the understanding, remembering, fancying of them, whereby the affections may be blown up, and impressions of a crucified Christ made upon our souls. Christ left behind him no other picture of himself but this. Here a wounded, broken, bleeding Christ is presented. Here we may see the sufferings of his body, his pains upon the cross; and here fancy may work about the unconceivable troubles of his soul, his heaviness to death, how his soul was made an offering for sin, Isa. liii. 10, the wrath of God, the cup of bitterness, which if men or angels had but tasted, they would have staggered and fell headlong into hell. Here fancy may represent the piercing his temples by the thorns, and the dints made in his body, which the psalmist compares to furrows, Ps. cxxix. 3.

This was the intent of

(1.) The ancient passover. The lamb was to be killed, the flesh roasted with fire, not boiled, the head, legs, purtenance, Exod. xii. 6–9, which was to set forth the unexpressible sufferings of Christ in every part. Isaac on the wood, the sacrifices on the altar, the serpent on the pole, the striking the rock, were types prefiguring this, but differ from this sacrament. They were to prefigure what was promised, this to commemorate what hath been performed. They were not properly memorials of this. They might in some sense be memorials to remember God of the promise, but this is a memorial to mind us of the performance.

(2.) Of the elements of this sacrament. Bread signifies this suffering, as passing through various kinds of alterations (a sort of sufferings) to be made fit for food: reaped when ripe, thrashed when housed, ground to powder and baked to be made fit for bread. The actions testify the painfulness: bread broken discovers a broken Christ; wine poured out discovers a bleeding Christ. The bread testifies the sufferings of his body; the blood, the agonies of his soul, because the spirits whereby the soul acts are in the blood.*

2. The intention of this death for us. It is in this ordinance represented as a sacrifice-death. He is 'our passover sacrificed for us,' 1 Cor. v. 7, 8. In his institution it was, ' my broken body for you, my shed blood for you,' as an expiatory sacrifice for the satisfaction of justice, appeasing of wrath, and thereupon the remission of sin, and collation of everlasting righteousness. On the cross it was given for us; in the sacrament it is given to us, to mind us what he did for us. It is to shew forth, not only his death, but the intention of his death for us; not for himself, or any sin of his own, for he was 'harmless, undefiled,' Heb. vii. 26, and a 'lamb without spot,' 1 Peter i. 19. There was no more need of his dying for himself than there is a necessity of our being glorious to make God happy. His sole intention was to be an offering to God for the removing of our guilt, the answering the charge of the law, the silencing the terrors of justice, which we were obnoxious to, had not Christ interposed himself as a sacrifice for us that both justice and mercy might be our friends.

3. The sufficiency of this death for us. It would never else be remembered. We remember no more than what was done; we remember a whole

* Goodwin's Peacemaker, pp. 56, 57.

Christ broken. God by covenant with Christ could challenge no more ; and justice, after the striking of that match, could demand no more. Christ paid all that he had to pay ; his whole body was broken, his whole soul bruised, his blood shed ; he gave up all the treasures he had : and this is represented in the supper. The cup Christ drank was full, and by his death he brought a greater glory to God than ever he had before ; whence ariseth a redundancy of merit, an overflowing merit for ten thousand worlds, were they in being and in a sinful state.

4. The acceptableness of this death to God. All that Christ did, he did by order as his Father commanded him. Had not his death been acceptable to his Father, he would not have ordered us to remember it. The great actions God hath done for his people, and by which he hath got most glory, and which have been most delightful to him, he would have commemorated : the passover once a year ; but this, as being the memorial of a thing more pleasing to him, often. It was ' a sacrifice to God for a sweet-smelling savour,' Eph. v. 2. He would have it remembered in heaven in the person of Christ, and remembered on earth in the symbols of his own appointment. His resurrection God would have remembered by the change of the Sabbath, but his death by a new and peculiar institution. Spices smell sweetest when pounded : his death is the greatest pleasure to God ; he would have heaven and earth filled with the savour of it. The acceptation was laid in the cross. In the supper we remember his death to plead the acceptableness of it to God.

5. The present efficacy of this death. It is now of efficacy, and will be to the second coming of Christ. Why else should it be remembered ; to what purpose should we commemorate it, if it did not retain an everlasting efficacy ; if his blood, like wine, had lost its spirits, and his body, like bread, were putrefied and consumed since the departure of Christ out of the world ? Some affirm that that blood of Christ which was shed, was not drank up by the ground, or dried up by the sun, or steamed into the vapours ; but was gathered up again by the power of God, and put into his veins.* ' His body saw no corruption,' Acts ii. 31 ; therefore no part of his body, not his blood, which was sacred, the blood of God, therefore not to be lost. As the soul and body of Christ, though separated, were united still to the person of the Son of God, his body being the body of the Son of God, his soul being the soul of the Son of God ; so also his blood, though separated from the body when shed, and had not its natural motion to perform its natural end for the supply of the body, as the soul of Christ did not perform its natural end for the informing of the body when separated from it, yet not a drop of his blood was divided from his person. But howsoever this be, not a drop of that blood is lost as to the virtue and efficacy of it ; and therefore when either pardon of sin is sealed, or purifying grace conferred in this ordinance, it is not by the sole remembrance of his death, but by the power of it efficaciously operating for and in the soul. Therefore this blood is opposed to corruptible things, 1 Pet. i. 18, intimating that the blood of Christ, in regard of its power and efficacy, doth not corrupt. As the sun sheds his light every day about the world, yet remains a fresh spring of new light in the air every morning, so this blood shed upon the cross loseth not its virtue, but is as operative as if we had stood under the cross, and had it dropping upon our souls at the instant of his sufferings. He did once ' offer himself a propitiation for sin,' but he remains a propitiation for ever. The sacrifice was but once performed, Heb. ix. 28 and x. 14 ; that shows the reality of it ; but it is often commemorated, to shew the perpetual virtue of it. This efficacy is therefore shewn forth in this ordinance.

* Dr Jackson.

III. How we should shew forth and remember this death.

1. Reverentially.

(1.) With a reverence of the holiness of God. God's hatred of sin is as high as his love to Christ; he hates sin as much as he loves his Son. He would never else have dealt so hardly with his Son for sin, whom he loved so dearly. He lamented over the loss of Jerusalem, Jer. xii. 7–9; but to manifest his detestation of sin, he spared not his Son; had no relentings when he suffered for us.

(2.) With a reverence of the justice of God. It was more that the Son of God should thus pour out his soul, than if the whole world had been hurled into hell. God struck him till justice had a full revenge, and struck him with that wrath which would have tumbled us into unquenchable flames. Not the pleas of an infinite mercy, a mercy God delights in, could stop the pleas of an inexorable justice. What earthly father but would count the sufferings of his son as the rending of his own bowels, a destroying a model of himself? but to see an infinite gracious God rending the soul of a beloved Son, letting his enemies loose against him, standing by without any manifest relentings, and adding to that torture his own frowns, even that God who cannot see his people afflicted without yearning bowels and a troubled heart, yet to seem unconcerned at the death of his only Son; can we remember this without reverential adorations of the dreadful justice of God?

2. Holily. We must undertake such religious services with suitable dispositions of heart. Let none with irreverent hands touch those *tremenda mysteria*, which may make the hearts of sinners be broken with terror.

(1.) With mourning hearts for sin. A broken Christ must not be remembered without a broken heart; a bleeding Christ and a hardened spirit, a sighing Christ and a senseless heart, are unsuitable. Our passover must be eaten with bitter herbs, with sorrow for past transgressions; we should endeavour to be as much affected as if we had heard every piercing groan in the garden, and numbered every drop of that bloody sweat which trickled down upon him, and been present when the soldiers did so cruelly handle him and pierce him. The springs of our sorrow should be opened and gush out; for it was our sin he bore, and our debt he paid. The fixing our thoughts intently on the death of Christ would melt the ice in our souls. We should look upon him till our hearts be set a-mourning, ' as for a firstborn,' Zech. xii. 10.

(2.) With deep considerations of the cursed nature and demerit of sin. It must needs be bitter, killing, condemning, cursed sin, which brought Christ to such a bitter death. What a dreadful breach hath it made between God and us, that nothing but the blood of God can cement and solder? How are we able to answer for one sin, when Christ endured so much for the expiation of the least, as well as the greatest? For death was due to the least; had our sins had less guilt, yet since the least had been an offence against an infinite God, Christ could not have had a less suffering than essentially infinite to make an atonement for it. How can we poor potsherds stand under the stroke of an almighty arm, when the human nature of Christ, though united to the deity, furnished with an eternal Spirit, attended with a gracious assistance, and assurance of a glorious success, startled at it, and hung down his head? Our iniquities met upon him, Isa. liii. 6, like a mighty torrent that bears down all before it; and who but infiniteness could have stood against such a force? See how sin pressed him down, who upheld the whole fabric of the creation by the word of his power, Heb. i. 3, and could, without any pains, have bore the weight of millions of worlds. Had not sin deserved so great a punishment, Christ should not have suffered it; a God of infinite compassion (and were there *magis* and *minus* in that which is infinite, more stirred up towards Christ than towards all creatures) would not have laid so great a load of sufferings upon him had not sin deserved it.

(3.) With strong resolutions against sin. It is a sad thing to be Christians at a supper, heathens in our shops, and devils in our closets. To come with a heart resolved to go on in impenitency, is to be worse than Judas, who was struck with remorse at the beginning of Christ's sufferings, when he saw him condemned. Shall he have relentings for his treachery, when he saw him ready to suffer, and we cherish intentions to sin at the representations of his sufferings already fully executed? We should then be not the receivers, but the murderers of Christ, tread him under foot, and make the table of the Lord a shambles, and bring the guilt of that blood upon our heads, which, if sprinkled upon our consciences, would purify them from the guilt of all other sins. The Jews took the passover standing, to shew their intentions to leave Egypt; so must we resolve to leave all correspondence with those enemies which have murdered the Redeemer. The passover must be eaten with unleavened bread; no leaven of sin must be mixed with our services, no leaven of hypocrisy with our lives, 1 Cor. v. 7, 8. We must eat his flesh and drink his blood, that we may live to the praise of his grace; shew it forth in the supper, that we may shew it forth in our lives. The thoughts of Christ's death should be an antidote against the poison of sin.

3. Believingly. We should in this act look upon it by faith, as the meritorious cause of our good. If we cannot believe when we see the price laid down for us and the ransom paid, when shall we believe?

(1.) We should profess our adherence to him. The shewing forth his death is solemnly to cleave to him alone for the pardon of our sins, the justification of our persons, and sanctification of our natures. There was to be in the passover a solemn publishing the nature of that deliverance, the great kindness of God in it, and the ends for which he delivered them. The Israelites that descended from Jacob were 'partakers of the altar' by eating of the sacrifice, 1 Cor. 10–18; *i.e.* they professed themselves to be of the Jewish religion and worship by eating with them; as they that ate of things sacrificed to idols in the idols' temple did by that action profess themselves the worshippers of that idol, and had fellowship with devils in it.

(2.) Look up to Christ in his death as a conqueror. It is 'the *Lord's* death;' he was a lord in his death, he was a king upon the cross as well as a priest, as he is a priest in heaven as well as a king; he hath both his priestly garment and royal crown; the cross was his victorious chariot, as well as the instrument of his execution. He then nailed our sins to the cross; he then triumphed over the powers of darkness, sin, Satan, and hell, Col. ii. 14, 15. He was a conqueror in his death, spoiling the devil of his prey, and snatching the captives out of his hands; his death was his victory, his ascension his triumph. Regard it, shew it forth, not simply as a death, but a conquering death.

(3.) Plead this death with God. This is believingly to shew it forth. This ordinance upon the earth is a counterpart of what Christ is now pleading and urging to his Father. Our pleas on earth should keep company with Christ's pleas in heaven. It is the best argument to prevail with God, who, though he may deny our prayers, will not deny his Son's blood. It is the best argument to quicken our prayers. Present God with his covenant sealed: God will not deny his own hand and seal; present him with this performance of Christ's priestly office, which is the only office he hath confirmed by an oath, Ps. cx. 5. He is a holy God, and will not deny his own oath.

Plead this death, for such pleas honour his wisdom, glorify his love, own his truth ; plead it, and all God's attributes will plead it with you. God himself will join issue with you, for God's attributes are the same with himself. This time is the fittest time to prevail with God. When is a child most prevalent in his intercession, but when he is most exact in his obedience ? This was the highest testimony of Christ's obedience, Philip. ii. 8, and engageth God as a Father to shew the choicest tokens of his love. As Christ was most obedient when he suffered it, we are most obedient when we believe it, approve of it, and plead it. When Christ died, he deposited all his merits in the hands of his Father. Go therefore to God for the legacies Christ left at his death.

(4.) Plead this death against sin and Satan. Shew it against every charge. We are like to meet with many rubs, sharp and weighty accusations, too true for us to repel without the vigorous force of this death. Whatsoever accusation Satan can present against you is answered here. Have we sinned ? Christ hath suffered for sin ; have we sinned many sins? Christ hath shed much blood, not only a drop ; have we sinned great sins? the death of Christ for sin was the death of the Son of God. Can the sins of men be stronger to condemn than the blood of God is to save ? We have deserved hell, but Christ hath suffered it. The wrath of God, which is the spirit and quintessence of hell, lighted upon him. Christ's death will answer all the subtle charges of the devil, appease the terrors of a raging conscience, silence the curses of the law, and quench the flames of hell.

4. Humbly.

(1.) Consider in this representation what we should have suffered. Those strokes laid upon Christ were due to us ; on us should those vials of wrath have been poured. We should have been the mark of all the arrows of God's vengeance. The tragedy acted on Christ should have been acted on us. Had that justice which was due to us seized us, we should have been held prisoners for ever. What power could have rescued us from Almightiness ? Those terrors were marching against us. Christ then changed states with us, took our sins to answer for them, and gave us his righteousness to meet the justice of God withal. He suffered the pains of hell, the wrath of God, and purchased heaven for us, which he might have kept without emptying himself, and sent us down to hell. The sufferings were endured by him, but the right to them was ours ; it was ' for our transgressions he was wounded, for our iniquities he was bruised, for our peace that he was chastised,' Isa. liii. 5.

(2.) Consider the deplorable misery wherein we were. How deeply were we sunk into the mire, that nothing could pluck us out but the Son of God! How strongly was the stain of sin impressed in our souls, that nothing could wash it off but the blood of God ; how enthralled to the devil, that nothing could give us liberty but the death of Christ ; how obnoxious to the wrath of God, that not the entreaties of Christ, but the voice of his blood only, could procure our redemption from the anger of that God, who had infinite compassions as well as infinite justice !

5. Thankfully. Such mercies as the death of Christ require high and raised thanksgivings. It is the greatest disingenuity not to pay thankfulness for a free mercy. The supper is a feast upon a sacrifice, as feasts followed the Jewish sacrifices. Christ was offered to God as a sacrifice, and returned to us as a banquet. He was ground by the wrath of God to be bread fit for us to feed on.

(1.) Blessing God for his love in offering up his Son to death. In this death God set open the flood-gates of mercy, and showered down the choicest blessings on the heads of believers. What is creating to redeeming love ? In creation God gave us a being, in redemption he gives us his Son, not only to live with us, but die for us, and afterwards to live for ever for our happiness.

(2.) Blessing Christ for his love in dying. Had not he drunk this bitter cup, we had not tasted a drop of mercy ; we had never triumphed if Christ had not died. What thankfulness is due to him because he died for us ? How much greater thankfulness is due, since he bore our sins, which is more than death ? Who can express that dreadful conflict, when he did sweat clots of blood ? He bore the torments of hell *in pondere*, if not *in specie ;* the *tantundem*, if not the *idem.* The remembrance of it being commanded by him, witnesseth the solemn pleasure he took in suffering death for us ; unwelcome and forced things would not be delightfully remembered by him, or ordered to be remembered by us, as a mark of favour.

(3.) The costliness of this redemption by the death of Christ should excite us to shew it forth with thankfulness. Our redemption this way cost God more than thousands of millions of worlds would have cost him. There was no need of shedding any blood to make them ; but the best that ever was or can be was shed to restore us : a word would create them, blood must redeem us. It hath cost God more than all the angels in heaven ever cost him ; and should it not be remembered with thankfulness ?

(4.) The gain we have by it should excite us to it. Death was bitter to him, but comfortable to us. His punishment was our discharge ; and he died for us that we might live with him. What gain we have by his resurrection and ascension is originally from his death. It is ' by the blood of the Lamb' that the devil is ' overcome,' Rev. xii. 11. By his blood are the promises sealed ; by his blood all the treasures of grace, mercy, peace, happiness, riches of glory are gathered together for us.

Use 1. If the Supper be a shewing the death of Christ, it is then no sacrifice, but the commemoration of a sacrifice. Sacrifices imply some kind of expiation and atonement ; this is a natural notion. The heathens thought by them to appease the anger of their gods. But the Supper is not intended as an expiation of sin, or a satisfaction to God, but a representing that oblation which Christ made of himself by death, which was propitiatory, and therefore is rather a feast upon a sacrifice, than a sacrifice. In a sacrifice, something is offered to God ; in a sacrament, something is exhibited to us.

2. How should the death of Christ run much in our thoughts, and our affections be raised! Such affections we should endeavour to have, as we believe those good disciples that stood by him, and saw him hanging and bleeding on the cross, had. And our affections should be of another nature ; for it is a question whether they understood the ends of his death, because none of them expected his resurrection. If we can see Christ pierced and not mourn, we may well question whether we have a spirit of grace in us, for such a frame is a proper fruit of this spirit, Zech. xii. 10. We should travel to the Mount of Olives, where Christ prayed and wept ; enter into the garden, the place of his agony. See how humbly he went, bearing the cross ; take notice of the pains he endured, the mocks and scoffs flung at him ; conceive, if we can, the dolorous cries of Christ, when he had lost the sense and sweetness of his Father's love ; and from thence let our affections get warmth. How should we set Christ before our eyes, and have the freshest remembrance of his dying love !

Doct. 2. The Lord's Supper is to be frequently celebrated and participated of. *As often*, implying, it ought often to be done.

For explication.

1. How often is not determined. There is no fixed time for the administration of this prescribed by any precept, no day commanded for it; but the celebration of it on the Lord's day was the primitive practice. No day fitter, in regard of its separation to God, in regard of public meeting, in regard of remembrance, both of the death of Christ and his resurrection; the battle and the victory, his death in the supper, his resurrection in the day. Nor how often on that day is it determined by any precept, whether weekly or monthly. The performance is commanded by Christ: 'Do this in remembrance of me,' is urged by the apostle in this chapter, but how often is not prescribed. God was more punctual in the Jewish sacraments: circumcision was fixed the eighth day, the passover annually in March.

2. Nor can there be a constant time fixed for every particular person; because there are varieties in the cases of good men, who may, by some emergency, find themselves hindered one time, and not another. Sometimes men's various callings administer to one more distractions than the calling of another, that they cannot rightly dispose themselves, nor spend so much time as is necessary to a due preparation; and there is more fruit by one sacrament, when men come with a suitable frame, than by a hundred slightly approached to. Though the passover was annually fixed, and under a severe penalty to be celebrated, yet there was a dispensation allowed to those that were under ceremonial uncleanness, or engaged in business on a journey, Numb. ix. 13; but those were diversions brought upon them by the providence of God, not contrived by themselves, which rendered them excusable. If any man had left his journey to that time, which he might have performed at another, and had delayed it on purpose that he might avoid the attendance on that ordinance, I question whether he had been within the compass of God's indulgence. Yet in those cases, though they were dispensed with at the first celebration of it on the fourteenth day of the first month, they were ordered to keep it the fourteenth day of the next month, and not to stay till the next annual revolution, Numb. ix. 10, 11. Yet we find the passover omitted all the time they were in the wilderness, as well as circumcision; and some observe that there was but one passover kept all the time of Joshua. And so great were the corruptions in the Jewish church, that when Josiah came to the crown in the eighth year of his age, and began in the eighth year of his reign to ' set his heart towards God' (2 Chron. xxxiv. 3), yet it was ten years before he could prepare them to keep the passover, which was kept in the eighteenth year of his reign, 2 Chron. xxxv. 19. It was commendable in him to restore it, sinful in the people to neglect it, since it was settled by a plain and standing command.

3. It was anciently often participated of. Some* think every day, from that of Acts ii. 46, ' They continued daily with one accord in the temple, and breaking bread from house to house,' in analogy to the daily sacrifice in the temple. Others understand it of their frugal and charitable entertainments of one another. That it was every Lord's day, is out of question by the ancient writings declaring the custom of the church. And Acts ii. 42, the breaking bread, which is understood by most of the sacramental bread, is joined with doctrine. They would lay in a *viaticum* and provision in those hard and stormy times, when they expected to be snatched away by the fury of persecutors before the next day of public meeting. And this was their custom, to join this to other acts of worship on the Lord's day: Acts xx. 7, ' And upon the first day of the week, when the disciples came

* Mr Joseph Mede.

together to break bread.' And this was afterwards kept up in the church in the time of Justin Martyr, and by some in the time of Austin, long after the other, which practice was perhaps grounded on Ezek. xliii. 27 : 'And it shall be upon the eighth day, and so forward, the priest shall make your burnt-offerings upon the altar, and your peace-offerings, and I will accept you, saith the Lord;' a prophecy of gospel times, and the cessation of the ceremonial law of daily sacrifices; by burnt-offerings being meant the Lord's Supper, the remembrance of the great burnt-offering whereby our peace was made; and by peace-offering, prayer and thanksgiving, which are called sacrifices in Scripture, Heb. xiii. 15; and on the Lord's day, being the eighth day, following upon the seventh, the Jewish Sabbath. It is likely it is not absolutely necessary that it should be administered every Lord's day, when the word is preached. The passover, the Jewish sacrament, was but annual, though Moses, the law of Moses, was read every Sabbath in the synagogue. The celebration came to be more seldom, because the frequency of it begat a coldness in the affections of the people, and the commonness occasioned too much contempt of it. The esteem and reverence of this ordinance was dashed upon this rock. The duty is extraordinary; they are *tremenda mysteria*. Great preparations are necessary to great duties; affections must be much exercised, which are wound up to a higher pitch by the novelty and rarity, and flag by the commonness of an excellent thing. The commonness of fasts in our days, and even at this time, hath driven true humiliation almost out of doors.

4. Yet to be frequent in it is agreeable to the nature of the ordinance, and necessary for the wants of a Christian. By too much fasting we often lose our stomachs. The passover indeed was annual, God fixed it to that time; but they had their daily sacrifices in the temple, which were types of Christ, and remembrancers to them of what was in time to be exhibited. We have none but this settled by Christ as an ordinance of commemoration of what hath been exhibited; therefore we ought not, for the time, to conform ourselves only to an annual custom. It is not to be neglected out of a wilful contempt, or a pretence of humility. Disobedience is not a part of humility, but the fruit of pride against God; and though a sense of unworthiness may be so great as to hinder a free and cheerful approach, and deter for a time, yet there ought to be endeavours to get rid of those clouds. We must not rest in lazy and idle complaints. That is no true sense of our own unworthiness which hinders us from a necessary duty.

Frequent it should be. The too much deferring doth more hurt than the frequent communicating. The oftener we carefully and believingly communicate, the more disposed we shall be for it.* Abstinence from it can never be good, but *ex accidenti*, either for defect of a due disposedness, or to excite a greater reverence; but to communicate believingly is good, *per se*, in itself. Now that which is good in itself is to be preferred before that which is good accidentally. If we abstain from it for reverence, we may the rather come for reverence; for if it be worthily received, it increaseth our reverence of God, and affection to him. That is the best reverence of God which owns his authority.

It ought not to be neglected, upon these reasons :

1. Because of the author. It is a feast of God's providing, to which he invites us; to neglect it is a contempt of God's rich provision and gracious condescensions. The great God appointed not any trifling ordinance; his wisdom appoints none but what his power can make worthy instruments; his goodness will appoint none but what his love will make highly beneficial:

* Suarez, vol. xv. disp. lxix. sect. iv. p. 889.

the contempt of it is a slighting both of his wisdom and grace. It is a command immediately from Christ, and therefore the command of God, who hath approved of him and everything he did, and set his seal to this commandment of our Saviour's, and all the rest. Had it not been agreeable to his Father's will, he had not been advanced to his royal dignity to sit upon his throne. It is Christ's command, whom we are bound to obey, by virtue of our allegiance to him, by virtue of the salvation we hope for by him, by virtue of the affectionate obligations we have received from him. It is his command, whom we must own as our Lord, if we expect him as our Saviour : Luke xxii. 19, ' This do in remembrance of me.' It is not left at liberty, *do if you will,* but *this do.* He is our Lord, and he is our Saviour ; not only our Saviour, but our dying Saviour. If his death be to be valued as the ground of our happiness, his legacies are to be esteemed as a part of our privilege. He that was going to lay down his life for us, would not appoint what was unnecessary for our present state ; yea, were it of no use to us, it is enough that it hath his sanction, whose sole authority deserves to be remembered by us. It was the breaking a positive command, in the eating the forbidden fruit, lost Adam paradise. If God pitcheth upon any means, though never so weak in themselves, they shall be effectual, and means seeming more powerful in themselves shall effect nothing. If the blast of rams' horns be ordained for the overthrow of the walls of Jericho, Josh. vi. 5, they shall do that which he hath appointed. If they be thought contemptible after God's order, all the battering engines in the world shall prove ineffectual to gain the victory. If Jordan be appointed for the healing Naaman's leprosy, 2 Kings v. 10, the waters of Abana and Pharpar, rivers of Damascus, shall never be medicinal. When God appointed lamps for the defeat of the Midianites, Judges vii. 20, had Gideon slighted them as too weak, and assaulted them with his numerous host, he had received a rout instead of a victory. When God orders any instrument of conveyance, all other means will be successless ; and not only so, but God will be offended, because his institution is contemned ; and what can then reasonably be expected from a slighted God ?

2. The time when Christ instituted it shews it not worthy of our neglect. It was a little before his death : 1 Cor. xi. 23, ' The same night in which he was betrayed he took bread.' Good men (much less would a good and bountiful Saviour) do not use to employ themselves in trivial concerns, when they are near expiring. That which was instituted, when wrath began visibly to march against him, Judas upon the point of betraying him, and is to continue till his second coming, is not without a desirable fruit. Had it been a needless ceremony, he would not have breathed out a word for its institution ; had it been an institution of a light concern, some other time would have been chosen by him for the settlement of it. We may gather the necessity, as well as the value of it, from the time of its institution, which shews that there is something worthy in it of our esteem, and undeserving our neglect. The last words, actions, legacies of dying friends, are never thought matters wholly to be neglected. Joseph's brethren questioned not their pardon from Joseph for the injury they had done him, when they used so powerful an argument as the command of their dying father : Gen. l. 16, 17, ' Thy father did command before he died ;' and shall we undervalue, by a wilful neglect, the commands of a dying Saviour, settled by him just before he went to remove the wrath of God from us upon himself ?

3. The ends of it declare the unworthiness of neglecting it.

(1.) The remembrance of Christ. This was the end, and twice repeated, 1 Cor. xi. 24, 25. In the giving the bread, ver. 24 ; in the cup, ver. 25. We are naturally unmindful of God, ungrateful to Christ; we need something to renew our remembrance of him. He hath left us this dark glass, wherein we may see his face till he return with a full glory; and is it an affection to him never to look upon his picture, the medal of himself, wherein he hath engraven the tracks of his dying love; all that he did, all that he purchased, all his fulness, all his treasures, wherein we may behold him as a Redeemer, pouring out his blood for us, as a sanctifier pouring his blood into us, as a benefactor opening his enriching treasures to us, as a supplier providing for all our wants? How can we say we love him, if we do not mind him? What value have we for him, if he be not in our thoughts? Well, but we may remember Christ otherways without this ceremony. We may, but do we? Do you frequently ponder upon him; are your thoughts of him edged with choice and ravishing affections to him; doth not the body of death hinder you from thinking of the Lord of life? But suppose you are not one minute forgetful of his love, doth it consist with your professed affection to him to choose your own ways of remembering him, and neglect his? Suppose we h·d a friend who had redeemed us from the galleys, restored us from servitude, redeemed our lives, instated us in a large inheritance, and was to take a long journey, promising to return again, leaving with us his picture, which he would have us look upon at some special seasons, and express in that method a particular mindfulness of him. Though we could not without an excusable ingratitude forget him had we not that picture, yet it were but an unworthy return to deny the observance of so small an order to a friend to whom we owe ourselves. This is all the picture Christ hath left of himself; he never appointed any images or crucifixes, never imprinted the features of his face upon Veronica's napkin. Is it not ingratitude to neglect the remembrance of him in his own method, when he might have put hard conditions upon us; and when it is not a mere sight of him, but a spiritual feast with him, wherein we may suck his very blood into the veins of our souls, as well as the wine into those of our bodies? The primitive Christians used commemorations of the martyrs, whose blood they counted the seed of the church; and shall the stated commemorations of that blood be neglected, which is the foundation, the price, and the purifying fountain of the church?

(2.) It is a seal of the covenant. This is the common nature of a sacrament, to be a seal of the righteousness or justification with God by faith in Christ, Rom. iv. 14.* As a seal affixed to a writing conveys to a man the lands and goods named in the writing. It is not only a sign which represents, but a seal which confirms, the benefit; not a bare picture, but a seal whereby pardon and the whole design of salvation is passed over to us: Luke xxii. 28, 'This cup is the new Testament in my blood, which is shed for you.' It is a confirmation of the rich charter of God. There is a conveyance, take, eat; take, drink; take Christ with all his treasures, with all his graces. This is a pledge of the promise, a pawn given you for the glory to be bestowed upon you. He seals it to the eye by the elements, and to a believing heart by the Spirit. It seals not the truth of the death of Christ, or the truth of your faith. It supposeth faith in the communicant, and supposeth the death of Christ in the institution; but it seals the right of faith, and the interest of faith. It is a seal of the righteousness of faith, of the interest of faith in that righteousness it lays hold on, as the seal of a deed seals the right and interest of the person in that land conveyed to him by the deed. What there is in Christ, is sealed to us in the sacrament for our comfort; the privileges he hath purchased, and the graces he is endowed

* Vines on the Lord's Supper, p. 324.

with ; and when you have this seal you have arguments for prayer, and power
to enforce them.   Lord, here is thy bow in the cloud, a sign that thou wilt
not drown the world ; here is thy seal in the sacrament, a sign that thou
wilt not charge my sin upon me, which hath been charged upon my Saviour.
It was told me that it was a body broken for me, blood shed for me.   I
have taken it upon this account, I have taken this seal, I have covenanted
to obey thee, I am willing and desirous, and I will be industrious to do
it ; be a God keeping covenant with me and truth for ever.   The honour
of God lies at pawn in his seal, whereby strong consolation cannot be denied
to those that lay hold upon Christ in it.   As the passover was a pledge as
well as a memorial, a pledge of a spiritual as well as memorial of a temporal deliverance, so is the supper a pledge of what is to come, as well as
a memorial of what is past ; a pledge of all the fruits of the death of Christ
yet behind.   Should this then, that is so desirable and confirming a seal,
be neglected, which we may believingly plead as God's act and deed, when
it is not a bare stamp of a seal, which signifies nothing but the image
upon the seal ; a seal to a deed which gives the assurance of the advantages in the deed, and an interest in the contents of the deed, and what
is conveyed by it.

(3.) It is a renewing our covenant with him.   It is a federal rite wherein
God exhibits, on his part, Christ and his benefits to us, and we profess our
subjection and obedience to him, laying more solemn vows upon ourselves ;
whence they were called sacraments, the word signifying a military oath,
whereby soldiers oblige themselves to be true to their general and the cause
they fought for.   And Pliny saith,* he learned it of some Christians, that
at their meeting they did *sacramento se obstringere, ne furta, ne latrocinia,
ne adulteria committerent,* &c.   Covenants are always mutual, something to
be done by us as well as for us.   God seals the benefits of the covenant on
his part, and we seal to the duties of the covenant on ours.   It strengthens
us in the assurance of the benefits promised, and engageth us to a performance of the duties required.   The exhibiting the signs is the seal on God's
part ; our receiving the signs is the seal on our part.   By taking them we
acknowledge that we stand to the conditions, and restipulate with God again
that we will be his ; and upon this striking hands with God, we claim a right,
and lay hold upon his seals and plead them.   You avouch God to be your
God, Deut. xxvi. 16–18, obliging yourselves to a greater distance from sin,
and detestation of it ; divorce from it to a more quickened obedience, vigorous faith, holy life, and exacter service; fetching strength from the death of
Christ in the supper to this end.   Is not this desirable, to be in covenant
with God, to have God in covenant with us, to have it more assured on both
parts, which is the felicity and security of a creature ?

(4.) It is a communion with God.   As the partaking of things sacrificed
to idols was a fellowship with devils, 1 Cor. x. 20, so the partaking of that
which was sacrificed to God, is a fellowship with God.   There is in this
action more communion with God (though not the sole act of communion,
as some say) than in any other religious act.   Prayer is an act of homage ;
praise an act of gratitude.   We have not so near a communion with a person, either by petitioning for something we want, or returning him thanks
for a favour received, as we have by sitting with him at his table, partaking
of the same bread and the same cup.   In all nations the nearest fellowship
consists in acts of this nature.   The eating of the supper, as the eating of
sacrifices, is a federal rite between God and the believer, signifying that
there is a covenant of friendship between him and them.   It is the Lord's

* Plin. lib. x. epist. xcvii.

table, and what feasted and cheered the heart of God in heaven, viz., the body and blood of Christ, God gives us to feast our souls on earth, so that we do in a manner eat and drink with him in this love banquet. Take, eat, manifests a communion; Christ is really presented to us, and faith really takes him, closes with him, lodgeth him in the soul, makes him an indweller; and the soul hath a spiritual communion with him in his life and death, as if we did really eat his flesh and drink his blood presented to us in the elements. Eating signifies taking in Christ as our own, his righteousness, and whatsoever is his in communion with him. Is this a privilege to be neglected? To sit at God's table, partake of his dainties, that which he doth most highly value, and deserves the value of the creature infinitely above the sitting at the table of the greatest monarch on earth; that which was the sweet savour to God upon the cross, is offered to us as a feast upon the table; and we eat that body and drink that blood which atoned God, and thereby have a communion with him in his pleasure and delight.

4. The benefits of this ordinance require frequency. As everything hath its use in creation, so likewise in redemption; God made nothing in vain in the one, and appoints nothing in vain in the other.

These benefits are many.

(1.) Weakening of sin; not physically but morally. The lively representation and consideration of the death of Christ, with all its circumstances, is a strong incentive and assistance to the mortifying sin in us; and there is no branch of the body of death, but some consideration or other fetched from the death of Christ, hath a virtue to destroy. How can any be proud when he sees Christ lay down his life in the form of a mean man; how can he be covetous, when he sees Christ turning his back upon the profits of the world? Christ upon the cross, viewed by a sparkling eye of faith, would work the same effect in our souls, which the looking upon the serpent in the wilderness wrought in the Israelites' poisoned bodies, expelling the venom from the vitals and out-works of the members, and abating the fury of a corrupt paroxysm. Now as feathered arrows will fly further, and pierce deeper, than when they are carried by their own weight only,[*] so such considerations, when helped by sensible representations, do more excite the faculty to a vigorous operation by a more sensible affecting the mind. The word declares the evil of sin, and the sacrament shews it in the person of our Saviour; sin is known by the word to be deadly, and it is seen to be so in the supper. Then is the soul most affected against sin, when God's indignation against it is manifested, when it beholds Christ made a curse, and bearing all that the law denounceth against sin, and sees the desert of sin and the terrors of wrath. Never doth sin look so ghastly, and repentance so sorrowfully, as when Christ and the soul meet together in this ordinance. The looking upon Christ opens the spring of sorrow, Zech. xii. 10. In this we take a crucified Christ that we may have crucified sins. The very approach to this ordinance, kindles resolutions against corruption, and smothers the flames of sin in the soul. Who that understands the nature of sin, and the evil consequents of it, would be without such a benefit? Are there no invading temptations to be rooted, no indwelling sins to be expelled, no distractions to be settled; is there not still a root of bitterness always sprouting, an inward serpent always brooding, an Egyptian furnace in our hearts, sending out its sparks; must not the root be more withered, the poison cast out, the indwelling sin tamed, the furnace quenched? Do we not then need all the assistances to faith in the mortifying death of Christ? As Christ upon the cross expiated sin, so Christ in the supper

* Amyrald, Thes. Salmur.

mortifies sin by his Spirit, and purgeth those iniquities which are as a veil between the face of God and the joy of our souls. Faith acts more lively against its enemy, when it considers that the blood was shed for the soul, as to justify, so to sanctify. As there must be a removal of those humours which lurk in the body, whereby the vital principle is stifled, and growth rebated, so there must be a removal of those spiritual diseases which hinder the raising our heads higher towards heaven.

(2.) Nourishment of the soul. In regard of the insensible decay of the spirits of the body, there is need of a continual supply to recruit them, and keep them up in their due vigour; our souls stand in no less need of being succoured by a feast of fat things full of marrow. The flesh hath its provisions, and grace must have hers. In the nourishment of the body, the meat, by the vital heat in the stomach, is turned into the substance of the body; so by a believing participation of Christ in the sacrament, we are turned into the image of Christ, and nourished up by it to eternal life. His flesh is meat indeed, and his blood is drink indeed, John vi. 65; he is given to us as nourishment: 'Take, eat, This is my body,' as nourishment to be incorporated with us; the bread is the sign of his body, and his body is the bread of the soul; the element conveys vigour to the body, and the thing signified strength to the soul, and recruits it with new spirits. What bread and wine do physically convey to the body, which is strength, comfort, nourishment, that doth the body and blood of Christ by faith convey to the soul, quickening, comforting, strengthening, cherishing grace. As the new creature is brought into being only by the power of Christ, so it is maintained by the blood of Christ only, and Christ hath provided this to be both our meat and our medicine, our food and our antidote, to revive our soul, and cure and prevent our diseases, to repair the decays which the remainders of sin and evil humours cause in our souls. It is not a naked remembrance; that would be in breaking the bread, and pouring out the wine, by which actions are signified the death of Christ; but nutrition is intended, therefore the bread is eaten, the wine drunk; our bodies need daily bread; the maintaining the life cannot consist with a total abstinence from food. Who but a madman would be so cruel to himself as to deny his faint body its ordinary relief, and its stated meals? Are any of our souls so fat and flourishing as to need no more spiritual food; are we grown up to the degree and state of angels who never eat nor drink? If we would not contemn the food of our bodies, which common providence prepares for us, have we any more reason to contemn the food of our souls, which rich grace provides for us? As we cannot expect healthful nourishment from corn, but as dressed according to various methods, so we cannot expect nourishment from Christ but in the way of his own appointments.

(3.) Increase and exercise of grace. Christ is the storehouse and fountain of all the treasures of life and peace, but his ordinances are the channel. Though Christ hath treasures to enrich us, yet he will choose the way of conveyance himself. By virtue of that principle whereby bodies live, they grow up to that stature which is convenient for them, and their growth is promoted by those means which maintain life in them. It is eaten, it is drunk, to promote our growth as well as maintain our lives. Grace is increased by Christ; he is the finisher as well as the author, Heb. xii. 2; and therefore the increaser of it, laying by degrees one stone upon another, till he completes it by the top stone; dressing the plant to a greater flourishing. This ordinance, therefore, is of frequent use for the building up and bringing forth more lively and juicy fruits. The elements, bread and wine, are not only nourishing, but strengthening, and so is the thing signified by them.

Some speak of a garden of balsam trees in Egypt which bring forth no fruits unless they be watered with a neighbouring fountain, wherein the blessed virgin was reported often to have washed our Saviour. It is true of grace, the balsam-tree in the soul, which will not thrive unless watered by the blood of Christ. Faith is increased thereby; as the oftener the word is heard, so the oftener sacraments are used, the more doth faith thrive. The same arguments which first persuaded us to assent to the truth of a thing, the more they are impressed upon us, the more sensible they are made to us, the more they do continue and increase that persuasion; and according to the thriving of faith is the vigour of all other graces. Where should we find this vigour for our graces, but in the body and blood of him who is the fountain of all grace to us? This was instituted, indeed, while our Saviour was mortal, but it conveys a spiritual immortality to our souls, because it receives its strength and efficacy from his resurrection. It is here the smoking flax may rise into a flame, and the bruised reed find its support and repair; and the spirit may be renewed even in the infirmities of the flesh. If we come with weak grace and strong breathings, we may return with strong grace and full satisfaction. Do not little sparks need frequent and gentle blasts to blow them up? Proficiency is our duty; we must press forward towards the mark, we must run our race; it is our duty, then, to take our *viaticum*, or provision, to enable us thereto. Why do we come to the word but to have grace either wrought or increased? Why should any believer, then, neglect the other means of God's appointment? Sacraments are the marts wherein we trade for an increase of our stock, as well as the word. Since, therefore, we are subject to decays, and liable to changes and wants in our spiritual condition, we stand in need of a rooting and establishing ordinance. If we would maintain the fire, it must not be by removing the fuel. If our stomachs be lost, it is a sign our growth is stopped. Is our faith so strong that it needs no further confirmation; our grace mounted to that height that it needs no further steps; our desires so sharp as that they cannot receive any keener edge? It is an ordinance wherein grace is much exercised, and more unitedly about its object, Christ; and were there no other advantage than this, to have an opportunity to strike up all our graces together, our clasping faith and our melting repentance, our flaming love and our nimble desires, it were enough to make the ordinance itself desirable to a Christian, since there is an unspeakable comfort in the very sound of him. But so excellent an ordinance cannot be without a more excellent benefit.

(4.) Sense and assurance of love often comes in by it. Wine is comforting. In no ordinance is Christ so particularly applied, 'Take, eat, this is my body.' It concerns Christ to make them welcome to his table that come with hearts thirsting for him. Christ was known by the breaking of bread, when the disciples knew him not before in his opening the Scripture, Luke xxiv. 30 ,31. Gladness attended the keeping of the passover, 2 Chron. xxx. 21, 26. Great joy, then, in Jerusalem, not in the neglect of it. The primitive Christians continued in their ' gladness of heart' by ' breaking bread from house to house,' Acts ii. 46. Much more surely by breaking bread with Christ in the supper. It is the most probable time of the Spirit's performing the great office, which is to bring things to remembrance, when we are engaged in an ordinance, whose chief design is to bring Christ in his expiatory death to remembrance; when the office of the Spirit, and the end of the institution meet together, it is the most likely time for the Spirit to exercise his office and join in with the end of the sacrament, to shew the high and heavenly things of our Saviour. There is a sweetness in a promise, but more in a promise drawn into covenant with all its ramifications.

God's seal, as well as his oath, is for confirmation; his word is sufficient, but lest that should be staggered at, he hath added his oath; if that should leave any doubts, he hath fixed his seal, all which are the highway to a comfortable assurance. The sin within us, and the devil without us, are always raising vapours, which gather into clouds, filling us with doubts, and hindering the sense of God's comfortable face, staggering our hopes, and making us question that love which is grounded upon so many promises. God hath in this given us a pledge of his love, and a ground of assurance, when we have Christ printed clearer in his sufferings and his love, visibly represented as made a curse in our stead, a sacrifice bearing his sins in our body, and expiating them by his blood, and this Christ taken into our souls, and pleaded to God as our security. Thus hath Christ given his body for us, and left his body with us as a pawn, a pledge for all we want, for all the good we can hope for. Sense of his love must be great, when the soul considers that his blood satisfied God, and may well satisfy it. When we eat and drink believingly, our souls delight themselves in fatness. And as the heart of God was satisfied with him upon the cross, so the heart of a Christian is often replenished by him at a sacrament. What the gospel presents in words, the sacrament doth in signs; what the word presents to the ear, the supper doth to the eye, to the taste, that we may have comfort come in at all our senses. How often have drooping spirits met with comfort in the very action; and met with hidden manna in sacramental bread, like a glorious Christ in a human body, and have had a full sense of a Saviour's love accompanying the visible representation of it? How often have his people heard him in it speak peace, peace; speak peace to them, and breathe peace in them, and kiss them with the kisses of his mouth? How often have their consciences been pacified, and their creeping joy found an elevation? There have been mutual glances; Christ hath struck a beam upon the soul, imprinted a clearer stamp of love, and the soul hath clasped its arms about a Saviour. And is such an ordinance fit to be neglected?

(5.) Union with Christ is promoted. As the bread and wine, being turned into our nature, become one with us, so the body and blood of Christ, being by faith turned into our substance, make us one with Christ. As the bread and wine are physically united to us, so we are spiritually united to Christ, Christ incorporating himself with us in a sacrament. He was our surety upon the cross, he is our advocate in heaven; and incorporated with us in the supper in a spiritual, not a transubstantiate manner: 'I in them,' John xvii. 23, 26. Can we too often clasp about him; can the union be often renewed, and become too close and strait?

Use 1. How much is the neglect, if not contempt, of this institution to be bewailed! How sad a thing is it, that many for many years have turned their backs upon breasts full of milk! How hath it been regarded as if it were an abrogated law, a seal out of date, torn off from the covenant, as though the institutions of Christ were miserable comforters, and it were a despicable privilege to receive entertainment at God's table.

(1.) It concerns such to inquire, whether the reasons of their neglect be valid against a positive command. Since it is a command, *Do this*—not only to remember Christ, but to remember Christ in this method, *Do this in remembrance of me*—it is worthy their consideration, whether the ground of their neglect be such as will bear a divine scrutiny, and sustain the force of God's inquisition. They must be evasions past understanding that can hold water against a divine order. Though it may not always be frequented, yet it is not always to be omitted. No excuse was valid against the passover, but uncleanness or a journey, and that not for an annual but a month's omission, Num. ix. 13. But what light excuses have we to keep us off from a feast with God for many years, which we would not admit of to hinder us from a feast with man ?

(2.) Was it appointed to be neglected ? Did Christ take such care to institute it, and we take care to avoid it ? did he give such a positive order for no other end but that we should never regard it ? can we say we value his word, when we slight his seal ? is your faith so strong in his word, that it needs no strength from the seal ? was not the faith of the apostles as strong at that time of institution as any man's, or at least in some few days after ? Yet it was not left *ad libitum:* you *may* do this, but *do it.* Christ is a better judge of the weakness of our hearts, our proneness to forgetfulness, the difficulty to preserve faith as well as obtain it. And he instituted it as an act of kindness as well as authority, that it might be observed, not neglected by us. Were there no end of it, but only an act of his will, acceptance is a civility we owe our Saviour. If he had said, I pray you, do this, could you have refused to him that died for you ; could you refuse it to him that endured the wrath of God for you ? What had become of you if he had not died ; all the angels could not have removed that load of wrath that lay upon you ? If it be a command to do it, to neglect it is a sin ; for what is sin but a breach of God's command ? It is a direct command, not drawn by consequence, as plain a command as any in the decalogue, ' Do it in remembrance of me ;' not, may do it, do it if you will, or, do it when you will.

(3.) How can such free themselves from unworthy reflections upon Christ ? It is either an act of wisdom or folly in him. If of wisdom, why are we so foolish as not to observe it ; if of folly, why do we at all believe in him whom we count a foolish Saviour ? It was either an act of love in him or disdain. If of love, why are we so ungrateful as not to regard it ? if of disdain, why should we depend upon a person whom we virtually charge with leaving a mocking ordinance to us just before his going out of the world ? We must either quite discard our faith, or discard our neglect. There is no doubt but it was both an act of wisdom and love in Christ ; the wisdom that conducted the course of his life was not absent from him when he was so near his death, nor had his love which animated him to death the next day, forsaken him the night before ; had he left his love, he might have prevented his death. To neglect it, then, is to vilify Christ's institution, to disparage his skill and care of his church, as though there were no need of any representations of him, or as if something might have been ordered better. It is to charge Christ with a trifling institution, it is to charge him with the greatest folly, that when he was to encounter with wrath and death, he could not find something else to busy himself about ; that he could not pitch upon a better thing to recommend to you, as a token of his care, and a support for your souls. If we will thus undertake to prescribe Christ what he should do, this is to be, not his servants to be guided by him, but his lords to rule him, and give him his instructions, as though he were our, not his Father's, ambassador. How can we hope for the benefits he hath purchased, while we cast such reflections upon him, as if he were busy about just nothing ?

(4.) Is it neglected because the elements are so mean, and the thing so easy in itself ? Had any Israelite neglected to turn his eye upon the brazen serpent, the poison in his blood had digged his grave. What might they not have objected against it ; what good can a look upon a brazen figure do my wounds ? I want a plaster for my sore, more than a cast of my eye. Brass will naturally inflame my distemper, not assuage it. Can the picture of a serpent cure the biting of a real one, and at such a distance ? This and more might have been objected against that, than against this; but such logic would have destroyed the dispute. Or is it easy, and therefore fit to be neglected? It was our Saviour's mercy to make it so easy, who might have imposed harder conditions on us; and shall we slight his tenderness, who was loath to burden us, and careful to relieve us? What would have been said, had it been as painful as the circumcising the flesh, or as distasteful as the bitter herbs of the passover? It is true, it is common bread, it is common wine in itself; but it is consecrated bread, and consecrated wine in its use. It hath the stamp of Christ upon it, as the wax taken out of the shop hath the seal of the conveyer, which the purchaser would not part with for all the wax left behind in the hands of the seller.

(5.) Or do we think Christ is come again, that we neglect it? The command was dated from the night before his death, and is to be in force till he return again. Was it his resurrection that is meant by his coming? Would Christ at such a time appoint an ordinance, that was to last but three days, and never like to be put in practice after his institution? Or was it till he came in Spirit? He was come in Spirit at Pentecost, before the apostle in the text urged the institution; therefore *come again* cannot be meant of that. The ordinance then had ceased before Paul writ to the Corinthians; and he would never have restored an abrogated institution, who was so vehement an opposer of an abrogated ceremonial law. Or till he come in Spirit into the soul? Was Christ in Spirit in none of the Corinthians, who were a church of great graces and great gifts, as well as great corruptions? Paul rectifies their corrupt mixtures, but exempts not any from a due observance.

(6.) Why doth any one neglecter of it, who hath faith, observe any other command or institution? Those that make not conscience of all known duties, make conscience of none. He that offends in one point, breaks the whole law; he that contemns one point of the gospel, violates the authority of the whole. I do not see how any part of the Christian religion would be dear to any who have so slight a regard to that which may claim an equality with any ordinance, and a precedency in our esteem in some respects, in regard of the positive command of our Saviour, the time when he appointed it, and the length of its duration, ' Till I come.' I doubt the apostasies of many, and the unfruitfulness in the lives of professors, may be charged upon either the neglect of this, or an unworthy carriage in it. He hath little desire to gain Christ, or preserve Christ, that will have him in his own way, and not in Christ's way. What we desire, we should take a course to enjoy in the method of that person who only can fulfil our desires.

(7.) Or is it unfitness that is the cause of neglect? Hath any man heard of repentance, and faith, and holiness, and yet hath nothing of them? What a miserable case is this! If you are not fit for this ordinance, you are not fit for heaven. What will you do when you come to die? He that is not fit for the supper, is not fit for heaven, for the marriage day of the lamb. Is not the unfitness from sloth, laziness, and unwillingness to take pains with the heart? If any man can say he hath used all his industry, by prayer and repentance, to fit himself for heaven and for the ordinance, and done what he can, God requires no more than men are able to do. If unfitness to come be dangerous, is not a total omission as dangerous? Will you plead your unfitness to God at the last day, as an excuse for disobedience? What an excuse will this be, Lord, I would have been often at the supper, but I was unfit, I gave way to a constant course of temptation, I never had an eagerness of desire for it, I was torn with various distractions, I let sin reign in me, the care of a farm or a trade diverted my thoughts from it;

what self-condemning excuses are those? You know how firm they were to stave off the anger of the king from those that made them in the Gospel to excuse their not coming to his wedding, Mat. xxii. Or is it a perfect fitness that is not to be found within the circumference of the earth? You will make God a hard master under the gospel, to receive none but those that have a perfect fitness for him. If any would be perfectly fit, the course is not to reject the means for it. Diseases can never be cured with a slighting, but by using the remedy.

(8.) Consider what you lose, and what danger you incur. Whatsoever benefits are stored up in a sacrament we lose by neglects; whatsoever obedience is in observing it, we lose the reward of; we lose the fruit of his love in it, and we deny the obligation of his authority, and the honour of obedience to it. God will not calmly and coldly suffer neglects. To detract from any ordinance of Christ, is in part to diminish the Scripture, to deny part of his will and testament. Why was the neglect of the Jewish sacraments so severely punished, that the persons were cut off, not by a civil punishment, but by the hand of God, as the Jews interpret it? Is not the grace offended in ours as good as was in theirs? Ours may claim the precedency of them in benefits, and therefore should in estimation. It is much, that when Christ hath graciously condescended to us, we should not thankfully ascend to our own privilege. Well, then, why shall not the inconceivable love of a Saviour move you to the obedience of a command so easy, so beneficial, so alluring? You are bound to profess Christ, to remember him in your lives, who remembered you at his death. Do you think yourselves his members within the great charter of salvation which he hath purchased and sealed? How can any be members of his corporation, and disobey his orders? Are you not entered by baptism; have you not vowed and promised your allegiance; and is the neglect of a known and positive command the way to perform it? Consider it is a law made by the purchaser of our salvation.

Use 2. Is of exhortation to observe it, and that frequently. Though a dying Saviour is remembered, yet a living Saviour is sought for in it; and shall not we be as ready to seek a living Christ in the sacrament, as the women were to seek a dead Christ in the sepulchre? Mat. xxviii. 1. The neglect of it doth speak some light thoughts of it. Is it because of the meanness of the elements? We may as well despise a great Redeemer, because clothed with the infirmities of a mortal body, as despise the spiritual representations of him, because clothed with the meanness of earthly elements. God doth always delight to convey great things through mean mediums. Gideon shall route a Midianitish army with potsherds, with earthen pitchers; and the jaw-bone of an ass shall be more successful in the hand of Samson, than a massy sword in the hand of Goliath. By the weakness of the cross God redeems the world; by the foolishness of preaching he converts a world, and conveys through earthen vessels a treasure wherewith to enrich his people, and a strength that makes confusion in the kingdom of darkness; and by these elements, mean in appearance, he doth nourish the believer, still making those ordinances the pipes of his invisible grace. Or is it for want of a disposition? If there be no faith at all, the cause is sad; if there be no fitness for heaven, there is no present fitness to converse with Christ in his supper. Or is it but a weak faith? The more need then of a strengthening ordinance. Would we have a more elevated frame of heart? The way to ascend to the top of a pinnacle is not to run from the steps which lead to it. Who is sufficient for these things? But the more spiritually sensible we are of our own insufficiency, the more confidence we may have in the sufficiency of a Saviour; the more sensible we are of our disease, the more confident of the skill and affection of our phy- sician, and the more we should apply ourselves to his prescriptions.

Let us consider some questions.

(1.) Will any believer be guilty of disobedience to the author of his faith? *Do this*, is a word of command, Luke xxii. 19. Not left *ad libitum*, it is not, *you may if you will*, as was said before; but *do it* in remembrance of me. Do it, if you will remember me; I will account you no rememberers of me, unless you do it. The command was given to the apostles, but to deliver it to the church: 1 Cor. xi. 23, 'For I have received of the Lord that which also I have delivered unto you.' We must obey the commands given to the apostles, so far as they are practicable by us, as well as think to share in the comforts of the prayer Christ put up for us and his apostles, John xvii. 20. The influence of what was spoken in their presence extended to all believers, and the observance of what was instituted in their presence is to be regarded by all believers. God would not only have the Israelites cleanse themselves, but be circumcised and eat the passover, when they were upon the borders of Canaan, before he would bless them with the victory, Joshua v. 2, 10. God would have them renew covenant with him, in the way of his own appointment, before they should have possession of Canaan. Suppose there were no benefit to be expected, 'though every institution of Christ is a mark of his love, as well as a fruit of his authority,' yet doth not the greatness of Christ's love deserve our tenderness of his authority in his commands? If they had nothing of privilege but all of duty, love to Christ would make us often remember him, and obedience would make our love choose the way of his own ordering, and not ways at our own plea- sure. *Deus voluit* is a sufficient motive, and we cannot free ourselves from the censure of disobedience, if we observe not his commands in the same manner that he enjoins them, in their circumstances as well as their substance.

(2.) Is Christ so mean a friend as not to be remembered? The memory of a good friend should be very precious. Is there any friend we have in the world can outstrip him in affection, and deserve a greater share in our first-born thoughts? What was ever more advantageous to us than the death of Christ, by whom we have our life; than the agonies of Christ, to which we owe our freedom from the wrath to come? Do we not remember our own benefit in remembering our gracious benefactor, who bore our sor- rows that we might enter into his joy? groaned under the curses due to us, that we might triumph in his Father's love and in his own glory; who emptied himself to fill us, and received the wrathful strokes to free us; who took our sins upon himself, and cast upon us the robe of his righteousness; bore the load of our transgressions to enrich us with the treasures of his merits; endured our death to procure our life, and hung upon our cross to advance us to sit upon his throne. Is it not a great unkindness to be un- willing frequently to remember so cordial and choice a friend? Besides, is it not fit to remember him frequently, who remembers believers perpetually? He regarded such in his last prayer, he remembers such in heaven to plead for them, he remembers them under their bespotting corruptions. Shall not believers remember him, who hath laid in his blood a perfect foundation for their perfect happiness? He remembers them that were enemies, and have too much enmity still; and shall not they remember him who is a clear and perfect friend? He bears their names upon his breast, as Aaron did the ten tribes on the ephod, Exod. xxviii. 12, and remembers even those who have crucified him; and shall not they remember Christ who were never wronged by him ? Should we not rejoice to see the rainbow in the clouds, which is a sign of God's securing covenant against a destroying deluge ? And shall we neglect the signs of God's securing covenant against an overflowing wrath ?

(3.) Why should we not often be in those ways where we may meet with our best friend ? Certainly he is as graciously present in this as in any other ordinance. He is present with us in observing every thing which he hath commanded, Mat. xxviii. 20; and shall this be without a more special presence, when it was instituted for a more special remembrance of him ? He is present symbolically, as a man by his picture ; he is present spiritually, the soul sees him by faith, as Abraham saw his day at a distance, and that with joy ; he is present by his efficacy, as the sun is present in the earth, though many hundred miles distant in its body. ' This is my body,' ' this is my blood ;' as sure as this is bread and this is wine, so surely by faith are you partakers of my body and blood in this ordinance. Can this be said of any other ordinance ? Where is Christ so particularly present, so closely applied as in this ?

(4.) Have you no graces that need strengthening ? Have we not need of all the means to strengthen that faith, which we shall have all the need of in the hour of death, to keep our souls from fainting under the stroke ? Is it not a desirable thing to have the benefits of Christ often applied to us, and our faith confirmed ? Is all our leanness removed, that we need no more marrow and fatness ? Are we so provided for heaven, that we need no more *viaticum* in our journey thither ? Who would come but seldom to his stated meals ? He that would fast one day would scarce fast two, but by force. We are yet in a journey, and we need strength to go forward ; we are beset with diseases, and we need medicines to cure us ; we are often faint, and we need cordials to revive us. Are our souls so fully established, our affections so ready at our call, as not to need sensible objects sometimes to raise them ? A vigorous fancy, helped by the sight of a picture, mounts to a greater activity ; so doth a spiritual faith. Can you, then, too often embrace the cross, drink down the blood of Christ, and put your hands into his wounds ? Is your faith so hearty, that it needs no cordials ; your love so hot, that it needs no breath for an higher flame ; your hopes so certain, that they do not sometimes reel ; and your obedience so quick, that it needs no spur ; and your standing so secure, that it needs no further settlement ? It is certain, that as we would have faith, we must attend upon converting ordinances, so if we would have strength of faith, we must frequent strengthening institutions. How would this Sun, shining upon our souls in his own orb, enrich us with his heat and light, suffer nothing to stand before it, and put out all those lesser fires, those foolish desires which aspire to other things, and weaken the soul ? After the Israelites were circumcised, and had eaten the passover, then did Christ, as captain of the Lord's host, appear to Joshua to encourage his heart, and strengthen his hands against those enemies in Canaan, by which our spiritual enemies are represented, Joshua v. 7, 10, 14. It is by a frequent exercise of faith, according to the methods of Christ, that believers would be as lions (as Chrysostom saith) breathing fire terrible to the devils themselves. Have you not found your own experience, or at least the experience of others, bear witness to this ? How often hath the empty soul been filled, the palsy hand cured, the thirsty heart satisfied, the feeble knees strengthened, a creeping love changed its pace, and a cloudy soul been brightened ? The more believing at a sacrament, the more vigorous is the faith afterwards. As in eating corporal food, by the assimilation of meat to our substance by the chemistry of nature, and converting it into blood and spirits, the body is strengthened ; so by the feeding upon Christ by faith, the soul is strengthened, and Christ becomes more and more mystically incorporate in the believer, ' Christ in them the hope of glory,' John xvii. 23 ; I in them, and thou in me.'

(5.) Why will any true believer gratify Satan ? The motions to hinder those that are gracious, must either be from God or Satan ; from God they cannot be, who is no enemy to the ordinance he hath appointed for them. It cannot be thought that God should decry his own institution, or call back his own invitation, or discourage a believer from the remembrance of his Son in that ordinance, which hath been enjoined for that end. The Spirit in his motions acts according to the word, not contrary to it. They must then be from the devil, who is an enemy not to be listened to. He endeavours to hinder the believer from the most spiritual duties, whereby he may gain the greatest profit. He kindles our corruptions, shoots in his temptations, fills us with scruples, exhorts us to omit, defer anything to stave us off from that which is the strengthening of our souls, and a weakening of his kingdom. Swallow not therefore this poison ; spit it out, lest you please the devil, and displease the Redeemer. How will the devil triumph if he can keep you in a constant omission of a known duty ! If the frequent attendance be a means to strengthen grace, the neglects are a means to weaken ; and the devil rejoices in the decays of grace, next to preventing any grace at all. He feeds himself with hopes that at last he may make such utterly insensible.

(6.) Why should any believer deny to pay Christ the debt of thankfulness for his great love, in that way which he hath appointed ? It is a thanksgiving, a thankful remembrance, therefore anciently called the *eucharist*. It is appointed as a feast to rejoice before God for the benefits we profess to enjoy by the death of Christ ; as the eating of the sacrifice offered to an idol was a profession that all that they had came from the kindness and powerful influence of that idol. Shall not our souls be filled with hosannas for the greatest mercy that can be bestowed upon us, viz. a redemption from guilt, death, hell, and the wrath of God ? Shall we refuse a thankful acceptance of that honour to sit at his table, and to sup with our prince ? Would not that person be accounted ungrateful, that should delight in the picking of straws when his king calls him to his presence ?

To conclude. Let the benefits of this ordinance persuade every believer to a frequency in it. They must needs be great and desirable upon a worthy and believing partaking, because the sin and danger are dreadful in an unworthy approach. If indeed we have no enemies to conquer, no weakness to strengthen, no sin to trouble us, no temptations to surround us, no damps to smother our assurance, no ebbs in our graces, no totterings in our faith, no coolings in our love, no emptiness to be filled, no doubts to be resolved ; if we are in heaven, and are as angels in assumed bodies, then we are lifted above the end and intendment of it; but this is no man's case in the world. It is a command, to neglect it therefore is to despise his authority ; it is for our good, to neglect it therefore is to contemn his mercy ; his institutions are attended with promises, to neglect them is to deny his truth.

We have handled two doctrines from the words. There is one more yet behind, concerning the *duration* of this ordinance ; from the last clause, ' You shew the Lord's death till he come.'

There is especially a twofold coming of Christ mentioned in Scripture.

1. His coming in the flesh; 2, his coming to judgment. Both mentioned

Heb. ix. 28, ' Christ was once offered to bear the sins of many, and he shall appear the second time without sin unto salvation.' The one was to bear our sins, the other to glorify our souls; the one to expiate our guilt, the other to present us to God without any filth; the one to begin salvation, the other to perfect it; the one to seal the promises, the other to perform them; the one to put an end to the remembrance of sin, by substituting himself as a sacrifice in the room of the legal ones, whereby there was a remembrance of sin every year, the other to put an end to the fruit of sin, afflictions and sufferings of his people.

It is not his coming in the Spirit which is here meant; this had not consisted with the interest of Christ, the wisdom of Christ, or the end of the sacrament.

(1.) Not with the interest of Christ. Christ came in Spirit after his ascension, at the time of the liberal effusion of the Holy Ghost upon the apostles, Acts ii., which was his coming to them as he had promised: John xiv. 18, ' I will not leave you comfortless, I will come unto you.' Would he so solemnly assemble the apostles at such a time, when that wrath, which he saw marching out against him, called for the employment of all his thoughts, and his greatest care in the management of that work? When it was come to that issue, would he neglect his present interest and business to settle an ordinance so short-lived as the space of fifty days, when most of that time he intended to comfort them by his personal presence after his resurrection? It had not consisted with his interest at that time to employ himself about that which should so suddenly expire.

(2.) Nor with the wisdom of Christ. To institute that so solemnly for his remembrance, that should be of so little use. It was to remember him in his absence all the time he should be in his Father's kingdom. A greater absence than that of twelve days must be meant; for he was absent from them only during the time of his lying in the grave, and the time between his ascension and the descent of the Spirit, if by coming here be meant his coming in the effusion of the Spirit: Acts i. 3, ' He was seen of them forty days, speaking of the things pertaining to the kingdom of God' (it is likely he was with one or other of them every day in that space), which, it is probable, were not to be put in execution till the coming of the Spirit, which they were to wait for at Jerusalem, which was to endue them with power from on high, Luke xxiv. 49, Acts i. 8. And though after the descent of the Spirit, they ' continued in breaking of bread,' yet not before, but only ' in prayer and supplication' (Acts i. 14) for the power of the Holy Ghost, which was to commission them. And would Christ take such care to have a church before the fall of the Jewish church, and enable his apostles by his Spirit in so miraculous a manner to settle his commands among those that should believe in him; and this, which is one of the greatest and most in favour to the church, so lately instituted, and for the commemoration of the fundamental benefit, to expire just after the promulgation of it? That did not cease at the coming of Christ in the Spirit, which we have no evidence that it was put in practice from the time of the first institution till the coming of the Spirit. Did it consist with the wisdom of our Lord to give a command which was never to be practised?

(3.) Nor with the end of the supper. It was to be done *in remembrance.* How could they in so short a time forget him, in whose hands and sides they had seen the marks of the nails and spear? How could they forget him whose death they had seen, and whom they had enjoyed again by a miraculous resurrection? Besides, the Spirit was come, and so this ordinance ceased before Paul writ to the Corinthians, and he who had been so vehement an opposer of an abrogated ceremonial law, would never have restored an abrogated institution.

Nor is this coming again to be understood of the Spirit's coming to a particular person. Then,

(1.) As soon as ever men come to be fit for this ordinance, they must waive it. If the coming of Christ here spoken of be his coming in Spirit to a soul, as soon as ever he is come in Spirit they ought not to observe it, because they would break the command which is limited to such a time, the time of his coming. The Spirit comes in the work of regeneration, in the work of faith. To what purpose did Christ institute this, if the only subjects capable of it were *ipso facto* deprived of it, when they were first in a capacity for it? None receives good from this ordinance but those that have faith. Indeed, men in a crowd may press upon Christ and touch him, yet only that person that touches his garments and takes the elements by faith, receives virtue from him. What a madness it is to feed a dead man; and if he should be restored to life to deprive him of the means and nourishment to preserve that life.

(2.) It would then be instituted only for the refuse of the world, for such as had no mind to remember him, nor could remember him with any affection to him or comfort to themselves, since they were alienated from him by their unbelief. We cannot suppose that Christ, that night wherein he was betrayed, should take care only of his enemies. He prayed for his disciples, not for the world; he gives the supper to them, and in them, as the foundation of the church, to all that were to believe on him, not to the world. It is the second coming of Christ to judgment that is here meant, when he comes in perfect majesty to bestow a perfect glory; when he shall come ' in that manner as he was taken up into heaven,' Acts i. 11; when the remembrance of his death shall be swallowed up in the vision of his person, and fruition of the ripe and complete fruit of his sufferings. In the mean time it is a standing memorial of the sufferings of our Saviour.

The doctrine then is:

Doct. The Lord's Supper is a lasting and continuing institution, not to be put down at the pleasure of any men. It will not be repealed till Christ come. Another gospel is not to be expected, Gal. i. 6, 7, &c.; and therefore while the gospel endures, the appendixes, the institutions annexed to it, will endure. The times of the gospel are called often in Scripture ' the last days;' no other dispensation is to supersede it, and the ordinances in it are immoveable things, not to be shaken till Christ comes. He is not yet come, the institutions therefore he transmitted to us by the apostles are still of use. Nothing can put a period to them, but the coming of Christ, which no man can say is yet accomplished. The ordinances of Christ are like the pillar of fire and the cloud which guided the Israelites in their journey through the wilderness, and did not withdraw from them till they entered into Canaan. When the church shall be perfected, when Christ shall appear to put the crown upon the head of the glorified church, and bring it into the promised inheritance, the clouds of ordinances will vanish; there will be no more need of them, the ends of them will be completed; there will be no weak grace to need strengthening, nor any indwelling sin to need mortification. In the reformation of the church, prophesied of in Rev. xxi. 3, ' The tabernacle of God is with men, and he will dwell with them.' The ordinances are not to be abolished; while God hath a tabernacle among men, he will have a worship, an instituted worship to help us in our natural worship. The tie of homage the creature owes to God cannot be unloosed. If a worship, then some modes and rites of worship. The tabernacle was the place of worship. This cannot be meant of a state of glory in heaven, because, ver. 1., it is a ' new

Jerusalem which comes down from heaven,' a state distinguished from the state of glory in heaven. In the time of the reformation of the church, which is there promised, the Lamb is said to be the light of the church : Rev. xxi. 23, ' The Lamb is the light thereof.' Christ is always called a lamb in allusion to the paschal lamb, and in that title, his death as a sacrifice is always included. If the lamb, as a sacrifice, be the light of the city in that glorious state which the church doth expect in the full and thorough reformation, the memorials of him as a lamb, and so the memorials of his death, will be preserved till earth give place to heaven. And whereas it is said, ver. 22, ' There shall be no temple,' *i.e.* no human and legal ceremonies, but pure ordinances. And ' the city had no need of the sun and of the moon to shine in it.' Men shall not serve God according to the equinoxes and the course of the moon, as the Jews had their passover about the vernal equinox in March, and the observations of the new moon to shew to them the times of worship.* There shall be no earthly constitutions, inventions of man, anything that smells of the legal ceremonies, but God shall be glorious in his own institutions, and the Lamb shall be the λύχνος, the candle of it. The simple institutions of Christ shall be the light of the church. All those ordinances which signify to us the love of the Lamb, the death of the Lamb, the benefits by that death, shall be kept up in purity and vigour. In the reformation of the church the ordinances shall no more cease than they did in the second temple, which was a reformed church after their captivity in Babylon, and so reformed that they never ran again to idolatry. But the ordinances of God continued in the temple till the coming of the Messiah to tabernacle among men ; so in the reformation from the idolatries and corruptions of antichrist, which will be, as it were, the erection of a second temple, the ordinances shall continue till the coming of Christ to judgment. Christ intimates the continuation of this ordinance in the church till the consummation of all things, and the investing his people with the glory he had promised them, in his words after the institution of it : Mat. xxvi. 29, ' I will not drink henceforth of this fruit of the vine, till I drink it new with you in my Father's kingdom,' which he speaks to shew the nearness of his death, and to comfort them under the apprehensions of it, assuring them they should be with him in his Father's kingdom, partakers of his glory. It also implies that no other institution was to intervene between that time and their being with him in his Father's kingdom. The communication of himself should then be in a new manner. But till that time they must not expect any converse with him but in those ways he had settled. The nearer Christ's coming is, the more will his ordinances be in practice. When the Israelites were upon entering into Canaan, circumcision and the passover were celebrated, which had been omitted all the time of their wilderness condition.

1. All the ordinances of Christ are to continue in his church, then certainly this. The institutions of Christ in the gospel are said to be immoveable, such as cannot be shaken : Heb. xii. 26, 27, ' He hath promised, saying, Yet once more I shake not the earth only, but the heavens. And this word, yet once more, signifies the removing of things that are shaken, as of things that are made, that those things which cannot be shaken may remain.' ' Yet once more,' Hag. ii. 6 ; for it is taken out of that place, the apostle following the Septuagint translation. *Once more*, supposeth that that time being past, there should be no more change of laws in the church. The old institutions under the law are called τὰ σαλευόμενα, things that are shaken or fluctuating, uncertain. The evangelical institutions are opposed to those, as things that cannot be shaken, τὰ μὴ σαλευόμενα. *Once more*, clearly intimates that the

* Grot. in loc.

ordinances introduced by the Messiah should be unalterable, as long as the scene of the world, heaven and earth, endures. He would change but one time, not many. The new laws of the gospel will not be changed by God's authority, but be left in the same state wherein they were established by the Messiah, and not be subject to change, as the legal administration was. The order appointed by Moses was to be shaken, and give place to a better administration ; but the order settled by the Son of God is to stand as firm as a mountain of brass, as the foundations of the earth, or the arch of heaven. If not shaken by God, no reason they should be shaken by man. The faith is said to be ' once delivered to the saints,' Jude 3. Once, *i.e.* unalterably the doctrine of faith is delivered ; as God is said ' Once to swear by his holiness,' Ps. lxxxix. 36 ; once for all, never to be altered. The doctrine of faith, and institutions of the gospel, are monuments of God's grace, not to be demolished or defaced till God puts a period to the world, and wraps up the persons of all his elect in the bosom of Christ. It is his injunction to his apostles, when he commissioned them to teach men to observe all things that he had commanded them ; and he promiseth his presence with them in so doing to the end of the world : Mat. xxviii. 20, ' Teaching them to observe all things whatsoever I have commanded you ; and lo I am with you always, even unto the end of the world.' The things Christ hath commanded, are then to be observed till the end of the world, for he promises his presence with them to the end of the world in the teaching of those things. The things therefore that Christ hath commanded must be taught. If they be not, no men can have any comfortable hopes of the presence of Christ with them. If Christ will have a ministry to the end of the world, he will have a church to the end of the world ; if a church, which is the seat of ordinances, then ordinances to the end of the world ; if ministers, who are the ' stewards of the mysteries of God,' then mysteries there are to be dispensed to the end of the world. Observe the universality of the subject twice repeated, *all things*, and *whatsoever I have commanded you*. Everything that Christ hath commanded must be taught ; everything therefore that Christ hath commanded must endure. Observe also, that the extent of the duration is repeated twice too, *always*, even *to the end of the world ;* it includes also the extent of the duration of the things commanded, because his presence is promised to them in the teaching of whatsoever he commanded. The ordinances therefore of Christ are to be perpetually observed. And they are those evangelical dispensations which are here commanded to be taught and observed, because they are those which Christ, as mediator, hath appointed, ' which I have commanded,' I that have power given me in heaven and earth, for that is the ground of this command : Mat. xxviii. 18, ' All power is given unto me in heaven and in earth ; go ye therefore and teach all nations.' And lest any should take upon them to determine the time of their continuance, because the first word, *always*, is πάσας τὰς ἡμέρας·, he explains what he meant by it, and adds, ' even to the end of the world.' So that it is not meant to the end of the Jewish state, but the end of the frame of heaven and earth. The presence of Christ in the way of his ordinances is here promised. Christ will be present with them after the end of the world, but in another manner of presence than now ; a special presence here in the weakness of ordinances, a glorious presence hereafter in the fulness of vision. Observe also, if ministers cannot promise themselves the presence of Christ, but in teaching all things whatsoever Christ hath commanded, other men cannot promise themselves the presence of Christ with them, but in observing all things whatsoever Christ hath commanded ; and this institution is one of those *all things*. And since the apostles did not live to the end of the world, this promise looks further than the persons of the apostles; it looks to the church which they should settle in such order as he had appointed, founded upon such doctrine, and observing such institutions, according to his command; he would be with that church that should observe their doctrine, and preserve it successively to the end of the world. As in his prayer, John xvii. 20, he did not only pray for the apostles then with him, so he doth not promise this only to the apostles then with him, but to the church. All the institutions settled in the Jewish church are often said to be ordinances *for ever*, *i.e.* during that dispensation, till God should give them their passport and send them away. But the gospel ordinances are to be in force till the conclusion of all things in the world.

2. Sacraments were thought by God needful for men in all their several states in the world. Sacraments were judged necessary by God in innocent nature. The tree of life had a sacramental signification of life upon Adam's obedience. Much more in lapsed nature have we need of those sensible things for the support of our faith in the promises of God. After the fall there were various institutions brought in by degrees. Adam, and Abel, and Noah, had their sacrifices as significant of the Messiah promised to them, and expected by them. Abraham had an addition of circumcision. The passover and other rites were added under Moses. The Messiah takes away them and introduceth others which are to continue, since they are the last days wherein God hath spoken to us by his Son, Heb. i. 1, and are not to be thrust out by any other dispensation. Not but these sacraments under the gospel are changeable in their own nature, if it seem agreeable to the good pleasure of God. For there is a difference between natural laws and positive laws;* natural laws do not proceed merely from the will of the lawgiver, positive do. Those things which are evil in their own nature, are not evil because they are prohibited by the will of God, but because they are contrary to a rational creature as rational; so that God cannot dispense with them, for then he would dispense with evil as evil, and so would deny his own righteousness, if he should allow that which is unjust in its own nature. But for positive laws, which are not innate in nature or grace, but proceed from the will and authority of God solely, they may be changed by the will of the lawgiver. So the ceremonial law was changed, because it was neither good nor evil in itself, but had its authority solely from the will of God. But the moral law cannot be changed, because the duties it enjoins are naturally good in themselves, and the things it prohibits are evil in themselves; and this God cannot dispense with, for then he should call good evil, and evil good. But God hath declared he will never change these. The end of all ordinances was to bring the worshippers to real holiness, which is the perfection of the soul; in innocency, to preserve men in it; in lapsed nature, to discover the necessity of it, and the way to it; and therefore they must be observed under every dispensation, for that end for which they were instituted. Now if these rudiments, proportioned to the Jewish infancy, were not to be violated by them under the severe penalty of the soul's being cut off from among the people (which the Jews understand of a cutting off by the hand of God), sure the more noble institutions of the gospel, settled by the Redeemer, being clearer representations of the love he hath shewn to us, and the benefits we may expect from him, stand more stable, and are big with greater motives to persuade men to the use of them, than those under the law, which were grievous in regard of their multitude and chargeableness, and obscure in regard of the distance of the thing signified by them. They may seem to have had more reason to despise the

* Rivet. in Genes. Exercit. xiii. p. 54.

institutions in those several ages, than we to slight the evangelical ordinances, since they are dignified by the more excellent dispensation they are
annexed unto. And God always had some conduit-pipes, through which to
pour out the blessings of his grace upon the souls of his creatures.

3. All laws once settled are of force till they be repealed by that authority
which did enact them. Christ, as Lord of the church, hath power to appoint
institutions, and none but he hath power to remove them, and even he hath
not power to remove them by any act but by that of his coming. Christ
hath settled this till he comes; since his word is past, nothing but his coming
can repeal it. His command is therefore in force, and ought to be observed,
and it is in force till he comes ; so that if an angel from heaven should bring
us word of a repeal, we ought not to believe him, because Christ is not
come, to which period of time it is to endure. Had it not been a high presumption for any to abolish the ceremonial law among the Jews, till the
promised seed was come, which was the period of its duration ? Gal. iii. 19.
And is it not as high a presumption to look upon gospel institutions as null,
before the time appointed for the coming of Christ, to put an end to this
scene of things, be fulfilled ? But doth not every man who looks upon this,
or any other ordinance, as out of date, assume the power of abrogating, as
much as in him lies, the laws of Christ. It is the obedience we owe our
Lord not to entrench upon his prerogative in the abrogation of his laws, any
more than to usurp the authority of enacting any. It is enough it is his
law, and while it is so we ought to observe it, till he gives us a dismiss by
giving that a repeal. All ordinances have their sanction and establishment
from Christ's authority. The first patriarchs, Adam and Noah, lived without circumcision, Abraham without the laws of Moses. But had God commanded the one to be circumcised, as he commanded Abraham and his
posterity, and enjoined the other to observe the legal institutions, was his
authority to be slighted ? Had they not been as much bound to use them
as the Israelites were ? God never gave power to any man to change his
ordinances, or to dispense with them. The passover continued till God
superseded it by another institution ; circumcision till God changed it into
a more easy. The supper on earth must hold, by Christ's authority, till it
be changed into the marriage supper of the Lamb, and never-fading delights
in heaven ; it must hold till earth be left for heaven, elements for substance
and the person they represent. Who can upon a better account challenge
an exemption from the observance of positive institutions than our Saviour,
who had no need of them ? Yet how observant was he of them, because
they were established by divine authority. So that he calls his submitting
to be baptized of John a ' fulfilling of righteousness,' Mat. iii. 15. If therefore we do acknowledge that Christ is come, and that he will come again,
and believingly look for this coming of Christ, we ought to acknowledge it
by such testimonies as he hath appointed.

4. The covenant is perpetual, and therefore the seals are perpetual.* The
covenant, indeed, God made with Abraham and the Israelites, was the same
covenant, and perpetual in regard of the substance of it ; for God promised
to be their God, and that they should be his people, and to give them eternal
life, whereof Canaan was a type. But because the Mediator, in whom this
covenant had its confirmation, was not yet exhibited, therefore it was not
yet perpetual in regard of the accessories, and those institutions which were
appointed for the confirmation of their faith in it ; as the priesthood, sacrifices, and sacraments, which could not remain, but must be abolished at the
coming of the Mediator, the band of the covenant. The rites belonging to

* Zanch. in Hos. ii. 9, pp. 44–36.

that were but 'shadows of things to come;' and when Christ, whom they shadowed, came, the shadows must necessarily pass away, and some others be instituted in the room of them. When the Aaronical priesthood fell, their sacraments fell with it; and the priesthood being changed, the law is changed also. But Christ, being 'a priest for ever after the order of Melchizedec,' 'hath an unchangeable priesthood,' Heb. vii. 24. And therefore the seal and laws belonging to that priesthood are unchangeable, and will continue to the end of the world. In the supper, God doth witness that he doth give us the flesh of Christ, and blood of Christ, and unite us to him, and incorporate us with him: and on our parts, by the receiving them, we witness our embracing God's favour, and return to him, and faith in him, and obedience to his law. Since there is no more exhibition of him to be expected in order to eternal life, but God hath summed up all his will in Christ, settled him an everlasting priest, these seals will endure as long as there is any exercise of that office of priest, which will be till his second coming; wherein all his elect shall be perfected, and no more need of sacrifice or intercession. If it were a type of something to come, when the substance is come the shadow should be done away; but it is a memorial of what is past, and no other administration is to succeed in the room of Christ, and therefore it is to be continued till his coming, and resigning all to his Father.

5. The state wherein we are requires the continuance of it, and of other ordinances.

(1.) In regard of our constant decays. Our bodies would moulder to dust were they not daily nourished; and is there not as much need of nourishment for our souls? Our souls need such institutions, as well as our bodies need food. A man may expect as well to grow without food, or that his vine should bring forth fruit without sun, and rain, and dressing, as that while he is in the world he should thrive in grace, that doth not take in the fructifying showers of Christ. Our sin is struggling, and needs something to conquer it; our faith is staggering, and needs something to confirm it; the sin that clogs us must be removed; the grace that burns dim must be brightened. We need pardon, here we may behold it sealed; we need straiter union to Christ, here it is promoted. The conjunction between Christ and a believing soul is as close as between us and the bread we eat, the wine we drink. There is need, while we are in the wilderness of this world, to be fed with manna; when Canaan is possessed, this will cease. We have a journey to go, a battle to fight. Is it not necessary we should, with Jonathan, take some honey by the way to recruit our spirits? God always conveyed his grace by some pipes, and these he hath appointed in the times of the gospel.

(2.) In respect of our weakness. Some intercourse there must be between God and us, if we be happy. Immediately we cannot have it; such communications are reserved for heaven: these are shadows fitted to the weaknesses and dimness of our sense. We could not look steadily upon Christ's glorified body; but we may behold him in a sacrament as in a glass without twinkling. The object is not primarily and immediately presented to our eye; but by the mediation of a glass, we have some broken beams, some glances of his presence. And in those shadows we may see Christ crucified before our eyes, embrace him in our arms, and carry him in our hearts. Our state must be changed from earth to heaven before sacraments can well be abolished. If the sacraments be necessary as seals to confirm the truth of the covenant to us, as pledges of Christ's love and his conducting presence, and as instruments to convey strength, vigour, and all the blessings of the covenant to the heart, they are therefore needful till the doubting and staggerings of the soul be removed by full vision, and till we are got to the top of the mount of blessing.

Use 1. Christ will always have a church in the world. A church is the seat of ordinances. Privileges conferred by charter suppose a corporation. If Christ hath left a standing legacy, there shall be some persons in the world to whom it shall be paid. It is his royal prerogative to appoint them. He will not be a titular king, without a kingdom, without subjects. Christ will maintain his interest. And since he hath established his ordinances till he come, he will have a generation to serve him in the observance of them till he come. The church and ordinances cannot constantly be separated, though for a time they may, as the Israelites had not circumcision in the wilderness, and the passover also was omitted, but renewed by them before their entrance into Canaan. Yet it will not follow from hence that ordinances must always continue with us. They may be taken from a particular church, though not from the catholic church. God may have a church in the world, when he hath it not in this or that particular nation. Our day may be turned into a black night. Our manna may not always fall. God sometimes takes away his ordinances from a people to pull down the house, and 'pluck a people up by the roots,' 2 Chron. vii. 20. Sometimes he takes away his influences from them. *Urim* and *Thummim* may continue, but he will not answer Saul by them; the house may stand, but darkness may fill it when the glory of God departs: though there be a temple and sacrifices, yet but husks of ordinances only.

2. It is in no man's power to add to, or detract from, Christ's institutions. Not a pin in the temple he will have altered till he gives order. God is a jealous God, and careful of his sovereignty. It is not for any inferior person to alter the stamp and impression the prince commands. None can coin ordinances but Christ, and till he call them in, they ought to be current among us.

3. See Christ's love and bounty. Christ would not leave his people without a durable legacy. As Christ prayed for all that were to believe, so he provides for them. The apostles were not only to have the benefit, but all. He spreads a standing table for his people before he enters into his purchased glory, provides to feed them till he comes to take them home to himself. He entrusted it not to others, leaves it not to the apostles to appoint what they pleased; but writes the bill of fare himself, and directs what dishes we were to feed on till his return.

4. This ordinance must not be contemned. The passover was to be observed, much more the supper settled by Christ. It is to continue till his second coming. Is Christ yet come? Doth not the creation yet groan under vanity, doth not the heaven and the earth look with their old aspect? Have they yet put on new apparel? Doth not the sun run its ancient course? Are there yet the nearest signs of his second coming? Then no signs of the cessation of his institutions. All commands must be kept till the appearing of Jesus Christ, 1 Tim. vi. 14. Certainly then this that is so nobly circumstantiated, let not any man think himself above it upon a conceit of a greater measure of the Spirit. It is an impiety to pretend the Spirit of Christ can overthrow the institutions of Christ, which are to have the same duration in the world with the influence of the Spirit; to pretend that Spirit, whose office it is to bring the things of Christ to remembrance, to overthrow a grand memorial of him, contrary to the design of his mission; this is to set Christ and his Spirit at variance. To 'despise prophesyings' is to 'quench the Spirit,' 1 Thess. v. 19, 20. Will not the despising a great

ordinance of Christ be attended with the same dreadful effect? The Spirit doth not do all things in us without means, but directs us how to use the means, as he did Solomon to build the house.* He that contemns it, after so positive a command of remembering him this way till he comes, regards little Christ's authority, and presumes himself wiser than Christ; as if he could have given him directions how to have settled his church in a better method. Is it not a great ingratitude to God to despise what he commands as a privilege? Were not the apostles men of an extraordinary measure of the Spirit, because of their extraordinary employments? and did they not exercise themselves in the institutions of Christ? How have many proceeded from the slighting of Christ's institutions to the denying the authority of his word; a slighting Christ himself crucified at Jerusalem, to set up an imaginary Christ within them!

5. It is a standing ordinance till he come, no longer. The happiness of believers is great in attendance on the institutions of Christ, but greater afterwards. It is then there will be a full sight of that which is now in dark resemblances. It is then believers shall see the original copy of this picture. It is but till he come; he will not always have his people subject to ordinances, or show himself in a glass, but face to face. Then must this deputed light give place to a greater; then must these shadows fly away when the sun appears. It is a privilege to sit with him at his table here, but a greater to drink of the fruit of the vine new with him in the kingdom of his Father.

* Holinsworth of the Spirit, p. 42.

A DISCOURSE OF THE SUBJECTS OF THE LORD'S SUPPER.

But let a man examine himself, and so let him eat of that bread, and drink of that cup. For he that eats and drinks unworthily, eateth and drinketh damnation to himself, not discerning the Lord's body.—1 COR. XI. 28, 29.

HAVING discoursed of ver. 26, I now proceed to those which I have read. The substance of ver. 27, will come in in handling ver. 29, where the apostle mentions the greatness of the punishment of unworthy receiving; as vers. 26, 27, he had spoken of the greatness of the sin. Something we insisted on the last day, in the discovery of the sinfulness of unbelief, and more will upon the same subject be coincident with what might be spoken in this case. The apostle here exhorts the Corinthians to a worthy participation of that great ordinance of the Lord's Supper, and (1) lays down the rule of self-examination, before their approach, that they might not contract so great a guilt as that of the body and blood of Christ. But if he would not be guilty of the body and blood of Christ, 'let him examine himself.' (2.) The manner of participation: 'So let him eat, and so let him drink.' (3.) He backs and enforceth it with a reason: 'For he that eats and drinks unworthily, eats and drinks his own damnation.' A great danger is incurred by the neglect of this manner of proceeding.

Let a man, ἄνθρωπος, ἑαυτόν. An Hebraism for *every* man.* The apostle speaks it, saith Grotius, in regard of the disorders which were in the Corinthian church, in matter of discipline. Do not believe, because no censures are passed upon you, and the foundations of government are razed up in your church, that therefore you shall escape punishment for the contempt of those mysteries. No, God requires a worthy receiving, and will punish an unworthy one. So that it is an universal duty upon every Christian that desires to approach the Lord's table, to set upon a serious examination of his heart and life, which the excellency of the mystery in its own nature requires; an excellent ordinance requires a peculiar preparation: every man, not every man in the world, but every man in the church; not every heathen, but every man that pretends a right to the supper.

Examine himself, δοκιμαζέτω. Some understand the word of an artificial examination, as goldsmiths try metals by the touchstone, to discern between

* Estius.

what is true gold and silver, and what is counterfeit; but it is rather to be understood of a judicial trial, a trial of matter of fact, a trial of state, a trial of graces.

1. A trial of grace, whether it be inherent or no. It is a shewing the death of Christ; there must be therefore a search whether those graces which suit the death of Christ, and answer to the ends of it, be in the subject, as repentance, faith, love to God and to our neighbour; whether there be, not a legal, but evangelical worthiness, and a suitableness between the master of the feast and the guest; whether the heart and life agree with the precepts of Christ; what stamp of the Spirit upon the soul and conversation.

2. A trial of the state wherein those graces are. Since the supper is not worthily received, but by an exercise of repentance, faith, and love, it is necessary to inquire into the state of those graces, and their vigour or languor in the soul, that they may be excited to manifest themselves in a suitable carriage to the master of the feast, and the grandeur of the ordinance we are to attend upon.

By this are excluded from this ordinance,

1. All persons incapable of performing this antecedent duty. Either in regard of natural inability, as children, infants, who though anciently in the time of Austin, were admitted to this ordinance, yet against the rule of the apostle, because by reason of the imperfection of their age, they were not capable of performing this necessary duty which was to precede. As children are not the subjects recipient of the supper, because they are not risen to a suitable degree of understanding, so neither are madmen, because they have lost that understanding they had, and the great mysteries of religion must not be exposed to contempt. And in regard of a negligent inability, as ignorant persons who neglect the means of knowledge, or improve them not to furnish themselves with a sufficient stock of knowledge to this end, so a man grown in age may be a child in understanding, and upon the same account is as incapable as a child of this ordinance; men, therefore, are unfit to come without a distinct knowledge of the doctrine of the gospel.

2. All persons who cannot find upon examination anything of a divine stamp upon them in the lowest degree. Such are all unrenewed men, who have not one bruise in their souls, not one breath of smoke and gracious desire towards Christ in their hearts, and consequently all scandalous persons in life, who are as uncapable, by their spiritual madness and contracted vicious habits, as men that are mad naturally, by a distemper of their brain. This trial is for the finding fit qualifications for this ordinance, τί δοκιμον, something sound and worthy, which such persons cannot upon examination find.

This command of self-examination evidenceth to us,

1. That a Christian may come to the knowledge of his state in grace; otherwise it would be wholly fruitless to examine ourselves. If we may know by the want of saving conditions that we are in a state of nature; we may know by the presence of them, that we are in a state of grace.

2. No necessity of auricular confession; to tell all the secrets of the life to a priest.

So let a man eat of this bread, and drink of this cup. *So,* not otherwise; it is a hedge planted against every intrusion. *So,* not without examination, and a fitness upon it. It is not an ordinance appointed for every man; there is a manifest distinction between persons capable of the *word,* and capable of the *supper.* Preaching is to be to every creature, every rational creature, Mark xvi. 15, 16. Unbelievers are capable of the word, believers only of the supper. The one is to bring men into the family, the other to nourish them after their entrance. If any man find himself in a state of death, let him repent, believe, resolve a new and serious life, and so let him come, not else ; for without those he can receive no fruit of spiritual grace in this ordinance.

So let him eat, so let him drink. The apostle* here obviates an error crept into the Romish church, the taking away the cup, a custom unknown in the purest and primitive times of Christianity. 'Let him eat and *drink*,' saith the apostle ; 'Let him eat, but *not drink*,' saith the church of Rome. How soundly doth the Romish church accord with the primitive church ! 'Drink ye all of this,' saith Christ, Matt. xxvi. 27 ; 'Let the people not touch the cup,' saith Rome. How valid with them is the authority of that Christ they profess to be the Son of God, and the supreme head of the church ! The apostle, saith Estius, commands that none should partake without examination, but doth not command that every one should drink. I answer, either it is a command or a permission ; it seems to be a command. As the apostle commands the self-trial, so he commands the end of that trial, which is drinking the cup as well as eating the bread. If he commands the trial, he commands much more the participation, because in enjoining the means, he enjoins the end. We are bound to the use of means only in order to the end of those means. If the apostle commands the eating the bread, he commands also the partaking of the cup, the word *so*, &c., being grammatically to be applied to both. It would be ridiculous to think that the apostle's language was in this strain : Let a man examine himself, and if he finds himself fit for this mystery, let him choose whether he will either eat or drink ; he may do one or both if he will, or he may let it alone if he will. Who would dare to put such a sense upon the apostle's words ? If *let* be a word of command in the former sentence, it is no less in the latter. If therefore, he commands examination as a means, he commands communion as the end ; and communion much more, since the end is nobler than the means, and the means desirable for the sake of the end. But if it be a permission of the apostle, (for that it must be at least in the judgment of any man), that every one finding himself fit upon a trial, may drink of the cup as well as eat of the bread ; what power on earth should deny that, which the inspired apostle and great doctor of the Gentiles permits ? What pope or councils have authority to deprive any Christian of that which the founder of the Gentile church hath upon record allowed unto them ? What reason can be alleged that it is not as proper for the church now, as it was for the church of the Corinthians ? It was of use many centuries after the apostles' times, and is practised in all churches but that of Rome, wherein the denial of the cup was introduced about two hundred sixty odd years ago. What a blessing do we enjoy, to be freed from the antichristian yoke, and enjoy those privileges which the wickedness of men would deprive us of !

Bread and Cup. The doctrine of transubstantiation was not then known in the church.† The apostle calls it bread and cup three several times, vers. 26–28. Our reason, our sense, our sight, our taste, informs us it is bread and wine. The papists tell us, against reason and sense, that it is not bread, though it have the colour and taste of bread, but it is really the flesh and blood of Christ; it is changed and transmuted into his body and blood. It is indeed a sign of the body of Christ, a memorial of his broken, crucified body, and of his blood shed. The water in baptism represents the blood of Christ for the washing the soul, as the wine doth his blood for the nourishment and comforting the soul. Can any man say against his sense that it is not truly water ? The church is called 'the body of Christ,' Eph.

---

* Daillé, Melange des Sermons, Serm. xviii. p. 287, &c.
† Daillé, Melange des Sermons, Serm. xxviii. p. 283, &c.

i. 22, 23. But have not those men and women that make up the church, distinct persons from the person of Christ, distinct substances from the body of Christ? Are they upon their union to Christ as his members changed into the nature of Christ, and corporally his members, as his hands, and feet, and fingers were his upon the earth, and are his now in heaven? Why should the apostle call it so often bread, if it were not bread, if the nature and substance of it were changed into another substance? The Scripture gives both the names of bread and wine, and the body and blood of Christ, to the elements. They cannot be both properly; it cannot be bread properly, and the body of Christ properly; one therefore must be figuratively understood. Our sense tells us, and the apostle informs us, that it is bread; therefore it is called the body of Christ by a figure, since it hath nothing of the qualities of the flesh, but the essential qualities of bread. Besides, had it been properly the body of Christ, the apostle had discoursed far below his intention, which was to correct the irreverence of the Corinthians in this ordinance, and to recommend to them the sober and venerable use of it. He had neglected the main argument to enforce his main design, had it been properly the body of Christ, which would have made their irreverence more unreasonable, and of the highest guilt imaginable. He had been imprudent to have neglected acquainting them that this was the substance of the body of Christ, his very flesh and blood, and had been unfaithful in his trust, and silent in the most considerable argument. This had been more for his present purpose; but there is not a syllable of any such thing.* The apostle might have argued in a higher manner from that, to convince them of the sinfulness of unworthy receiving; but he makes a manifest distinction between the bread and the cup, and between the body and blood of Christ: 'He that eats this bread and drinks this cup of the Lord unworthily, shall be guilty of the body and blood of the Lord.' The bread and wine may be received unworthily, but the body and blood of Christ cannot be received unworthily. That implies a contradiction; for Christ assures us that 'every one that eats his flesh, and drinks his blood, hath eternal life,' John vi. 54. The papists say,† that because he that receives unworthily is guilty of the body and blood of Christ, therefore the body and blood of Christ is really in the sacrament. Saul's persecuting the disciples of Christ was, in the account of Christ, a persecuting of himself, Acts ix. 4. Was the body of Christ, glorified in heaven, really present in the bodies of his disciples persecuted by Saul? And when the apostle speaks (Heb. x 29) of 'treading under foot the Son of God,' who is so foolish as to imagine that the Son of God was really in his person and body under the feet of those apostates, as the body of an enemy they had thrown down might be under their feet? The bread is called the body of Christ representatively and sacramentally. And it is an ingenious observation of a learned man,‡ that the word, 'This is my body,' refers to the supper in distinction from the passover, which Christ put an honourable end unto: Matt. xxvi. 26, 'As they were eating' (*i. e.*, as they were eating the paschal lamb), 'Jesus took bread, and blessed it, and brake it, and gave it to his disciples, and said, Take eat, this is my body.' The paschal lamb was Christ's body in a figure, Exod. xii. 46. Speaking of the paschal lamb, 'Neither shall you break a bone thereof,' which is applied to Christ, who had not a bone of his body broken upon the cross, which John takes notice of as a 'fulfilling of the scripture,' John xix. 36. 'These

* Slichting in 1 Cor. xi. 27.
† Daillé, Melange des Sermons, Sermon xxviii. p. 297.
‡ Lightfoot, Gleanings out of Exod. sect. xviii.

things were done that the scripture should be fulfilled, A bone of him shall not be broken;' which can refer to no other but the command about the paschal lamb in that place of Exodus. To this it is that the word τοῦτο doth refer in the speech of our Saviour: 'This is my body.' The passover had been a sacramental type of the body of Christ to the Jews. He was the Lamb of God, and he is 'our passover sacrificed for us.' But now Christ takes bread, and tells them, This is my body under the gospel. The paschal lamb shall no more be a representation of my body, as it hath been hitherto, but this shall be the sign of it. The bread upon this account is no more really the body of Christ than the paschal lamb was the body of Christ for so many ages, wherein it had represented it, which none of the Romanists will acknowledge to be transubstantiated into the body of Christ. They differed not in their representation, but only in the circumstance of time; one representing Christ to be slain, the other representing him cruci-fied and slain already.

In ver. 29 the apostle describes the punishment, as he had (ver. 27) described the sin : 'For he that eats and drinks unworthily, eats and drinks damnation to himself, not discerning the Lord's body.'

He that eats and drinks unworthily. (1.) In an unworthy state. (2.) In an unworthy frame, not actually discerning the Lord's body.

Eateth and drinketh damnation to himself. Κρῆμα signifies sometimes *judgment,* Gal. v. 10, 1 Pet. iv. 17. Unworthy receiving is such an act as deserves damnation, and if not repented of, will bring damnation. The state may be changed, and so damnation avoided; but believers themselves, for their unworthy frames, shall not avoid the stroke of God, which the next verse manifests, ver. 30: 'For this cause many are weak and sickly among you, and many sleep.'

Not discerning the Lord's body. Not discerning the end, subject, and mystery of this sacrament; putting no difference between that and common bread. There is putting a difference between things, in regard of opinion and judgment.* As God is said to put no difference between the Jews and Gentiles, in regard of purification by faith, Acts xv. 9: 'And put no differ-ence between us and them, purifying their hearts by faith;' so men put no difference between the body of Christ and the body of a mere man, between bread as representing the body of Christ, and bread, the ordinary staff of life, when they make no solemner preparation for it than they do for an ordinary repast. When a man doth not regard the person and merit of Christ according to the true value of him, and comes to the Lord's table as to common bread,† and considers not to what end the elements are des-tined, nor the greatness and glory of that body which they represent, he violates in those signs the honour due to the majesty of Christ. If a man did rightly understand the dignity of the body of Christ, and how much it suffered for our sins, and that we should die to sin, he would certainly pre-pare himself by a strict survey of his own heart, that he might not come unworthily to so great a mystery.

In the verses we see,

1. The antecedent duty, examination.
2. The subsequent duty, participation.
1. The antecedent duty, which is laid down,
(1.) In the extent of the subject, *A man,* i.e., every man.
(2.) The nature of the duty, *Examine.*
(3.) The object of it, *Himself.*
(4.) The necessity of it, *So let him come,* not else.

* Daillé, Melange des Sermons, Sermon xxviii.   † Amyraut in loc.

2. The subsequent duty described in its two parts.

(1.) Eating the bread.

(2.) Drinking the cup.

3. The enforcement to this duty, ver. 29.

(1.) The danger of unworthiness, *Eats and drinks damnation.*

(2.) The nature of unworthiness, *Not discerning the Lord's body.*

(3.) To which we may add, The sinfulness of unworthiness: ver. 27, *He that eats and drinks unworthily, is guilty of the body and blood of the Lord.* To which the particle *but* (ver. 28) refers, as the means to avoid that sinfulness : ' But let a man examine himself.'

Doctrine :

1. All men outwardly professing Christianity are not in a capacity to come to the great ordinance of the supper. The apostle writes not to the heathen, but the Christian Corinthians.

2. It is every man's duty solemnly to examine himself about his interest in Christ, and his right to this ordinance, before he come.

3. Without due examination, and by unworthy receiving, a man commits a great sin, and incurs a great danger.

1. For the first. All men outwardly professing Christianity are not in a capacity to come to the great ordinance of the supper. If all men were capable, pre-examination were not then necessary. But because this duty is enjoined as a precedent, therefore those that cannot examine themselves, and those that find no good issue of that examination, ought not to come ; for the word ' so ' excludes all such. Christ preached to a multitude, he excluded none from hearing, no not the worst of the Pharisees. But this ordinance he administered in a select company ; he preached openly, he celebrated this privately in an upper room, whence the custom of celebrating in the chancel or upper part of the church, not in the body of it, took its rise. The word is more extensive, this more contracted. There were multitudes in the Jewish church owned him as the Messiah ; but not all were admitted by him at this his first institution, but the apostles, and perhaps some few other disciples. For though he said to ' sit down with the twelve,' Mat. xxvi. 20, yet (ver 26) he is said to ' give it his disciples.' If there were only apostles there, it signifies that he gave it to them, not as apostles, but as disciples, to shew thereby that all those that give up themselves sincerely to his instruction are capable of this ordinance in all ages of the church, and that it is not common to all that only make a mere profession of him. Anciently the catechumens, or persons entering their names to Christ to be instructed, stood a long time upon their probation before they were admitted into the more secret mysteries of the Christian religion, whether with good reason, I will not here determine ; superstition lies principally in excess.

In prosecution of this doctrine, we shall lay down some propositions.

1. Only regenerate men are fit to come to the Lord's Supper. No man in a natural state but must needs eat and drink unworthily, for he retains his enmity and hostile disposition against God and Christ. Sanctified persons only are the proper guests. This was prefigured by the ceremony of washing the disciples' feet, which Christ used before the supper, John xiii. 8, 10. Without sanctification we have no part in Christ, and therefore no right to his supper. An unregenerate man cannot perform the duties necessary, drag out his sins, arraign them before God, mourn for his abominations, with a hearty contrition. By examination in the text, we must not understand a bare examination, but that which ought to be the consequent upon it, a judging ourselves, and performing those acts consonant to the state we judge

ourselves in. For so the apostle means, as appears by ver. 31, following the text, 'For if we would judge ourselves, we should not be judged.' To what purpose is this commanded examination necessary, but for any man to see whether he hath those dispositions which are essential requisites to this ordinance ?* The children of Habaiah, the children of Koz, and of Barzillai, were not to eat of the most holy things, because they were not in the register of the genealogies, Ezra ii. 61–63. If our names be not written in heaven, and are not to be found in the genealogies of the new born, we are not fit to eat of this holy feast. Those that were uncircumcised in heart as well as in flesh, were not to enter into God's sanctuary, Ezek. xliv. 9. Though an unrenewed man may be a great moralist, and his moral virtues may look like some pieces of a wedding garment, yet they are not the wedding garment till they be wrought into a right fashion by faith. It is a feast, and therefore only for God's friends. It is bread belonging to children; unrenewed men are not yet in a state of sonship. Circumcision was to precede the passover, Exod. xii. 44 ; baptism to precede the supper. But this is but a symbol of an inward grace, without which no right to participation. The Israelites were baptized in the Red Sea, before they fed on spiritual manna, 1 Cor. x. 2, 3.

(1.) Faith is a necessary qualification, but unrenewed men have not faith. *Take, eat,* implies something spiritually to be done. There must be the hand of faith to receive and apply Christ, the mouth of faith to take in Christ. Natural men want both a spiritual hand and a spiritual mouth. An unbeliever receives the elements, not the life and spirit, of a sacrament. Faith is as much a condition requisite to a spiritual partaking of the sacrament, as to everlasting salvation. No salvation without believing, no taste of Christ without believing. Without faith, a man receives no more the body of Christ, than a chicken that should come into a room after, and pick up some fallen crumbs of bread from the ground, receives the body of Christ. The main qualification which makes sacramental bread spiritual food is wanting. We can no more turn the bread and wine into the body and blood of Christ without faith, than a chemist can transmute one metal into another without the operation of fire. Christ dwells in the heart by faith only, Eph. iii. 17. The paschal lamb was not to be eaten till the posts of the house were sprinkled with the blood of it, Exod. xii. 7. The soul must be sprinkled with the blood of Christ by faith before it is fit to partake of this ordinance. As God doth not promise salvation absolutely to man, but upon condition of faith, so the sacrament doth not seal absolutely remission of sins to man, but upon the condition of believing. If there be no sealing therefore of the counterpart to God by performing the condition upon which God doth found his grants, there is no right to the seal. The promise is made to the penitent and believing sinner. What interest can he think to have in the seal, who hath not yet embraced the promise ? It seals in particular to a person what the word proposeth in general upon such a condition. Pardon of sin is sealed to faith ; there must be a performance of the condition on our part, before there can be any ratification by the seal to us. God seals no more than he promises, nor in any other manner than he promises. He promises only to faith, and therefore only seals to faith. Covenant graces therefore must be possessed and acted before covenant blessings can be ratified to us. As in covenants between man and man, the seal annexed to the writing seals no more than what is contained in the writing, and upon the acceptance and performance of such conditions, which

* Bolton of the Sacrament, pp. 87, 88.

are mentioned in the deed. Where there is not therefore an acceptance and performance of the conditions between the parties, the seal is no more than a blank, as to any real advantage. The sacrament is a seal *in actu primo*, in its own nature, but not *in actu secundo* to a wicked man; a faithless impenitent man hath not the beneficial fruit of it. It doth seal an unbeliever his damnation; for 'he that believes not shall be damned,' is part of the gospel, as well as 'he that believes shall be saved,' Mark xvi. 16. The question is not, whether the condition of faith may not be infused at the time of partaking by the extraordinary grace of God. The supper seems not to be a renewing, converting ordinance. That there must be faith, if there be any true fruit of it, is out of question, and that no unrenewed man hath, nor can have, any hopes he should be there inspired with so noble and necessary a grace; and therefore in that state he is not a capable subject of this ordinance. For such therefore to approach the Lord's table, is a mocking of God, to come to God to seal the remission of sin, when they have no mind to come up to the conditions wherewith that pardon is proposed; as it is for a man to come to a prince for pardon, who hath not yet laid down his arms against him. God in his seal testifies his approbation of the promises upon the conditions expressed; man in receiving testifies his approbation of the condition. He that hath no principle of approbation in him, mocks God in his approach. Faith is a necessary moral qualification to the receiving of the sacrament.

(2.) An unrenewed man is not in covenant, and therefore no capable subject. This follows upon the former. If he hath not faith, the condition of the covenant, he is not in covenant with God; and what right hath such an one to the seals? All men by nature are 'strangers to the covenant of promise, aliens from the commonwealth of Israel,' Eph. ii. 12. What have they to do with the privilege of the free denizens of Israel? They that are not included in the deed have nothing to do with the seals of the conveyance; it is but fruitless wax to them, not a confirming seal. The covenant runs thus, 'My beloved is mine, and I am his,' Cant. ii. 16; it is mutual between the parties. By covenanting with God, we become the Lord's: Ezek. xvi. 8, 'I entered into covenant with thee, saith the Lord, and thou becamest mine.' There is an appropriation of Christ to us, and a consecration of ourselves to Christ. What hath he to do with the ordinance, that wants the essentials of the covenant, who hath no valuation of Christ, no breathings after him, nor makes any dedication of himself to Christ? Those that never gave up themselves to God, receive no seal, but mere bread, mere wine. Unregenerate men are under a covenant of works. The covenant of works was made with the whole nature of man in Adam; the curse of the covenant seized upon all, Gal. iii. 10; the duties of that covenant are incumbent upon them who are under the curse of it; the violation of that covenant freed not man from his obligation to duty, though it brought upon him a new obligation to punishment. It is a privilege only of believers to be freed from the covenant of works; for they are 'not under the law, but under grace,' Rom. vi. 14. And 'there is no condemnation' only 'to them that are in Christ,' Rom. viii. 1. But where men do not believe, God deals with them upon the terms of the first covenant; he expects a full righteousness from them in their own persons, as being without Christ, and having not accepted of his blood upon his own terms, to take away the guilt of their sins. It is true, unregenerate men are under the offers of the covenant of grace, but not within actual acceptation of the covenant of grace. They enjoy some benefits of the covenant made with Christ; for they enjoy their lives, have worldly comforts, the fruits of God's patience, all which are upon the account of the Mediator; and they have been entered in by baptism; yet since they practically disown the terms of that covenant, they put themselves back under a covenant of works, to stand upon their own bottom; and therefore refusing a consent to that covenant, the benefits of the covenant belong not to them. For if a seal (as some affirm) be of the same nature with an oath, whereby God confirms his promise, yet it is so only to the heirs of promise, not to those that are rejecters of the covenant and promise.

(3.) This sacrament is a sacrament of nourishment. Unrenewed men therefore are not fit for it. They are dead, Eph. ii. 1; and what hath a dead man to do with a feast? Men must be alive before they be nourished. It is *eat, drink*. The principal intent is not to eat corporeally, but spiritually; words not to be spoken to a dead man. Meat and drink may be put into a dead man's mouth, but he can swallow down neither one nor another in a vital way, nor concoct either of them. He that wants the life of grace can make no use of the nourishment of grace; so that the sacrament is at best but a vain thing to such. But besides, the very end of the sacrament is perverted, when the richest viands are taken by a man spiritually dead; as the end of bread, which is to nourish the body, is perverted, and the creature abused by being used contrary to the end of it, when it is put into the mouth of a dead man, to whom it can be no advantage. The body of Christ conveys strength and growth to his own members only; to living members, not to dead. Dead branches receive no sap from the vine.

(4.) This sacrament is an ordinance of inward communion with Christ. But unrenewed men can have no inward communion with him. They cannot have that joy which ought to be in a converse with Christ, because they cannot taste any of those spiritual dainties which are in this feast. They may eat the sacramental bread, but regenerate men only have a new relish, spiritually, to taste the body and blood of Christ; they only relish the milk of the word, and the sweetness of a sacrament. What communion can Belial have with Christ, or darkness with light? Christ will have no converse with his enemies, till they are prepared for his reception by the stamp of his Spirit. Christ must be let into the heart before he sups with it: Rev. iii. 20, 'If any man open the door, I will come in to him, and sup with him.' The door must be opened by conversion, before Christ will feast with the soul in a spiritual communion. Those that are not graciously fit for a spiritual communion with him in heaven, are not fit for a spiritual communion with him in the earth: 'Unless we be born again, we cannot enter into the kingdom of God,' John iii. 5, and therefore have no right to those privileges which are the foretastes of glory. Bosom-communion belongs only to bosom friends; others are but intruders, and will receive no countenance from Christ.

(5.) This ordinance is to be received by true Christians only. But renewed men only are such. Christianity is an inward powerful work, not a paint, an image. The *form* of godliness doth not constitute a man a Christian, but the *power* of it, 2 Tim. iii. 5. All natural men are 'without God in the world;' they are ἄθεοι, Eph. ii. 12, atheists, and may as well be called ἄχριστοι, not Christians, being 'without Christ.' There is not only required an assent of the understanding to make a man a Christian *in foro Dei*, but a consent of the will; there must be the accepting as well as the assenting part. It is not a bare knowledge, or the profession of religion, demonstrates a man a regenerate man, either in the presence of God, or to himself, though to others in the judgment of charity it doth. It is a work of the will that is required; he is no Christian who barely knows Christ to be king, priest, and prophet, and cordially accepts him in none of those offices. Now this ordinance being the proper badge and privilege of Christians, none ought to partake of it but Christians. These evidences belong to the proper tenant, not to the counterfeit; to those that are his real friends, not to his lip friends and heart enemies. Freemen only have a right to the privileges of the city, and true Christians to the privileges of the church.

Obj. But it may be said, By this, none but those that have assurance of their being in a state of grace ought to come to this institution; and certainly there is many a true Christian wants this comfort; and the supper is a privilege due to grace, not to assurance; to Christians as Christians, not to Christians as comfortable Christians.

Ans. I answer, Caution is to be used in this, lest some doubting Christian should be left in a maze. Many humble souls are most backward; the presumptuous spur on apace; the baser metals are most volatile.

(1.) Penitent persons mourning for sin, though wanting assurance, are regenerate, and have a right. Contrite hearts are the most acceptable sacrifices to God, next to the bruised body of our Saviour, Ps. li. 17. Those that have bruised hearts, and cannot call to mind their former sins, but the pulse of their indignation beats quick against them, to such Christ appears first. He shewed himself to Mary Magdalene before he appeared to any of the apostles after his resurrection, yea, before he appeared to his own mother, Mark xvi. 9; and possibly some of her former sorrow began to spring afresh, and her speech seems to discover some sorrow and astonishment in her, and a great affection to Christ, John xx. 11, 13, 15. Such bleeding, contrite souls doth Christ love; and such as he loves shall be as John, lying in his bosom, and leaning upon him at a sacrament. Where there is a true repentance, a detestation of all sin, a resolution to avoid sin for the future, and a lying at the feet of Christ, there is true grace, though it may not be always visible to the soul. These are the sour herbs we are to eat the passover withal.

(2.) Regenerate persons cannot always say positively that they have grace, yet find so much ground as that they cannot absolutely deny it, unless in some sharp fit of desertion. It is not easily discerned sometimes, because of the weakness of it. Faith, like a grain of mustard seed, may lie sometimes in a heap of rubbish; clouds of sin, withdrawings of the Spirit, and injudiciousness of conscience, may obscure the work upon the heart at some seasons; yet a strong will, and an earnest breathing to please Christ, whispers something in the soul to cherish it. A strong and prevailing will is the proper evidence of conversion, and in Scripture it is expressed by will: Rev. xxii. 17, ' Let him that is athirst come, and he that will, let him come.' The acts of the will and the thirst of the soul are easily discernible, enough to keep the heart from a denial of the work of grace, though not enough to clear it up against all oppositions. The work of grace may be clouded; the sun does not always send forth its beams. The thorn in Paul's flesh seems to be a present cloud upon his spirit, hindering him from a sight of his own evidences, since it is put in opposition to the revelations he had in his rapture into the third heavens, 2 Cor. xii. Mary knew her own affection to Christ, and her sorrow for her sin, and could not deny those affections so palpable in herself and visible to others; but had not assurance of her state till Christ spake that comfortable word to her, Luke vii. 38, 48, ' Thy sins are forgiven thee.' Every man that is regenerate may be able, upon a perusal of his own heart, to say, I am sincere in this or that; my ends are right, and the bent of my heart stands towards God. In grace there is some light discovering of it, though not perfectly, yet so as the soul can say, I am no hypocrite.

(3.) A perfect assurance is not required. It is said, ' Let a man examine himself' as to the frame and temper of his heart ; not let him be assured of his being in Christ and of an happy state, but let him take a survey of his heart, and see that his frames are suitable, and so let him come. The supper supposeth men not to have a full assurance ; it is a seal, and seals are for confirmation, where there may be matter of doubt. It is a question, whether a perfect assurance be in the world. As grace is not perfect, but hath its ebbs and floods, so hath assurance. As faith is mixed with unbelief, so is assurance with doubtings. As the soul saith, ' Lord, I believe ; help my unbelief,' so it hath often said, Lord, I hope ; help my doubts. The needle stands right to the North Pole, but not without its tremblings. In the greatest doubtings, we should have recourse to those sparklings and sprightly leaps of our souls, when we found the first touches upon our hearts, and stay ourselves upon those presents we had in the day of our espousals.

2. Ignorant persons are not in a capacity for the supper. The subjects capable of it are men and women professing Christianity, and understanding the grounds of that which they profess. Light in the mind, and the true knowledge of God, was part of the image of God, and our original righteousness in the creation, as well as rectitude in the will, and the right standing of it towards God, Col. iii. 10. Ignorance being a privation of that ornament of the soul, a fruit of our apostasy, the root of all our dishonouring of God, cannot render us fit guests for his table, or procure a welcome from him. Blind offerings can be no more acceptable to God under the gospel than they were under the law. He is a great king, Mal. i. 14. Those that approach to him are bound to know what belongs to the honour of his name.

By this ignorance we are not to understand,

(1.) An ignorance of the abstruse controversies in religion, which are often too knotty for the sharpest and most industrious understanding to unloose. A man may be unable to understand thorny and intricate disputes, yet with a sanctified knowledge of the fundamentals of religion, be in a nearer capacity for the benefits of this ordinance, than those that by their subtle wits can divide a hair.

(2.) Nor a scholastical knowledge of fundamentals, so as to be able to give an exact definition of those things which are necessary to be known. It is sufficient if he knows them as a Christian, though not as a scholar. A house may be strong, and keep out wind and weather for the security of the inhabitant, though it be not so neatly built and skilfully garnished. A man may know the fundamental articles, yet not know all the consequences rationally deducible from those articles.

(3.) Nor a perfect knowledge of all the ends of the death and resurrection of Christ. To know that Christ died, what he was, and for what he died, is necessary, but a perfect knowledge none have. As graces have their spots, so our knowledge hath its mixtures of darkness. The wisdom which the wise angels are daily learning, cannot be grasped by the largest and most elevated understanding upon the earth. The disciples in the time of Christ's being in the flesh, had but little knowledge of his death and resurrection, Luke ix. 44, 45, John xx. 9. Peter understood him to be the Son of God, but was ignorant of God's design to redeem the world by his blood, Mat. xvi. 16, xxii. 23. They afterwards knew something of it, and had an habit and disposition to believe whatsoever Christ should reveal to them. Yet that knowledge which was sufficient for the apostles, till a fuller manifestation by the Spirit, is no plea for our ignorance in the same thing, since the pouring forth of the Spirit, the taking off Moses his veil, and penning the truths of the gospel with a sunbeam. A little knowledge at the time of

Christ's being in the world, and in several ages of the world, where the means have been less, would be more acceptable than a greater knowledge now, disproportioned to the means of knowing.

(4.) There must be an understanding and believing in some measure the fundamentals of religion. We must have some understanding of the nature and attributes of God, especially those that are more bright in the sufferings of Christ, and they are to be particularly respected in all our acts of worship: as the holiness and justice of God, the power and faithfulness of God, the omniscience and omnipresence of God, the sovereignty and goodness of God. We must know the fall of Adam, the fruits of it upon his posterity, the exactness and spirituality of the law; there can be no motion to God without a sense of our misery. We must know Christ in his nature, God-man; in his design, redemption; in his commission, sent; in the manner of effecting it, by the shedding his blood, resurrection from the dead; the manner of applying it, by his intercession in heaven, and his Spirit on earth; in his offices, as king, priest, and prophet; the efficacy, value, and merit of his sufferings, the purifying virtue of his blood, the necessity of salvation by him, that there is no justification but by his righteousness, no sanctification but by his Spirit, and that one is as necessary as the other; the one for our acceptance with God, the other for our communion with God: the necessity and nature of faith for the enjoyments of the benefits purchased. There must be some knowledge in all those things, else we know not to whom, or how, or for what to apply ourselves in this great mystery of Christianity, which exhibits and represents to us on God's part the whole scheme of redemption, and requires on our parts the exercise of faith about its proper and particular object. There must be some knowledge of those things; the quantity cannot be determined; the quality is, that it be a sensible knowledge; not such a knowledge as a parrot hath, that may be taught to rehearse the creed, without reason or sense to understand or believe a word he speaks. A modest and a sensible ignorance, provided it be not total, is more tolerable than a puffed and insensible knowledge.

(5.) A knowledge of the nature and ends of the ordinance. The Lord's body cannot otherwise be discerned, ver. 29. The mysteries of the ordinance would be as Arabic letters to him that understands not the meaning of them. The master of the family was to teach the use and ends of the passover to the receiver, and all that were present were to understand the ground of the first institution, and the nature of the ordinance. The supper being a contract between God and man, a man must understand the nature and terms of that covenant, and also the nature and end of the seal; he cannot else be a worthy contractor with God. The body of the Lord cannot be discerned without an understanding of the nature of the ordinance, and the nature of the ordinance cannot be understood without a knowledge of those principles of religion upon which it is built.

Ignorant persons are not fit to come.

(1.) They are uncapable of performing the duties requisite. The antecedent duty of self-examination enjoined by the apostle as essentially necessary, 'So let him eat,' not otherwise. Those therefore that are unskilful in this work, by reason of their ignorance of the universal depravation of nature, the obnoxiousness of all men to the curse of the law, and the impossibility of avoiding the terrors of it without an interest in that mediator, in and by the way of his own appointment, are uncapable of performing this duty, and so unfit subjects for this ordinance. They cannot repent, for they have no spiritual eye to discover their own filthiness. The prodigal never ' came to himself' till his understanding was enlightened, Luke xv. 17. By the same ground that infants and children are excluded (who were anciently admitted to this ordinance), because of their defect of reason, not being able to perform this duty, ignorant persons are to be excluded. In them there is a natural, in ignorant persons a moral, inability, and under means of grace a sinful indisposition. There is as much reason for children in age to partake of this ordinance as for children in understanding. Both have a want of knowledge in those things which are of a concern to a right participation of this ordinance; nor can they perform the concomitant duties. Those who understand not the nature and ends of the death of Christ, cannot commemorate it in a right manner. All our service of God ought to be a reasonable service; not only as having the highest reason for a motive to urge it, but in regard of the *modus*, the manner of doing it. It must be done with an exercise of reason. We must serve God as Christians; but in our service we must not put off the nature of man. The right manner of partaking of this supper consists in repentance of sin, and faith in Christ; what repentance can there be for sin, when the evil of sin and the deplorable consequents of it are not known? What faith can there be in one ignorant of the cause and ends of the death of Christ? They cannot come with desires suitable, that know nothing of their own wants. They who know not themselves empty, cannot desire spiritual fulness; who know not themselves sick, cannot desire spiritual cordials; who know not themselves under the curse of the law, cannot desire a satisfying Christ; they have no sense of that for which his body was bruised, wounded, and crucified. Nor can they perform the subsequent duties, which are a walking in holiness; there is no foundation in blindness for any regular walk.

(2.) All ignorant persons are unbelievers. None formerly entered into covenant by a solemn profession * but those that had knowledge: Nehem. x. 28, 29, 'Every one having knowledge and having understanding entered into an oath to walk in God's law.' How can any believe the glorious things of the gospel, which they know not, nor desire to know, but stop their ears, blind their eyes like bats and owls, love the darkness of the night better than a clear sunshiny day? If we know not the firmness of the ground, we will never set our foot upon it. A man in ignorance is in the 'chains of darkness.' 'Darkness' and the 'power of the devil' are the same thing, Acts xxvi. 18. He that hath ignorance in his head and heart is alienated from God. An alienation from God is a friendship with the devil. Is it fit for the voluntary captives of Christ's greatest enemy to come rattling with their chains of darkness, and under the conduct and power of the devil, to a feast appointed for the friends of God?

(3.) Such know not how to value this ordinance aright. It is not fit a jewel should be bestowed on him who understands not the value of it, and would part with it for a song to the next cheat he meets. An ignorant person would part with any spiritual excellency upon the next temptation of the devil. As want of strength makes the body, so want of knowledge makes the minds of children capable of being moulded into any form. An eye unpurged from the films upon it can never discover the beauties of divine mysteries, or entertain them with any spiritual delight. He that understands not his original corruption knows not how to prize a medicine. You may sooner make one born blind admire the sun, which he never saw, than make a blind soul have an estimation of Christ, to whom he hath a natural enmity.

(4.) Ignorant persons are always under the command of some secret lust. Ignorance itself is a great sin. The not knowing what we may easily know, since it is revealed, is so far from excusing that it rather aggravates; be-

* Ignorantis non est consensus.

cause it is not a defect in the faculty itself (as in the case of madmen), but a defect in the improvement of the faculty, and such a defect as is voluntary, which man hath a power to remove. It stifles the notion of God rather than is dispelled by it: John i. 5, ' The darkness comprehendeth it not,' *i. e.* the light. Besides the evil of its own nature, it is the ground of all wickedness. If they are only ' filled with goodness' that are filled with knowledge, Rom. xv. 14, they must be filled with evil that are filled with ignorance. Where the mind is dark, the motion must needs be irregular. The ignorance contracted by the fall hath been the root of all the corrupt inclinations and miscarriages in Adam's posterity. Ignorance first brought lust into fashion, and keeps up the mode : 1 Peter i. 14, ' Not fashioning yourselves according to your former lusts in your ignorance.' A fashion, course, and form of sin renders men unfit guests for the Lord's table.

And this leads to the third proposition.

3. Proposition. Men guilty of a course of sin, though secret and unknown to others, are unfit for this ordinance. This injunction, ' Let a man examine himself, and so let him come,' bars out such. By examination is not to be meant a bare act of examination, but that which ought to be consequent upon it ; not let a man examine himself, and in whatsoever posture he finds his soul let him come ; no, let him examine himself to find out the nest of vipers in his soul which hiss against Christ, and cast them out. Let him perform the acts consonant to that state wherein, upon inquiry, he finds himself. What man would be so wretched as to make this conclusion: I am a swine, a beast, I live in such and such sins unrepented of, yet I have performed my duty, I have examined myself, which is all the apostle requires of me, and I rest in this act ; nothing more is enjoined me. Is there no end of this act ? All things are commanded, not for themselves, but for some end. The apostle enjoins it not to make the sacrament a license for sin, or to encourage the wearing of Christ's livery to keep men's lusts warm. Every secret gross sinner stands anathematised both by law and gospel ; the law curseth him because of his sin, and the gospel condemns him because of his unbelief. What excludes a man from admission when it is known to others, excommunicates him in his own conscience when it is only known to himself. All things in the ordinance bespeak purity ; the place was fitted for the first institution, the soul must be fitted for the participation ; the place was trimmed for Christ's entertainment, the heart must be trimmed for his reception. The grave of Christ was free from corruption ; no putrefied body was ever lodged there ; the soul must be free from any affection to filth. Though Christ had not a hole where to lay his head, he will not have a sty or a swine-trough wherein to lay his body. His humanity is advanced above the highest heavens, and the signs of it are not to be received by an earthly and polluted soul. Such ought not to approach, though they seem to have a repentance, till it appears that their repentance is serious and thorough. Those that have been stained with some secret gross crime ought not to approach upon a sudden and late begun contrition.* To mourn one day and come to this ordinance the next, argues but little care to dispose themselves for so great an institution. A soul glutted with sin, though beginning to vomit it up, cannot so suddenly gain a spiritual taste for the body of Christ. How many have had sudden qualms, and discharged themselves of some sins the better to swallow more ! Imaginations of repentance are not always realities. He that offends another, and saith he is sorry for it, and a short time after offends again, affords no reason to believe that he is a penitent in earnest.

* Cajetan. Sum., p. 59.

Quest. What sins debar a man from this ordinance ?

(1.) Not such which are infirmities incident to human nature. Every sin doth not impede the operation of faith about the proper object. Every breach of the command is not a hindrance. Sins of daily infirmities are breaches of the command, otherwise they are not sins. There is no perfection of virtue, while remission of sins is to be daily petitioned for ; the state of perfection is reserved for a state of glory. There is a blackness mixed with the church's comeliness, Cant. i. 5, a blackness of sin as well as of affliction. The wheat ceaseth not to be wheat, though tares are mixed with it. In the best mines there are earth and dross as well as gold ; precious stones have their flaws, which cannot be removed without the destruction of the substance, nor infirmities abolished without the destruction of the body. The disciples were not without corruptions at the institution ; ambition bubbled up in them, Luke xxii. 24, and fear quickly made them forsake their Master ; but they were not naturalised or rooted in this evil, neither did the devil enter into them as he did into Judas. As the Father of mercies doth not discovenant us for every infirmity, so neither should we exclude ourselves from partaking of the seal : 1 John ii. 1, ' If any man sin, we have an advocate with the Father.' The office of advocacy erected in heaven supposeth sin after regeneration, and during our continuance in the world. But there is a great difference between the indwelling of sin and the rule of sin. To sin is to decline from that rectitude in an act which the agent ought to observe. In this respect we sin, according to the tenor of the law, in everything we do, though not according to the tenor of the gospel.

(2.) But a course in wilful and frequent breaches of a known command debars a man. That which is against the principal intent of the command, and the main office it requires of us, such as omissions of known duties. When family duties are omitted, and the house, which should be as a little church, is rather a synagogue of Satan ; when there is a total or frequent omission of secret prayer, which disowns that worship of God which is due to him by the light of nature, and is the note of a wicked man. ' Will he always call upon God ?' Job xxvii. 10. Those that forget Christ all the week are not likely to be devout in the remembrance of him upon a Sabbath. And such sins of commission as are enumerated, 1 Cor. vi. 9, 10, ' fornicators, adulterers, effeminate, thieves, covetous, drunkards, revilers, extortioners,' are a bar if not repented of, 2 Cor. xii. 21. The heart that is an habitation of any of those kinds of devils is not a member of Christ, and can bring nothing but a mystery of iniquity to fit it to partake of the mysteries of Christ. This is a blaspheming Christ in the heart, while he is received with the hands ; like the reviling thief that hung beside him on the cross, not like a loving or beloved disciple that looks upon him by faith while he is bleeding to death. These have no right till their guilt be unbound by repentance and faith.

Such ought not to meddle with this ordinance.

[1.] Moral uncleanness is a greater bar than ceremonial. If a man were defiled with a dead carcase, he was to forbear eating the passover, Num. ix. 6. If any man, unclean by the touch of a dead body, came into the tabernacle, he defiled it, and was threatened with a cutting off from Israel, Num. xix. 13. How much more ought they to abstain from the table of the Lord, that are not only defiled, but dead, who bear a dead putrefied soul in a living body ? 1 Tim. v. 6, ' She that lives in pleasure is dead while she lives.' If ceremonial uncleanness, without any mixture of a moral, were hateful to God, much more hateful to him is moral uncleanness. The worship of God is more precious than to be sacrilegiously invaded by impenitent sinners; every work of the hands, and that which is offered is unclean, as well as when offered by one that had touched the dead, Hag. ii. 13, 14. Lepers who had a natural disease were not to come into the congregation, that they might not defile the place wherein the Lord dwelt, Lev. xiii. 46, Num. v. 2, much less ought they to approach this ordinance, where the Lord is solemnly present as master of the feast, who have running sores, and stink above ground in the nostrils of God. If for those outward uncleannesses men were to abstain from those institutions which the apostle calls 'worldly rudiments' and 'carnal ordinances,' they are too foul guests for so rich a feast, who can bring nothing else but the loathsome exhalations of hell to spiritual ordinances. The livery of the devil becomes not the table of the Lord.

[2.] All the right which they may claim by baptism is forfeited *in foro Dei*. It is a repentance, profession of faith, resolution to walk accordingly, and the answer of a good conscience towards God, which are the foundations of any man's right to the supper; but secret impieties are a disowning repentance, violating good resolutions, denying the faith which hath been before professed. Where the terms of the covenant are not observed, there is a forfeiture of any right to the benefits and seals of it. All rebellion is of right followed with an attainder and deprivation of birthright. A continual breach of covenant by commission of known sin attaints the soul in the court of heaven, and the charter is not to be enjoyed but by the parties that fulfil the conditions required. He that 'hates instruction' hath no part in the covenant, Ps. l. 16, 17. What claim can he be supposed to have, that declares to God by his practice that he will not be ruled by his law, or own him as his chiefest good? A rebel separated from Christ in affection and will hath nothing to do with an ordinance of peace. He that takes no care of the honour of God who created him, nor of his own soul, which is to run parallel with the endless line of eternity, is a much worse infidel than he that neglects provision for his own family; yet of such an one the apostle pronounceth that he hath 'denied the faith,' 1 Tim. v. 8. Dogs they are in the account of God, more deservedly than the believing Canaanite was in the account of Christ. And wicked men are called so in Scripture, Rev. xxii. 15, 2 Peter ii. 22. What right have dogs to the children's bread, to the legacy of choicest love? Can such be supposed to be included in his will? If they have any right, it is to the table of devils, not to that of the Lord. And it may well be wondered how any men can come securely to a communion with Christ, who bring such evil dispositions and full-blown sins unrepented of, which they know will for ever deprive them of any communion with God in heaven, unless they think that great sins should merit glory!

[3.] Such cannot in that state perform the duties requisite in this ordinance. Faith is a necessary qualification; but a denial of subjection to Christ is an evidence of a gross infidelity. Practices are the clearest indexes of faith or unbelief; evil works deny God in his promises and precepts. If any man tells you he believes that to be fire which is before him, and that it will burn, and yet wilfully runs into it, you must either conclude he hath no assent to what he doth affirm, or else that he is mad, and hath a mind to destroy himself. And those that believe neither the promise nor command of the word, will not be induced to believe it because of the seal, when they give no credit to the writing. Repentance is necessary to this ordinance, but this and a course of sin are utterly inconsistent: repentance is a 'breaking off iniquity by righteousness,' Dan. iv. 27, and a secret sinner breaketh off righteousness by iniquity. An unwearied practice manifests a fixed resolution, but repentance is a change of the purpose of the heart, not to commit the same iniquity again, nor any other: Job xxxiv. 32, ' If I have done iniquity, I will do no more.' A purpose of sin cannot consist with repentance, nor is a flashy purpose of repenting a true remorse. A bird may soar high towards heaven, and presently descend as low as earth; as Saul resolved not to persecute David, but was quickly bent upon his old game. He cannot have a sense of sin, which is a necessary qualification to a worthy receiving: he understands not, believes not the vast breach sin hath made between God and the world, who every day is resolved to make it wider. He is not in the least truly affected with the greatness of that God against whom he sins, with the kindness of that Christ whom he freshly murders, the curse of the law which he hath incurred, nor the wrath of God which he hath provoked. Where any one sin is loved, that soul hath not a sense of the justice of God against it, or the unexpressible sufferings of Christ for it; and can such a man have a fundamental right, who hath not a grain of the fundamental graces, or celebrate in a right manner the memorial of Christ, who walks every day as if the devil were his redeemer?

[4.] Such contemptuously undervalue the blood of Christ, and therefore are unfit for this heavenly ordinance. It is no better than a mocking of God to come to his table with a professed enmity in the heart against him; a Judas's *Hail, Master*, while he is playing the traitor; the soldiers' *Hail, King of the Jews*, to Christ, while they design to crucify him. This is to be his executioner, not his guest. To hold in the heart any one sin, which is the enemy of Christ, while we partake of the supper, is no other than to design the murder of him; as he that invites a prince to his house, wherein he lodges a desperate enemy to the prince he invites, may well be supposed to have a design against his life. We may as well profess our love openly to the nails that pierced him, and the spear that ran into his side, and adore them in our thoughts for such an action, as bring a love and zeal for those sins which were more bitter to him than the nails in his hands, or the reproaches of the rabble. A remorselessness in sin is a killing the Son of God afresh. What is it to be guilty of the blood of a man, such a man's blood as Job would not set with the dogs of his flock, or the blood of a Lazarus, who would be happier by a mortal stroke than a painful and beggarly life? What is it then to have the guilt of the blood of the glorified Son of God, the blood of him that came to be our Saviour; and thereby to do more than approve of the cursed action of the Jews? Is it not as great an affront, as if one fallen into a jakes should, in that filthy condition, intrude himself into a prince's company, sit down at his table, and dip his bemired hands in the same dish? He that knows himself to be a secret enemy to God, undervalues Christ by an approach to this ordinance, as if the body and blood of the Redeemer were food fit for a viper, or a swine good enough to wear his badge. Such is every man that hath a rooted affection to any one sin under a profession of Christ; he puts a disgrace upon him, while he prefers his sin before him.

[5.] Such cannot receive any good from this ordinance. He can design no good to himself with a resolution to continue in his sin. What can his end be, but to see Christ bowing under sin, that himself may live more contentedly in it? To attend upon any means of grace, that sin may abound, and be more at ease, is equivalent to continue in sin, that grace may abound, which the apostle mentions with *God forbid*, Rom. vi. 1, 2. Whosoever lies impenitent in any gross sin is dead, and can receive no more nourishment from any spiritual ordinance, than a dead man can by meat put into his mouth. His sin petitions against him, as Esther against Haman at the banquet of wine,* and his death, as his sin, is more increased. He makes his sin more bulky by the addition of that of unworthy receiving, and hastens his death by a fresh provocation. It is as impossible such a man can obtain any beneficial end of the institution, as it was for a Jew to be purified, who held in his hand an unclean thing which defiled him, while he dipped himself in the purifying water; and he gets just as much good by the supper, as Judas by the sop, a part of the paschal sacrament, Job xiii. 17; to have not only one devil enter into him, but seven more, and return more proud, covetous, unclean, unbelieving, impenitent than before, with his sins more strengthened, as a believer's graces are, and more contented to lie in the mire, and increase sins to lay upon the cross of Christ. Judas did no more than this. I suppose he came only with a resolution to maintain that peculiar beloved sin of his, his covetousness, not dreaming of the consequent of it, the death of his Master, nor with any intent to procure it; for he was sorry when he heard Christ was condemned, and therefore in all likelihood aimed, not at the loss of his Master's life, but the filling his own purse; yet the devil took possession of him. A resolution to continue in any sin after the fit of devotion is over, settles Satan's throne faster in the heart. A wicked man's sacrifice is always ' an abomination to the Lord, much more when it is offered with a wicked mind,' Prov. xxi. 27. And what more wicked mind can there be than to resolve to preserve the enemy of a bleeding Christ found, while he is exhibited as broken and bleeding for it?

[6.] Such as lie in the mire of any secret sin are not fit for this ordinance, because it is not a converting ordinance, neither in the intention of God nor the ordination of Christ in the first institution. None but visible professors were counted capable of it in the primitive times; they first continued ' in the apostles' doctrine,' and then ' in breaking bread,' Acts ii. 42.

I will grant first,

(1.) That it may be the instrument of a second or partial conversion. There is a conversion from a natural state to a state of grace, which is the renewing of the mind; this is ordinarily wrought by the word, as the cord whereby God draws men; and a gradual conversion after some fall, as Peter was converted by a look of Christ: Luke xxii. 32, ' When thou art converted.' This latter may be caused by this ordinance, and that grace which hath been suppressed by sin receive the virtue of a resurrection by the sacrament. The representation of a broken Christ reminds a man of his sin committed against so dear and loving a Saviour. The remembrance of Christ in that ordinance, being the great wheel to set all the other wheels in motion, causes an actual conversion by exciting the grace which was habitually there before; and this may be called a conversion, as conversion is an exerting those principles of grace infused by the Spirit, and habitually resident in the heart, though under some languor by the prevalency of some sin.

(2.) I do not question God's absolute power. Not what God may do, but what he hath revealed to be his ordinary instrument, whereby he will work this or that effect. Who can limit the Holy One of Israel? His ways are unsearchable, and his paths past finding out. He hath an almighty power to create millions of worlds, it doth not follow therefore that he will do it. God by his absolute power may infuse the first grace into the heart at this ordinance; but God hath not discovered any such intention, or declared in his word, or in the nature of the institution, that this is the end of it.

(3.) I do not deny but that it is possible, that a man that hath some dispositions and previous preparations to grace, may have the first renewing

* Trap on Cant. vii. 7.

grace bestowed upon him at the supper.* For an unregenerate man may by a serious precedent examination rake into his own heart and life, search into his state how matters stand between God and his own soul, whereupon follow some convictions, contrition, and disaffection to his darling lust, and some resolutions against it; and God may come in with converting grace at the sacrament, and make an utter divorce between the soul and the sin, and the new name may be given together with the manna, and grace infused at that instant. Where there are such dispositions to the receiving a new form, why may it not be introduced at that time as well as another? Yet if any such effect be, I should rather ascribe it to the word attending the signs, than to the signs themselves, or the act of receiving; the beginning of grace being the proper end of the word, and not of the supper.

(4.) I will not deny but that it is possible that a man, seeing the passion of Christ represented in the supper, may have such an impression made upon his heart, and his affections united to Christ. The exhortations may be instrumental to the converting a spectator of the action and a hearer of the word. The sight of miracles hath been instrumental to the conversion of some (though I do not remember any particular instance of any man's conversion by the sight of a miracle without the word preached before, and then miracles added for confirmation of the word). The sight of things makes a deep impression upon us. The whole creation is a book of God's printing, and presents us with instructions worthy our notice, and generative of reflections in us. God doth teach by the eye as well as by the ear, and sacraments are called *verbum visibile*. This may be; but there is no example of any such conversion in Scripture, nor doth the end, manner, and nature of the institution credit the opinion of its being a converting ordinance, nor hath Christ discovered his will that it should be so. If any man hath been converted by it, I should rather attribute that effect to the word, the proper instrument of it. We say *sol et homo generant hominem*, yet we do not call the sun but the man the father of the child. Suppose a man had been converted by the supper by the good pleasure of God, must men unfit for it plead a right to it? Because one walking in the way hath found a treasure, must every one expect the like hap by walking in the same path? I have heard of some, and knew one, who dated his first spiritual awakening from a dream, but would not he dream that should look upon that as an institution of God to that purpose? Because one hath been cured of an ague by running into water as cold as ice, must therefore all under the same distemper follow the same course, where they may as well expect their death as their cure? No man can reasonably expect his conversion by coming in such a posture, whereby, contracting more than an ordinary guilt of the body and blood of Christ, he incurs a greater damnation. But it is not likely to be a converting ordinance, because,

(1.) If baptism be not a converting ordinance, much less is this of the supper. That supposeth faith in the adult person, and the profession of faith in the parent for the child. The Jews did not admit a proselyte to circumcision before he was instructed in the law; then upon his own profession he was admitted to the seal, and his children upon the profession of the parent; and the apostle admitted no adult persons to baptism but upon their profession of Christianity. Circumcision was a seal of the righteousness of faith, Rom. iv. 11; it was a 'seal of the righteousness of faith which he had, being yet uncircumcised.' The circumcision at the first institution supposed faith in the party. Baptism hath the same relation, much more the supper; a seal supposeth something to be sealed. If it be appointed

* This is Suarez his opinion.

for ratifying the covenant and promises of it to the receiving soul, it sup-poseth that condition in the receiver which the covenant requires, otherwise it seals nothing. Anciently they did admit the baptized person immediately to the supper, though they kept them long in instruction before they ad-ministered the former.

(2.) This sacrament is appointed for nourishment, and that supposeth life. A sacrament doth not suppose the effect which it was instituted to produce, but this sacrament supposeth grace in a participant.* And indeed, bread and wine are not ordered to enliven a dead man, but to nourish and maintain life in a living man. The bellows kindle not the wood, but sup-pose fire kindled before. This sacrament is instituted as a part of refresh-ment, with meat and drink; and though Christ, who is exhibited in this sacrament, can raise a dead man, yet he is offered in this ordinance for pro-ducing such effects which are agreeable to the nature of it. He is offered as spiritual food, and spiritual food supposeth a new birth.

(3.) Pre-examination implies it to be no converting ordinance. If it were so, what need this bar, ' So let him come,' and not otherwise ? What need such a strict examination, whether they did repent or whether they were regenerate ? He must examine himself whether he be a sincere professor of Christianity, whether he have true repentance and faith, whether Christ be in him. That which is pre-required to the Lord's supper it was not pro-perly instituted to effect.

(4.) The nature of excommunication speaks as much. Had it been a converting ordinance, should not the incestuous person rather have been kept in the Corinthian church for his amendment and reformation than thrown out ? 1 Cor. v. 13, ' Put away from among you,' &c. It being in-tended as a medicine to reduce him to repentance and humiliation, did not deprive him of that which was the chief remedy to bring him to repentance. Though it be a cutting off from communion with the church and church pri-vileges, yet not from hearing the word, which is not properly a church pri-vilege, but the privilege of all where the gospel comes. An excommunicate person is to be held in the same rank as a heathen or publican, Mat. xviii. 17. Who would deny Turks and Pagans access to hearing the word if they would come, or not rather invite them to it and gladly receive them? Converting ordinances may be dispensed to known impenitent sinners. Christ preached the word to the pharisees, his stout-hearted enemies, who, he knew, conspired against his life. But he instituted and administered the supper only among his disciples.

(5.) The word was appointed to work faith. Rom. x. 17, ' Faith comes by hearing'; but where is it said, Faith comes by receiving the sacrament ? There is plain proof for the one, none for the other. Paul was sent by preaching to open men's eyes, Acts xxvi. 18. We find many converted by the word, none by the sacraments : the jailor by the word, Lydia by the word, the eunuch by the word, three thousand by the word. Faith is necessary to a right hearing the word : not absolutely, for men hear that they may believe ; but the word doth not profit us unless mixed with faith, i. e. unless that which they hear be believed and assented to by them. If either this or baptism had been converting ordinances, Paul's commission would have run that way; but he was sent 'not to baptize, but to preach the gospel.'

Since then it is no converting ordinance, those that are unconverted, who never yet repented of and forsook their secret sins, are not fit guests for Christ.

* Suarez somewhat enlarged.

But some will conclude the approach of secret sinners from Judas his partaking of this ordinance ; but that is a question.　Some think Judas did receive, others conclude he did not, and that he went out before the supper.　Zanchy thinks it thwarts the story of St John's Gospel ; Beza gathers that he was not there from John xiii. 30, ' He then having received the sop, went immediately out,' εὐθέως ἐξῆλθεν, which was at the end of the second supper, after which Christ instituted the sacred supper. The sop was properly a part of the rite belonging to the paschal lamb, dipped in the sauce of bitter herbs, which the master of the family reached to every guest, Exod. xii.　But the sacramental bread was broken, not dipped in any liquor.　Gomarus* hath this argument : Christ (Luke xxii. 19, 20) tells them his body was given for them, and his blood shed for them, without making any exception of Judas, which it is likely he would if he had been present, as he did in his prayer afterwards, John xvii.　Judas had no interest in the body and blood of Christ for remission of sin ; his sins could not be remitted, neither could he have any profit by the body and blood of Christ, for Christ calls him, John xvii. 12, ' the son of perdition, that the Scripture might be fulfilled.'　And consider, Judas was in hell before Christ suffered death, for he hanged himself as soon as ever he heard Christ was condemned, and Christ's blood could not be shed for him any more than for any other in hell.　It is not likely that Christ, who never admitted Judas to the choicest familiarities, should admit him to this standing token of his love.　When he whipped buyers and sellers out of the temple, he would scarce suffer a devil to be partaker of his body and blood.　If he would not pray for Judas, it is not likely he would give the symbols of his body and blood to Judas.　As to that, Luke xxii. 21, ' The hand of him that betrays me is with me on the table ;' being put after the relation of the supper, it is no argument for Judas his receiving it ; for the evangelists do not observe always in their relations the order of things as they were done.　Mark (chap. xiv. 23, 24) relates the passage of the supper as if the words of institution were delivered after they had drunk the wine and ate the bread without knowing to what end, and the institution had been after their participation of it.　According to the other evangelists, this speech concerning Judas was before the institution, Mat. xxvi. 21, &c. ; Mark. xiv. 19, &c.　But suppose Judas did partake of the supper, what encouragement is it to a secret sinner at any time to venture upon it, when he may fear Judas his reward, and a greater power of the devil and his lusts over him.

Use. Let us look well to ourselves.　Privileges must not be rested in securely without inspection into ourselves and examination of our ways ; we may be odious in God's eye, though fair in men's.　The profession of faith may be without the grace of faith ; there may be knowledge without an internal and secret practice ; much light in rotten wood ; there may be a counterfeit integrity, a moral integrity without an evangelical ; a repentance to be repented of, and a faith not sincere.　Some shall come at the last day and tell Christ they have ate and drank in his presence, eaten his body and drank his blood in the sacrament, and be answered with a dreadful, *I know not whence you are*, Luke xiii. 26, 27.　God will shut heaven's gates against many whom the gates of the visible church cannot be locked against. Something else is required to give a title in the judgment of God than what gives a title in the judgment of man.　Ananias and Sapphira we may rank among the first of seeming converts, but made the examples of God's judgment for their sin.

* Vol. i. p. 471.

Doct. 2. It is every man's duty solemnly and seriously to examine himself about his interest in Christ, his habitual grace, his actual right and fitness for the Lord's Supper before his approach to it. It is not the first time of our partaking, but every time, 'so let him come.' Now, the second and third time as well as before; great preparations are necessary for great duties. The particle *so* bars men from coming without this previous work. Let him come in such a manner; if he neglects this self-examination, let him not venture upon this great mystery. Thus, Ps. xxvi. 6, 'I will wash my hands in innocency, so will I compass thy altar, O Lord,' alluding to the ancient custom of testifying the purity of their souls by the cleansing their hands, or to the washings used before sacrifices; or if we take Ambrose his gloss, I will with a purity of heart embrace the Messiah, signified both by the altar and sacrifice. ' *So* will I compass thy altar;' without such an inward purification, I dare not presume upon an approach unto it. There ought to be an inspection into ourselves, that there may be nothing disagreeable to the Master of the feast, or unworthy of his honour. If a care of our garb and carriage be necessary in our approach to the table of an earthly prince, much more when we come to the table of the Lord, where the mighty Sovereign of heaven invites us to feed upon those dainties which are the delight of his heart and the nourishment of our souls, the joy of heaven, and ought to be the pleasure of earth. Christ prepared himself for his sufferings; he examined his own strength before he engaged, had the assurances, security, and accepting testimony of his Father before he entered upon them, so that he had nothing to do but to suffer when he came to it; and we should have nothing to do but to feast with God when we approach to him to commemorate those sufferings. Adam's body was prepared by God before the inbreathing of a living soul, and our souls must be prepared before the entrance of a quickening Saviour. If we take physic, we prepare our bodies, that the medicine may have the freer and surer operation; when we sit down at our ordinary meals, we would have prepared stomachs. Shall we prepare vessels for our own service, and bring unprepared hearts to the table of the Lord? Would not we have meat but in a clean dish, and shall we lay the eternal food, the flesh and blood of Christ, in miry souls? Every ordinance hath a preparative; meditation is to usher in prayer, prayer is to sanctify the word, the word and prayer to sanctify other ordinances. This institution hath examination for its harbinger to prepare the way of its access to us, and our access to it.

1. This self-examination or preparation is necessary. God required it in all duties. Purification went before sacrificing. The preparation and examination of themselves as to ceremonial uncleanness was strict before the passover, which was inferior to this ordinance, as the legal state was to the evangelical. The mercy to be now remembered is greater, the duties of preparation and devotion ought not to be less. The death of Christ was then represented to be suffered in time, it is now represented both as suffered and accepted. The clog of legal administrations is knocked off by the gospel, but not the holiness, which is both the beauty of the soul and an ornament of divine institutions. The meanest vessel belonging to the sanctuary, the shovels, basins, flesh-hooks, and fire-pans, were not to be used without preparation by a holy oil, Exod. xl. 9–11. Much more ought we to be sanctified for the participation of the symbols of that body which was crucified for us on earth, and glorified for us in heaven. The circumstances at the institution require it; the room wherein it was instituted was prepared, Mark xiv. 15. Christ washed his disciples' feet before the institution, John xiii. 5. We must imitate him, and wash our souls before the

participation. The Spirit's sanctification gives a right to the benefits purchased by the blood of Christ. The heart, which is a vessel to receive the body of Christ, ought to be prepared, as well as the room wherein he first appointed and celebrated the symbols of it, or the grave, wherein his body was to be awhile enshrined. His body in the sacrament must be wrapped in a clean soul, as well as his body, by Joseph in clean linen. Our Saviour entered not upon his offices without preparation by prayer and fasting, Mat. iv. 12, Mat. xxvi. 36, to set us a pattern of the like practice before any great undertaking. If men were to sanctify themselves before they came to the sacrifice,—1 Sam. xvi. 5, ' Sanctify yourselves, and come with me to the sacrifice,'—and eat of the part appointed for the feast, there is as much reason for preparation for the commemoration of the greatest sacrifice that ever was, the substance of all those that were offered before it. This cannot be without a previous examination of the quality and measures of the habitual grace in us, and what filth remains to be purged out.

(1.) It is necessary to clear up a right. There is an outward acceptation of Christ and his laws without a true and inward change of heart. All the Corinthians were called saints by the apostle : 1 Cor. i. 2, ' called to be saints ; ' saints by an outward calling, not all so by an inward regeneration. There are blazing comets which may appear bigger and greater than a fixed star. A gilded metal and true gold are outwardly like one another, yet differ in their species. There is a sanctification which is common to apostates from the faith, Heb. x. 29. The Scripture mentions a ' dead faith,' James ii. 26, which is no more a faith than a carcase is a man. There is a ' repentance unto life,' Acts xi. 18, which supposeth a dead repentance, like the humiliation of Ahab, dropping tears without a mollifying of his natural hardness ; or Judas his sorrow, raised by the fire of his conscience, not by the look of his Master. There is a ' lively hope,' 1 Peter i. 3, which supposeth a dumpish and heavy-headed hope. There are ' lively stones,' 1 Peter iii. 5, which implies that there are some unhewn and rough stones, not fitted and prepared for the temple. There is a repentance towards God, and a sorrow which works death, differenced not in their outward acts, their shape and resemblance being alike, but in their inward aims. The building upon the rock and the sandy foundation might be of the same outward beauty, form, height; the foundations were different; the one firm, the other fading. Satan's children may appear angels of light as well as their father. There is a faith common with devils, there is a faith proper to Christians, *solis et semper*, always in the habit, though not always in the act.

(2.) It is necessary for the exciting of grace. That the soul may be excited before ; that there may not be an ebb in our affections when there is a flood of our Saviour's blood ; that our stomachs may not fail us in the presence of a full banquet ; that we may not have little thoughts in the presence of great and adorable objects. The paschal lamb was not to be eaten boiled, but roasted, Exod. xii. 8, 9. The Jews say they were not to baste it with water, but with wine or oil, both inflaming, to shew indeed the mighty agonies and scorching sufferings of Christ; perhaps, also, to mind us of the warm and glowing frame our hearts were to be in at the eating of our passover sacrificed for us, that we may have fervent affections, without any chillness to damp our heat. To think or speak of the work of redemption without a suitable devotion is unworthy of any that bears a Christian badge, much more to have slight and creeping affections, when the great mysteries of it, with all the parts, are presented before our eyes. An actual exercise of grace is necessary to the concocting this spiritual food, as an actual excitation by nature of that vitriol humour, or natural heat, or whatsoever other cause of concoction it is for the preparing our bodily food to be nourishing to the members. To give meat to one in a swoon is all one as to put meat into the mouth of a dead man ; the vitals in one are extinct, in the other oppressed and languishing, and unable to perform their office. This excitation and exercise cannot conveniently be without an antecedent preparation and examination. In the case of the body, it is the work of nature ; in the case of the soul, it is the act of the mind and will quickened by grace. The excitation of grace in the soul is not as natural as that of the concoctive faculty in the body, which is done without any act of our mind, as our breathing is. This will revive graces, which seem to lie buried under ashes, into a flame, and rouse up holy principles that lay dormant in a bed of laziness.

(3.) It is necessary to prevent sin. The apostle's direction to them to examine themselves, implies the want of it to be the cause of those miscarriages among them, which he taxeth in the preceding verses. After he had shewn them the danger, ver. 27, the guilt of the body and blood of Christ, he adds, ' But let a man examine himself.' To prevent the sin of unworthy receiving, and the danger accruing, let a man examine himself. As if he should have said, had this duty been practised, Christ would have had more guests and fewer executioners of him at his table. If this were always practised, none would dare (as too many in the world do) to approach the Lord's table only with a design to wipe off their old scores ; and, upon a presumption that their consciences are cleared of their former debts, begin the same sins afresh with more ease. As those in the poet,* who besprinkled themselves with the water sacred to Mercury, and begged of him that they might more securely cheat and cozen hereafter. This is to offer a sacrifice with a wicked mind, Prov. xxi. 27; to bring devils to God's table to grow up into a legion afterwards ; to make buds of sin to be full blown, which a serious and careful examination would prevent. Melting affections and an hungry sense are the fruits of this work, and antidotes against encroaching temptations.

2. As it is necessary, so it is universal. ' Let a man examine himself.' Not some men, but every man. The most substantial Christian, as well as the weakest, or one that lies drowned still in the deluge of the fall. All the Corinthians were not spots in the feast, certainly some were free from the common taint. If there be a Judas in Christ's family, the rest of the apostles were holy ; there is also an Elijah, and seven thousand more that have not bowed their knees to Baal, in the time of Israel's apostasy. Yet the apostle excludes none from this duty. ' Let a man examine himself,' i. e. every man. Gracious men are best fitted for this work of self-examination. They should not only consider whether they have the habits of grace, but whether the prints of the Spirit be as plain as when they were first stamped ; whether their grace be in such a plight and posture fit to meet the Lord Jesus in his great institution. A nobleman, when he comes to his prince's table, doth not only reflect upon his quality, kindred, and relation, but whether he hath a garb suitable to the presence of his sovereign. A believer in habit may want the act of faith; and partaking of the supper in such a posture, receive a frown instead of a smile, and bear away a mark of Christ's anger instead of a badge of his favour. Some of the good Corinthians, because of their carelessness in this, fell under God's stroke, had weaknesses and sicknesses sent among them, and some seized upon by death, which is called a chastisement, a temporal judgment, distinct from the condemnation of the carnal world,

* Ovid Fast. lib. v.

ver. 30, 32, ' For this cause many are weak and sickly among you, and many sleep. When we are judged, we are chastened of the Lord, that we should not be condemned with the world.' God intending by this means to reduce them to their duty, and a reverence conformable to his institution, he chastised them with the goodness of a father, that he might not condemn them with the rigours of a judge. Uzziah, a good king, as well as Uzzah, a good man, may be too bold with holy things, and may suffer a temporal punishment, while freed from an eternal judgment. Every man is his own governor, and ought to ride circuit in his soul to make inquisition, and set up a tribunal in his own bosom, and cite himself before it. We must not only examine whether we have a wedding-garment, but also whether it be well kept and brushed ; whether no moths be got into it, no new spots dashed upon it. A rich robe may be sometimes so besmeared and daubed with mire, that none of the gold-lace upon it may be visible, till cleansed. Graces are to be purified, as well as sins purged out ; grace, as well as metal, for want of rubbing and exercise, will gather rust. The act of grace is as necessary to a partaking the fruit of this ordinance, as the habit of grace is to a right to glory. There being, therefore, to be a special exercise of faith, repentance, affection to Christ, these graces are to be awakened and quickened by a self-reflection. But of this I have spoke before.

I shall only mention two things.

1. Let a man examine himself, as to his sentiments concerning the nature of the institution. The apostle intimates it in the motive he urgeth to press this examination : ver. 29, ' For he that eats and drinks unworthily, eats and drinks judgment to himself, not discerning the Lord's body.' Where he chargeth the not discerning the Lord's body, upon the neglect of this.* We must consider what an holy and glorious use those elements are destined to, and the glorious body of our Lord, which they represent, that we may not violate in the signs the honour due to his majesty. To discern the Lord's body, is to consider it as the body of the Son of God,† of God blessed for ever, the sovereign Lord of the whole world, the body of the Lamb who takes away the sins of the world, a miracle of goodness, the pavilion of the Sun of righteousness, the pledge of believers entering into heaven, a body purer than the heavens in holiness, and higher than the heavens in glory. Consider the design of this body : It was to be a sacrifice for the world, an expiation of sin, the ligature of the church to God ; it hath been loaded with our crimes, and borne the punishment of our sins upon the cross ; it hath undergone the chastisement of our peace ; it hath been the purchase of our peace, the price of our liberty, the cause of our life ; it bowed down upon the cross to purchase our happiness, and mounted up to heaven to insure it to us, and possess it for us. The death of this body was of universal influence to expiate our sins, the resurrection of this body was for the justification of our persons; it sunk into the grave loaden with our guilt, it rose out of the grave and ascended to heaven to be invested with an inconceivable immortality for our consolation. Angels cannot behold it without admiring our happiness, God cannot behold it without wiping out the sins of a believer, upon the account of the sufferings it underwent ; he cannot cast his eye upon it without remembering what, and for what it suffered. It is this body crucified, but now glorified, this Christ dying, but now living for ever, which the elements represent to us, and that as a sacrifice, not as suffering an ordinary death. We must therefore discern the gift God presents us with, as greater than if

* Amyraut Paraphr.
† Daillé Melange des Sermons, Serm. xxviii. pp 300–302, somewhat changed, but imitated.

he gave us the whole world, since the Creator, who infinitely surpasseth the creature, gives us his Son, and himself in his Son. How can we have full and clear sentiments of this, without rousing up our minds, fixing our considerations upon it, and reflecting upon ourselves, whether we understand the nature of those mysteries, the design of the death of his body, and the glorious end of its resurrection? We cannot, without it, have a faith, love, and devotion answerable to the greatness of the things which our Saviour hath done and suffered in this body for us.

2. Let a man examine himself what soil he hath contracted since the last time he was with God; whether the interest of God hath prevailed in our hearts above the interest of the flesh, or whether some secret lust hath not spread its wing and increased its empire, which may have strength to waylay the benefits we expect, and be as a wall of separation between the supplies of God and the wants of our hearts. We must enquire what violations there have been of the covenant we made before, and bewail them: he is not fit to renew a covenant with God who is careless of the former breaches of it. Dust will be contracted in a house if it be not daily swept: our houses are swept and cleansed more solemnly before the coming of invited guests. Do we invite Christ into our souls, and shall we not examine every corner, and search out the dirt and cobwebs which may be offensive to him? The Spirit of Christ is a dove, and doves love clean places. The Jews, before the passover, searched every hole and chink with a candle for any leaven that might lie hid, and threw it away as a thing to be abominated. Have we not much reason to inquire what old leaven hath swelled up our souls, find it out, and manifest our hatred of it? whether we have not stored up some new nails, new spears, new gall which may afflict our Saviour, and be as bitter to him as the crucifixion; whether anything hath crept in to impair our affections to God. The nature of the ordinance requires this inquisition. Filth is not fit for a feast. We look what dirt there is upon our hands before we take what is necessary for our ordinary repast. A Belial in the heart, and Christ at a banquet, have no alliance. A carelessness whether we are defiled or no is inconsistent with this feast; and if any trash be got into our stomachs, it may hinder our spiritual appetite, and a hearty feeding upon Christ. Let that be the matter then of a good man's inquiry, whether he hath kept to God as his sovereign, to Christ as his Saviour, and to the Holy Ghost as his comforter; whether grace hath attained more strength and sin more weakness; whether the soul be more straitly or loosely within the bonds of the covenant. And indeed true grace is like the angel of God's presence, which conducted the Israelites to Canaan; it will not countenance any intruding lust, or pardon any iniquity, though it will beg God's pardon for it. These two inquiries are necessary to every man that hath habitual grace and fitness for this ordinance.

But,

3. We should enquire whether we have habitual grace or no; whether there be those uniting glowing graces,* faith and love. He that comes to the supper without faith, saith good Mr Tindall, is like a man that thinks to quench his thirst by sucking the ale-bowl. It is but a piece of bread we receive without faith, the symbol of the body of Christ without the soul and Spirit of Christ; and so we have no more advantage by the ordinance than the Jews which crucified Christ would have had, if they had eaten of his flesh and drunk of the blood which then issued from his body, or than the beasts had which drank of the rock (which typified Christ) as well as the congregation, Num. xx. 11 1 Cor. x. 4, which had no more benefit by it than if

* As D. Preston calls them.

they had drunk of any ordinary water. There must be an inward grace as well as an outward ordinance to have a spiritual benefit. Plagues come out of the temple, Rev. xv. 7, great judgments from ordinances carelessly and sinfully used. The word is the savour of death unto some, as well as the savour of life to others. Habitual grace there must be; a perfection of grace is not required; if so, then none but the innocent angels and glorified saints were fit guests. The perfectest soul indeed is not too good a vessel to receive the Lord of life; but God requires only of us a disposition of heart suitable to the design of the ordinance: a deep sense of our misery, a lively sorrow for our crimes, a hearty embracing his Son, a strong resolution to be at enmity with sin, and at peace with God. It must be a diligent trial, as we would try metals by the fire. We may easily be deceived, and think that to be the echo of the Spirit, which is but the hissing of the serpent,* and the whispers of Satan.

The great grace which you should search for is faith.

We shall lay down some signs of it:

1. Negatively.

2. Positively.

1. Negatively.

(1.) Faith is not a general acceptation of Christ or profession of him. Many men's faith is built only upon human tradition, education, or the laws of a nation. Men's living in a Christian commonwealth, and owning the Christian religion upon a secular account, is no evidence of faith, because what is entertained upon the score of interest, will, upon the change of interest, be as soon cashiered as it was embraced. The ten tribes in Solomon's time professed the legal and temple worship; but after Jeroboam had set up the calves at Dan and Bethel, they were as superstitious in the observing of them, which is evident by the complaints of the prophets, especially of Hosea, throughout his whole Prophecy. They were not forced to it so much by Jeroboam as willingly revolted from God: Hosea v. 11, 'They willingly walked after the commandment,' i.e. after the commandment to worship the calves. So easily are the vulgar induced to step into the religion of authority, and make anything a God that their ruler would have so, though it be a calf. Faith is an act of the freest choice, not a disposition which is derived by inheritance and succession from generation to generation, as it is with people who will be of the same ways of their fathers; but it is a free election of Christ upon a sight of his excellency.

(2.) Nor is it a dogmatical faith, whereby we believe the truth of the Scriptures, and the divine authority of them. Indeed, there must be a knowledge of Christ, what he hath done and what he hath suffered, else there is no taking of him as God presents him. True faith is never without this knowledge, though this knowledge and assent seems to be often without true faith. There may be a faith to believe that Christ is the Son of God, without a faith to embrace him; there may be an ointment poured upon the head, which doth not, as Aaron's, run down to the skirts of the garment, to the heart and affections. Many may assent to the truth of a proposition that Christ is excellent and lovely, who never bring their will to consent to espouse him; and by a bare knowledge there is not an union to Christ, any more than by a sight and knowledge of a star there is an union with that star. Some scriptures seem to place faith in assent in the judgment of some: 1 John iv. 2, 'Every spirit that confesseth that Jesus Christ is come in the flesh is of God;' 1 Cor. xii. 3, 'No man can say that Jesus is the Lord, but by the Holy Ghost.' The apostle John in that gives only the note of a true teacher as to matter of

* Culverwell.

doctrine, viz. if he asserts that Christ is come in the flesh, is the true Messiah, the Son of God, and righteous. And the other place speaks of the gifts of the Spirit, not of the inward grace: the assenting to Christ that he is Lord is a gift of the Spirit by a common illumination. And indeed in that age, an assent to a new, vilified, and persecuted doctrine, was a greater testimony of faith than the highest external professions can be in the age wherein we live. An assent is the first step, but if it be not an approving, efficacious assent that overpowers the will, it is no more than a condemned devil may have. 'Putting on Christ,' Rom. xiii. 14 ; 'leaning upon God,' Isa. l. 10; believing in Christ implies more than a naked assent, which is expressed well enough by a believing God or believing Christ.

(3.) Nor is it a temporary joy in the doctrine of the gospel that is true faith. This is higher than the former, the other being a glow-worm light in the understanding, and this a flashy heat in the affections, and a joy in the matter revealed, Mat. xiii. 20. The seed that was received into stony places was 'received with joy,' which may be occasioned by the novelty of a thing, the suitableness of it to some interest or carnal affection upon some present necessity. Such have often been seen to revolt again. It is as a man's taking a servant whom he puts off again, or as the sending for a physician in a present fit, and rejoicing at his coming, and putting him off after some ease when the distemper is removed.

(4.) Nor is it a presumptuous persuasion of a secure and happy state. Many men's faith is a mere presumption. They take it for granted that they have faith, feed themselves with an empty conceit, without making an exact scrutiny, and bringing it to the touchstone of the word to try whether it be faith of the right kind. If faith were a persuasion of a man's salvation, then all that have not this persuasion are not believers ; and then many a gracious pilgrim in this world, who have lived many years without it, or with a few glimmerings of hope, would be excluded from that rank wherein he stands in the account of God. If it were only a persuasion, none of the 'children of the kingdom' (as Christ calls them, Mat. viii. 12, those that live within the pale of the church) can be cast into utter darkness. For the command of believing would be no more than the commanding a man to be persuaded that his sins are pardoned, which would be the easiest thing in the world to a carnal heart. And God would command an untruth contrary to his word, if he commanded us to believe that our sins are pardoned, before we have those qualifications which are by the word requisite to the passing a pardon to us. Faith is not an assurance, much less a common persuasion. Faith is our victory, assurance the triumph ; faith is an act of the whole soul, assurance of the mind only ; faith consists in a direct act, assurance in a reflex act. Faith is not a proud persuasion, for then one in arms against his Creator might be saved in that state, with his presumptuous confidence, as well as that soul that lies clasping the promises and embracing the precepts.

But, 2. Positively, true faith may be evidenced,

(1.) In regard of the object.

[1.] It is a taking Christ. The act of faith on Christ is as a marriage act. Marriage is an act between person and person : 'My beloved is mine, and I am his,' Cant. i. 16. The union between the soul and Christ is a spiritual union of persons, as in marriage, to which it is compared, Hos. iii. 3. The benefits by Christ are consequent upon it, as the estate follows marriage. The person of Christ is the object of faith ; the promise is the encouragement to faith.

[2.] Taking Christ as Christ, as appointed and anointed by God, as coming out from God : John xvi. 27, 'Ye believe that I came out from God.

Faith stands by the cross of Christ, beholds him bruised by the Father for sin, and ventures upon Christ, because the Father hath set him out as a propitiation. If Christ be made sin for us, we must receive Christ as one that takes our sins upon him from the date of the covenant between God and him concerning redemption : as the saints of old looked upon him as taking sin upon him, and then slain, which was set forth in their sacrifices, laying their sins upon the head of the beast before it was slain, and in the scape-goat, whereon their transgressions were put before he was sent into the wilderness, Lev. xvi. 21. This is one of the principal things faith doth eye ; for what warrant, what comfort, what encouragement to accept of Christ, were it not for this, that the offended God hath appointed him the Redeemer, and his death the way of restoration ?

[3.] Taking Christ entirely, and that upon his own terms ; to cleave to the cross and bear his yoke, as a prince and as a saviour ; taking him as God hath exalted him, Acts v. 31. Where Christ saves as a priest, he rules as a lord, and directs as a prophet. We are exposed to wrath by the guilt of sin, Christ is a priest to expiate it ; we are captives to the power of sin, Christ is a king to subdue it ; we are ignorant both of our misery and remedy, Christ is a prophet to dispel the fogs of our ignorance. If we will be under the power of sin, we must be under the guilt of sin; if we will keep our sins, Christ will keep his blood, and be no Saviour to them that will be servants to their lusts. In the work of faith, the soul feels the guilt of sin to burden it, and accepts Christ to satisfy for it. It sees the filth of sin that grieves it, and accepts Christ to purge it. It is sensible of armies of sin which overrun it, and fresh recruits from indwelling corruption, and accepts Christ to conquer them ; and such a faith gives glory to God, for by receiving Christ to satisfy for the guilt, it owns the justice of God which hath been provoked ; by complying with the directions of Christ for walking in the ways of God, it honours the holiness of God, which it had before vilified ; by bringing all the corruptions to be subdued by the royal authority of Christ, it acknowledges the power and sovereignty of God, against which it had before rebelled. It accepts Christ upon his own terms.

First. To serve him. Faith eyes Christ as dying, and eyes the end of Christ's dying. What was Christ's end in dying must be our end in receiving him. The great end was to ' redeem a people to himself,' *i.e.* to his service, a people ' zealous of good works,' Titus ii. 14 ; not only to do good works, but perform them with a zeal for the Redeemer. Faith hath always a holy ingenuity. To pay a service to him that hath paid the ransom, and lay out its strength for him from whom it hath received the mercy ; to own no other Lord but him from whom it hath received the soul, the life, and all that it hath and hopes for. Faith takes Christ for a Lord, not to change him or barter him away for any other master ; to perform the duties required, as well as to enjoy the dignities offered.

Secondly. To be saved by him. Many men would take Christ as a Saviour, but not upon his own terms ; they would join something else with him ; they would have Christ and salvation, but in their own way, that some glory may be ascribed to their endeavours, to the works of the law done by them : but faith is a willingness to be saved in Christ's way, merely by his grace. Faith is the band of marriage on our parts, marriage is but to one; since nothing is so excellent as Christ, he will have no rival. The bed of Christ must be kept undefiled. True faith, which works by love, is so ingenuous that it will never rob Christ of the honour he paid so dear for, and thereby own him but as an half and imperfect Saviour. It will not stand before God by any other claim than that of Christ.

[4.] Taking Christ's righteousness is the formal act of it. Faith puts a value upon the righteousness of Christ, and after a deep sense of sin, sings in a triumphant manner: Isa. xlv. 24, ' In the Lord have I righteousness and strength.' This righteousness is entertained by true faith, because by it the God whom the soul entirely loves is exalted in all his attributes. Saving ' faith works by love ' to God, Gal. v. 6 ; and therefore, as it is deeply sensible of sin, because it offends God, so it cheerfully accepts the righteousness of Christ, because it is acceptable and delightful to God. Love to God bubbles up in every act of faith : for since faith brings us to God, it brings us to affect that God ; and it is as impossible faith can act without love, as that a man can work without hands. The apostle, Philip. iii. 9, desires to be ' found in that righteousness which is through the faith of Christ, the righteousness which is of God by faith,' values the righteousness of Christ, because it was the righteousness of God by faith ; so that this righteousness of Christ is entertained by a true believer, because it is a righteousness which doth infinitely please God. As in the pleadings of this righteousness for itself, it useth the pleasure of God as an argument, so in the acceptance of it, it eyes it as a motive. And were there anything in the world that a believing soul could think it should honour God more, or please God better in, than in relying on Christ, it would do that. All true grace levels the intentions to the glory and delight of God.

(2.) Consider it in regard of the adjuncts of it.

[1.] It is a mourning and penitent faith. The strongest faith is so. The stronger the faith, the deeper the sense of sin. Paul cries sorrowfully out, ' Who shall deliver me from the body of this death ? ' after he had closed with Christ by faith. It is the work of faith to keep alive upon the heart the sense of the guilt, filth, and evil of sin, to make the soul have vile thoughts of itself, and high thoughts of its deliverer. When the law of faith is in the heart, the heart of stone is turned into a heart of flesh, and the lion-like disposition becomes lamb-like, and as a child before God. The horror of conscience is removed by the sunshine of faith; but the sense of the guilt and filth of sin is increased by the light of it. Abraham had the strongest faith and the deepest humility. How self-abasingly doth he plead with God for Sodom's safety, and receive the promise from God with his mouth in the dust: Gen. xvii. 3, ' And Abraham fell on his face, and God talked with him.' And is it not impossible for any believing soul to reflect upon the agonies, wounds, and dying groans of Christ, and his own vileness and sin for which Christ did undergo them, and not be filled with a godly sorrow and self-abhorrency ? A proud faith is as great a contradiction as an humble devil.

[2.] It is joined with a high esteem and valuation of Christ. The soul prefers him in the mind and judgment above anything that can pretend a claim to its affection; it sets such a rate upon him, that all the treasures of heaven and earth cannot work it out of that esteem : 1 Pet. ii. 7, ' To you which believe, he is precious ; ' but how precious, the tongue of an apostle, no, not of an angel, can express. So precious he is, that the promises of angels, the threatenings of devils, the allurements of the world, the pleasures of sin, yea, and the hopes of enjoying ten thousand worlds, shall never persuade him to part with Christ. Alas ! there is no loss dejects him so much as his absence, no purchase delights him so much as his presence. The weakest faith can appeal to Christ, ' Lord, thou knowest that I love thee,' would love thee, grieve that I can love thee no more. Faith and love are the two uniting graces, and therefore cannot be separated. To an unbeliever he is without beauty and comeliness, nothing desirable in him ; to others he is a pearl of great price, the head of the corner. Faith only sees the worth of Christ. It is joined also with high admirations of God for Christ, astonishments at the riches of grace and treasures of love. It works by love; it makes use of this affection to carry out all its services to God with thankfulness. The love of God is as a law within the heart of faith, which makes it return to God, as well as receive from him; and it can receive nothing without glorifying the donor.

[3.] It is accompanied with holiness; it is therefore called a holy faith, Jude 20. It must have holiness as a concomitant, though not holiness as an ingredient in the justifying act. Faith engrafts the soul into Christ, the root of holiness, and it draws from him sap for holiness. Our implanting into Christ, is rather to make us fruitful, than to make us joyful. Actions follow life, and actions of the same kind with that life which the creature hath ; as vegetative life produceth vegetative actions, sensitive life sensitive actions, a rational life rational actions, so a spiritual, believing life, spiritual and believing actions. Faith is not a name, a picture, but a real principle ; it is a working grace, and therefore obedience is called ' the obedience of faith,' Heb. xi. 8. Faith doth not only change a man's state, but alters his nature ; hence we are said to be purified by faith, Acts xxvi. 18. As it goes forth to Christ, it is justifying ; as it bathes itself in the blood of Christ, it is sanctifying. Education may wash the feet, but faith only washeth the heart. As we were in Adam, members of that corrupt root, we do partake of his guilt and of his filth. Being united to Christ, the second Adam, we partake of his righteousness and his fulness. It is a counterfeit faith which pretends to partake of the righteousness of Christ without a communication of the fulness of his grace. True faith employs the power of Christ in the subduing of sin. It is a fruit of the Spirit, and the Spirit doth not produce one fruit without the rest. It is the root grace, the root is dead if it have no branches, no fruit. Faith is seated in the heart, and spreads itself to the whole man and all the actions, as lines from the centre. It begins in the understanding, but hath its perfection in the will, descends to the affections; sends, like the soul, its influences out through the whole man. Though it be weak, it will have its motion. If it cannot go to heaven, it will cry to heaven. The remark Christ makes of Paul, an infant believer, is, ' Behold, he prays,' Acts ix. 11 ; as if he did not pray before in the time of his infidelity. His prayer now was of another colour and temper from his self-righteous, formal, cold praying before.

[4.] It is attended with growth. It is still climbing, and cannot get high enough till it end in vision. True faith is always joined with prayer against unbelief. It increaseth in its acts, and in the frequency and vigour of them. It first sucks the breast, and afterwards can chew the manna; it is looking much and often upon Christ. It is at first accompanied with tremblings ; ' it may be God may hear me ' and supply me; afterwards it comes more boldly, and loves to look Christ in the face. And there is a growth in all graces proportionable ; for where there is life, all the members grow, the head doth not grow in knowledge, and the heart decay in love.*

(3.) Consider it in the manner how it is wrought. The word works faith and preserves faith, and faith improves the word. It is not a gourd which grows up in a night; there is much tugging to persuade the soul to venture upon Christ. Great power would not create a world in a moment, but took time ; great power doth not produce faith in an instant ; there are preparations and conflicts before the hand of faith lays hold on a Saviour. And it may be said, as Isaac to his son, If this be venison, how camest thou by it

* Dr Reynolds.

so quickly? If this be faith, how camest thou by it so suddenly, without much travail and labour? The word is the seed, the Spirit the sun that quickens it. By the word, the Spirit discovers the vileness of a man's nature, the sinfulness of sin, the fulness of Christ, and the freeness of his righteousness. By the word, the Spirit opens our eyes to see our nakedness and misery; the word proclaims the articles of peace, silenceth our reasonings, answers our objections, stops the mouth of a cavilling sinner, justifies the terms upon which Christ doth offer himself. It is not a birth of nature, but by the operation of the Holy Spirit. That Spirit that conceived Christ in the womb of the virgin, doth produce faith in the womb of the soul; so that faith and Christ are produced by the same Spirit, by the same power, by the Spirit that conceived him, by the power that raised him from the dead.

As there is a necessity of faith in the habit, so there is a necessity of the acting of faith in this ordinance. God will have our recovery in a way contrary to that of our fault; the fall was by believing the devil rather than God; and God will have our recovery by believing God rather than the devil. By the ordination of God, there is as great a necessity of faith to partake of Christ at a sacrament, as there is of Christ to make a sacrament beneficial to us.

[1.] Faith is of absolute necessity to regeneration, and only regenerate ones have a right to this ordinance. Faith is a radical vital grace; as blood in the veins is to the body, so is faith to the soul. No regeneration without the Spirit, and faith is the first grace the Spirit infuseth; no regeneration without the blood of Christ, and faith is the hyssop which sprinkles that blood upon our souls. Faith engrafts us into Christ, whereas before we grew upon a dead stock; it is from Christ, who is life, that life is derived to us, and that by faith: Gal. ii. 20 'I live by the faith of the Son of God.' We have no right to the ordinance till we have faith; this only makes us members of God's family. Till we are his children, we have nothing to do with his table; they are as carcases that want faith, and what should carcases do with meat?

[2.] In all worship faith is to be acted, much more in this. As in worldly actions we stir up the faculties of our souls, and the members of our bodies, so in acts of worship we must stir up the graces of the Spirit. Faith must mix itself with every duty: 'Whatsoever is not of faith, is sin,' Rom. xiv. 23. It comes from corrupt nature, or refined nature, not from renewed and changed nature; so, instead of a welcome, we can expect to be entertained only with cloudy looks. To come to this ordinance without faith, is to draw water without a bucket, to work without tools, and to go to market without money. There is need of faith to give us admission into God's presence, Heb. x. 22. There is need of faith to give us acceptance.

[3.] Faith is the condition of the covenant of grace, the seal on our part, as the sacrament is on God's part. No other grace hath God culled out to make the condition of the new covenant, and indeed no other grace hath such a congruity and suitableness to that end as this. When two parties are fallen out, there can be no firm peace without mutual consent. God gives his consent by offering his Son and sacraments as a seal; we give our consent by faith only, whereby we own, approve of, and lay hold on the mercy set before us. There is no benefit by anything in the world, but by accepting and receiving. The altar is a sanctuary, but men must lay hold on the horns of it. There are cities of refuge for some sort of malefactors, but they must run to them. God sets forth Christ as a propitiation, as a treasure of mercy; there can then be no renewing the covenant, unless as

God on the one hand reacheth out his mercy, so we on the other hand put forth our hearts to receive it.

[4.] Christ in this ordinance is represented as the object of faith. The serpent, as lifted up, was the object of the Israelites' sight, and upon that they were to expect healing from it; so Christ as dying is the primary and immediate object of faith. And being here represented as dying, it is not a naked representation, but that we may exercise faith upon him under that notion. It is not Christ as glorious, but as crucified, is the object of faith; for as glorious, he is rather the object of love : but the *formalis ratio* of justification is Christ, as taking upon him the form of a servant, and becoming obedient to death upon the cross. In this sacrament Christ is represented as offering himself to God, and God offering that Christ to us; Christ's payment in performing the righteousness whereby we are justified, and God's accepting and imputing it to us. Christ's dying was intended by God as the object of faith when he set him out upon the cross, Rom. iii. 25. And now he sets him out in the sacrament, there is the same reason for faith; and he is here represented more familiar to our faith than the person of the Father, than the person of the Son of God in heaven, that we may have more distinct thoughts and apprehensions of him in all the business he did transact between the Father and us, which are the fuel to our faith. As he was set out in sacrifices under the Old Testament, that those that then lived might exercise their faith in the promised Messiah, so in the sacraments of the New Testament, that we may exercise our faith in the exhibited Messiah.

The second grace to examine ourselves about, and to exercise at this ordinance, is sorrow for sin.

This is necessary to the supper. The way to an heavenly repast, as well as the way to heavenly mansions, is 'through the valley of Baca.'

1. It is necessary to that which is required to the supper. It is necessary to every duty; all approaches to God without it are but impudent rushings into his presence; repentance is *sanguis animæ*, the blood of the soul. As no sacrifice was pleasing under the law without blood, so no service under the gospel is pleasing without this. Nay, it is the soul of all the rest; hence a broken heart is said to be above all sacrifices : Ps. li. 16, 17, 'Thou desirest not sacrifice, else would I give it, thou delightest not in burnt-offering. The sacrifices of God are a broken spirit.' God had appointed no sacrifice for presumptuous sins, but brokenness and contrition was of force. We perform duties most lively, when a sense of sin is kept alive upon our hearts. The viler thoughts we have of ourselves, the higher thoughts we have of God. There is nothing so much honours God in duties as an humble address. But in this it is very necessary that we may with a broken frame suit God's apprehensions of sin in the punishment of his Son, and Christ's apprehensions of it when he breathed out his dying groans. To be hard and insensible, then, is a sad sign of a distempered heart. The blood of our souls ought in a way of gratitude to be bestowed upon him, who hath bestowed upon us the blood of his body. As Mary washed the feet of Christ as a preparation to his death, we ought to do the like in a preparation to the shewing forth his death.

(1.) It is necessary to that state and frame of heart which every person ought to be in. Faith, indeed, is the condition of the new covenant, but repentance is a necessary ingredient; faith and brokenness join hands together in their beings and exercises. The matter of the new creation is a heart of flesh, which cannot be without a tenderness in the concerns of God's honour. The new nature cannot be without new affection, and a change of old sympathies into new antipathies. An insensible soul hath no spiritual life; a living member will feel pain. It is necessary to strong breathings after God; the humblest souls have the quickest flights heavenward. The fowls were created at first out of the water, Gen. i. 20; so are our winged desires from a flood of holy sorrow.

(2.) It is necessary to the ends of this ordinance.

[1.] Exercise and increase of grace. One end is to break the soul and the sin, and therefore there should be a preparation by repentance for such an end. If the soul be well heated before, a look of a dying Christ in the supper will melt it, and set the metal a running. There is in this ordinance the love and justice of God represented, folded in one another's arms; the strength of them single will do much, much more united. If we have not then a disposition to melt, we shall be more hardened, as things are by the sun that have no inclination in their nature to be softened. The end of this ordinance is to wound and slay sin by the power of Christ's death; and sin mourned for lies more naked to the stroke than when it is folded and sheltered in our affections. We come to have clearer and deeper impressions from God; and softened wax receives clearer and deeper stamps than that which is hard. Every grace receives a fresh verdure by a stream of repentance; the fruitfullest meadows have constant streams running through them. God's end is to represent to us the bitterness of sin, as well as his love in Christ; and, indeed, without a sense of the former, we cannot have a right estimate of the latter. What God aimed at in the death of Christ, he aimed at in the representation of it to us; and a part of our worthy receiving consists in our having suitable affections to Christ; and we cannot be affected with his sufferings unless we understand the gall and wormwood in iniquity. The bitterness of sin makes us taste the sweetness of pardon; mercy would be too cheap if given to an impenitent soul. While the taste of sin, the onions of Egypt, is in the heart, it will not relish the clusters of Canaan. We should have a suitableness to our Master. Christ is here represented as a man of sorrows, as one that with prayers, tears, and strong cries obtained an answer, and with blood obtained redemption; it is not fit we should be strangers to our Master's temper and disposition, and hug the spear in our souls that pierced his heart.

[2.] Comfort is another end, and communications of the love of God; and this is not to be had without repentance. The dejected, humble publican meets with God sooner in the temple than the flourishing Pharisee that rushed in. The sun refresheth the earth when it is softened by rain, but otherwise doth parch and scorch it. God will not smile upon persons hugging their sins at a sacrament. The wine of consolation is reserved by God for drooping spirits. Job must 'abhor himself in dust and ashes' before God will receive him, Job xlii. 6. Though he is as willing as able to revive the spirit, yet not till it be humble, Isa. lvii. 15, 17. The fatted calf is not slain, nor to be eaten, till the prodigal be penitent. The lowest apprehensions of a man's self are accompanied with the highest revelations. Moses and Paul were humble: the one a mourner for his own and the sins of the people, the other a great self-accuser, and both had the highest communications. If we would have a plaster, there must be a cutting off the dead flesh. Mary was bathed in tears when she heard that comfortable voice, 'Thy sins be forgiven thee,' Luke vii. 48. Dark colours are the best ground for gilding. If we therefore have a slight humiliation, only a little pang of sorrow, we may meet with a wound instead of a plaster, and instead of balm be put upon a rack. We must cry *peccavi*, before God will return an *Euge*. The soul that is most humble hath the first sight of God at the supper. It will make us prize comfort. That soul that thinks itself a dog will be sure to value a crumb. Repentance makes us have low thoughts of ourselves and our own deserts, and high admirations of Christ. When such an one meets with spiritual comforts at a supper, what wondering will there be! That I that did not deserve a smile, should have an embrace! I that did not deserve a drop, should lose myself in an ocean! Oh, that I that deserved to be damned with a witness, should meet with a seal of his love! that for the flames of hell, he should give me the clusters of heaven! A deep sense of sin is the most powerful rhetoric to prevail with God. He would deny Abraham nothing, when he prefaced his intercession for Sodom with 'I am dust and ashes,' Gen. xviii. 27. The comforts of Christ's blood are not dropped into, nor can they enter into, a heart that cannot weep and bleed for sin.

Since repentance is necessary, let us examine ourselves what of this grace there is in us.

(1.) What is the spring of our sorrow? Whether it be ingenuous, from a sense of what we have received from God, as well as what we have deserved at his hands; whether it is a scorched sorrow from a sense of the fire of justice, or a melting sorrow from the kindly heat of mercy. The father's kind reception made his prodigal son's icy heart thaw the faster: 'I have sinned against heaven and before thee,' Luke xv. 18. The prodigal is the emblem of the Gentiles, and their call to God and repentance towards him, which must be, because they have displeased him. Without a true spring, our cries and groans are of as little value as the howling of wild beasts in a toil. It is then right, when it hath such a temper as the prodigal: I have offended a kind and loving Father, wasted his goods, resisted his Spirit, listed myself in the service of the devil; this Father I have contemned, a bountiful hand I have kicked at, a heaven bespangled with stars of mercy I have turned my back upon. We may weep at the story of Christ's passion, when we are not really affected with our sin, the cause of his sufferings, and the displeasure of God. Our sorrow is right, when it is not merely for sin, as it is contrary to our happiness, but as contrary to God's holiness. This is a conformity to Christ, who mourned for the sins of men, as well as suffered for them; and mourned for them, not because he suffered for them, but because God was injured by them. There was not a grain of malice and ingratitude in sin but he understood; he had also a clear conception of the holiness of that God who was offended and injured by sin; and from those two parts of knowledge, joined with an ardent love to his Father, and charity to man, he could not but have the most enlarged sorrow for sin, and the highest detestation of it, both as it displeased God, and as it ruined the creature.

(2.) What is the subject of the sorrow; is it the sin of nature; do we judge that the greatest sin, and not regard it as the common people do the stars, imagining them no bigger than a candle, when they are of a vast bigness? To bewail outward sins, and not that of our nature, is to have a philosophical frame of spirit, not that of a Christian. Doth the body of death draw from us the loudest groans? Do we lay the axe to the root of sin, or are we mightily busied in lopping off the branches, without a regard of the root? Are inward and spiritual sins the subject of our grief? Can we mourn as deeply for those sins that none but God and our own consciences know, as for those which are visible to the eye of man? Doth our hardness of heart, formality, remainders of hypocrisy and unbelief most afflict us? Is our grief for all sins, and especially for that which hath been the master sin? Do we oppose that which we have the greatest temptations to, as David had to the killing of Saul, which would have helped him to a crown, which therefore he calls his iniquity? Ps. xviii. 23, 24.* Would we have the greatest Delilah no more spared than the smallest brat of Babylon? And is the enmity so great that we would destroy the power and strength of sin which lies in that master iniquity? Do we stop our ears against the strongest pleas it makes for itself, and wish as much its death as we do our lives? This is a testimony of repentance. Do we hate every sin because it is a falseness to God? Ps. cxix. 104.

(3.) What are the adjuncts of the grief? Is it in some measure proportionable to our sin, proportionable not to the law, but to the gospel? The first cannot be attained by us, because the injury done to God is infinite. What we cannot attain in the act, we should endeavour to attain in affection. Where the sin is great, great must be the sorrow: 1 Sam. vii. 6, 'They drew water, and poured it out before the Lord,' which some understand of the tears of the people. To drink in sin like water, and only to drop grief, will not agree. Is our sorrow permanent; is it a true grief, or only a pang; like heat drops or a rolling cloud, that goes away and never returns again? Is our sin, like David's, ever before us? Ps. li. 3. Have not many a slight kind of sorrow, sprung up only by the seriousness and solemnity of the ordinance; a seeming falling out with sin, but a quick reconciliation, and receiving it into a stronger favour than before? Transitory affections are too frequent. We find the Israelites in the temple weeping and lamenting, fasting and praying, because of their idolatries and false dealings with God, and shortly after returning to the commission of the idolatry they had bewailed. True repentance is always accompanied with a detestation and a 'revenge,' 2 Cor. vii. 11, which is indignation, as a furnace heated seven times hotter, not a faint and a dying kind of anger. Is the league between sin and the soul broken? As God seals in this supper a covenant of grace, we should be prepared to seal a counterpart of duty. As God is ready to seal a pardon, not to remember our sins to condemn us; we should be ready to sign a bill of divorce to sin, not to remember sin to commit it.

Love to God is another grace we are to examine ourselves about. There is a necessity of this.

1. Spiritual affections to God are required in all duties, much more in this. The highest representation of a loving Saviour suffering, ought to have a suitable return of affection. Duties are regarded not by the multitude (for hypocrites may be much in doing) but by the affection; sincere persons are only much in loving. All that God requires of us is summed up into this grace, love: Deut. x. 12, 'What doth the Lord thy God require of thee, but to love him and serve him?' Men may delight to pray from a natural eloquence, which is (if I may use the expression) but as the trimming of a mangy sacrifice, and delight to hear with such a kind of affection as they would a lovely song; but every duty ought to be kindled and inflamed by the fire of love to God; and a mite of service with this is better than a talent without it. This expels weariness in our duties, and makes God's injunctions our songs, Ps. cxix. 54.

2. The object proposed in this ordinance requires the strongest actings of affection.

(1.) Christ is here represented as the cause of our happiness, in the foundation of the benefits we enjoy, viz., his humiliation, death, and passion. Here is Christ undertaking our salvation upon the hardest terms; here are the arms of the Son of God open upon the cross, the spear reaching his heart, with his affections streaming out to us in blood, when we were his

* Musc.

enemies, and had not a grain of affection to him ; and is it not fit we should be prepared to cry out with holy ravishments of affection, ' Worthy is the Lamb that was slain to receive honour and glory ' ?   This affection must needs be due to him who reversed the sentence of our condemnation, made our peace and bore our curse, had his hands nailed, his head pricked, his side pierced, his heart grieved, that by those marks we might be induced to love him.   Who can challenge our affections if he cannot, who undertook our recovery when there was but a step between us and eternal death?   And how can we act such an affection if we be not possessed with it ?

(2.) Christ as appropriated to us in a way of union is here set forth. Union to him, communion with him, both depend upon love in each party. What can express a nearer union of Christ to the soul than to feed upon him, eat his flesh, and drink his blood?   Thus to have him incorporated with us, this is as the breaking of a ring, the renewing of a contract between Christ and our souls, a prologue to the great solemnisation of the nuptials to all eternity.   Hence the entertainment Christ makes his people is set out under the notion of a wedding supper, Mat. xxii. 3.   And being thus joined unto Christ, we are one body, yea, one spirit with him, 1 Cor. vi. 17.   Now as there can be no mystical union with Christ without faith, so there can be no moral union with him without love.   With what violence can we run to him, how can we be glued to him (κολλώμενος) without this affection ? As Christ in this ordinance makes over himself to the believer to be his in love, so the believer must make over himself to Christ, to be his in all service, affection, and obedience.

(3.) The excellency of God's love in Christ is here represented.   Here is God bringing his Son from heaven to earth, from the earth to the cross, from the cross to the grave, making his wrath find a passage to Christ's heart instead of ours, pouring out his blood to keep us from bleeding, and listening to the pleas of this blood in heaven to answer the pleas of sin against us. This being the highest elevation of the love of God, was intended to draw out our love to him.   Love therefore must be answered with love, not with enmity or a cold affection, we else run counter to the design of God.

(4.) All the promises are shewn to us in it sealed.   All the promises of God bound up in the covenant of grace are here confirmed and ratified. And is not this a time for the love of the soul to work ?

3. The graces to be exercised in this ordinance depend much upon love. Love is the spring of the soul which moves every grace, and therefore it is called the ' fulfilling of the law.'   Faith hath no operation but ' by love,' Gal. v. 6.   Faith and love are united, as well as uniting, graces ; faith is the hand, but love is as the spirits which move it.   And as faith and love in the habit, so in the operations they are inseparable ; we must cleave to Christ, and be cemented to him by faith, but love must strengthen the hand ; the more we love, the faster we hold.   Faith is not sincere but when it testifies itself by the operations of love.   True repentance flows from love.   Mary's tears were most free when her love was most hot.   The more inflamed our love to God is, the stronger will be our hatred of sin as that which is contrary to him ; the sweeter the remembrance of Christ is to our affections, the more bitter is the remembrance of any offence against him ; and indeed without it, we may see the print of the nails, and put our fingers into his wounds without any remorse.   Delight in Christ cannot be without it.   Christ cannot be much in our thoughts till he comes to lie nearest our hearts, and will never be our delight till he be our beloved.   We cannot have high and raised thoughts of him, which are necessary for a transformation into his glory, without this.   Strange imaginations will intrude them-

selves, and be welcome guests, unless this grace stand at the door to thrust them away. We cannot burn in our converses with God unless this grace set us on fire, nor can we have any heavenliness in this duty ; for it is by this affection that we have our conversation in heaven in any service. Nor can we have a strong appetite to Christ in a sacrament without it ; the stronger the apprehension of, and affection to, any good, the more importunate will be our longings for it, and the quicker our motions to it, and the less can the soul brook any distance between that good and itself.

4. The nature of the ordinance requires it. It is an heavenly banquet, and requires an heavenly frame. As love is the greatest grace in heaven, so it ought to be highly operative here. It presents us with God's love to us, and therefore calls for a suitable return from us. The heathens observed a suitableness in their sacrifices to the idols they worshipped. They would not offer a slow-paced creature to the sun, but an horse, because of the quick motion of that creature. God here wills the greatest good to us, and shall not we will the greatest good to God ? An enlarged God should make an enlarged heart. Nothing is more becoming than that love should be recompensed with love.*

5. No benefit can be by a sacrament without this grace. Communion with God is entailed upon it : John xiv. 21, 23, ' He that loves me, shall be beloved of my Father, and I will love him, and manifest myself to him.' Not that our love precedes the love of God in the first efflux of it, but the degrees and acts of our love, kindled at first by the love of God, are rewarded with greater declarations of his love. Where love is acted to God, there both the Father and Son will combine together for such a soul's satisfaction ; they will come and dwell there by the Spirit in a more close, familiar, and strict communion, and more certain possession. Where there are the actings of love, though there should be no sense of any new income, this grace would bring a satisfaction in the very exercise.

Now for the trial of this love.

1. Let us not judge ourselves by a general love. As there is a general love of God to man, a general love of Christ to mankind in dying, and giving a conditional grant of salvation upon faith and repentance, and a particular love to the soul of a believer, so likewise in man there is a general assent, and a particular serious assent to the truth of God, and accordingly a general love upon the apprehensions of what Christ hath done in general. There is a common love to God, which may be so called, because the benefits enjoyed by men are owned as coming from that fountain ; a love arising from the apprehensions which men commonly have of the goodness of God in himself, and a common love wrought in them to God, as to other things that are good. Again, men may have a false faith, and a false apprehension of pardon of sin, when indeed no such pardon is granted to them ; so they may have proportionably a false love upon such an ungrounded belief.

2. Nor let us judge ourselves to be lovers of God because of our education. Many have no higher reason of their love to Christ, but because their forefathers professed him ; and so upon the same score that any heathen loved his idol, an Egyptian his Apis and onions, or a Turk his Mahomet, or a papist his images, do many titular Christians love Christ. As among the papists many cleave to the popish principles, because their fathers did so, so among us, many have no other reason of their adhering to the Christian profession, and seeming affection to Christ, but the tradition handed to them by their parents.

3. Nor let us judge ourselves by any passionate fits of love, which may

---

* Nihil decentius quam ut amor amore compensetur.

sometimes stir in our souls. There is a love in the sensitive part which is the passion of love, a love rather stumbled on than judicially taken up ; and those violent kinds of affections, whether of love, joy, or sorrow, are not long-lived. But there is a love in the will, which is a rational love, which consists in a consenting to, and choosing of, Christ, and is always accompanied with a true faith.

But let us examine,

(1.) The motives and object of our affection. Do we love God for himself, or for his benefits ? To love Christ for the loaves, is common to the multitude. To love God for his outward mercies, is a natural love ; to love him for himself, is a gracious love ; to love him for his benefits, is rather to love ourselves, and love our own ends, than to love God. When the inducements to it are human, and not divine, it is a human and not a divine love. Many love Christ's dowry, but not his beauty ; his merit, but not his person ; as in marriages, many love the portion without affecting the person. True love is between person and person, not between person and estate ; that is a true moral love, the other is a true physical love, but is defective in the due grounds and ends of it. Not but there is and may be a love of what God hath and promises, and the benefits he confers ; this is a love of the reward. But when we love God merely for this, it is then *amor mercenarius ;* when we love God for himself, and the reward in order to him, it is a genuine love ; it respects other things for God, and God for himself. True love is grounded upon a sight of God, a serious and deep consideration of him, comparing him with other things, viewing those unmeasurable excellencies which are in him, upon which the soul doth judiciously conclude, that there is infinitely more sweetness and amiableness in God and Christ, than in all the pleasures and profits of this world. Thus the spouse compares her beloved with other beloveds, Cant. v. 9, 10. She considers what the world affords, and wherewith it allures ; and after a diligent inquisition, the object of her love is Christ's person, the motive of her love is Christ's excellency ; and such a love will embrace a crucified as well as a glorified Christ, a condemned as well as an adored Christ. Where God is loved for himself, everything of God is highly valued, his word, his ways, his ordinances. Christ in his whole latitude is beloved in all his offices. In his death as a sacrifice, in his life as a pattern ; the power of his death, as well as the propitiation by it.

(2.) What is the nature of our love ?

[1.] In regard of the prevalency of it. Do we love Christ solely, supremely ; doth this affection swallow up all other affections ; as Moses his rod turned into a serpent, did the rods of the Egyptian magicians ? Doth it, like the sun, obscure the light of the lesser stars ? As God is the chief good in himself, he must be so in our esteem. A true conjugal affection to Christ excludes all other things from an equal interest in it ; an equal affection to Christ and the world are as inconsistent and prodigious as two suns in the world. The heathens knew the necessity of a prevailing love to their idols, to be at an expense for them. If the Israelites begin to be fond, though of a calf, they will deprive themselves of their jewels to serve it. This prevalent love of Christ is so necessary an ingredient, that it was the main lesson he pressed upon his disciples, Mat. xvi. 24, Luke xiv. 26. Self must be denied, if we follow Christ ; all relations must be hated in comparison of Christ, if we be Christ's disciples. The soul of a man is too narrow and limited to be intensely affected with, and strongly to pursue, at one and the same time, two different objects. The heart must be a throne reserved for

Christ, where other things must sit at his feet. For as Christ gives himself wholly to the soul, the soul must bestow itself wholly on Christ ; and as Luther, *Mallem ruere cum Christo, quàm regnare cum Cæsare*, I would rather perish with the interest of Christ, than reign in grandeur with Cæsar. A hypocrite wills Christ in subordination to inferior goods. A sincere votary to Christ wills inferior goods in subordination to Christ. Do we thus love Christ in that which crosseth most the carnal inclinations and interest of corrupt nature ?

[2.] In regard of the restlessness of it. Can nothing but Christ and the enjoyment of him content us ? Are there inquiries after him, industrious pursuits, unutterable groans, that nothing can satisfy us, no, not all the world, without him ? Are we importunate, that he may be as a seal in our hearts, as well as we as a seal in his heart, that there may be clearer engravings, stronger impressions ? A true lover rejoiceth that he hath any love to give to God, and grieves that he hath no more to bestow. His life is bound up in Christ, as Jacob's was in Benjamin. An hundred worlds cannot content him without his beloved. He is upon his watch and guard against all temptations which may disturb his affection or enjoyment, and accounts the missing of Christ worse than hell itself ; all other things will be abhorred, and accounted as loss and dung, Philip. iii. 8.

[3.] What are the effects and concomitants of our love ? Are we careful to please him, though with our own shame ? Christ's love made him take the form of a servant to pleasure man ; the soul's love will make it take up the meanest shape to please the Redeemer. Christ cared not how much he was emptied, so he might discover his love ; the soul cares not how much it is humbled, so it may testify its affection. It is like the string of an instrument strained to the same height with another, which will move when the other is touched. A true affectionate soul will be conformed to Christ in its motions : Gal. i. 10, ' If I yet pleased men, I should not be the servant of Christ.' In the state of unregeneracy he pleased men, but now as a servant he would please Christ his Master. Are we in our bent and resolution careful to please God, without regard to the oppositions of the world ? as the sun holds on its race, though the clouds gather to hinder the shining of it. Are we desirous of his glory, as well as our own happiness ? Would we rather lose what we desire, than defraud God of his right ? Our own happiness is but a created good, and therefore ought not to be loved for itself. Nor must we prefer the gift before the glory of the giver ; the glory of God is incomparably more amiable than our own happiness can be. If a man doth all for his own happiness more than for God's glory, it is certain he loves that more than God ; and if he serves God only for happiness, he sells his service to God, and he serves himself not God, for he intends only to advantage himself, not to glorify God. It was plain that Delilah loved not Samson, when all her projects were to enrich herself, and gratify the Philistines in betraying him ; so if our projects be to satisfy ourselves, we are not lovers of God. Are the duties he enjoins delightful to us ? Do the commands which were before burdensome cease to be grievous to us ? 1 John v. 3. Are our duties not so much pressed by natural conscience, as sweetened by love ? Do we esteem lightly of every service we do ? True love never thinks it can do enough. Are we tender of his honour ? Do we account the enemies of God our enemies ? Ps. cxix. 21, 22. The Philistines loved their Dagon, when they would not tread upon the threshold where he had received a disgrace, 1 Sam. v. 4, 5. How is it as to constancy ? True love will not be quenched by the waters of afflictions : Cant. viii. 7, ' Many waters cannot quench love, neither can the floods drown it.' It is a fire that triumphs over the waters of the sharpest dispensations. When storms hang over the head, there is no repentance that ever his love was bestowed upon Christ. In this there is a suitableness between Christ's affection and the soul, in regard of the constancy of it. The creature's love hath its ebbs and floods. It is sometimes circumvented by temptations, in regard of the acts and exercise, though not of the habit, which recovers itself; as Christ's love hath intermissions in regard of the discoveries of it, though not in respect of the reality and truth of it; both are constant.

Another grace to be examined is love of God's people. This is the badge of a disciple: John xiii. 34, 35, ' A new commandment I give unto you, that you love one another, as I have loved you.' This is the livery whereby men are known to belong to Christ, as a prince's servant is known by the badge he bears. It is not, as Erasmus notes, if you use this or that ceremony, have this or that habit; if you use the same meat, have the same title, but if you have the same affection. This Christ left as his last will and testament, as that which lay most peculiarly upon his heart to be observed by them. When Moses was to leave the conduct of the people,* he gives them a commandment not to depart from the law of God. When John the Baptist quitted his function, he recommended to his disciples the disposing themselves, by the baptism of repentance, to receive the Messiah; and by the observing this and their fasts, they were marked to be John's disciples. The commandment Christ gives them a little before his departure, is to love one another, as the special character whereby they should be known to be his disciples. Hence it is called *his* commandment, as peculiarly his as the commandment to believe, for they are both joined together: 1 John iii. 23, ' And this is his commandment, that we should believe on the name of his Son Jesus Christ, and love one another, as he gave us commandment,'—as that which he took a special delight in. As if those two, faith and love, made up the body of the Christian religion. In regard of this commandment the apostle tells the Thessalonians, 1 Thes. iv. 9, that they were taught of God; and this Christ presseth again and again; for he repeats it often in that last sermon of his, which he would not have pressed so much, when he had so many things to deliver, if it were not necessary. He calls it a *new* commandment, not only in regard of the renewal of it; it having been as it were out of date, and wholly lost among the Jewish factions; not only because it is more commanded in the gospel, as sacrifices were under the law more pressed than this; but in regard of the pattern. Before, it was ' Love thy neighbour as thyself,' but they had no such glorious exemplar, before the love of Christ came to be unfolded to the world. Now it is, ' Love one another as I have loved you. So powerful a motive was never affixed to the moral law, which commanded love; former ages never had so fair and so full a copy for it as this. And so punctual were the ancient Christians in this, that Tertullian saith, it was the amazement of the heathens to see them *Animo animaque misceri*, their souls and minds united and mingled with each other; and, indeed, the more believers love God, the more they will love one another; as lines, the nearer they are to the centre, the nearer they are to one another.

1. This is necessary in all duties. Would we pray? Our hands must be ' lifted up without wrath and doubting,' 1 Tim. ii. 8. Would we hear the word? If we are ' swift to hear,' we must be ' slow to wrath,' James i. 19. Would we offer a sacrifice at the altar? we must ' first be reconciled to our brother,' Mat. v. 25. Fire from heaven will not else kindle the sacrifice. One of the leading sins to be purged out of the church of Corinth, in order to a due preparation to this ordinance, was malice, 1 Cor. v. 8.

* Amyraut, in loc.

2. But more necessary in this ordinance.

(1.) It represents the union of believers together. The bread being made up of several grains compacted together: 1 Cor. x. 16, 'For we being many are one bread and one body.' As the bread is a mark and means of the communion we have with Christ,* and as we declare by the participation of the external signs, that we have a communion with the Lord, do we not also make, by the same means, a solemn protestation that we are of the same faith, the same religion, with those that partake of those symbols? And since it is the same bread which represents one Jesus, it also associates us into one body. This bread is appointed to be a band to tie us to Christ, and to tie us in affections to one another. This ordinance was instituted to solder believers together. They have the same nourishment, and therefore should have the same affection. *Eodem sanguine glutinati*, knit together with the same blood, as Austin saith of himself and his friend. The death of Christ is here represented, which is an engagement to this affection. In this his death is shewn, which did meritoriously purchase this unity; in this we partake of Christ, in whom all believers are made one, engrafted in the same stock. It was the end of Christ's death to reduce all to a harmony, to still the war, not only in the members against the mind, but in his people one against another. Since we are to remember the death of Christ, we are to remember his will and pleasure at his death; when we remember our friends, we would at least remember their dying charge, John xv. 17. Doth not Christ press this in his farewell discourse, 'These things I command you, that you love one another,' when he was making his will to man, and his will to God? This was part of that will he was to seal with his blood. As Christ upon the cross was the highest eruption of love, so this sacrament is the setting forth the highest pattern of it.

(2.) No benefit of the ordinance without this grace. We have no communion with Christ without keeping this commandment: 1 John iii. 23, 24, 'This is his commandment, that you love one another;' and 'he that keeps his commandment, dwells in him, and he in him.' Passion is like a leaven that corrupts this ordinance to the soul; as anger hinders the concoction of bodily food in the stomach. When Jerusalem is a quiet habitation, the tabernacle shall not be taken down, and God will be a place of broad rivers and streams to it, Isa. xxxiii. 20. The greatest gift next to Christ, was that of the Spirit, which descended when the disciples were ὁμοθυμαδὸν, of one mind, Acts ii. 1. This being the design of the gospel, to knit men's hearts together in peace and love, those that have not this love are not cast into a gospel mould, and therefore not fit to receive advantage by a choice evangelical institution.

Let us examine ourselves as to this grace.

And that we may not mistake, every difference in judgment is not a sign of the want of this grace. Paul differed from Peter in opinion about the Jewish ceremonies, without any breach of love, Gal. ii. 11. Paul and Barnabas jarred so as to part asunder; yet neither of them can be supposed to be void of this, which their Master had so particularly enjoined them, Acts xv. 37–39. It cannot be expected but differences in judgment will be among the most serious Christians, while the blindness of their minds is but imperfectly cured. The strings of an instrument are not all of one size, nor have the same sound, yet agree in a harmony; there may be an harmony in affections, though there may be a difference in opinions.

But this love is true.

(1.) When it is founded upon the grace of a person. That which is most

* Amyraut, in loc.

lovely in Christ's eye should be so in ours ; the grace and holiness of a person is respected by Christ, not his outward state and condition. It is a loving 'in the truth,' and 'for the truth's sake,' 2 John 1, 2. A love of a disciple 'in the name of a disciple,' Mat. x. 42. As there is a common affection to God in men, because of his benefits, so there may be also some common affection in an unregenerate man to godliness, which may be the fruit of education, or an enlightened conscience, in some measure convinced that holiness is good. Holiness and grace are so beautiful, that the wickedest man would have the appearance of it, and would be esteemed good. But it must be a choice and prevailing affection, out of love to Christ, whose image he bears, flowing from a love to God, a spirit of regeneration, from the seed of the gospel rooted in the soul : Gal. v. 22, 'The fruit of the Spirit is love, joy, peace, long-suffering, gentleness, goodness,' and is therefore set upon the meanest Christian, as the meanest box which hath a jewel in it, will be esteemed for the jewel's sake by those that understand it. The Corinthians were defective in this love, in despising the poor in their love-feasts, a miscarriage the apostle blames them for in this, 1 Cor. xi. 22.

(2.) It must be a fervent love. 'With a pure heart fervently,' 1 Peter i. 22, not in appearance and faintly. The word the apostle useth, Rom. xii. 10, which is translated, 'be kindly affectioned to one another,' φιλό-στοργοι, signifies a vehement affection. For as God loves nothing more in this world than his own image, so those that have the divine nature drawn in them are in this part like him; for God never draws any image unlike himself.

(3.) A love manifested most in their persecutions. To be ashamed of believers in their sufferings is, in Christ's interpretation, to be ashamed of Christ himself. At the last day, the trial of men is by their acts towards God's people in time of their persecutions, Mat. xxv. 41–43, &c., as if the neglect of that which he calls his commandment were the great sin to be answered for then. It is not whether we visited them when in their houses, in state and triumph, or fed them when they had wherewith to do it themselves, but when in a state of want. If a man loves the graces of a believer, he will love him in suffering ; for though suffering alters his outward condition, it alters not his inward relation or gracious disposition. Christ upon the cross was as dear to John, his beloved disciple, who would not leave him then, as when the people would have made him king.

Another grace to be examined and acted is desire, a holy appetite. The Israelites were to eat the Passover in haste, not *lento corde et ore languido*,* but with a greediness of mind.

1. This is necessary in all duties. In hearing the word, the desire must be as insatiable as the infant's cry for milk, 1 Peter ii. 2. Not the outward breast, but the nourishing milk conveyed by it, satisfies the infant. In prayer, there must be unutterable groans, strong sallies, and flights of the soul with a holy *impetus*: Ps. lxiii. 8, ' My soul follows hard after thee.' It would have an infinite enlargement of heart to God, suitable to God's infinite fulness. This desire is expressed by hunger and thirst. No desire so clamorous as that of a new-born infant for milk, or of an hungry man for meat, who will eat his own flesh, or offer violence to himself, rather than want nourishment. But this should not be so strong as our desires for Christ.

2. But in this ordinary more necessary.

(1.) It is a feast, and appetite is proper to that. Were it but a crumb,

* Gaudentius.

yet desire were fit, as long as it is from heaven. If there be life, there will be a nutritive appetite, and desire of those things which are suitable nourishment. Now what but Christ can be suitable nourishment to the new nature wherein this appetite is seated? To come without an appetite upon Christ's solemn invitation, is a wrong to the master of the feast, and the cheer he hath provided; it is a shame to come to such a feast, and leave our stomachs at home. It is not a fulness Christ expects we should bring to him, but an emptiness with an earnest desire: Rev. xxii. 17, 'Let him that is athirst come;' it is an heavenly feast, there must be a suitable appetite. Evangelical food requires evangelical hunger; marrow and fatness should whet our stomach.

(2.) The greater the longings the greater the satisfaction. In great desires the soul is said to pant as an hart, and in speedy mercies Christ is said to run as a roe. When desire opens the heart widest, then God opens the hand largest to fill it: Ps. lxxxi. 10, 'Open thy mouth wide, and I will fill it.' Mary comes to the sepulchre before the other disciples, and when she misseth her Lord, is more restless, John xx. 11. She stays, and weeps, and looks into the sepulchre again, when the other disciples were more remiss and went away, and missed of the sight of Christ, which Mary was blessed with. The wider the heart, the more triumphantly doth the king of glory enter. We have according to our desires, as Joash according to his strokes, 2 Kings xiii. 18, 19; had he struck six times, he had utterly destroyed his enemies, whereas striking but thrice, he had but a treble victory. He that is so tender of a bruised reed that he will not break it, or a smoking flax that he will not quench it, will not let an hungry soul go empty away. God scarce gives mercies in a sanctified way, but where there hath been a restless importunity before. Benefits would not be prized without this: Prov. xxvii. 7, 'The full soul loathes the honeycomb.' The chapped and parched earth sucks in the rain after a great drought.

(3.) This is the noblest affection we can bestow upon God. God being infinite should be loved, not with a finite, but infinite affection. But nothing but desire can stretch itself to a kind of infinity, and therefore is most fit to be exerted in this heavenly and eminent ordinance.

Let us examine our desires,

[1.] Whether they be vehement. An infinite being should not be faintly and coldly desired. There ought to be a holy distraction in the soul,* as scorched bowels are full of pain till they get satisfaction. There is no question but an imperfect velleity, a languishing and feeble desire, may be in unregenerate men; they may have more or less some apprehensions of the good, which stir up proportionable desires; but the longings of a gracious soul are strong, spiritual, and produce mighty inward operations. As there is all sweetness in Christ, so there should be all vehemency in the acts of the soul to him. Is our desire limited to God alone? Do we apprehend him and pant after him as the greatest good, and Christ as the choicest and only Saviour? Is it so earnest, that if all afflictions were removed from us, all outward mercies bestowed upon us, this should not satisfy, but Christ alone and the light of his countenance? This holy longing can no more be stopped by any creature, than the sun can be barred by clouds from running its race. The whole world is but as the drop of a bucket after all the water is poured out. Would a small drop quench the thirst of parched bowels? No more can all the world answer the desire of a gracious soul, any more than a drop can cool the tongue of a damned creature.

* Θεία μανία, as Basil calls it.

[2.] Whether they are constant. Doth the fire in the temple never go out? Do settled apprehensions of Christ keep our hearts alive in their motions, or are they only like the fits of a fever, or flashes of lightning, which quickly vanish? Are they as pilgrims lodging only for a night, and in the morning leave no footsteps of themselves, no signs that ever they were there? Or are they kept up in some life and vigour upon the heart? In an equal heat it cannot be expected in this life, but when they flag, are they quickly revived? O let us seek God with our whole heart and with our whole soul.

A DISCOURSE OF THE UNWORTHY RECEIVING
OF THE LORD'S SUPPER.

Whosoever shall eat this bread, and drink this cup of the Lord, unworthily, shall be guilty of the body and blood of the Lord. For he that eats and drinks unworthily, eateth and drinketh damnation to himself, not discerning the Lord's body.—1 COR. XI. 27, 29.

AFTER the apostle had laid down the platform of the institution, he makes his inferences suited to the case and miscarriage of the Corinthians. Since this ordinance was appointed by Christ as a memorial of him, and in the celebration of it ' we shew the Lord's death ;' an unbecoming frame and carriage in so great a mystery, is a reflection upon the authority of it, contrary to the ends of it, and a contracting the guilt of the body and blood of Christ. As if he should have said,* While you Corinthians come together in a rude manner to this ordinance, as if it were a common and profane feast, the abuse and contempt redounds upon the body and blood of Christ represented by those elements. Calvin thinks the apostle makes a digression from the particular Corinthian case to an universal one, not only comprehending under unworthy receiving the abuses crept into that church, but all other miscarriages which might in the future rise up in that or any other church whatsoever ; and indeed it is as a general case to be considered in our days, since the particular case of the Corinthians hath not its parallel.

He considers

1. The sin, (1.) in its nature, eating and drinking unworthily.
(2.) In its aggravation, a guilt of the body and blood of Christ.
2. The danger, ver. 29, eating and drinking damnation to himself.
3. The cause of all, not discerning the Lord's body.

Whosoever eats and drinks unworthily. Whosoever approacheth without a consideration of the dignity of that which is represented by those elements,† and the ends of their appointment, regarding it as a common thing of no great value, and brings not those dispositions of faith and repentance, doth not reflect upon the elements themselves, but vilifies that which they represent ; and offends not so much against the exterior signs, as violates the reverence due to the body and blood of Christ ; and is so far from gathering the blessed fruit of this ordinance, that he returns with the mark of the murderer of Christ upon him; for he contemns the condition of the covenant, and consequently the blood of the covenant. The argument whereby he urgeth it, is the relation it hath to Christ. It is the bread and cup of the

* Musculus. † Amyraut, Daillé in loc.

Lord. Though it be bread and wine, yet it is a sacred thing; it is the bread and wine of the Lord, instituted by him for his glory and our salvation. He doth not say, Whosoever eats the body of the Lord, or drinks the blood of the Lord unworthily, but *this bread, this cup*. The apostle was not so witless as to have termed them bread and cup, had the doctrine of transubstantiation been known in his days. His argument had run stronger: it is but bread and wine in appearance, it is changed into the real body and blood of Christ; and therefore your unworthy carriage is immediately and not relatively a violation of his person. But the apostle acknowledgeth it to be bread and wine;* but to distinguish it from bread of an ordinary use, calls it, ' the bread of the Lord.'

Unworthily. A worthy carriage respects either persons or things; persons, when our demeanour is suitable to the dignity of the person we converse with; or things, when we manage a business we undertake with a decorum and becomingness, according to the nature of it; as we say a man did this or that very handsomely. He that doth not observe a decorum and decency in a converse with a person or management of a business, doth it unworthily, awkwardly, rustically, or slovenly. So the word *worthy* is used: Luke iii. 8, ' Bring forth fruits worthy of repentance,' *i. e.* suitable to the repentance you profess. And Eph. iv. 1, ' Walk worthy of the vocation wherewith you are called,' *i. e.* let your conversation answer your calling, and be suitable to the dignity of it. It is not any precedent act meritorious of the vocation, but a worthy carriage after it, suitable to the dignity of the calling. The apostle doth not say, Whatsoever unworthy person eats and drinks of this cup, &c., for then he had excluded every man, himself too. For who is worthy enough for these things? as the apostle speaks in another case, ' Who is sufficient for these things?' The apostle requires not here a meritoriousness. Merit belongs to Christ dying, worthiness to the believer receiving. He speaks not of the worthiness of the person, but a worthiness of the action. A man may want a worthiness of person to be employed in a prince's service, yet not want a worthiness of parts which fit him, being engaged in it, to manage his employ for his own and his prince's honour. Or if a poor man be called to a prince's table,* he is, because of his poverty and distance, unworthy to sit with him; yet being invited he may come; but if he behaves himself uncivilly and indecently, he makes himself guilty of a contempt of the royal majesty, in whose presence he is. Unworthily here notes the want of an evangelical frame and disposition of heart.

Guilty of the body and blood of the Lord. He offers wrong to Christ. The Jews were guilty of his blood, when they crucified him; apostates are guilty of his blood, when they deny him, Heb. x. 29. An unworthy receiver doth such an injury to Christ, that God will account him in the rank of the Jews that crucified him, and charge him with no less a crime than the guilt of the blood of his Son.

He eats and drinks damnation. Κρῖμα, judgment, which differs from κατάκριμα.† He eats judgment or punishment, which is double, either eternal or temporary. Final unbelievers eat it to their eternal condemnation; those that have faith, and are negligent in due preparations, eat it to their temporary correction. It is the effect for the cause. An unbeliever doth not properly eat his condemnation; for condemnation is not naturally or sacramentally in the bread and wine, but he eats that which will be the cause of his condemnation,‡ because not considering the glorious

---

* Musculus.   † Rom. v. 16, κρῖμα εἰς κατάκριμα, ' judgment unto condemnation.'
‡ Estius in loc.

use these elements are destined to, he doth not consider how great and glorious a thing the body of the Lord is, which they represent ; and so violates, in those signs, the honour due to his majesty. Not but that this is of itself, and in regard of the institution, wholesome and quickening, but by the evil disposition of the receiver, and the abuse of the ordinance, that which was ordained to life brings death ; as the foulness of the stomach makes wholesome food turn to venom in the body, Therefore the apostle adds, ' He eats damnation to himself.' There is no such thing in the institution. The fault is wholly in himself, not in the ordinance. He abuseth that which would be useful to him, if he brought worthy dispositions with him. As our first parents ate their death in eating the forbidden fruit, when the fruit itself was not of a venomous nature, but by transgressing the command of God, they rendered themselves obnoxious to the death God had threatened. So we say of a man, that he hath swallowed his death, when he hath eaten something which makes way for the entrance of death; not only when it is poisonous in its own nature, but when it is unsuitable to the temper and state of the patient. So he that eats unworthily, makes himself obnoxious to the judgment of God, either to be tormented by his scorpions hereafter, or awakened by his scourges here.

Not discerning the Lord's body, Διαϰϱίνων. To discern a thing or person is to separate it from other things or persons,* and give it its due rank and order, which is either, (1.) in effect, when a man is endowed with qualities which elevate him above others. As the apostle saith, God makes us to differ, Τίς γάϱ σε διαϰϱίνει ; 1 Cor. iv. 7, *i. e.* he puts a difference between us and others, giving us graces more advantageous than unto them. (2.) In opinion and esteem, when we value one thing more than another ; so, Acts xv. 9, God is said to ' put no difference between the Jews and Gentiles,' οὐδὲν διέϰϱινε, *i. e.* he hath treated them indifferently. So not to discern the Lord's body is not to esteem and honour it as he ought, not to give it its due rank ; to entertain it not as a singular and divine, but a common and ordinary thing. When men disesteem Christ, they count his blood as common blood, Heb. x. 20. What is there translated *unholy*, is in the Greek, ϰοινὸν ; so after the apostle had discoursed of the two elements, as representing the two parts of the sacrifice offered upon the cross, his body broken, his blood poured out for a propitiation for sin, not to discern it, is to have no higher opinion of the body of the Son of God, the wonder of God's wisdom and goodness, than of a common thing, and a matter of no value.

Or not discerning the Lord's body, is when our sense sticks upon the outward elements, and our spirits rise not up to view the merits and propitiation of Christ through the veil of the bread and wine, as if the elements were the things only we were to feast upon. It is a spiritual feast, and therefore we discern not the Lord's body when we have not spiritual meditations of the dignity of Christ, the atonement he made, God's wisdom, justice, and mercy in the design of his death. As Christ doth not put us off with empty signs, so he would not have us rest upon empty signs, but acknowledge his body and blood represented in them, for those ends for which the one was broken, and the other shed. The papists, to prop up their doctrine of transubstantiation, draw an argument for it from this place. The body of Christ is in the sacrament in its proper substance, otherwise a man could not be guilty of his body and blood.† For no man could justly be condemned for not discerning the Lord's body from other meat, if that which he receives were not truly the body of the Lord, but another meat ; and the unworthy receiving of the naked sign cannot make a

---

* Amyraut, Daillé, Musculus. † Daillé Melange des Sermons.

man guilty of the body and blood of the Lord. But this is no argument.* Christ is wronged in that which hath a relation to him, as well as immediately in his own person. The rejecting the apostles, the messengers of Christ, is a rejecting Christ who sent them: Luke x. 16, 'He that despiseth you, despiseth me;' and he that despiseth the commands of God delivered by man, 'despiseth not man, but God,' 1 Thes. iv. 8. Was our Saviour therefore substantially present in the persons of the apostles? Were they not separated from his body, when he sent them to other parts, and gave them this as an encouragement? How could he be with them, and absent from them in his body? When he chargeth Saul with persecuting *him*, because he 'breathed out slaughter against his disciples,' Acts ix. 4, was the body of Christ therefore substantially in his disciples? He that hath received the knowledge of the truth, and apostatiseth from it, 'treads under foot the Son of God.' Is the person of Christ under the feet of these contemners! To tumble a king's robe in the dirt, to counterfeit his seal, tread upon his crown, daub his picture, break down his arms in despite, offer violence to his ambassador, is reckoned as a violation of the person and authority of a prince; yet neither the person nor nature of the person is really present in any of those things. They are indeed the marks of his dignity, and he that violates wilfully any of them is supposed to be willing to do as much against the person of the prince, if it were in his power, as against anything which bears his character. The substance of the body and blood of Christ, is not in the bread and wine of the sacrament; his exalted body is no more to be broken and sliced in pieces; nor doth it consist with his state of glory, to have his substantial body shrouded under such mean elements. But the bread and wine are memorials and pledges of his body and blood, instituted by him as signs to signify him; therefore he that receives them without a due respect to Christ, and handles them unworthily, despising those things which are signified by them, is a contemner of the Son of God, since he hath no value for that which is a mark of his authority and his love.

Doct. Unworthy receivers of the supper contract great guilt, and incur great danger. In the handling which doctrine I shall shew,

I. What unworthy receiving is.
II. The sinfulness of it.
III. The danger of it.
IV. The use.

I. What unworthy receiving is.

1. Something negatively.

(1.) Unworthy receiving is not proper only to a man in a natural state. The apostle chargeth here unworthy receiving, not only upon the professing, but the regenerate Corinthians, upon such as fell under the chastening hand of God for this cause, that they might 'not be condemned with the world' to an eternal punishment, 1 Cor. xi. 32. He sent temporal punishments upon them that they might not undergo an eternal damnation; they were redeemed from eternal punishment, renewed in their souls, yet some of them were guilty of unworthy receiving. The apostle also puts the unworthiness upon the want of a self-examination, which a good man may, by some supineness and negligence, be deficient in, and, as the sleepy church, Cant. v. 2, may contract some rust in his graces, yea, and fall into some bemiring sin, as a neat man may into a dirty puddle, rendering himself at present unfit for the entertainment of, and converse with some worthy friend. Sins of a higher magnitude, which a good man may fall into, make him at the present

* Daillé Melange des Sermons.

unfit for heaven, and therefore for an heavenly ordinance. David was no worthy attender upon the institutions of God while he lay in his impenitency, till his tears had washed away his iniquity. Nor was Peter restored to the sweetness of converse with his Master, till he had wept bitterly; while a great sin remains unpurged, or the soul through negligence untrimmed, it is no fit guest for God.

(2.) Unworthy receiving is not to be measured by our sensible joy or comfort after receiving. Two men that have perfect health have not equal stomachs, nor equal appetites, and consequently not the same joy in their meals, yet both in health. We should more consider how graces are acted, than how comforts are dispensed; the former is our duty, and necessary to a right participation; the latter is an act of sovereignty, and not our duty. God's dispensations are not equal to all; some have only tastes, others full draughts; some may have more joy than strength, others more strength than joy. Mary had a strength of love to Christ, before she had a joy of pardon from him, Luke vii. 47. Paul's grace was not weaker fourteen years after his rapture, though we read not of a second discovery of the third heavens to him. God was most pleased with our Saviour upon the cross, acting his faith in, and love and obedience to God, when he denied him sensible comforts from heaven, and was bruising his soul for sin. The life and exercise of grace is the root of joy, though the fruit itself be not always visible; we may seem to have a rebuke from God, when we are in the strongest exercise of grace. The woman of Canaan had no sense of Christ's kindness, while she was acting a faith stronger than others who had met with swifter rewards. Jacob had the honour to be termed a prince prevailing with God, in that wrestling wherein he received such a touch from God as made him halt all his life after, Gen. xxxii. 25, 28. If our souls can ascend, like Manoah's angel, in the smoke of thanksgiving and elevations of spirit, and be melted and softened by a flame of love, there is a worthy receiving, though there be not a sensible comfort.

But, 2. Positively; that is an unworthy receiving,—

(1.) When evil dispositions and beloved sins are not laid aside and forsaken. As there must be faith respecting the Christian doctrine, so there must be repentance respecting the conversation. He eats unworthily that hath different ends from what Christ had in the institution; and wants the qualifications which Christ requires, who hath neither faith nor repentance, no sense of sin, nor love to Christ, to hold up to God. Common infirmities render us not unworthy, but voluntary defilements: neither the poverty, blindness, or halting of one or other of those invited, Luke xiv. 21, Mat. xxii. 10, was charged upon them, but only the filthy rags that one of them came in; such sordidness as he might have mended, not the lameness which he could not cure. Common infirmities are inseparable in this life; but the great breaches and violations of the covenant are to be discharged. Every sin doth make some separation between God and us (as the smallest body hath its shadow); but they are the darling sins that are a thick cloud between him and us. Those then are unquestionably unworthy receivers, that approach with a love to their lusts; as Judas, who came with his covetous disposition and treacherous purposes. Such as lay aside their sins at present in the act, but not in the habit and affection, that shake hands with them for a time, to fondle them afterwards.

(2.) When, though beloved sins are discarded, yet there is not a due preparation suitable to the quality of the institution. The apostle implies it in the precept he enjoins immediately after the declaration of the sin: ver. 28, 'Let a man examine himself.' He that doth not trim up the graces he hath, that doth not search them out, and marshal them in order to entertain the master of the feast, as well as he who wants those qualifications necessary. An actual as well as an habitual sanctification was required of Jesse's sons before the sacrifice : 1 Sam. xvi. 5, ' Sanctify yourselves, and come with me to the sacrifice.' Christ did sanctify himself before he made himself a sacrifice, John xvii. 19, so should we before we commemorate it. If the lamps be not trimmed, they will burn but dimly. If that he counts the wedding-garment be not brushed, it will be a slighting the Lord not to appear in our best garb. The Corinthians were chastised, not for want of grace in habit, but for want of grace in act. It is a disrespect to Christ not to put on a wedding-garment which we have in possession, when graces and affections are not set on work which the ordinance requires. A natural man is unworthy for want of possessing those graces; a renewed man unworthy for want of acting them. The party that so offended was not sent out to clothe himself, but punished for his neglect : ' Friend, how camest thou in hither ? ' Christ's worthy care in the institution must be answered with a worthy carriage in the preparation. He washed his disciples' feet before the institution, John xiii. We should prepare our souls before the participation. When a good man's graces lie dead at the ordinances, he receives unworthily. What difference is there between a dead man and one that doth not exercise the acts of life ? When Christ reacheth out himself, and our hands are not ready to take, our hearts not ready to embrace, it is an unsuitable carriage. We have no great esteem of the gales that blow, if we will not prepare and hoist our sails to be filled with them, and stand not ready to suck Christ's breast in his ordinance.

(3.) It is an unworthy receiving when we rest only in the ordinance, expecting from the work done, what we should expect only from Christ in it. When we content ourselves with Elijah's mantle, without asking for the God of Elijah. Thus the Jews deluded themselves with their privileges, and displeased God with their neglect of him ; like Joab securing himself by laying hold of the horns of the altar without repentance for his murders. This is to derive from the sacrament the cause of our righteousness and justification, and ascribe that to the naked elements and signs which is only to be expected and desired at the hands of God. This is a wrong to God, when we prefer the shadow before the substance, the shell before the kernel, satisfy our appetite and take no notice of the Master. Doth not he slight both the physician and the physic, that expects a cure from a medicine in his pocket, which he was to take into his body ? The like it is to Christ, to think that a corporal feeding, without a spiritual relish, can nourish our souls ; a chewing the elements with the teeth, without feeding upon Christ with the heart. This is evident, when we answer not sacramental engagements, as well as when we come without sacramental preparations ; in that we slight the end of the ordinance, as in the other we slight the greatness of the institution.

(4.) When there is a garishness and looseness of spirit in the time of our attendance. Not discerning the Lord's body, say some ; not minding the Lord's body, but letting the thoughts run at rovers, which should be fixed upon Christ's dying ; not making a difference between this holy bread and common refreshments in the behaviour of our souls. Our spirits should be low in regard of contrition, not in regard of a sordid demeanour towards God. To have base ends and starts in his worship ;* to regard our own things in this act, and not the things of God ; to have unsettled and roving thoughts, crosses the end of this ordinance. It is unworthy not to remember Christ,

* Grotius.

not to shew forth his death; how can this be done without minding him? The Master of the feast is not remembered unless we look through the bread and wine to the broken body and the shed blood of Christ. We esteem not him that we do not mind, we value not him that we do not, with the weight of our souls, intently lean upon. Not that any man is free from roving while the flesh cleaves to him. (The involuntary startings of the flesh, the involuntary injections of the devil, do not make us unworthy receivers. God regards the willingness of the spirit to affect us, and the weakness of the flesh to pity us. ' He knows our frame, that we are but dust,' and dust is apt to be removed with a blast of wind.) But when the reins are let loose to the headstrong flesh, when we pull it not in, but follow rather than resist the motions; it is then that we make light of the dignity of this ordinance, and the great and glorious body of our Lord represented thereby. Neither can we understand every actual consent to such motions at the time of our attendance to be the unworthy receiving, which makes us guilty of the body and blood of Christ, though it be an unworthy carriage, unless we should count all the apostles to be unworthy receivers, who, if not in the time, yet presently after the first partaking of it, contended among themselves about earthly greatness in the kingdom of the Messiah, as it is probable from Luke xxii. 24. But when it is habitual, voluntary, and without a purpose of soul, and a ' setting the heart to seek the Lord,' 1 Chron. xxii. 19, such an one is not free from this character of an unworthy receiver.

II. The sinfulness of this. It is a contracting the guilt of the body and blood of the Lord. This unworthy carriage derives its original from that disposition which incited the Jews to a crucifying of him. Though there be not a blow struck at his person, there is the spring of as many blows as ever the Jews gave him. *Diversa peccata, par contumelia.* What hath been said lately about the sinfulness of unbelief might be applied to this case. I shall therefore say the less of it. Though there be a difference in the circumstances of the several sins, there is little or none in the contempt and indignity. He that doth despite to the image or arms of a prince, would do the same to his person, were it as much in his power.

1. It is an implicit approbation of the Jews' act in crucifying Christ. If we are not affected with that state of Christ, we consent to, and approve of, that act of his crucifiers; not positively, but privatively; not having that temper and affection of spirit which such an action doth call for from us. This is one way, among many others, of being accessory to another's sin, by not having a regret at it. He that makes light at the death of an innocent person,* confesseth him a malefactor, and that he deserves to be slain, since being slain, he deserves so little regard, or at least he makes him a malefactor, and gives just occasion of suspicion that he would have been ready enough to have imbrued his hands in that man's blood. The committing a sin is an approbation of all of the same kind that went before. Had it not been so, the guilt of the blood of all the prophets could not have fallen upon the heads of that generation which murdered Christ, Luke xi. 47. Whosoever hath slight thoughts of the death of Christ, and neglects those duties so great a condescension calls for, partly consents to the savage usage Christ met with from the Jews. They were the authors of the first crime, and an unworthy receiver the abettor.

2. It exceeds the sin of the Jews in some circumstances, as well as that exceeded this in others. That was against his person, this against his propitiation; they did it against one they accounted a blasphemer, we do it

* Pemble, p. 507.

against one we account not only innocent, but a Redeemer. The Jews tore his body, and an unworthy receiver, saith Chrysostom, defiles it, by putting the body of Christ into an unclean vessel. The sin is greater, by how much impurity and defilement is more against his nature than death and torment.

8. In regard of the relation the ordinance hath to Christ. There is an analogy between the bread and the wine, and the body and blood of Christ. The nearer relation anything hath to God, the more heinous is the offence. To kill a debauched man unjustly, innocent of any crime to deserve death, is an affronting God in his image, Gen. ix. 6. To neglect uncharitably a member of Christ is greater, because it is a despising of Christ in his mystical body, Mat. xxv. 45. This is greater, because it is an affront to his body and blood in the picture and representation of him. To fling the picture of a prince into the kennel, and stamp upon it with contempt, is treasonable in some places. A man of quality is not injured so much by breaking his earthen vessels, as by defacing and defiling his arms, the marks of his honour. It disparageth the whole covenant of grace in unworthy usage of the seals of it. How base a disposition is it to sit down at the table of a man with an hostile mind against him! to stab the master of the feast at his own table, while he is treating and entertaining us with dainties!

4. It is a great sin, as it is against the greatest testimony of his love. That hand which was afterwards pierced and nailed upon the cross for us, did first break this sacrament to us. He appointed it when he was to go out of the world, when he knew all things were given into his hands, John xiii. 3; when he knew he was to leave the world, and sit down at the right hand of his Father; he would then do a work worthy of himself, to declare his own liberality to us. It was the first fruit of the power granted to him. It is a violation of that marriage knot whereby Christ would have us be joined to him, and become his spouse. He only was the author of this. His crucifixion could not be without other hands, and the wickedness of many persons in bringing him to his sufferings. But this acknowledgeth him only the author. The motive of his sufferings was the satisfaction of his Father's justice, as well as his love to us; this hath purely his own love for the spring of it. His suffering was a part of his obedience; but the only motive of this institution was his kindness. And the apostle prefaceth this institution (as it may seem) with a manifestation of his love, 'having loved his own, he loved them to the end,' John xiii. 1, as if he could not leave a higher pledge of his love than this; since he could not leave himself, he would leave his picture.

III. The danger of this sin, he 'eats and drinks damnation to himself.' As the sin is set forth in the greatest blackness, so is the punishment in the greatest dreadfulness. The sin subjects us to the same punishment that was reserved for the crucifiers of Christ. God inflicts upon his own temporal corrections, upon final unbelievers eternal; he useth his rods on some, his axes on others. It is but reason the severity upon the offender should be proportionable to the communications to the worthy receiver. Where his liberality is unworthily used, his severity shall be justly felt.

He eats and drinks damnation to himself. Damnation is not the end of the ordinance, no more than it is the end of the gospel, or of Christ's coming into the world. The supper was appointed for holy and beneficial ends, but the unworthiness of the receiver turns that into a sword which was intended for food. Worms grew from that manna which was intended for a blessing, when they used it not according to the command of God, Exod. xvi. 20. Rain is to make the earth fruitful; and where it meets with a good soil, it opens the womb of the earth to bring forth wholesome plants; but where it lights upon a bad soil, it brings forth briars and thorns. It is not the fault of the rain, but the disposition of the ground, which produceth hurtful and venomous plants which are ' nigh unto cursing,' Heb. vi. 7. So the ordinance is bread to strengthen, wine to refresh ; but where the wickedness of a man is mixed with it, there is poison in it, a piercing hook under a delightful bait. The word is a savour of life and a savour of death, 2 Cor. ii. 16 ; a savour of life when mixed with faith, a savour of death when mixed with unbelief. Where the blood of Christ doth not cure, it inflames a wound ; where it doth not save, it condemns ; that which is not melted by the sun grows into a greater hardness. Christ, as a sacrifice on the cross, was pleasing to God, as the murdered innocent a burden of guilt on the Jews ; so as he is grateful food in the sacrament to a worthy receiver, he is the bane of an unworthy communicant by reason of his unholiness. It was a sad cut to David to be guilty of the blood of Uriah, whose blood, though not shed by his hand, was designed by him to be spilt in the service of his country ; yet how was his soul galled for it, and his son afterwards in the head of an army against him for his punishment ? What a crime is it to kill a child in the womb, who never yet saw the light ? What is it then to murder the Son of God in the signs of his body, the Saviour of the world, the king of glory, whose blood is unconceivably more precious than the blood of all men, the life of all angels ; doth not this deserve a severe correction ?

IV. The use.

1. The manner of duties must be regarded as well as the matter. The matter of this ordinance is participated by both the worthy and the unworthy receiver. The manner makes the difference. The same matter of prayer may be put up by two several persons, the one accepted, the other rejected ; one offers it with a wicked, the other with a sincere mind, Prov. xxi. 27. The eating the passover ' otherwise than it was written,' was dangerous, and needed Hezekiah's prayer to God for a pardon of them, 2 Chron. xxx. 18. He that came ' without a wedding garment ' could have relished the sweetness of the meat, but, intruding in an unbecoming garb, was turned out as unfit for the king's table. As God hath the love of a friend, so he hath the greatness of a sovereign. He will not be treated with as an ordinary friend, but ' sanctified in all that draw near to him,' Lev. x. 3. His gracious indulgence must not diminish our awful thoughts of his majesty. Though it is a crucified Christ we remember, one clothed with infirmities, yet it is one that hath dropped his mantle, and is exalted at the right of the majesty on high. Since he is God in heaven, we must not be hasty to present ourselves in an unbecoming garb before him : Eccles. v. 2, ' Let not thy heart be hasty to utter anything before God, for God is in heaven.' Circumstances in worship are more than ciphers ; but if they were no more, take away all the ciphers joined with an unit, how is the sum curtailed to nothing ?* The voluntary omission of a circumstance necessary to an action doth not excuse but aggravate.

2. The holiness of an ordinance will not excuse a miscarriage in it. Some are nourished by this ordinance, others pollute themselves. The fruit is not according to the holiness of the ordinance, but the disposition of the receiver. Before the destruction of the temple, Ezek. x. 2, God saith, ' Fill thy hand with coals, and scatter them over the city.' The fire in the temple, which they thought was to serve for the expiation of their sin, should serve for the destruction of the city. The temple hath thunders and lightnings in it as well as music, Rev. iv. 5. The most wholesome food sinks† under the power of corrupt humours in the stomach. Nadab and Abihu were the true priests of God ; they intended to offer incense to the true God.

---

* Durand.   † Qu. ' stinks '?—ED.

The incense was according to the mind of God, and the censers were of the consecrated vessels. They erred only in taking strange fire, which God had not commanded, and this cost them their lives, Lev. x. 1, 2. We may have right ordinances, direct our addresses to the true God ; but the holiness of those will not excuse the want of heavenly fire, the grace of the Spirit, and the want of a due value of the mediation of Christ.

3. The sins of those that draw nearest to God are the blackest. Never was anything termed a guilt of the body and blood of Christ but the Jews' wickedness in crucifying, men's apostasy in denying him after knowledge, and the abuse of this ordinance, and that not only in the unregenerate Corinthians, but in the best that were guilty of those miscarriages ; he taxeth whosoever eats and drinks unworthily. An universal particle.

4. The ground of our mischief is always in ourselves. It is not from the emptiness of the ordinance, that is a full cistern ; nor from the shortness of God's grace, he is an overflowing fountain ; but from want of those graces, or of exercising those graces, which are the bucket to draw and the mouth to drink. The plantain is not poisonous in its nature, but the venomous nature of the toad turns it into poison. Misery ariseth not from the insufficiency of the sacrament, but the unworthiness of the receiver. That judgment is conveyed to one, when grace is conveyed to another, is our own fault. The door is open, but unbelief pulls to the door and locks it. The miseries rained down upon us are but the ascended vapours of our own sin. Christ hath an hand to reach the benefit to us upon our worthiness, and a hand to inflict the punishment on us upon our abuse ; he makes himself a feast for the believer's faith, but the unbeliever makes himself a feast for the Redeemer's wrath.

5. We see here the base nature of sin. It changeth the brightest ordinances, makes the waters of the sanctuary bitter, turns food into poison, and a cup of salvation into one of damnation. We frustrate God's expectations when he looks for fruit ; then it is just he should frustrate ours when we look for food.

6. If an unworthy receiver be guilty of the body and blood of Christ, a worthy receiver hath a special interest in the body and blood of Christ. He hath as much advantage thereby as the other hath guilt. The apostle speaks this to put a bar to the Corinthians' sin, to make them sensible of their unreasonable miscarriage, not to scare them from the ordinance, but to excite them to come to it in a becoming manner, so as to honour God and benefit themselves ; that they might sheathe God's sword, and not draw it against themselves. Though the Red Sea swallowed up the Egyptians that would venture into it, yet it was a wall to preserve and deliver the Israelites from the hands of their enemies. He that receives worthily, eats and drinks salvation to himself, by the rule of contraries. The ordinance comes upon him like rain, fitting him to bring forth herbs meet for the use of him that dressed him ; and such a person receives blessing from God, Heb. vi. 7. Certainly that Christ, that never turned away a little faith without a blessing when he was upon earth, will much less now disappoint it when it is exercised on him. Since in heaven there is no diminution of his compassion, there can be no increase of his severity to such an one.

7. Should not all of us, that have at any time of our lives been partakers of this ordinance, reflect upon ourselves, yea, the best of us ? Can any of us say that we never contracted the guilt of the body and blood of Christ ; that we always had some worthy dispositions for him ; that our minds were never wavering, our hearts never cold, our affections never languishing, our spirits, that should have been in heaven, never sunk to the earth ? Is there not then a partial guilt ? Yet God hath admitted us again and again, spread

his table, filled his cup, put manna into our mouths, and his cup into our hands. Wonderful patience in God, to bear with a wonderful sin in us! ' Deliver me from blood-guiltiness, O God,' may be the cry of every one of us, as it was David's, Ps. li. 14. How often have we wounded him that hath delivered us, killed him that hath saved us, abused that blood that was the price of no less than the redemption of our souls and bodies! Who doth not condemn the Jews for crucifying the Lord of life in his infirmities? And ought we not as well to condemn ourselves for crucifying the Lord of life in his glory?

8. How, then, should we take heed, whenever we approach to the Lord's table, of any unworthy demeanour towards him, whereby to contract such guilt and incur such displeasure? How should we endeavour after as clear affections to Christ as he bears to us, with meltings of heart and faintings of soul for him? We receive benefit according to our worthiness. As we prepare our souls for God, so he prepares himself for us: Isa. lxiv. 5, 'Thou meetest him that rejoiceth and works righteousness, that remembers thee in thy ways.' He is a feast of fat things to them that have faith to receive him. If we value not the pledges of his love, we shall bear the marks of his indignation. Adam, the first rebel of mankind, had the sweetness of a promise, and was not given up to that justice of God which he had provoked, and the malice of that devil whose temptation he had swallowed. Nor was Peter, who, in the denial of his loving Master in so base a manner, had gratified the devil, given up to be winnowed by him. But the first that ever offended in an unworthy receiving the Supper (if he did receive it) was, without remedy, given up as a possession to that devil who had animated him to his treacherous design. It is a dreadful eating when attended with such a sin and such a judgment. To receive worthily is to be affected with the sufferings of Christ; the cause of those sufferings, sin; the end of those sufferings, redemption from the guilt and filth of sin; the acceptation of those sufferings by God, the confirmation of the fruits of them; to cast ourselves into the arms of a crucified Saviour, washing our souls in his blood; pleading his merits before God, humbly and believingly applying them to ourselves. Let us, then, raise up our spirits, drink deep of the cup of salvation, drink abundantly of that love which is sweeter than wine. If we come before him in a becoming posture, with our hearts burning, our souls thirsting, our drooping faith may be then revived, our closed eyes opened, dark shades may fly away. The disciples that knew not Christ in the way, neither by the features of his countenance, nor the spirituality of his discourse, yet knew him in the efficacy of a sacrament, if that were the celebration of it, as some think, which is mentioned Luke xxiv. 30, 31. He withheld his grace before, to honour this ordinance with it. Let, then, the bounty of Christ engage us.* He hath not given us a hand or an arm, his head or his feet, a few drops of his blood, but his whole body, his whole soul, his graces, his virtues, the fruits of his death, to be participated by us, to be insouled with us. He hath given himself wholly for a sacrifice; he hath given himself wholly in a sacrament; a greater gift could not be given on the cross; a greater gift cannot be given at a table. He is given for our comfort, our refreshment, our physic, our victory. The relation the sacrament hath to the sacrifice, and the benefits conveyed to us, call for a becoming carriage from us. Let us discern the Lord's body, which is the mystery and subject of the sacrament; value it in its due rank as the price of our redemption, the delight of God, the admiration of angels, a body that hath nothing comparable unto it in the whole world.

* Lingend. de Eucharist. p. 185.

A DISCOURSE OF SELF-EXAMINATION.

Examine yourselves, whether ye be in the faith; prove your own selves: know ye not your own selves, how that Jesus Christ is in you, except ye be reprobates?—2 Cor. XIII. 5.

THE apostle having blamed the Corinthians for some enormities among them, and knowing there were some that had not repented of them, comes now to a conclusion of his epistle, and assures them, that if he should come again to them, he would not spare them, but be sharp against them with his ecclesiastical censures. And as for such who had not been guilty of those crimes, yet had mean thoughts of the apostle, and would have some eminent proof of his apostleship, or of Christ speaking in him, ver. 3, he refers himself to them, and makes them the judges of it, whether they had not found the mighty operation of Christ in him. For as though Christ's being crucified evidenced his being subject to the infirmities of man and the penalty of the law, yet his resurrection and his glory is an evidence of the power of God in him and with him; so though I be weak, yet you yourselves bear arguments in you of the power of God, working in the apostleship, which I have exercised among you, and therefore 'examine your own selves,' and try whether there be not a mighty change wrought in your souls, 'whether you are not in the faith,' and quite other men than you were. If you find not such effects, assure yourselves you are not yet in the state of true Christianity.

Some understand this of Christ being in them in regard of the miraculous gifts, the gifts of miracles, tongues, and healing; and understand by faith here, a faith of miracles, which was a special gift, and very resplendent in the primitive church. But that doth not seem to be the sense of it, for the possessing such gifts is not a sign of election, nor the want of them a presage of reprobation, or a testimony of insincerity. Miracles may be wrought by those that have not a justifying and saving faith. Judas had the same commission with the rest of the apostles, at Christ's first sending them out in the time of his life; and we may well conjecture, that miracles were wrought by him, as well as by his colleagues, in that employment. Besides, it cannot be manifested that those gifts were bestowed upon every member of the primitive church, but only upon some called out by God for that purpose. And if by faith be understood here a faith of miracles, whereby they should try themselves whether Christ was in them, those that had not that gift conferred upon them had no evidence of their being in Christ; or at least, had not so illustrious an evidence as the others had, who outstripped the rest of their brethren in those miraculous powers. The gift of miracles was an evidence that Christ was in those instruments, in regard of his power, but true faith only is an evidence that Christ is in a man in regard of his grace.

Examine yourselves, Πειράζετε. Tempt yourselves. The word *tempting* is sometimes taken for trying, as when God is said to *tempt* Abraham in commanding him to sacrifice his son, to know or make known to him that he feared God, Gen. xxii. 1, 12.

Prove yourselves, Δοκιμάζετε. Try yourselves as goldsmiths do metals; prove yourselves, that you may know experimentally what is in you. Δοκιμὴ is used for experience, Rom. v. 5.

The phrase speaks diligence in this work, the repetition intimates both diligence and frequency; what is not known in one act, may be known in repeated acts. Self-examination is a duty in all cases, the repetition speaks necessity; it implies also men's natural backwardness to it.

Know you not your own selves. It implies the folly and unreasonableness of the neglect of it, also the possibility and easiness, upon a due and diligent inquiry, to know whether Christ be in us or no.

How that Christ is in you. Whether the power of Christ hath not wrought in you to the transforming your soul.

Unless you be reprobates, 'Αδόκιμοι. The apostle doth not understand by the word reprobates, such as are eternally rejected by God, as reprobates are opposed to the elect. Those that had not Christ in them at that time might have him afterwards, the work of conversion being daily promoted in the church; but *reprobates*, *i.e.* counterfeit, adulterate, not yet purified and refined from your dross, or, unless you are unapproved or void of judgment, or unexperienced in the ways of Christ. And he puts μή τι, a diminutive term, *unless* you be somewhat and in part sincere. Or it may go further, and the apostle might mean thus: if after the power of Christ, which hath appeared so gloriously among you, you find no strong operation in your own souls towards him, you have reason to suspect that you are not owned by him, that he may give you over to yourselves.

The protestants confirm the doctrine of the possibility of assurance, and a man's knowledge of himself to be in a state of grace from this text, which doctrine the papists impugn.* It is strange that some of the schoolmen, who assert that a man may by the strength of pure naturals love God above all things, yet deny that a man can know that he loves God above all.

In the verse, observe,

1. The duty expressed: *examine yourselves, prove yourselves.*
2. The matter of it: *whether you be in the faith.*
3. The enforcement and motive: *except you are reprobates.*

Doct. Self-examination is a necessary duty, belonging to every one in the church, and requires much diligence in the performing of it.

Hence some observe, that when it is expressed that God created man in his own image,—Gen. i. 27, 'In the image of God created he him,'—the word is *Elohim*, which is a name of God belonging to his judicial acts, which imply trial and examination; in the image of *Elohim* created he him, *i.e.* with a power of self-trial and self-judging. This self-examination is an exact and thorough search into a man's self, an exquisite consideration in what posture he stands to God. The word is the rule, a glass wherein we see God's will; and conscience is the examiner, that is, the glass wherein we see our lives and the motions of our hearts, and which, by the help of the word, doth dissect and open the soul to itself.

* Catharin. in loc.

I shall not prosecute this doctrine fully, only lay down some conclusions.

1. It is a necessary duty, in regard of our comfort. What good doth it do a man to hear that a Christ is sent to redeem, that a ransom is paid, that sin is pardonable, hell avoidable, heaven attainable, upon the conditions of faith, and not know whether he hath so advantageous a grace in him, which only entitles him to such glorious privileges? What comfort in Christ, in his meritorious passion, in his triumphant resurrection and ascension, in his prevalent intercession, unless we know that by faith we are united to him, and consequently have an interest in all the gracious fruits of his different states of humiliation and exaltation? If we can find this grace in our souls, what a joy unspeakable doth result from thence? Christ as a king will protect my soul, Christ as a priest hath expiated my sins, Christ as a prophet will remove my ignorance; my soul was in his mind upon the cross, my concerns are in his breast in heaven, my name is enrolled in the register of his subjects.

It is necessary,

(1.) Because there are common graces. As there is an outward and inward call, so there is an outward profession and an inward transformation. There are some virtues come from the hand of God as creator, and some immediately from the Spirit as a renewer; some common virtues for the preservation of human society, and some special graces for the fabric of an invisible church. There is an acceptation of the law for an outward practice, without an affection to the lawgiver, or an esteem of the spirituality of the law itself. There is a sanctification in opposition to Judaism, or Paganism, or some erroneous opinion; which is common to those that may apostatise, Heb. x. 29. The apostle calls the church of Corinth saints: 1 Cor. i. 2, ' called to be saints;' saints by vocation outwardly, not all saints by a new vocation inwardly.

(2.) Because there are counterfeit graces. There is much false coin in the world, washed pewter and gilded brass; there are sepulchres garnished outwardly, and full of rottenness and stench within; there are many that want not their artifices in religion as well as in common converse. Good things may be imitated when they are not rooted. We have heard of some limners that have represented Christ so to the life as to deceive artists as skilful as themselves. The apostle speaks of ' a dead faith,' James ii. 26, which is like the carcase of a man without life, a faith that deserves no more the name of faith than the carcase doth the title of a man when the enlivening and principal part is fled. There is a ' repentance unto life,' Acts xi. 18, which supposeth a dead repentance, such as Ahab's humiliation, like marble sweating tears in moist and rainy weather without any mollifying of the natural hardness, or Judas his sorrow, raised by the fire in his conscience, not like Peter's, by the spiritual influence of his Master. There is a ' lively hope,' 1 Peter i. 3, which supposeth a dead hope; there is a ' lively stone,' 1 Peter iii. 5, which implies that there are lifeless stones, that are not inwardly fitted and prepared for the spiritual building. The building upon the rock and the sand might have the same beauty, form, and ornaments, but not the same foundation; one was stable and the other tottering. There is a ' repentance towards God,' Acts xx. 21, when the dishonour of God afflicts us, which implies there is a repentance towards ourselves, when the danger of our own persons starts a pretended sorrow for sin. There is a faith that is sound and lasting, a faith that is temporary and perishing, a faith that starts up like a mushroom in a night, and withers at the next scorching temptation. There is a faith common with devils, and a faith proper to Christians; there is a faith *of* Christ and a faith *in* Christ.

(3.) Because every man is in a state of grace or nature. There is a state of grace, Rom. v. 1, a state of wrath, Eph. ii. 3. The world is made up of receivers of Christ or rejecters of him, true subjects to God or rebels against him. There are two families, the family of God and the family of the devil. The visible church was not without its distinction. The ark contains unclean as well as clean beasts. There is a Cain in Adam's family, a Ham in Noah's ark, an Ishmael in Abraham's house, and a Judas in our Saviour's retinue; and at the last day the whole world will be distinguished into two only kinds, of sheep and goats. It is necessary therefore to inquire whose we are, whether we belong to the God of heaven or the god of this world; whether we have the renewed image of God,' or still retain the old stamp of the devil.

2. It is a duty that requires diligence and care. That which is of infinite consequence in the state of your souls, ought not to be built upon sandy and slight foundations. It is called communing with a man's own heart, Ps. iv. 4, not a slight glance and away; sweeping and looking with a candle, Luke xv. 8, wherewith every cranny and chink is pried into; trying of the reins, which are parts of the body hidden with fat. There must be a careful removing of several things to come at them; a searching for some precious filings of gold in a heap of dust; an employing all the faculties of the soul in a diligent search: Ps. lxxvii. 6, ' My spirit made diligent search.' It is expressed by counting, Ps. cxix. 59, ' I thought on my ways,' חשבתי; he looked over the acts of his soul one by one. The heart is called the ' inward parts' or depths ' of the belly,' Prov. xx. 7. As the bowels are folded together in many coats and coverings, that they are not easily come to, so the heart of man is full of devices.

(1.) Diligence is requisite, because the work is difficult. It is no easy matter to be acquainted with ourselves. The soul is not well acquainted with its own features, and preserves not the species of itself. ' We behold our faces in a glass, and soon forget what manner of men we are,' James i. 23, 24. As man is apt to know anything but himself, so it is more easy for him to know anything than himself, as the eye sees everything but itself. There must be diligence to discern the rational workings of our soul, to know whether we truly understand such a thing, or really and firmly will such a good. The judgment of man is corrupted, and misrepresents things like a cracked glass.* We can more easily judge of a bodily than of a spiritual disease, because the understanding which should judge of the state of the soul is sickly and ill-affected itself. Our wills also being so changeable, sometimes set on one thing and sometimes flitting to another, the spiritual workings of them are not so readily discernible. This work is done by a reflex act; and reflex acts, in spirituals as well as naturals, are weakest and more languishing, whereas direct acts are more powerful and vigorous. Where grace is small and corruptions many, it must be hard to discern it, as it is for an eye to discern a small needle, especially if in the dust and rubbish. The roots of sin also lie deep, like Achan's wedge of gold in the earth, not easily to be found without good directions. Lust lies in secret corners; there is a deceitfulness of it, subtle evasions, and specious pretences: consideration is requisite to the discerning of them. External acts discover themselves, but the inward acts of the soul, which are the surest evidences, are not discernible without a diligent inspection. The natural inconstancy and levity of our spirits divert us, and the streams of our corruptions cloud and bemit† us, and control our endeavours in self-examination, that we cannot sometimes any more fixedly behold the motions of grace than we can see the beams of the sun in a black and mourning sky.

(2.) Diligence is requisite, because man is naturally unwilling to this

---

* Preston.   † Qu. 'bemist'?—ED.

duty. He would live anywhere but with himself, think of anything but himself, delights most in those things which hinder him from a consideration of his own state. Men are more willing to have their minds rove through all the parts of nature than to busy themselves in self-reflection, would read any book or relation rather than the history of their own heart. We are nearest to ourselves physically, and furthest from our own selves morally. Men whose titles are cracked and unsure are loath to have them tried before the judge, and come under the siftings of conscience. Ever since the fall we run counter to God; it is the property of the divine nature first to know himself, and then to know other things; but we are cross, would know any other thing but not ourselves, would read others, and not so much as spell ourselves. We naturally abhor any actions wherein we may be like God, though they are the most proper operations for our souls, and suitable to the nature of them, as reflex acts are. There being in us a contrariety to God and his law, to God and his gospel, there results from thence an unwillingness in us to bring our hearts under the examination of conscience, that power which acts by authority and deputation from God. And when grace doth egg us at any time to the performance of the duty, do not our hearts hang back, and our corruptions check us in it? Satan is no mean instrument in this: he is said to blind the world, that they might not know their state. He hath lost his likeness to God in his primitive happiness, and ever since envies man the recovery of that likeness which is possible to man and impossible to himself, and therefore diverts him from all glances towards it, and endeavours after it, the first step to which is self-reflection.

This unwillingness ariseth,

[1.] From carnal self-love. It is natural to man to think well of himself, and suffer his affections to bemist or bridle his judgment. A biassed person cannot be a just judge. Every man is his own flatterer, and so conceals himself from himself. Very few that are uncomely in body, or deformed in mind, but think themselves as handsome and honest as others. David so loved himself that he saw nothing of his sin, but was fair in his own eyes till Nathan roused him up by telling him, 'Thou art the man.' Every man would be 'right in his own eyes,' Prov. xvi. 2. Every blackamore fancies himself to have a comely colour. This self-love may so far bemist a good man, that he may not believe such an act to be a crime, such an excuse to be a fig leaf, such a mark to be unsound. And this self-love keeps men off from this work, for fear they should behold their own guilt, and their souls be stung with anguish. Men that are bankrupts are loath to cast up their accounts, lest it should appear to them that they are undone. Some are loath to see their ugly faces in a glass. Conscience, awakened by this duty, bites and stings, and men are loath to impair their own ease because they would escape the din of an accuser in their own bosoms; they turn fugitives from their own hearts, and would rather go to hell in a feather bed than to heaven in a fiery chariot. While man seeks nothing more than himself in a sinful way, he conceals himself and flies furthest from himself in a reflexive way.

[2.] From presumption and security. Some walk as securely as if there were no heaven, and it concerned them not; others walk as presumptuously as though they were heirs-apparent unto it, and yet have no title. Many will have a false persuasion of their faith and interest in Christ at the last day, Mat. vii. 22, and cry, 'Lord, Lord!' and the foolish virgins will knock as confidently and expect entrance to the feast as well as the wise, will not believe but they have a title to heaven till Christ himself clap the door upon them, and manifest the contrary. Had they raked in their own souls and been plain dealers with themselves, they could not but have found them-selves in a lost condition. Those that thus presume cannot endure to hear of the differences between hypocrisy and sincerity, how far a castaway may go in religion. This was the reason the pharisees were such enemies to Christ, because he raked in their consciences; they could never come near him, but he brought some indictment against them of hypocrisy. As Ter-tullian called heretics *lucifugæ scripturarum*, because they would not be cured of their errors, so are such men also afraid to bring their hearts to the test of the word, because they would not be cured of their false presumptions. As Ahab hated Micaiah, so these their own consciences, because they expect to hear that from them which they think evil, and cannot have such a view of themselves in that glass as they desire to have.

(3.) Diligence is requisite, because man is hardly induced to continue in this work. That self-love which makes them unwilling to enter upon it, ren-ders them unfit to make any progress in it. When we do begin it, how quickly do we faint in it! How soon are our first glances upon ourselves turned to a fixedness upon some slighter object! Every man's heart is like an unruly horse, that will be going out of the way if there be not a resolution to check it in its first starts, and bring things to a judicial trial. The heart itself is so light and fluttering, that it wants the stability of grace to fix it in the trial of grace.

(4.) Diligence is requisite, because we are naturally apt to be deceived and to delude ourselves. Our natural blindness and dimness render us liable to mistake, and our deceitful heart may sing a *requiem* to us while we are fools. We have a subtle enemy that lies in wait for us, who can transform himself into an angel of light, and disguise his serpentine hissings to make them appear like the breathings of the Spirit. If Adam in innocence, who had an ability to discern his methods, was deluded by him, much more may we be deceived by him in a state of corruption, when our hearts naturally have his stamp, and are inclined to take his part and join with him in a self-deceit: 'The heart of man is deceitful,' Jer. xvii. 9. It is the great impostor and cheat of the world, the antichrist within us, the deceiver of our souls, as the great antichrist is called the deceiver of the nations. How apt are we to take upon trust what our heart first speaks! James and John could tell Christ that they were able to drink of his cup, and no ques-tion they meant as they spake, Mat. xx. 22; but had it come to a trial, they would not have endured to sip of it; and the issue manifested it: they turned their backs upon him, as well as the other disciples. The Israelites, had they tried themselves by their present resolution, Deut. v. 27, 'All that the Lord our God shall speak unto thee we will hear and do it,' might have subscribed themselves as pious as any in the world; they spake no other than they meant. But God had a further inspection into them than they had into themselves: ver. 9, 'Oh that there were such a heart in them that they would fear me, and keep my commandments always!' Natural conscience is often silenced by a pretence and a show, and a man is naturally apt to make his own corrupt judgment, sometimes also his pas-sion, the standard of good and evil, and not only to frame grace according to his own affections, but a god also: Ps. l. 21, 'Thou thoughtest that I was altogether such an one as thyself.' The apostle intimates it in that signal mark of caution, when he presseth a truth to which natural conscience will subscribe, that 'neither fornicators, nor idolaters, nor adulterers, nor effemi-nate, nor covetous, nor drunkards, shall inherit the kingdom of God;' 1 Cor. v. 9, 'Be not deceived,' saith he: even in these things men may deceive themselves with false hopes, much more in moral righteousness. Many boast themselves rich in spirituals when they are really poor ; so did Lao-dicea think herself rich when God gave her another inventory of her estate, that she was ' poor and miserable, and blind and naked,' Rev. iii. 17. There is too much resting in the world upon outward privileges,* and often beggars conceit themselves princes because they dream of sceptres. How many extend their hopes as far as their wishes, and these as far as a fond fancy and imagination !

(5.) Diligence is necessary, because to be deceived in this is the most stinging consideration. To drop into hell when a man takes it for granted that he is in heaven, to dream of a crown on the head when the fetters are upon the feet, will double the anguish. It is better for a rich man to dream that he is a beggar, for when he awakes his fears vanish, than for a beggar to dream that he is rich, for when his dream ends his sorrow begins. The higher the false conceit, the lower do men sink when they fall ; the higher men's expectations of heaven are without ground, the more stinging is their loss of it.† To have vain hopes, till God puts us into the scale and weighs us, will be a miserable disappointment. For a man to deceive himself aggravates this ; as self-murder is accounted a greater sin than the murder of another, because it is against that charity to ourselves which is the copy and rule of charity to another.

(6.) Diligence is necessary, because many have miscarried for want of it. Thousands that have thought themselves in the suburbs of heaven, have been cast down to the depths of hell. If all should be saved that think they shall be saved, the strait way would be that which leads to hell ; for what man is there almost that doth not confidently believe he shall be happy ? How many dream they are going to paradise, and when they awake find themselves in the devil's arms !

II. The use.

1. If this be our duty, to examine ourselves, then the knowledge of our state is possible. If we are to examine ourselves, we may then know our-selves. Reflection and knowledge of self is a prerogative of a rational nature. We know that we have souls by the operations of them.‡ We may know that we have grace by the effects of it, if we be diligent; as we may know by the beams of the sun that the sun is risen, if we shut not our eyes. Grace chiefly lies in the will, and it discovers itself in actions. The more raised any being is, the more active it is. The being of a God is known by the effects of his power in the world, and the being of faith is known by the operations of it in the heart and life. Though gold and that which is gilt be like in appearance, yet the true nature of each of them may be discerned by the touchstone. Hypocritical grace is like true grace, but it is not the same. Sincerity may be known. If we cast but a glance upon our hearts in any word or action, we may know whether we mean as we speak or do, or whether we have any by-ends in it. The discerning of habitual sincerity is not so easy as the knowledge of an integrity in a particular act; yet if we keep a due watch over the motions of our hearts and the actions of our lives as they come upon the stage, and consider what their ends are, it will not be so difficult to know ourselves. It is impossible a man's will should steal by him in all the actions it produceth, and a man be ignorant and insensible of it. The spirit and conscience of a man may know such things as are in it, both the habits it hath and particular motives to this or that act: 2 Cor. ii. 11, ' The spirit of a man that is in him knows the things of a man.' If men would be more inward in conversing with their own hearts, they might

---

* Vaughan, Serm. p. 6, 7   † Miserum est fuisse felicem.
‡ *Cogito ergo sum* is the first principle in the new philosophy.

have an acquaintance with the concerns of their souls, as their sense hath with outward objects. There can be no sufficient reason given why the understanding should not as well know the acts of the soul and will, as the acts of the sense and the motions of the body. We know our particular passions and the exercises of them. There is no man that fears a danger, or loves an amiable object, but he knows his own acts about them, as well as the object of those acts. If a man have faith and love, why should he not be as able to know the acts of faith and love as to know the acts of his particular affections? This is easy, if we did live more with ourselves, and oftener exercise that prerogative of reflection which we have above beasts. It is difficult indeed in regard of our corruption; as the law is said to be weak, not in itself, it was able to answer the end for which God appointed it, and man by the endowments of his creation was able to observe it; but it became weak to make men happy, and man impotent to conform to it, through the flesh, Rom. viii. 3, by the entrance of corruption. It is the same corruption of man which renders this knowledge of himself difficult. He lives too much abroad out of his own soul, and too little within, otherwise there is no doubt but he may know his own will, and the habitual inclination of it.

2. How foolish is the neglect of this duty! How many ramble about the world without acquainting themselves with their own hearts, or considering whether Christ be in them! What advantage can there be in the knowledge of other things, if we know not whether there be any operations of grace in our own souls! How few give themselves the opportunity of a serious retirement! How unreasonable is it to rest satisfied with underground hopes of heaven, to call ourselves citizens of Jerusalem above, and have no copy of our freedom to shew, nor any living witness in us to bear testimony for us! It is against nature to desire to be in any company rather than our own, to endeavour to know everything in the world rather than ourselves, which is the first object of knowledge. Should that reason which God hath given us, more excellent than the nature of beasts, be employed about examining everything but ourselves?

3. Use of exhortation.

It is our highest advantage to know what should become of our souls in eternity. Is it a small thing to be within the verge of the wrath of God? And is not the knowledge of this necessary, if we be in such a case that we may avoid it? Or is it a small thing to be an heir of heaven? Are justification, adoption, acceptation, small privileges; faith, love, repentance, small graces? Is not the knowledge of them necessary, that we may have the comfort of them? May not some convenient space of time be every day spent in this? May I not say, as Christ to his disciples, 'Can you not watch one hour?' Can you not spare one hour for so great and necessary a work? Let us enter therefore into the bosom of our heart, and see whether we have a true faith, such as Abraham's; whether it be such a lively faith that hath freed our souls in part from the mud of our corruptions; whether it be a faith resting upon Christ for salvation, without giving indulgence to the least offence to him? Such a faith that purifies the heart, reforms the life, inflames the soul with a love to God, causing us to rejoice in him, and in any further degree of conformity to him? Whether it engenders in us a serious desire and a suitable endeavour to obey Christ? Such a faith that relies upon his promises without slighting his precepts?

III. I shall, lastly, give you some directions about this duty of self-examination.

1. Acquaint yourselves with those marks that are proper only to a true

Christian. Overlook all those that are common with the hypocrite, such as outward profession, constant attendances, some affections in duties. Let us not judge ourselves by outward acts; a player is not a prince because he acts the part of a prince. But we must judge ourselves by what we are in our retirements, in our hearts. He only is a good man, and doth good, that doth it from a principle of goodness within, and not from fear of laws, or to gain a good opinion in the world. Grace is of that nature, that it cannot possibly have any by-end. As it is the immediate birth of God, so it doth immediately respect God in its actings. In the very nature of it, it aims at God, as to love him, believe in him. The great accusation the devil brings against Job was, that he served not God for nought, that his service was not sincere, that he acted a righteous part for his own ends, and to preserve his worldly prosperity, Job i. 9, 10. But if our ends be right, and our actions in the course of them according to his rule, if our hearts in them respect God's law and his glory, how will the devil's arrows drop down, as shot against a brazen wall! The inward bent and the habitual delight and affection of our hearts, is chiefly to be eyed, whether they are in God or in other things. This was the apostle's way of trial: Rom. vii. 22, 'I delight in the law of God after the inward man;' and what the incitements are to your profession and service, whether they are not bare affections, moveable passions, carnal interests, a good education, a working fancy, &c. Take those marks, which are inconsistent with hypocrisy, 'such as accompany salvation,' Heb. vi. 9, and necessarily infer a truth of grace. Begin at the lowest step of true and sincere grace, inquire not at first into the marks of an high and towering faith, of the eminent degrees of it. This would be to put a giant's suit upon an infant's back, and judge ourselves not men, because the garments fit us not. A small beam will manifest that the sun doth peep out of a cloud; but larger ones, and more spread, evidence that it hath got a full victory. Have a right notion of true grace, and though grace be little, yet you may know it; as if a man hath a true notion of a diamond, though never so small, he can truly say that is a diamond as well as if it were bigger. Though a gracious spirit may not have grace enough to satisfy its desires, yet it may find grace enough to settle its soul. There may be grace enough to give a man an interest in Christ, though there be not a full strength to answer all the obligations of the gospel. Let us examine, first, the *truth* of grace, and afterwards the *height* of grace. A little of the coarsest gold is more valuable than much of the finest brass. See how the habitual frame and inclination of the heart stands. A heart set upon heaven discovers the treasures of the heart to be there. See whether we have David's temper, to 'hate every false way,' or Paul's, to 'have a conscience void of offence towards God' in regard of his service, as well as towards man in regard of his converse; not to neglect anything towards God that conscience tells us is our duty to him. One sound and undeniable mark is better than a thousand disputable ones.

2. Let us make the word of God only our rule in trials. This is the only impartial friend we can stick to, and therefore it ought to be made our main counsellor. The word is the principle whereby grace is wrought, and it is the medium whereby grace is known.* The word is that whereby we must judge of doctrine, 'to the law and to the testimony.' If an angel from heaven speaks any other thing than what God hath delivered, he is not to be heard. It is also the rule whereby we must judge of graces. If conscience speak anything for a man's comfort, that is not according to the word, it is to be silenced; if conscience presents us with anything as a grace,

* Priucipium essendi et cognoscendi.

that will not hold water before God, it is to be rejected in that case; bring it to the touch-stone to see if it, be current coin. As we are to try other men's spirits, so our own, by this rule; it is a part of man's sinful ambition to be his own judge, and so to make his own fancy his rule. The Scripture beam is like a sunbeam, it will discover the most inward, and the most minute, thing, Heb. iv. 12; it will reveal the deceitful contrivances and sophistry of the heart. This word must try us at last, it is to be the rule of the last judgment, to salvation or condemnation; let it be the rule of our self-judgment. It is safe for us to take that rule which God himself will take, and take in good part whatsoever the word saith; if it shew us our evil, let us change our course; if it speak good, let us be thankful to God, and give him the rent-charge and tribute due to him for it.

3. Take not the first dictates of conscience. 'He that trusts his own heart is a fool,' Prov. xxviii. 26, *i. e.* without a diligent inquisition, it is not wisdom to do so, ' but he that walks wisely shall be delivered;' he that makes a strict inquiry into it, shall be delivered from its snares and his own fears. It is a searching, examining, proving our hearts, that is required, not taking them at the first word. There may be gold at the top, and dross at the bottom. We are naturally quick of belief of those things we would have and desire; we should be jealous of these hearts which have so often deceived us, as we are of those who have often broken their word. Whatsoever it speaks, suspend your belief of its sentence, till you have well examined the ground and reasons why it gives in such a report; if it tells you, you are in a good state, that you are penitents, believers, have a choice love to God, an eye fixing on the glory of God as your end, bring it to the test, examine why it saith so. We have here to do with the greatest impostor, and in other things we will not give credit to a cheater. Therefore our searching often in Scripture is joined with trying. We must not only search out our graces, but try whether they be of the right stamp, and have the mark of God upon them. Examination and proof must go together in this act, as they do in the text.

4. In all, implore the assistance of the Spirit of God. Natural conscience is not enough in this case, there must be the influence of the Spirit; it is God's interpreter that can only ' shew unto a man his righteousness,' Job xxxiii. 23. The sun must give light, before the glass can reflect the beams. Grace cannot be discerned, if the Spirit obscure and hide itself. In the night, the beautiful colours in a room are by the darkness, as it were, buried from the sight; but when the sun discharges its beams into the chamber, they are enlivened, and affect our sense. There may be graces in the soul which appear not, if the Spirit withdraws his light; but when he displays himself, they will appear in their true lustre. In all our trials of ourselves, let us beg of God to try us. When David had been ransacking his heart, he would not rest in his own endeavours, but begs of God to open his heart more fully to his knowledge, and bless him with a perfect discovery of it: Ps. cxxxix. 21-23, ' Do not I hate them which hate thee? I hate them with a perfect hatred.' I think, I conclude I do; but lest my conclusions may be wrong, do thou, O God, ' search me and know my heart, try me and know my thoughts,' *i. e.* make my heart and thoughts, and bent of them, visible and fully discernible to me.

5. Let us take heed that, while we examine our graces and find them, our hearts be not carried out to a resting upon them. We may draw some comfort from them, but must check the least inclination of founding our justification upon them. Graces are signs, not causes, of justification. Christ's righteousness only is our wedding-garment, our graces are but as the fringes

of it.   Liberty is a sign the malefactor is pardoned, but it is not the cause of his pardon, but the king's merciful grant.   God is a jealous God, and is likely there to withdraw his hand, where the glory of his works shall be attributed to anything below him, and his gifts made equal with his Son; and therefore as one saith,* in our trials of ourselves we should do as men with a pair of compasses, fix one foot in the centre while they move the other about the circumference; so let our souls rest in Christ, and hold him with one hand, while with the other we turn over the leaves of our hearts, and be inquisitive after our evidences.   Our justification is not by any inherent grace, but our justification is known to us by the grace we find in ourselves.

6. In case we find ourselves not in such a condition as we desire, let us exercise direct acts of faith.   Let us not deject ourselves, and make so bad a conclusion as Peter did, and say to Christ, ' Lord, depart from me, for I am a sinful man;' but let us cast ourselves upon the truth and faithfulness of God in the promise of life in Christ.   Lay hold on the promise of life, as if you had not laid hold of it before.   When comfort is not fetched in by reflex acts, let faith be exercised in direct acts; when there is darkness and no light, ' trusting in the name of the Lord,' and 'staying upon God,' is the proper business of the soul, Isa. l. 10 ; we should then drink of the waters of life, groan under our sin, and go to a Saviour; ' forget,' as Paul, ' the things that are behind, and press forward to the things which are before,' Philip. iii. 13, 14.   We naturally would believe God upon his deed, and trust in him, because we find something wrought in our own souls ; God therefore sometimes hides a man's own ·graces from him, to draw out the soul in acts of faith, which indeed gives the most glory to God.   God will be believed upon his word, and God turns it often to the great advantage of the soul, and puts it upon the exercise of faith, when he denies it the comfortable sight of faith.   In this case we should make use of such Scriptures which may foment and nourish faith, and put us upon the casting out that filth and mud in our souls which we discerned.   When we can find no grace to present Christ with, we should fetch grace from him.   A city of refuge is for a malefactor, a physician for the sick, and a Christ for those that groan under the burden of sin ; a Christ lifted up and dying, for those that are stung by the serpent.

To conclude.   Let us be frequent in this work.   Let us not neglect a privilege God hath invested us with above other creatures below us.   There is nothing can reflect upon itself, inquire into the nature of its own being, but man ; and shall we only resemble the beasts, to see those things which are without us, and not turn our eyes inward, and see what workmanship of God there is in our souls, and what conformity there is between us and our Creator, between us and our Redeemer ?   Shall we put such an affront upon ourselves, as to banish the noblest part of our souls from its proper operation ?   A frequent examination of ourselves would ballast our life, keep faith and repentance fresh and vigorous.   Let us take heed of a spiritual laziness, and saying, ' There is a lion in the way ;' let us remember it is necessary, and though it be difficult, it is not so in itself, but by reason of our averseness to it.   The difficulty may be cured by diligence ; the necessity of it, and the advantages of it, should both inflame our desires to it, and increase our pains in it.   Certainly there can be no more dreadful sign of no grace at all than a neglect of trial whether we have grace or no.   If we examine not ourselves, prove not ourselves whether we be in the faith, we are reprobates, *i. e.* unsound, insincere, not in a state of true Christianity.

* Dr Manton.

A DISCOURSE OF THE KNOWLEDGE OF CHRIST CRUCIFIED.

For I determined not to know any thing among you, save Jesus Christ, and him crucified.—1 Cor. II. 2.

The church of Corinth, to which the apostle directs this epistle, was a church as flourishing in gifts as any, yet as much crumbled into divisions as eminent in knowledge. A year and six months the apostle had been conversant among them, planting and watering with expectation of a plentiful harvest; but no sooner had he turned his back, but the devil steps in and sows his tares. It was a church still, but divided; it had the evangelical doctrine, but too much choked with schismatical weeds.

1. Observe, The best churches are like the moon, not without their spots. The purest times had their imperfections; a pure state is not allowed to this, but reserved for another world.

2. Church antiquity is a very unsafe rule. Other churches, at some distance from the apostles, were as subject to error as this. Pride and ambition were less like to keep out of them than out of Christ's family. Had the history of this church's practices and tenets, without this corrective epistle of the apostle, been transmitted to after ages, they would have been used as a pattern; not the church, but Scripture authority is to be followed. Fathers must not be preferred before apostles; church practices are no patterns, but as they are parallel to the grand and unerring rule.

The apostle, laying to heart the rents, draws up the whole doctrine he had before preached unto them into a short *epitome*, but first declares the manner of his first carriage among them, ver. 1. He came not to them ' with excellency of speech, or of wisdom, declaring unto them the testimony of God.'

To come with man's wisdom,

1. Would detract from the strength and excellency of the word, which, as the sun, shines best with its own beams. The Spirit's eloquence is most piercing and demonstrative, and quickly convinceth a man by its own evidence. Carnal wisdom charms the ear, but this strikes the heart.

2. It detracts from the glory of God, who is more honoured by the simplicity of the gospel than luxuriances of wit. It was his honour, by the doctrine of a crucified Saviour, to nonplus the wisdom of the world; and the glory of his wisdom, as well as strength, to confound, by impotent and weak

men, the power of Satan, which so long had possessed the hearts of the Corinthians.

3. It would be an argument of hypocrisy to use any other arguments than divine. Men in this would but seek themselves, not God's glory. It would be pride to think that their fancies could be more prevalent than evangelical reason; and therefore the apostle would do nothing but endeavour to set out Christ in his own colours, as he hung upon the cross, that their souls might be captivated to the obedience of a crucified Lord.

I determined, Οὐ γὰρ ἔκρινα. I judged it most convenient for me, most profitable for you. It was a resolution taken up deliberately. It was not for want of the knowledge of those principles which are cried up in the world for true wisdom. I understand them as well as others; but what things I counted gain before, I now count loss, for the excellency of the knowledge of Christ, and think it not worth the while and pains to make much inquiry about them.

To know nothing, to believe nothing, to approve of nothing, to make known nothing.

(1.) Not your traditions, which have for themselves the plea of a venerable antiquity, and have been handed to you from your ancestors. What I chiefly determine to know is as ancient as the oldest of those mysteries you so much admire, even ' the Lamb slain from the foundation of the world.'

(2.) Not your philosophical wisdom, so much admired by you and the rest of the world. I come not to teach you a doctrine from Athens, but from Jerusalem, and not so much from Jerusalem, as from heaven. I come to declare him in whom are hid all the treasures of wisdom and knowledge.

(3.) Not your poets, wherein the chief mysteries of your religion are couched. I come to teach him to you which your sybils and their prophetic writings pointed at long ago.

(4.) Not your mysterious oracles, which had so long deluded the world; but I come to declare him by whose death they were silenced.

But Jesus Christ, and him crucified. Christ in the deity and glory of his person; but also as crucified, in the ignominy of his passion, and the advantages of his office.

This is the sum of the gospel, and contains all the riches of it. Paul was so much taken with Christ, that nothing sweeter than Jesus could drop from his lips and pen. It is observed, that he hath the word *Jesus* five hundred times in his epistles.

Others understand it thus : I will know nothing but Jesus Christ, though he were crucified ; I will boast of him whom others despise.

Among you. You Corinthians, though learned, though rich, I would not know anything else among you than Christ, who is the wisdom of God and the treasures of God.

Observe,

1. All human wisdom must be denied when it comes in competition with the doctrine of Christ.

2. Christ and his death is the choicest subject for the wisest ear.

3. As all Christ, so especially his death is the object of faith.

4. As all of Christ, so more especially his death, in all the mysteries of it, ought to be the main subject of a Christian's study and knowledge.

Doct. For the last, as all of Christ, so more especially his death, in all the mysteries of it, ought to be the principal subject of a Christian's study and knowledge. This is the honour of the gospel, and therefore the preaching of the gospel is called the ' preaching of the cross,' 1 Cor. i. 18. Which should be considered by us,

I. In the first spring.
II. In the person suffering.
III. In the fruits of it.

I. In the first spring. His death was ordered by God.

Peter, as the president of the apostles, delivers it as the sense of the whole college of apostles then present: Acts ii. 23, ' He was delivered by the determinate counsel and foreknowledge of God.' It was decreed and enacted in heaven, resolved before time, though done in the fulness of time. Therefore Christ is called ' the Lamb slain from before the foundation of the world,' *determinately*, in the counsel and decree of God ; *promissorily*, in the promise and word of God passed to Adam after the fall ; *typically*, in sacrifices which were settled immediately upon that promise of redemption ; *efficaciously*, in regard of the merit of it, applied by God to believers before the actual suffering. He was made sin, not by us, not only by himself, and his own will, but by God's ordination : 2 Cor. v. 21, ' He hath made him to be sin for us,' by a divine statute, *i. e.* he was ordained to be put into the state and condition of a sinner in our stead ; not into the practical and experimental state of sin, but the penal state of a sinner; to be a sacrifice for it, not to be polluted with it. Indeed, had not God appointed it, it had not been meritorious ; for the merit was not absolute for us, but pactional and conditional. It was capable of meriting, because of the worth and dignity of the person ; but not actually meritorious for us, but upon the covenant transacted between the Father and the Son, that it should be performed by him for us, and accepted by the Father for us, and applied by the Spirit to us.

And as it was appointed by God, it was,

1. An act of his sovereignty. Suppose God might have pardoned sin, and recovered man by his own absolute prerogative, had not his word been passed that, in case of man's transgression, he should die the death. As a word created the earth, and cast it into such a beautiful frame and order, so by one word he might have restored man, and set him upon his former stock, and have for ever kept him from falling again, as he did the standing angels from ever sinning. Yet God pitcheth upon this way, and is pleased with no other contrivance but this, and in a way of sovereignty he culls out his Son to be a sacrifice ; and the Son, putting himself into the state of a surety and Redeemer, is said to have a command given him on the part of God as a sovereign : John xiv. 31, ' As the Father hath given me commandment, even so I do ;' and received by him as a subject, John x. 18. And as God owns him as his servant, Isa. xlii. 1, so he ' took upon him the form of a servant,' Philip. ii. 6, *i. e.* the badge and livery of a servant ; and the whole business he came upon, from his first breath to his last gasp, is called the will of God ; and at the upshot he pleads his own obedience, in ' finishing the work given him to do,' as the ground of his expectations, and the glory promised him, John xvii. 2.

2. An act of the choicest love. God, at the creation, beheld man, a goodly frame of his own rearing, adorned with his own image, beautified with his graces, embellished with holiness and righteousness, and furnished with a power to stand ; and afterwards beheld him ungratefully rebelling against his sovereign, invading his rights, and contemning his goodness, forfeiting his own privileges, courting his ruin, and sinking into misery. So blinded is his mind, as not to be able to find out a way for his own recovery ; so perverse is his will, that instead of craving pardon of his judge, he flies from him, and when his flight would not advantage him, he stands upon his own defence, and extenuates his crime ; thus adding one provocation to another, as if he had an ambition to harden the heart of God against him,

and render himself irrecoverably miserable. God so overlooks these, as in immense love and grace to settle a way for man's recovery, without giving any dissatisfaction to his justice, so strongly engaged for the punishment of the offence. And rather than this notorious rebel and prodigious apostate should perish according to his merit, he would transfer the punishment (which he could not remit without a violation of his truth, and an injury to his righteousness) upon a person equal to himself, most beloved by him, his delight from eternity, and infinitely dearer to him than anything in heaven or earth. Herein was the *emphasis* of divine love to us, that 'he sent his Son to be the propitiation for our sin,' 1 John iv. 10. It was love that he would restore man after the fall ; there was no more necessity of doing this, than of creating the world. As it added nothing to the happiness of God, so the want of it had detracted nothing from it. There was no more absolute necessity of setting up man again after his breaking, than of a new repair of the world after the destructive deluge. But that he might wind up his love to the highest pitch, he would not only restore man, but rather than let him lie in his deserved misery, would punish his own bowels to secure man from it. It was purely his grace which was the cause that his Son ' tasted death for every man,' Heb. ii. 9.

3. An act of justice. As his love to us proposed it, and Christ, out of his affection to the honour of the Father and our welfare, accepted it, and was willing to undertake for us, and interpose between us and divine wrath, to stand in our stead, and bear our sins, so it was then an act of justice to inflict ; for God being the governor of the world, the great lawgiver righteously exacting obedience from his rational creature, upon the transgression of his law becomes a judge, and his rectoral justice demands the punishment due for the transgression to be inflicted upon the offender. To preserve the rights of justice, and to give a contenting answer to the cry of the bowels of mercy, to wipe off, as I may say, the tears of one, and smooth the frowns of the other, God lays our iniquity upon Christ, Isa. liii. 6. Christ takes the punishment upon himself, to bear our sins in his own body on the tree, and becomes responsible for our transgressions. And though he never sinned, nor stood indebted to God in his own person, yet becoming our surety, and being made under the law, putting himself in subjection to the law, and standing in our stead, he put himself also under the obligations of it to punishment. And thus the weight of the whole punishment due to man was laid upon Christ by God as a just judge. That which he could not have from the debtors he might have from the surety, who had put himself under that obligation of payment, and so was bound to undergo all those curses the law might have inflicted upon us ; and pursuant to this obligation, God imputed our iniquities to him, and punished them in him.

II. Consider the person suffering.

1. In regard of his dignity. The Son of God became man ; the Lord of glory emptied himself. It was the Lord of angels that took upon him the nature of a servant ; the Lord of life shed his blood. It was the Son of God that stooped down infinitely below himself into our nature, to be a sacrifice for our redemption ; he that was greater than heaven became meaner than a worm.

2. The willingness of his suffering. He being equal with the Father, could not be commanded to undertake this ; he willingly consented, and willingly accomplished it. He was not driven, as the legal sacrifices were, to the altar. His enemies were not so desirous to make him a sufferer, as himself was ' straitened ' till he was a sufferer, Luke xii. 50. The cup was

as willingly drunk by him as it was tempered by God : and his enemies did not so maliciously ' put him to shame,' as he joyfully endured it, Heb. xii. 2. The desire that the cup might pass from him was the struggles of his human nature ; not an unwillingness in his person, or a repenting of his undertaking this office. It was a natural motion, evidencing the truth of his humanity, and the greatness of what he was to suffer.

3. The greatness of his suffering. His death had all the ingredients of bitterness in it. It was a grievous punishment, because the holiness of God would not have been so manifested in a light one.

(1.) Ignominious. It was a death for slaves and malefactors : for slaves, whose condition rendered them most despicable ; and for malefactors, whose actions had rendered them most abominable. The Lord of heaven endured the punishment of a slave, and was numbered among transgressors. It is called shame, Heb. xii. 2. Each suffering was sharpened with shame ; he was buffeted, spit upon, wounded in his good name, accounted an impostor ; the most odious terms of blasphemer, Beelzebub's agent, &c., were put upon the Son of God.

(2.) Cruel and sharp ; lingering, not sudden ; from his scourging by Pilate to his death was six hours, all that while in much torture ; he suffered from heaven, earth, hell, in his body, in his soul.

(3.) Accursed. As under God's blessing all blessings are included, so under the notion of a curse all punishments are contained : Gal. iii. 13, he was ' made a curse for us.' There must be something more dreadful than a bare outward pain, or bodily punishment ; Christ wanted not courage to support that, as well as the most valiant martyr ; he bore the beginnings of it till he saw a black cloud between his Father and himself. This made him cry out, ' My God, my God,' &c. The agonies of Christ were more than the sufferings of all the martyrs, and all men in the world, since God laid upon him the sins of the whole world.

III. Consider the fruits of this death, which will render it worth our study.

1. The appeasing the wrath of God for us. God was willing to be appeased (hence the sending of Christ is everywhere in Scripture ascribed to the love and grace of God), but his justice was not actually appeased till the death of Christ. As a merciful God, he pitied us ; but as a holy God, he could not but hate our transgression ; as a God of truth, he could not but fulfil his own threatening ; as a God of justice, he must avenge himself for the offence against him. He gave Christ as a God of mercy, and required satisfaction as a God of justice. He ' set him forth as a propitiation, that he might be just,' Rom. iii. 25, 26. His mercy rendered him placable, but his righteousness hindered the actual placation. He had a kindness for man, but could not have a kindness for his sin ; he had bowels for his creature to free him, but no bowels for his transgression to let that go unpunished. That justice whereby he can no more absolve the guilty than condemn the innocent, was an obstacle to the full issues of his mercy. But when an offering for sin was made by an infinite person, and our near kinsman, who had a right of redemption, there was no plea in justice against it, since the sacrifice was complete ; no plea in divine veracity, since the penalty was suffered ; no plea in divine holiness, since that was infinitely manifested ; no bar to mercy to come smiling upon the world. The wrath of God was appeased upon the death of the Redeemer, and this reconciliation is actually applied upon the acceptance of the believer. If God had not been placable, he had never accepted a substitute ; and if he had not been appeased, he had never raised this substitute after his passion, nor ever held out his hand of grace to invite us to be reconciled to him. There is nothing now remains to be done but

our consenting to those terms upon which he offers us the actual enjoyment of it. This crucified Redeemer only was able to effect this work. He was an infinite person, consisting of a divine and human nature; the union of the one gave value to the suffering of the other. The word of God was passed in his threatening; his justice would demand its right of his veracity; a sacrifice there must be to repair the honour of God by bearing the penalty of the law, which could not be done by the strength and holiness of any creature. All the created force in the earth, and the strongest force of the angelical nature, were too feeble for so great a task. Justice must have satisfaction; the sinner could not give it without suffering eternal punishment. He then puts himself into our place to free us from the arrest of justice, and bear those strokes which, by virtue of the law, wrath had prepared for us. The dignity of his person puts a value upon his punishment, and renders it acceptable for us, it being a death superior in virtue to the death of worlds; it was a death which justice required, and at the sight of it justice was so calmed, that the sharp revenging sword drops out of its hand. God hath smelt in it so sweet a savour that hath fully pleased him. He can now pardon the sins of believers with the glory of his righteousness, as well as of his grace. He can legally justify a repenting sinner. God hath been served in the passion of the Redeemer, his justice and holiness were glorified and the law accomplished, the honour of God is salved, and the author of the law righted, the justice of God sweetened. By this propitiation for sin, God is rendered propitious to guilty man, and stretcheth out his arms of love, instead of brandishing his sword of vengeance. The ancient believers lived in the expectation of this, but they beheld not the consummation of it: they thirsted for it, but were not satisfied with it till the fulness of time. It solely depended upon the passion of Christ; it is by the cross that God is reconciled and all enmity slain, Eph. ii. 14. He was then wounded for our iniquities, and being cast into the furnace of divine wrath, quenched the flames; as Jonah, the type, being cast into the raging sea, quelled the storm. He bore our sins by bearing the wrath due to them, and satisfied justice by suffering its strokes. It could not stand with that justice to punish him, if he were not placed in our stead to be the mark and butt of that justice for us and our sins. Doth not then a crucified Christ deserve to be known and studied by every one of us, who hath done that upon the cross which the holy law, sacrifices divinely instituted, the blessed angels, the purity and strength of universal nature, had never been able to effect? He hath expiated our sins, and by his blood hath secured us from the sword of divine vengeance, if we refuse not the atonement he hath made.

2. Silencing the law. Christ crucified, by satisfying the justice of God, brake the thunders of the law, and dissolved the frame of all its anathemas: 'Being made a curse for us, he hath redeemed us from the curse of the law,' Gal. iii. 13, i. e. from the sentence of the lawgiver, denounced in his law against the transgressors of it; so that 'now there is no condemnation to them that are in Christ Jesus,' Rom. viii. 1, because they are 'dead to the law by the body of Christ,' Rom. vii. 4. By the body of Christ as slain and raised again: for this 'handwriting of ordinances, which was contrary to us, is taken out of the way by God, being nailed to his cross,' Col. ii. 14. He hath abolished the obligation of the moral law, as to any condemning power, it being the custom to cancel bonds anciently by piercing the writing with a nail. The ceremonial law was abolished in every regard, since the substance of it was come, and that which it tended to was accomplished; and so one* understands ver. 15, 'Having spoiled principalities and

* Pearson on the Creed, p. 424.

powers, he made a show of them openly,' of the ceremonies of the law, called principalities and powers in regard of the divine authority whereby they were instituted. These he spoiled ; the word ἀπεκδυσάμενος signifies *unclothing*, or unstripping ; he unveiled them, and shewed them to be misty figures that were accomplished in his own person. The flower falls when the fruit comes to appear ; grace and truth came by Jesus Christ, grace to obey the precepts, and truth to take away the types. But it is also meant of the condemning power of the moral law, which was nulled by the death of Christ, who, upon his cross sealing another covenant, repealed the former. The settling a new covenant implies the dissolution of the old. That was nailed to his cross which was contrary to us, a law that was a charge against us, and by virtue whereof we were sued ; and this was the law as sentencing us to death, which was pierced and torn by those nails, that did discover that debt and denounce the sentence, which cannot be meant so properly of the ceremonial as the moral law. The ceremonial law of sacrifices was the gospel in shadows, and appointed for the relief of men, and as a ground whereon to exercise their faith till the appearance of the substance, and therefore cannot be said to be contrary to us, but an amicable discovery, that we are to have that relief in another which we wanted in ourselves ; and that we were to be freed from the sentence of death by some grand sacrifice represented by those sacrifices of animals. Besides, the apostle writes this as a cordial, issuing out of the blood of Christ to the Gentile Colossians, who never were under the obligations of the ceremonial law, that being appropriated to the Jews. The apostle brings it to back his assertion, that their trespasses were forgiven. This argument had been of no use to the Gentiles, who sinned not against the ceremonial law, but the moral law ; and if one only had been cancelled, and not the other, the Jews themselves, whose offences were most against the moral law, had had little or no comfort in having the fewest of their sins forgiven. Our Saviour died by the power and force of the moral law: that brought him to the cross for the fulfilling it in its penalty, as well as he had done in his life by his obedience ; and he receiving the full execution of its sentence upon himself on the cross, as a substitute in our place, nulled that sentence as to any force upon those that believe in him. The plea against it is, that it hath already been executed, though not upon our persons, yet upon our surety ; so that, being nailed to his cross, the virtue of his cross must cease before the killing power of the law can revive. This crucified Christ, who disarmed the law of its thunders, defaced the obligation of it as a covenant, and, as it were, ground the stones upon which it was writ to powder, is worth our exact knowledge and studious inquiry.

3. Upon this must follow the removal of guilt. If God, the judge of the world, be appeased and satisfied; and the law, upon which our accusation is grounded, and which is the testimony of our debt, be cancelled, the removal of our guilt must necessarily follow. And this forgiveness of sin is the chief and principal part of our redemption, and ascribed to his blood as the procuring cause ; Eph. i. 7, ' In whom we have redemption through his blood, even the forgiveness of sin.' He bearing our sins in his own body on the tree, there necessarily follows a discharge of every believer from them. The payment made by the surety is a discharge of the principal debtor from the pursuit of the creditor. As he took away the curse from us by being made a curse, so he took away sin from us by being made sin for us. The taking away the sins of the world was the great end of his coming. There had been no need of his assuming our nature, and exposing himself to such miseries for our relief, had we been only in a *simple* misery, for then we might

have been rescued by his strength; but being in a *sinful* misery, we could not be relieved but by his sacrifice to remove our guilt, as well as by his strength to draw us out of our gulf. Our sin was a bar upon the treasures of divine blessings; this must be removed before those could be opened for us, and could not righteously be removed by bare power, but by a full payment and satisfaction of the debt. It is a violent oppression to free a creditor from the hands of a debtor by force; it is righteous only when it is by legal payment. Well, then, Christ was 'made sin for us,' 2 Cor. v. 21, and that in his death upon the cross; to what end? that sin might remain in its guilt upon us? No; for him to be made sin, and that by God, without respect to the taking away of sin, had been inconsistent with the wisdom and righteousness of God. The justice of God would not permit him to take our debt of another, and yet to charge it upon ourselves. He was therefore 'made sin for us,' that we might 'become the righteousness of God in (or by) him.' He was made sin, that we might be counted without sin, by the imputation of the righteousness of the mediator to us, as if it were our own; that as he represented our persons, and bore our penalty, we might likewise receive the advantages of his righteousness for the acquittal of our debts, the sin of our nature, and the sin of our persons, the removal of the guilt contracted by Adam, and imputed to us, and the guilt contracted by ourselves; for it is 'of many offences unto justification,' Rom. v. 16. He was the true person, figured by the scape-goat, that took away our sins and carried them into a land of forgetfulness, where none dwells to take notice of them, and censure us to death for the crimes. Is not, then, this crucified Christ worth the knowing, who took such heavy burdens upon his own shoulders, that they might not oppress ours, and suffered as a victim in the place of our guilty persons, to 'obtain an eternal redemption for us'? Heb. ix. 14. He that gives so great a ransom for us as that of his life and precious blood, rather than we should remain in our chains, deserves the choicest place in our understanding as well as affections. Were it a bare deliverance, it would challenge this; but he is said not only to deliver us, which speaks power, but to redeem us, which speaks price, and a buying what was passed into the possession of another; a payment of that which we were never able to pay.

4. Another fruit is the conquest of Satan. The empire the devil exercised over man did not arise from any dignity in his person, or any right he had to him in himself, but it was first founded on sin, and granted to him by the justice of God, and was not the power of a prince, but of an executioner. Had not sin first opened the door, his venom could not have infected us, nor his power have hurt us. He could never have been our accuser without some matter of charge from us; nor ever have been our executioner, had we not fallen under the hands of divine justice. His power is erected upon our crimes, whereby he becomes the minister of divine vengeance. But a crucified Christ hath bruised the head of this old serpent, and wounded the prince of this world; he hath displaced him from his power, snatched from him the ground of his indictments, by cancelling the law upon which his accusations are founded; and despoiled him of his office by satisfying divine justice, which conferred an authority upon him of executing divine vengeance: Rev. xii. 10, 'The accuser of the brethren is cast out,' and 'destroyed him that had the power of death,' and that through his own death, Heb. ii. 14, 15. That the devil had not a total power over Adam after the fall, proceeded from the intervention of this surety, and the absolute credit of his future victory over him; yet that promise, that the serpent's head should be bruised, did not, through the weakness of their faith, and the

long delay of performance, preserve them from the fear of death; notwithstanding, that they were all their lifetime subject to bondage; for since the devil's empire was reared upon the ruins of men by sin, he could continually object to them that their sins were not expiated, that death remained as a punishment of sin; but the cross of Christ hath disarmed him of this weapon; his grand plea whereby he kept men in servile fear is completely answered. In bruising our Saviour's heel by the death on the cross, he felt a fatal blow on his head; his conqueror got above him out of his reach, without any hope left in him to touch his heel again. The devil's right was legally taken from him by Christ's death on the cross; the foundation of his authority, viz., sin, was taken away. He was 'destroyed,' that is the apostle's expression, not in his person, but in his authority; he was irrecoverably expelled from his dominion, which he had by his false oracles usurped over the world, John xii. 31; and it is by this crucified Christ that we are more than conquerors over him. And should we not know this crucified Christ, who hath weakened the venom of the serpent, broke the force of the tempter, vanquished him on the cross by the merit of his blood, and conquers him in us by the efficacy of his Spirit?

5. Sanctification is another fruit of the cross of Christ. To be delivered from the guilt of sin, that bound us over to punishment, had been a great favour; but it would not have been a perfect favour without being delivered from the venom of sin that had infected our nature. Though God willed man good by a love of good will, yet he could not delight in him with a love of complacency. If the contagion and filth of sin had deformed and sullied our souls as much as before, if our guilt were only removed, we had been freed from punishment, but without restoring the divine image we had not been fit for any converse with God. It was necessary that our souls should be washed, and our faculties put into a state to serve, in some measure, the glory of God and the end of our creation. God would have seemed to deny his own holiness, if he had regarded only the reverence of his justice, by appointing a sacrifice for atonement, and not consulted the honour of the other by renewing his image in the nature of man. But this is purchased by the death of Christ: 'He came by water and blood,' 1 John v. 6; by blood to expiate our sins, and by water to purify our souls, answerable to the Jewish state wherein it was typified, where there were sacrifices for guilt, and washings for filth. These two things come to us by the death of Christ, the remitting our crime, and the removing of our spot. He gave himself that he might save us, Eph. ii. 25, Titus ii. 14; when he came to purchase the blessings we had forfeited, he would not omit this, which was one of the chief. By him the conscience is purged from dead works, from sin which brought death, and being worse than a pollution by a dead body, hindered us from access to God, as that did from an entrance into the temple. He hath broke our chains, as well as blotted out our crime; healed our natures, as well as procured our pardon; purchased our regeneration, as well as remission. It is by his cross that 'the old man,' which had incorporated himself with our souls, 'is crucified,' Rom. vi. 6. By this he gained the power of sending a saving Spirit, which had not entered into our souls had not Christ's blood flowed out of his veins. The effusion of this blood was the cause of the effusion of the Spirit; it was shed upon us through Christ alone. He hath by suffering for sin on the cross rendered it a detestable thing, and shewed how dreadful that is, that could not receive its fatal wound without a wound first in the heart of the Son of God. This is the most powerful motive to quicken us to a hatred of sin, and a love of holiness, and his life the most illustrious pattern. But all this had been of

little efficacy to us, had not the water of the Spirit flowed out from the rock when it was struck, to cleanse the filthiness of our souls. This is given upon the account of his death to believers, to purify their hearts from the mud of the world, and to form them to a new life for the honour of God; and it is not denied to those that will ask, and seek, and knock, Luke xi. 13. Had Christ only purchased remission without sanctification, it had not been for the honour of God's holiness, nor would our condition have been elevated, heaven had been no place for defilements or slaves. It was necessary the filth of sin should be removed, the dominion of sin be abolished, that we might as holy persons approach to God, and as free men converse with God. Is not a crucified Christ, then, worth the knowing, that hath not only destroyed Satan our enemy without us, but can destroy sin our enemy within us? As he hath snatched us from punishment by expiating our sins, so he can bring us to communion with God by razing evil habits out of our hearts; without this latter, we are not capable of enjoying a complete benefit by the former.

6. Opening heaven for us. What is this life but a wallowing in a sink, a converse in the dregs of creation, in an earth polluted by the sin of man, wherein we every day behold fresh affronts of God, and find motions in us dishonourable to ourselves? But Christ by his death hath provided a better place than this, yea, a place more glorious than Adam's paradise, which was designed for our habitation by the first creation; a place not only built by the word of God, but cemented and prepared by the blood of Christ. By the law against sin we were to have our bodies reduced to dust, and our souls lie under the sentence of the wrath of God. But our crucified Saviour hath purchased the redemption of our body, to be evidenced by a resurrection, Rom. viii. 23, and a standing security of our souls in a place of bliss, to which believers shall have a real ascent, and in which they shall have a local residence, which is called the purchased possession. As Adam brought in the empire of death, so Christ hath brought in the empire of life: Rom. v. 17, ' Shall reign in life by one Jesus Christ.' He hath not purchased for us a paradisaical life, or restored us to the mutable state wherein Adam was created; he hath not linked us for ever to the earth, and the use of the creatures for our support; he hath purchased for us an eternal life, and prepared for us eternal mansions, not only to have the company of men, or the society of the blessed angels, but to be blessed with the vision of God, to reside in the same place where his glorified person is adored by the happy spirits, to ' live with him,' Rom. vi. 8, a life wherein our understandings shall be freed from mists, and our wills from spots, and our affections from disorder. We lost a paradise by sin, and have gained a heaven by the cross. And should not this crucified Christ be studied, who hath settled the regions above for our reception, and procured an entrance into that place which justice, by reason of our sin, had else made for ever inaccessible to us?

I might mention more, as the establishment of the covenant, access to God, perseverance, and the conquest of the world.

Use 1. Let us be thankful to God for a crucified Redeemer.

There is nothing in heaven or earth such an amazing wonder as this, nothing can vie with it for excellence. All love and thankfulness is due to God, who hath given us his Son, not only to live, but to die for us a death so shameful, a death so accursed, a death so sharp, that we might be repossessed of the happiness we had lost. All love and thankfulness is due to Christ, who did not only pay a small sum for us as our surety, but bowed his soul to death to raise us to life, was numbered among transgressors, that we might have a room among the blessed. Our crimes merited our sufferings, but his own bowels made him a sufferer for us ; for us he sweat those drops of blood, for us he trod the wine-press alone, for us he assuaged the rigour of divine justice, for us, who were not only miserable but offending creatures, and overwhelmed with more sins to be hated than with misery to be pitied. He was crucified for us (by his love) who deserved to die by his power, and laid the highest obligation upon us who had laid the highest disobligements upon him. This death is the ground of all our good, whatever we have is a fruit that grew upon the cross. Had he not suffered, we had been rejected for ever from the throne of God, salvation had never appeared but by those groans and agonies. By this alone was God pleased, and our souls for ever pleasured ; without it he had been for ever displeased with us, we had been odious and abominable in his sight, and could never have seen his face. Nothing is such an evidence of his love as his cross ; the miracles he wrought, and the cures he performed in the time of his life, were nothing to the kindness of his death, wherein he was willing to be accounted worse than a murderer in his punishment, that he might thereby effect our deliverance. If he had given us the riches of this world and a greater, had he given us the honour of angels, and made us barons of heaven, without exposing himself to the cross to accomplish it, it had been a testimony of his affection, but destitute of so endearing an emphasis. The manner of procuring is more than a bare kindness in bestowing it ; he testified his resolution not only to give us glory, but to give it us whatsoever it should cost him, and would stick at nothing rather than we should want it. The angels in heaven, in their glistering lustre, are the monuments of his liberality, but not of so supreme an affection as is engraven on the body of his cross.

2. Let us delight in the knowledge of Christ crucified, and be often in the thoughts and study of him. Study Christ, not only as living, but dying ; not as breathing in our air, but suffering in our stead ; know him as a victim, which is the way to know him as a conqueror. Christ as crucified is the great object of faith. All the passages of his life, from his nativity to his death, are passed over in the creed without reciting, because, though they are things to be believed, yet the belief of them is not sufficient without the belief of the cross : in that alone was our redemption wrought. Had he only lived, he had not been a Saviour. If our faith stop in his life, and do not fasten upon his blood, it will not be a justifying faith. His miracles, which prepared the world for his doctrine, his holiness, which fitted himself for his suffering, had been insufficient for us without the addition of the cross ; without this, we had been under the demerit of our crimes, the venom of our natures, the slavery of our sins, and the tyranny of the devil ; without this, we should for ever have had God for our enemy, and Satan for our executioner ; without this, we had lain groaning under the punishment of our transgressions, and despaired of any smile from heaven. It was this death which as a sacrifice appeased God, and as a price redeemed us ; nothing is so strong to encourage us, nothing so powerful to purify us ; how can we be without thinking of it ! The world we live in had fallen upon our heads, had it not been upheld by the pillar of the cross, had not Christ stepped in and promised a satisfaction for the sin of man. By this all things consist ; not a blessing we enjoy but may put us in mind of it ; they were all forfeited by our sins, but merited by his precious blood. If we study it well, we shall be sensible how God hated sin and loved a world ; how much he would part with to restore a fallen creature. He shewed an irresistible love to us, not to be overcome by a love to his own bowels.

(1.) This will keep up life in our repentance. We cannot look upon Christ crucified for us, for our guilt, and consider that we had deserved all that he suffered, and that he suffered not by our entreaty, nor by any obligation from us, but merely from his own love, but the meditation of this must needs melt us into sorrow.   Should we not bleed as often as we seriously thought of Christ's bleeding for us ?   You cannot see a malefactor led to execution for a notorious crime, but you have some detesting thoughts of the fact, as well as some motions of pity to the person.   A strong meditation on Christ will excite compassions for his sufferings, but a detestation of our sins and selves as the cause of it.   It is a ' look upon Christ pierced ' that pierceth the soul, Zech. xii. 10.   Would not this blood acquaint us that the malignity of sin was so great, that it could not be blotted out by the blood of the whole creation !   Would it not astonish us that none had strength enough to match it, but one equal with God !   Would not such an astonishment break out into penitent reflections !   Would not the thoughts of this make us emulate the veil of the temple, and be ashamed that it should outstrip us in rending, while our hearts remain unbroken !   Should we not be confounded, that a lifeless earth should shake in the time of his sufferings, while our reasonable souls stand immoveable !   Could any of the Israelites, that understood the nature and intent of sacrifices, be without some penitent motions, while they saw the innocent victim slain for their sin, not for any fault of its own ; and should we be unmelted, if we considered the cross, the punishment of our crimes, not any of his !

(2.) It would spirit our faith, when we shall see his blood confirming an everlasting covenant, wherein God promises to be gracious.   All the promises centred in the cross, received their life from his death, and are from thence reflected on us.   Where can faith find a vigour but in the royalties of mercy, displayed in the satisfaction of justice ?   Where can it find a life but in the views of its proper object ?   When we behold a Christ crucified, how can we distrust God, that hath in that, as a plain tablet, writ this language, that he will spare nothing for us, since he hath not spared the best he had.   What greater assurance can he give ?   Where is there anything in heaven or earth that can be a greater pledge of his affection ?

(3.) This will animate us in our approaches to God.   Not only a bare coming, but a boldness and confidence in coming to God, was purchased by a crucified Christ, Heb. x. 19.   God was before averse from man, and man unwilling to approach to God.   Now God invites, and man may come ; man calls and God answers.   What can be more encouraging than to consider, that ' by his blood he hath made us kings and priests to God,' Rev. v. 9, 10, to offer up sacrifices with a royal spirit, since the curse which should have fallen upon our heads has been borne by him.   We should think of it every time we go to God in prayer ; it was by this death the throne of God was opened.   This will chase away that fear that disarms us of our vigour.   It will compose our souls to offer up delightful petitions.   It is in this only we see the face of God appeased toward us.

(4.) This will be a means to further us in a progress in holiness.   An affection to sin, which cost the Redeemer of the world so dear, would be inconsistent with a sound knowledge and serious study of a crucified Saviour. We should see no charms in sin, which may not be overcome by that ravishing love which bubbles up in every drop of the Redeemer's blood.   Can we, with lively thoughts of this, sin against so much tenderness, compassion, grace, and the other perfections of God, which sound so loud in our ears from the cross of Jesus ?   Shall we consider him hanging there to deliver us from hell, and yet retain any spirit to walk in the way which leads thereto? Shall we consider him upon the cross, unlocking the gates of heaven, and yet turn our backs upon that place he was so desirous to purchase for us, and give us the possession of? Shall we see him groaning in our place and stead, and dare to tell him by our unworthy carriage that we regard him not, and that he might have spared his pains? It must be a miserable soul, worse than brutish, that can walk on in ways of enmity, with a sense of a crucified Christ in his mind. Could we then affect that sin which appears so horrible in the doctrine of the cross? Can we take any pleasure in that which procured so much pain to our best friend? Can we love that which hath brought a curse, better than him who bore the curse for us? For want of this study of Christ crucified, we walk on in sin, as if he suffered to purchase a license for it, rather than the destruction of it. The due consideration of this death would incline our wills to new desires and resolutions. It would stifle that luxury, ambition, worldliness, which harass our souls. We should not dare to rush into any iniquity through the wounds of Christ; we should not, under a sense of his dying groans, cherish that for which he suffered; we should not do the works of darkness under the effusions of his blood, if we did in a serious posture set ourselves at the feet of his cross.

(5.) This will be the foundation of all comfort. What comfort can be wanting, when we look upon Christ crucified as our surety, and look upon ourselves as crucified in him; when we can consider our sins as punished in him, and ourselves accepted by virtue of his cross? It was not an angel which was crucified for us, but the Son of God; one of an equal dignity with the Father; one that shed blood enough to blot out the demerit of our crimes, were they more than could be numbered by all the angels of heaven, if all were made known to them. He was not crucified for a few, but for all sorts of offences. When we shall see judgments in the world, what comfort can we take without a knowledge and sense of a crucified Christ! What a horror it is for a condemned man to see the preparation of gibbets, halters, and executioners! But when he shall see a propitiation made for him, the anger of the prince atoned, the law some other way satisfied, and his condemnation changed into remission; all his former terrors vanish, and a sweet and pleasing calm possesseth him. With this knowledge and sense we should not be much terrified at the approaches of death in our last gasps, when we consider itself gasping under the weight of the cross. The blood of Christ is as a balsam dropped upon the points of the arrows of death. That, by removing the guilt of sin, pulled out the sting of death. When we tremble under a sense of our sins, the terrors of the judge and the curses of the law, let us look upon a crucified Christ, the remedy of all our miseries. His cross hath procured a crown, his passion hath expiated our transgression. His death hath disarmed the law, his blood hath washed a believer's soul. This death is the destruction of our enemies, the spring of our happiness, the eternal testimony of divine love. We have good reason, as well as the apostle, to determine with ourselves, ' to know nothing but Jesus Christ, and especially him crucified.'

A DISCOURSE OF OBEDIENCE.

Ye are my friends, if ye do whatsoever 1 command you.—JOHN XV. 14.

THE words are a part of Christ's discourse after the supper he had instituted. The chapter begins with a parable, wherein Christ likens himself to a vine, and the disciples (and consequently all believers) to branches. The using this parable was occasioned, as some think, by Christ's passing by some vineyards, whence he raises a discourse to spiritualise their meditations upon the view of the creatures. Whether this were so or no, yet the discourse is excellent, both to shew the near union and relation of Christ and believers, and the way and means of a spiritual growth in sanctification and holiness. Christ was sent into the world to publish a new religion, but not a lazy, but a fruitful one. God the Father is the husbandman, who both dresseth the vine, and purgeth the branches to render them fruitful. Several arguments he useth to engage them to abide in him, and consequently to be fruitful.

(1.) From their misery without it, ver. 6. The fire is the portion of unfruitful branches. 'If a man abide not in me, he is cast forth as a branch, and is withered, and men gather them, and cast them into the fire.'

(2.) From the prevalency of their prayers with God, if his words did practically and fruitfully abide in them. Ver. 7, 'If you abide in me, and my words abide in you, you shall ask what ye will, and it shall be done unto you.'

(3.) From the glory of God and honour of Christ which are furthered by it, ver. 8. When what you ask is in order to your own fruitfulness and consequently God's glory, you need not fear the grant of your requests. 'Herein is my Father glorified, that you bear much fruit ; so shall you be my disciples.'

(4.) From gratitude; since he had given them, and was yet further to give them, the highest demonstration of his affection to them, ver. 9. You have had evidence of my Father's love to me, in his witnessing my mission from heaven by multitudes of miracles, and such a kind of love as my Father bears to me, I do, and will bear to you if you continue to be my disciples. And all the proof of it I demand of you is, the continuance of my commands and the performance of them : ver. 10, 'If you keep my commandments, you shall abide in my love, as I have kept my Father's will, and abide in his love.' If you would have such a kind of love from me as I have had from my Father, you must perform such a kind of obedience to me as I have performed to my Father ; you must make me a pattern of imitation, and my precept the rule of your actions. And ' do not think,' saith he, ver. 11, that what I have spoken of to you is so much out of an authority or an imperiousness, as out of an affection to you and your interest. It is not that I should have an advantage, but that you should have a joy ; that such a joy as you have felt in my presence with you, and in my redeeming work, may constantly remain in you. Now the way to have this joy is to keep my commandments. Fruitfulness will clear up your interest in me, and especially the observance of that command of a mutual love to one another, ver. 13, for ' greater love can no man shew than to lay down his life for his friend ;' and you shall see I will not go backward to discover the highest affection to you ; and as I discover my affection to you in laying down my life, so you can discover your affection to me only by observing my commands.

So that the verse lies between two arguments to urge them to it.

(1.) His own love to them, which was of the highest stamp, ver. 13.

(2.) The revelation he had made to them, which was the fullest, ver. 15. ' All things that he had heard of his Father,' and the clearest, those that he had made known to them ; so that you have my love to oblige you, and my revelation to direct you. As I have had love to purchase what you want, so you must have love to perform what I order : ' Ye are my friends if ye do whatsoever I command you.' He invites them to it by an honourable title of friends. You shall be ranked in the number of them, and continue in this dignity, if you keep my commands. I do not press this of loving one another, that you should perform this only and neglect the rest, for you are not my friends in the practice of one of my precepts unless you join the practice of other precepts to it.

Ye are my friends. Actively, you will declare and manifest yourselves to be my friends in conforming yourselves to my mind. Passively, I will declare myself to you. I have treated you as friends* in imparting the counsels of God to you, not known to others. It is fit you should treat me as your friend in gratifying me in obedience to my commands. The dignity of a friend to Christ may well soften the hardness of a command. He doth not so call them friends as that they should forget that they are his servants and he their Lord ; for as he mentions friendship as their privilege, so he mentions his will by the way of a command to make them sensible of their duty : ' If you do whatsoever I command you.' It is a great honour (saith Austin) to call those his friends whom he knows to be his servants.

Ye.

1. All of ye. It is universal. Men are too narrow to have many intimates, but the heart of Christ is large enough for all. Friendship with Christ is the privilege of every obedient person.

2. Ye, though poor, considered as men. Outward distress is no hindrance to spiritual relation.

3. Ye disciples, apostles employed for God, yet not my friends unless you obey me. Not gifts, but grace ; not the highest employment, but exact practice interests men in this privilege.

Are, not *shall be*. *You are* doth not exclude the future, but assures them of it. They shall be because they are. It is not a thing to be waited for, but at present possessed.

If you do whatsoever I command you. Adam had a precept,† which, if he had kept, he had continued in the love of God ; and Christ hath given us precepts which, if we keep, we shall continue in the love of Christ. Obedience is necessary, not by way of merit, but condition. He shews how grateful

* Muscul. † Ibid.

obedience is to him, because he dignifies the practiser of it with such a title, which how honourable is it for us, and how necessary for our welfare.

The text is made up of privilege and duty, relation and action.

1. Privilege and relation : *friends*.

2. Duty and action : *if ye do*.

Observe, 1, how glorious is the relation of a holy soul to Christ ! He doth not say, I love you if you keep my commandments. A man may love his servant or his beast, but admits them not to special friendship ; the condition of the one and the incapacity of the other will not suffer it. This title is higher than an assurance of a bare love ; he loves them as friends as well as servants.

2. How condescending is the love of Christ ! He calls the worms of the earth the friends of God. We cannot be his servants unless we keep his commands ; and by keeping his commands we commence a higher degree than that of servants, even that of friends.

3. Christ's commands, not his deeds, are the object of our obedience. Set not before you what I do, but what I order you to do. Our conformity to Christ consists not so much in an imitation of what he did as in an obedience to what he prescribes ; the example of Christ is not our rule without the precept of Christ. Some actions of Christ are unimitable, but all his commands are obeyable.

4. Privilege is entailed only to duty.

That which I intend is only the nature of obedience, as deducible from these words, ' If ye do whatsoever I command you.'

1. *Do*.

(1.) Obedience must be positive. Not only avoid what I prohibit. It consists not merely in not bringing forth bad fruit, but in bringing forth good. It is not enough to forbear the commissions of sin, if we are guilty of the omissions of duty. The fig-tree was not cursed because it brought forth bad fruit, but because it brought forth no fruit, Mat. xxi. 19. No father will be content with his child in forbearing what he forbids, unless he also performs what he prescribes. Many, like the pharisees, please themselves with negatives, I am not profane, a drunkard, swearer ; but what title is procured to the privilege in the text, if as much cannot be spoken of positives as may be of negatives ? We must be as careful to do what he wills, as to shun what he hates. He never 'puts off the old man' cordially, that hath not also put on the new, Col. iii. 8, 10. It is not a true friendship to omit what may displease a friend, if we do not also what may gratify him. God would have an obedience from us suitable to the happiness he promiseth us. He doth not only free us from hell and wrath, but invest us with heaven and happiness, so he would have us not only delivered from sin but created to good works. And you know that our Saviour is not only called Jesus because he 'saves from sin,' Mat. i. 21, but Christ, because he is appointed by God to govern, fit, and prepare souls for heaven.

(2.) Do it as friends. Obedience must be sincere. An action may look like a friendly act when there is nothing of friendship and good will in the heart. Every precept requires not only an outward but an inward conformity, not only a bodily action but a spiritual frame. God would not have the skin of a sacrifice without the flesh and entrails, nor the carcase of obedience without truth in the inward parts, Ps. li. 6. Christ intends not only an outward appearance, but respects the form of every action. Duties are not differenced by the outward garb, but inward frame. Waters may have the same colour, yet one may be sweet and the other brackish. Two apples may have the same colour, yet one may be a crab, and the other of a delightful relish. A serpent hath a speckled skin, but an inward poison. We must look to the rule, that the matter of our actions be suited to it, otherwise we may commit gross wicke ss, as they did who thought they did God good service by killing hi. righteous servants, John xvi. 2. We must also look to the frame of our hearts, otherwise we may be guilty of gross hypocrisy. A friendly action cannot come from the heart of an enemy, no more than good fruit from a corrupt tree. It may have a specious appearance when the heart is rank, as a man with a stinking breath holding a perfume in his mouth smells sweet; the sweetness is not from his breath, but the perfume, which takes not away the foulness of his stomach, or the corruption of his lungs. Christ cannot count any service from a rotten heart of any worth. A multitude of them are but as cyphers, signify nothing without a figure in the front: Prov. x. 20, ' The heart of a wicked man is little worth.' Sound actions cannot spring from a corrupt heart, no more than sweet water from a bitter fountain. He that considers not how his heart stands, whether it were wound up, whether it were in tune, whether it were melted, or whether it were frozen, that doth not care how drowsy and unsavoury his spirit was, doth not anything as a friend to Christ.

(3.) Do as friends; obedience must be affectionate. It must be love ' out of a pure mind,' 1 Tim. i. 5. In the command of charity, which is the special command before the text, the greatest outward assistances are of no value without this ingredient, but the least with it are highly accepted. A cup of cold water, Mat. x. 42, a little box of ointment with an affectionate respect to God, are valued and registered. As mercies are not welcome to a good man without God's love in them, so our services are not welcome to God without our love in them. A little bread and drink with God's love is better than great riches with his displeasure. Job's boils and rags with God's love were richer than his enemies' robes, and a starving Lazarus better than a rich epicure. A drop of service with affection to God is more worth than all the works of men without it. It is no argument of friendship for a man to send a rich cabinet to another with something in it, to which he knows his friend hath an antipathy. Splendid services to Christ without glowing affections are of the same nature. Christ would have us imitate him; he gives himself with his special mercies, and we must give ourselves with our special duties. But how often are some duties performed, not out of love to Christ, but love to ourselves? Judas his carrying the bag might be one cause of Judas his obedience to Christ, that he might get some advantage by it; and when he saw a greater offered by the pharisees, he deserted and betrayed him. *Fac me Episcopum Romanum,* saith one, *et ero Christianus.* When men pretend service to God to catch preferments from men, when they make a profession of religion to cheat more craftily, *Ut sub Christiano nomine lucrosius pereant,* this is not to do what Christ commands, but what we affect.

(4.) *Do.* Not be constrained to do, but do willingly, freely. What Paul would not have servants give to their masters, Eph. vi. 6, that many men give to God, an eye-service. While men have some serious thoughts of God's omniscience, they may pay him some service, as a servant may work while his master's eye is upon him or his feet at the door, but make a mock at him when his back is turned. Or they may do it out of fear of judgment. This may be a motive to quicken, but not the spring to give the first life to our obedience. A man may be very free in obedience, but upon a wrong motive, as schoolboys may get their lessons well one day, not out of love to their books, but that they may play the next; or as a child at play, called by his father to go upon an errand, runs faster than his father would have him, puts himself all in a sweat. This might be thought a very free and willing obedience, but it is not so much obedience to his father as a gratifying himself in a speedy return to his game, and pursuance of it without any more disturbance. Or there may be a readiness when an obedience will suit to corruption. This is such an obedience as the devil is for. He was much for Job's trial, which God was also for. God orders him to deprive Job of his estate, that thereby his sincerity might be evidenced to the world, and the devil conforms himself to God's order out of malice to ruin him, hoping that hypocrisy would issue out instead of sincerity.

[1.] There is a freedom as opposed to constraint. It is not the act itself, but the naturalness of it, is a sign of obedience. A constrained obedience may consist with a devillish nature, and therefore cannot be a sign of a friendship to Christ. The devil obeys God, but by force; he is forced to a negative obedience, and sometimes to a positive obedience, not by any conscience of a command, but by a constraint by God's power; as Luke viii. 28, when Christ commanded him to come out of his long-possessed habitation. There may be a constraint by education, which is scarce sensible, when that upon a profane man is more visible. As a rugged stone will move no further than a strong arm will throw it, so a profane man moves no farther than his conscience, or some fear of man, throws him in any duty of obedience. But a man that hath the advantage of a religious education is like a stone smoothed into a right figure, that moves upon a plain at the least touch, yet there is constraint goes to that motion, though not so sensible, because the parts are by an outward smoothness fitted for such a motion; so it is with a man that is smoothed by education.

But the obedience Christ requires is to be free. Good actions are therefore called fruits of righteousness, fruits of holiness; because as a tree brings forth fruits naturally, so doth a true Christian bring forth righteousness. The gardener helps, indeed, by watering and digging, but doth not constrain the tree. God helps the man at the first conversion, but doth not force the soul. In Gal. v. 19, 22, it is observed that sins are called works, and graces called fruits, to shew the freedom of a holy, and the servile frame of a wicked, man. A good man is not put upon a duty merely by a sudden fit and importunity of conscience; as wicked men naturally lay in provision for their lusts, so do good men labour to lay in provision for their obedience and graces. The law, like a schoolmaster, scourgeth some truant souls to obedience, but the gospel gives a willingness of spirit in the day of power, Ps. cx. 3. The difference between these two powers is, the law is a powerful constrainer, mixed with severe threatenings that drive to fear, and the gospel is a powerful constraint, mixed with kind promises which help to love.

[2.] Freedom, as opposed to dulness and heaviness. God's delight in a holy person is rendered as one reason of his mercy: Ps. xviii. 19, 'He delivered me, because he delighted in me;' and our delight in Christ should be the reason of our duty. 'If ye do whatsoever I command you.' It is not a lumpish and heavy action that Christ requires; he requires such an obedience of us as himself performed to his Father: John xv. 10, 'If you keep my commandments, you shall abide in my love, as I have kept my Father's commandments, and abide in his love.' That was not a heavy motion; it was his 'meat and drink to do his Father's will,' John iv. 34. Meat and drink are not only naturally desired, but delightfully received. Cheerfulness accompanies election of a thing: Ps. cxix. 173, 174, 'I have chosen thy precepts, and thy law is my delight.' Lumpishness is a sign we never chose it, but were forced to it. Sin is sweet to a wicked man, as a dainty to a glutton's palate, Job x. 12. He accounts duty his burden, and a true disciple accounts it his honour. He, like the sun, rejoiceth to run, and when he is in service, his heart cries out, with Peter in the mount, ' It is good to be here.' Such cheerfulness in service procures cheerfulness in mercies : Isa. lxiv. 5, ' Thou meetest him that rejoiceth and works righteousness.' He puts to his hand to help such an one. Christ loves not melancholy and phlegmatic service ; such a temper in acts of obedience is a disgrace to God and to religion : to God, it betrays us to have jealous thoughts of God, as though he were a hard master ; to religion, it makes others think duties are drudgeries, and not privileges. Well, then, so much of cheerfulness in obèdience, so much of a Christian temper ; so much of dulness, so much of an antichristian frame.

The disciples of Christ have not this liveliness in a constant equality. The wings of the soul drenched in sin, as well as the wings of a bird bemired, will flag. A good man's heaviness is from infirmities and distempers. A strong, active man may be laid upon his sickbed, and be loath to be stirred, but a carnal man's heaviness is from nature and willingness. A wicked man's heaviness is at his duty, a good man's heaviness is at his own deficiency ; his delight consists in the spirit, for the flesh is weak, and will never in this world be otherwise.

(5.) Do *whatsoever*, &c. Not lazily ; obedience must be diligent. God cares not for a slow obedience ; he would not therefore have an ass offered in sacrifice, Exod. xiii. 13, but would have it redeemed with a lamb, or the neck of it broke. A true Christian is like a seraphim, that hath six wings to fly upon God's errands, Isa. vi. 2 ; or like the living creatures, Ezek. i. 14, that ran and returned at the appearance of a flash of lightning, which is the quickest motion. Sound members move at the command of the will, whereas palsy members must be dragged along. Man naturally would have a ready God, and not a ready heart ; he would have a God ready to attend his complaints, but would not have a heart ready to attend God's commands. But good men take God at a word of precept, when he hath any work for them to do, as well as at a word of promise, when they have any wants for him to supply. Hypocrites may be obedient in promises, as the son in the Gospel, Mat. xxi. 29, 30, that promised to go into the vineyard. A good man doth more without open resolving, another resolves more without open doing. A master will take it ill if a servant disputes his commands. Paul set about the work he was ordered quickly : Gal. i. 16, ' I consulted not with flesh and blood ;' he called not flesh and blood into a cabinet council. What we do for Christ, we must do without advising with corruption, which is an enemy to God and his ways. Such counsellors will furnish us with evasions to slip from our duty, and represent things either impossible or unseasonable ; either that it cannot be done at all, or else it may be done better at another time ; and as it is said of our own nation, we lose more by treaties than we gain by war, so it may be said of our corruption, we lose more by such treaties than we gain by an open war against it. God would employ Moses though he had a slow speech, but checks him for his slow obedience. Abraham was as quick in his observance of God's command as Moses was slow : Gen. xvii. 23, ' The self-same day' wherein he had received the command of circumcision he put it in practice ; he would make no pauses, lest carnal reason should step in with objections. The readiness of the Gentiles to obey Christ is expressed : Ps. xviii. 44, ' As soon as they hear of me, they shall obey me ;' like Elisha, who, upon Elijah's spreading his mantle over him, leaves his father, and oxen, and plough, and runs after him. The more of fire there is in anything, the more active it is ; the more of a divine Spirit, the more vigorous.

(6.) Do *whatsoever*, &c., constantly; not do it for a spurt, or by fits and starts. Obedience must be constant; it is that which God longs for: Deut. v. 29, ' Oh that there were such a heart in them, that they would keep all my commandments always, that it might be well with them!' and it will never be well with a man till he doth it.

[1.] In sinning times it should be most conspicuous. Good men should ' shine as lights in the midst of a crooked and perverse generation,' Philip. ii. 15. The stars shine clearest in the darkest, if unclouded, nights. Good men are like fountains, hottest in the coldest seasons. When did David love and esteem God's precepts, but when men had made void his law? Ps. cxix. 126–128. He would double his valuation of, and obedience to, God's commands, when he saw them most violated by others. He brings in a double *Therefore*, ' Therefore I love thy commandments above gold; therefore I esteem all thy precepts concerning all things to be right.' The more men despised them, the more he valued them, because he knew they were most dear to God, since they were most hateful to man. David had been refreshed by God when he was afflicted, and he would most please God when he was dishonoured. Wisdom, *i. e.* Christ, justifies her children in the sight of her adversaries; they should therefore justify wisdom in the sight of her enemies. Christ would have his people bear witness, by their profession and practice, against the sins of the times, as well as he will judge and condemn the world at last with them by their approbation. Thus Joseph of Arimathea would go boldly to Pilate to beg the body of Jesus, though the malice of the age had risen so high as to put him to death, when he was never mentioned in Scripture till that action. Sinful times increase the wickedness of the wicked, but strengthen the graces of the godly, for they make them more watchful, and watchfulness makes them the more practical. We then declare ourselves most the friends of Christ, when we own him among a multitude of enemies. Opposition makes God take notice of our obedience in a special manner. Probably Judas his repining at Mary's kindness in anointing Christ, was the occasion that the scent of that ointment was spread about the world.

[2.] In suffering times. In suffering times from God, as in desertion. Christ's obedience was eminent, he would obey God when God had forsaken him. A true disciple is not, like Saul, impatient to wait upon God when he hides his face, and run to a witch for counsel: ' Though he slay me, yet will I trust in him,' Job. xiii. 15. To obey Christ when he manifests his love, is obedience to ourselves; to obey him when he veils himself, is pure love and obedience to him.

In suffering times from men. Many would be obedient to their advantage; but to be obedient to death, is the property of a true disciple, Rev. iii. 21, as it was of his Master, Philip. ii. 8. Misery makes men oftener forget their virtues than their vices. Many are like the Jews, to cry *Hosanna* when Christ rides in triumph; and presently after, when he is condemned, either fly from him or vote against him; like snakes that come out of their holes in a hot day to sun themselves, and at night retreat to skulk in their caverns. Many come to live by Christ, but not die for him. Shame, mocks, scoffing, did not hinder Christ from dying for us; why should shame and reproaches hinder us from dying for Christ. The apostle speaks of cleaving to that which is good, Rom. xii. 9, κολλώμενοι; things glued are not easily separated. We should cleave so close to him that nothing should part us from him. Wind will not blow a snail, or any other glutinous substance, off a tree.

Well, then, constancy is an ingredient in the obedience Christ requires. His trees bring forth fruit in old age, Ps. xcii. 14. Age makes other things decay, but makes a Christian flourish. Some are like hot horses, mettlesome at the beginning of a journey, and tired a long time before they come to their journey's end. A good disciple, as he would not have from God a temporary happiness, so he would not give to God a temporary obedience ; as he would have his glory last as long as God lives, so he would have his obedience last as long as he lives. Judas had a fair beginning, but destroyed all in the end by betraying his Master.

2. The subject of this doing. *Ye*, it must be the whole man. Not *do* with a part of yourselves, but your whole selves ; there must be a resigna- of the whole soul to God. The tables of the law were written on both sides, Exod. xxxii. 15, 16, so must obedience be upon every faculty. Ahab, Herod, and the stony ground were partial in their obedience, like 'Ephraim, a cake not turned,' Hosea vii. 8, baked on one side and dough on the other ; *Intus Nero, foras Cato*, saith Jerome. But our obedience to Christ must answer our former enmity ; as that was spread over the whole soul, so must this. There must be an enlightened understanding, flexible will, tender conscience, regulated affections, watchful members to go upon the errands of God. As the father said to the prodigal, ' All that I have is thine,' so must the soul to Christ, Lord, all that I have is thine, understanding, will, affections, &c. The holocausts among the Israelites were wholly burnt ; so are we wholly to sacrifice ourselves.

3. The object. *Whatsoever*, Ὅσα, as many things as I command you. Not think it enough to perform one or two, but every one whatsoever. And so he taught the apostles to teach others, Mat. xxviii. 20. Christ performed every command of his Father, and we must perform every command of Christ. He is not a man after God's own heart that doth not ' fulfil all his will,' it is David's commendation that he did so, Acts xiii. 22. Josiah hath the same character left upon record, both for the universality of the subject, and the universality of the object : 2 Kings xxiii. 35, ' He turned to the Lord with all his soul, according to all the law of Moses.' An habitual disposition there must be, that must pass into act, where a particular command, and an opportunity of observing it, meet together. No command but is so good, so just, so holy, that it deserves our compliance with it in the highest pitch, and when we cannot equal it we are to bewail our defects. Obedience is quite out of tune if any one command be slighted. The lute is incapable of making music if one string, the treble, be broken. When the people went to gather manna on the Sabbath, and so broke the law, God taxes them with a violation of the whole, Exod. xvi. 27, 28. To neglect any one command is disingenuous. Would we have all our sins pardoned, and shall we not be willing to have all God's commands performed ? It is also dangerous. If a man be to go ten miles, and only go nine of them, he had as good never have set out, he will never come to his journey's end.

(1.) Whatsoever I command you, in the true meaning and design of it. Not like the pharisees, who, though they do not blot out the law, yet enervate it by false glosses and interpretations, and so make it insignificant, taking away the life and soul of a command.

(2.) Whatsoever I command you, though it may seem mean and low in the eyes of men. As Christ did not think anything too low to do for us, we must not think anything too mean to do for him. Whatsoever is accounted vile that is for the honour of Christ, we should endeavour to be more vile in it. We have David's vote for it, that it was ' better to be a doorkeeper in the house of God, than to dwell in the tents of wickedness.' The least duty must be performed ; art shews itself most in little works, so doth grace its excellency in the performance of the least commands. *Natura triumphat in minimis*, a fly shews God's power as well as the world. The least mite in sincerity is acceptable to God, as well as the greatest hecatomb, or a sacrifice of the beasts upon a thousand hills. The least command should be as dear to a gracious soul as the greatest. We are not to waive the greatest because of its difficulty, nor despise the least because of its littleness. A jewel is not accounted vile because it is little, nor should a command because it is mean. He that breaks the least command, shall be least in the kingdom of heaven.

4. The person commanding: ' Whatsoever *I* command you.'* The authority of Christ must be eyed in all obedience, and his command be made the rule. When we do the matter of the law, without an eye to the authority that enacts, it is an obedience to the law, but not to the lawgiver. Men may perform the matter of a law, yet despise the authority of the lawgiver in their hearts. We are not so much to consider, saith Jerome, *imperii quantitatem*, as *imperantis dignitatem*. We are not only to observe Christ as a friend, but obey him as a sovereign. He that is the king's friend must not forget that he is also the king's subject. What he doth as a friend in a way of kindness, he must perform also as a subject in a way of duty. We must glorify Christ as Christ, *i. e.* in all the relations wherein he stands to us. Now he is not only our Saviour, but our king, and we are not only his friends, but his servants. What we receive from God should be received as from him : 1 Thess. ii. 13, ' Ye received the word as the word of God.' What we do to God, should be done as to him, suitable to his divine greatness and majesty. Obedience must be performed because Christ commands, and as Christ commands it.

Use 1. It informs us of the excellency of the Christian religion. It demands the greatest purity, and confers the greatest privilege. It brings us to the rule of God, and invests us with the friendship of our Creator. No religion hath so much of benefit, and so much of duty. Nothing enforceth such exactness in the ways of God. Nothing bestows so much of happiness upon the creature. In other religions something is indulged to gain proselytes, and carnal rewards are proposed to invite them. The precepts of this are holy and the rewards high ; other religions consist in negatives, this in positives. The gospel discovers more sin, and exacts more holiness. It affords us matter of love, not fear, for our principle ; not force to constrain, but grace to persuade. Gospel obedience is not the fruit of bondage, but the fruit of love and friendship.

2. Obedience is our privilege as well as our duty. It admits us into the friendship of Christ. The bitterest duty is sugared with this unspeakable comfort. Those that stand idle in the market-place meet with no such reward. It is no small honour to be a king's friend ; how unconceivable is the honour to be a friend of Christ ! ' In keeping his commands there is great reward.'† This is a reward above the highest descent. Enoch was descended but the seventh from Adam, yet this was not his honour, but his walking with God. To be a friend of Christ in rags, is a greater honour than to be king of the whole world in purple robes. Jerome, speaking of a Roman senator, saith, He was noble, not because *Consularis*, but *Christianus*. The very act of an holy obedience gives a sweeter reflection than all the pleasures of the world. Christ, indeed, calls the gospel a yoke, but an easy one. He calls it a yoke, as natural men think it, not as gracious men

* 'Εγώ emphatically added.
† Imperium Dei beneficium est.—*Hierom.*

find it, for it is a privilege more than a yoke. Christ discovers the glory of his love in the heart, as God did the glory of his presence in the temple.

3. How inexcusable are disobedient professors. The greater the honour proposed as an invitation, the greater the sin in refusing the terms upon which that honour may be enjoyed. It had been worth the enduring the torments of some thousands of years, to come at last to the privilege of being the friends of Christ. But no such thing is required; it is not parting with the first-born of our bodies, or searching out thousands of rams, or ten thousands of rivers of oil; it is not suffering the flames of hell for a finite multitude of years; no impossible or rigid penances are enjoined; only 'Do whatsoever I command you,' and his 'commands are not grievous' in the experience of those that have tried them, 1 John v. 3. What an unreasonable thing is it not to part with dung for gold, with rags for robes, with misery for happiness, with hell for heaven, with sin for Christ! He that would refuse to be a prince's favourite upon the performance of an easy task, deserves, without pity, to be spurned out of the court; and what excuse can that person have that will not exchange the slavery of the devil for the friendship of the Redeemer? Can any blame Christ at last for refusing any relation to them, and bidding them depart from him, when they here refused his friendship, and would have nothing to do with him?

4. How much comfort and encouragement may be drawn from hence under all reproaches. Who would regard the barking of dogs in the doing of that which hath an excellent honour entailed upon it? The devil regards not the opinions men have of him; he looks not upon their curses as his loss, because he is of an higher nature; he pursues his business. Shall a diabolical nature slight that which a divine nature shall not surmount? Shall not curses here, and torments at the end, discourage him from venting his malice against God, and prosecuting his devilish designs? and shall reproaches discourage any from that obedience which is attended with so great an honour? What is it to be reproached and scorned here a little time, while the favour of God is enjoyed, and after a few nights' sleep we are to be raised out of the dust to glory, to enjoy his friendship for ever, and to be in glory where he is? This would be a support when the bullets fly fast about our ears. It is impossible to be faint-hearted with lively thoughts of so great an honour. Weigh seriously this honour, and then weigh the obstructions, and see whether the latter be not overbalanced by the former. Would a glorified saint, incarnate again in the world, decline the practice of obedience upon such a gallant encouragement, because of reproaches? Men might as soon persuade him to fry in hell as to part with so great an honour upon so light an opposition. The rolling of a black cloud over a traveller's head will not cause him to break off a necessary journey to court, to become the king's friend or his son-in-law.

5. What an incentive have we, then, to an exact obedience! This is the delight of Christ, and so high a delight to him that he thinks fit to reward it with no less than a special friendship. Christ looked upon the young man's morality with an eye of love, much more will he upon an evangelical obedience. It is not the pomp of the world, or the glittering vanities man's heart runs after, that can lay any claim to this dignity. Obedience, though low, if sincere, is the delight of Christ. He loves to go into his vineyard and look upon the 'tender grapes,' as well as upon the 'ripe fruit,' Cant. vii. 12; viii. 2. It is by this you shew yourselves the friends of Christ; by this you maintain his honour in the world. This is a silent conviction upon others, and makes them have some veneration for religion. Men judge

usually of principles by practices, and you never heard any speak against the principles of religion, but they first fell upon the practice of the professors of it. It is by this obedience we glorify God and Christ, Mat. v. 16, *i. e.* make others speak well of the ways of religion. Let this honour of being the friends of Christ engage us to obedience as the means. It is a shame for such that may attain such a privilege to pursue anything lower; an Alexander watches for kingdoms. It is a poor-spirited Domitian that loves to catch flies. How many will conform to men's principles, to their will, for a small reward, yea, for no reward; and shall not we conform to our Redeemer's will for so glorious a title? We must first be Jacobs, supplanters of vice, before we be Israels, seers of God.

Let us close all with a few directions.

(1.) Let us walk as those that have the eye of Christ upon us, to see whether we act as friends to him or no. Let us consider in every action that it is registered by conscience, laid up in Christ's remembrance, and will be censured by him either as the act of a friend or an enemy. Men look upon the bark of the action; this may appear fair, and have a gloss upon it: Christ looks upon the inward part, upon the spirit, to see how the heart is conformed to the command. We may hide our deformities from men, but not from an all-seeing eye. Now I am going to this or that action, I have a watchful eye over me that pierceth into all my thoughts, discovers the principles whereby I am conducted, the end for which I move, and sees how my heart answers the command.

(2.) Let us walk as though every action were an inlet to the favour or enmity of Christ. What know I but this action may open a door to the favour of Christ, or his endless refusal? What do I know but at the end of this I may either be in Abraham's bosom or in a gulf of misery, and launched into a blessed or miserable eternity?

(3.) Let us walk as though the glory of Christ depended upon every action. If our credit, estates, relations, worldly advantages, depended upon one action, how careful and diligent should we be in the doing of it! Let us act as though the honour of Christ, and our relation to him, depended upon what we go about.

(4.) Let us walk as if we were to give an account immediately of what we have done. Let us set before us Christ's tribunal, and imagine ourselves called to judgment. I am going about a business, but if Christ should send for me at the end of it, what account can I give him of my friendship and obedience to him in it? Is this such an action that, when I look Christ in the face, I can challenge him upon this promise to own me as a friend?

(5.) Let us walk as though Christ stood before us crucified, with all the obligations of love on his part; as if we saw him with his wounds open, and love and blood distilling from his heart upon us; and consider whether the act we are going about be suited to such inestimable kindness, or a putting him to an open shame. Hath not Christ had wounds enough, but must I increase them? Hath not he had misery enough, but must I add more? Shall I break his heart who breathes kindness towards me, and behave myself as an enemy towards him who offers me a favour which cannot be merited by a creature? Shall I wound him whose heart is open for me, and strike him that woos me? Shall I be a Judas to him that would be my friend, and pull him down that would lift me up to the highest privilege of a creature?

(6.) Let us walk as we think a damned soul would walk, if he were again to live under the knowledge of such a promise. How would he obey, and obey heartily! How would he pray, and pray fervently! How busy might we suppose him to be in inquiring what those commands were, and how diligent in the performance of them ! How would he by violence take all opportunities to pursue his duty, and attain his privilege ! What if any should see a damned soul stand before him when he was going into an unclean bed, and tell him it was for less than this he was judged an enemy to Christ, and a miserable wretch for ever ; would any man's fear suffer him to go on in his intended evil ? We have not those objects of fear before our eyes, but we have this promise in the word, suited more to ingenuous natures, to be accounted the friends of God and Christ, ' if we do whatsoever he commands us.'

www.ingramcontent.com/pod-product-compliance
Lightning Source LLC
Chambersburg PA
CBHW060446100426
42812CB00025B/2711